D1065324

John Davis Lodge

A Life in Three Acts

JOHN DAVIS LODGE

A Life in Three Acts

Actor • Politician • Diplomat

Thomas A. DeLong

SACRED HEART UNIVERSITY PRESS
FAIRFIELD, CONNECTICUT
1999

Library of Congress Cataloging-in-Publication Data

DeLong, Thomas A.
    John Davis Lodge: a life in three acts: actor, politician, diplomat /
    Thomas A. DeLong.
        p. cm.
    Includes bibliographical references and index.
    ISBN 1-888112-03-04
    1. Lodge, John Davis, 1903-1985. 2. Legislators—United States—Biography.
3. United States. Congress. House—Biography. 4. Ambassadors—United
States—Biography. 5. Governors—Connecticut—Biography. 6. Actors—
United States—Biography. I. Title.

E748.L816 D45 1999
973.9'092—dc21
[B]
                                                                99-049123

To Francesca Lodge,
who invited me back through time
and into a timeless friendship,
and
To Richard Gentile and Wally Woods,
who led me forward
and across the finish line

Contents

Preface

John Davis Lodge might have remained a faceless New York lawyer had it not been for an attraction to the theatrical career of his wife Francesca and the lure of his "family business," which was government service. The grandson of Senator Henry Cabot Lodge of Massachusetts, one of the Republican Party's most influential leaders in the early 1900s, John grew up in an atmosphere of patriotic duty, dynastic privilege, and unequivocal accomplishment. Often overshadowed by his grandfather's political heir and his older brother, Henry Cabot Lodge, Jr., John struggled for his own place in the sun, a platform where he could use his skills as a public speaker, writer, linguist, and debater.

Meeting dancer Francesca Braggiotti while an undergraduate at Harvard, Lodge took the first steps that would one day remove him from trusts and estates and take him to Hollywood as a potential star. He put aside the law for acting in early talking pictures. Proficient in French, he went on to starring roles in fourteen films in France, England, and Italy.

The outbreak of war interrupted his screen work. Following three and a half years of military service, he returned home and entered Connecticut politics, winning a seat in Congress in 1946. Four years later, he became Governor. Defeated in 1954, Lodge began a new "act." President Eisenhower appointed him as ambassador to Spain. He later served his country in Argentina, Switzerland, and at the United Nations.

Lodge's full and active life encompassed three segments of major accomplishment: acting, politics, and diplomacy. His wife often observed that she had five or six husbands because he successfully changed careers and jobs time after time during their fifty-six years of marriage.

Who, then, was this public figure—lawyer, actor, legislator, governor, diplomat? Politically, he stood out as a conservative among Republicans, yet he spoke up for broadly progressive legislation and believed that politics is the art of inclusion for varied schools of thought and action. As a diplomat, he represented the United States at its best, but met criticism when he seemed to dwell too much on the cultural and social aspects of his posts. On screen, he played his parts well, yet often projected a stiff, unbending demeanor that generally lost audience favor. He was a man of puzzling contradictions. An undisguised Brahmin, he could on occasion indulge in cajolery and self-promotion, or break into light-hearted song and humorous repartee. Controversy and conflict were always close by, as were the envy and guile of embassy aides and political ward heelers, in part because he did not go up the political or diplomatic ladder. And all too frequently, his party cut him loose at key moments and left him dangling as he struggled to retain or regain a foothold.

A chronic sibling rivalry fostered by brother Cabot and his ambivalence toward John's public service frustrated John. This competition began in their early schooldays, and contributed to John's momentary periods of a facial tic and nervous stutter.

With the untimely death of his father, John unremittingly relied on his mother for direction, comfort, and praise. But it was Francesca who gave his life purpose, fulfillment, joy, and adventure. While both were willing to discuss virtually any subject on the table, the matter of the unknown and youngest Lodge daughter would never be addressed.

Veracious and intelligent, proud and sensitive, John Lodge always wanted to be wanted by his country and his party. He is remembered as a hard-working, conscientious, and articulate citizen—a man of achievements who never turned down a job and who never sought retirement.

Setting forth a life as sweeping and complex as John Lodge's inevitably involves placing the biographical narrative of actions and events within a broad panorama of the social, political, and geopolitical activities of much of the twentieth century. However, my focus is only intermittently on an analysis of the nuances of politics and foreign affairs of his times. *John Lodge, A Life in Three Acts* is more the story of a man, his wife, and their families as he ventured forth in a life of service, a life that he characterized as well spent.

In the 1960s John Lodge gave serious thought to writing an autobiography. But at age sixty or so, he concluded that his public service careers and contributions were far from over. In fact, for another two decades, he would serve his country, virtually to the very end of a long and momentous life.

Lodge built up an enormous mass of papers and correspondence covering his various callings and travels. Before his death, he made arrangements for the inclusion of this material in the Hoover Institution archives at Stanford University. It was his hope that this material would become the pivotal research source for his biography, a story that had not been published in extensive book form.

In the 1970s his brother, Henry Cabot Lodge Jr., a distinguished U.S. Senator and Ambassador, had written two memoirs, and author Alden Hatch had recounted the story of six generations of the New England Lodges. But John felt Cabot's book barely acknowledged a sibling and his place in the family, and Hatch's narrative skipped over many achievements and contained numerous factual errors.

Two years after Lodge's death in late 1985 at age eighty-two, I was asked by his widow, Francesca Lodge, to help organize and inventory the papers of both John and Francesca as well as thousands of photographs. As these arduous archival tasks unfolded, it readily became clear that the life of John Lodge needed to be told.

From 1988 to 1994, I spent untold hours in interviews and conversation with Francesca Lodge at her homes in Connecticut and in Spain. She had known John since his undergraduate days at Harvard, nearly a decade before their marriage in 1929. Their lives together formed a unique and successful partnership in the arts, politics, and diplomacy. Her observations and insights, although often laced with broad hyperbole and limited by diminishing recall, proved an invaluable frame of reference and source of dramatic acumen. Albeit there were structured interviews with Francesca Lodge, information was increasingly gleaned piecemeal across a dining room table or en route to destinations near and far, by car, plane or foot. The unattributed quotations from Francesca in the text come from these conversations. Francesca also directed me to scores of individuals to interview. Ultimately, I contacted nearly 300 persons who had known the Lodges in some capacity or were family members.

In addition to the Lodge Papers at the Hoover Institution, initially contained in more than 550 large boxes, I utilized the Governor John Lodge Papers at the Connecticut State Library, Hartford; Former Members of Congress archives, Washington; various Lodge family papers at the Massachusetts Historical Society, Boston; Alden Hatch Collection at the University of Florida, Gainesville; and the Francesca Braggiotti Lodge files, Villa Santa Matilda, Marbella, Spain. The Acknowledgments section provides a full summary of collections and special libraries used in my research and a list of those individuals interviewed or consulted. The ultimate narrative stands as my own interpretation of the life of a remarkable man whose life spanned most of the twentieth century and who touched and was touched by many of its major figures and events.

Thomas A. DeLong
Southport, Connecticut

Acknowledgments

A wide range of institutional archives and libraries, as well as government collections and units, and their staff members, contributed to the narrative: Hoover Institution, Stanford, CA (Carol A. Leadenham, Elena Danielson, Grace Hawes, Katherine Reynolds, Charles G. Palm); Oral History Research Office, Columbia University; Alden Hatch Papers, Rare Books and Manuscripts, University of Florida, Gainesville (Carmen Russell Hurff); Former Members of Congress Oral History Collection at the Library of Congress; Connecticut State Library—Archives, History and Genealogy Unit, Hartford (Mark H. Jones); Dacor (Diplomatic and Consular Officers, Retired), Washington; Motion Picture Division, Library of Congress (Patrick Loughney, Rosemary Harris); Richard Nixon Library and Birthplace, Yorba Linda, CA (Amanda Fish); Ronald Reagan Library, Simi Valley, CA; Harvard University Archives (Brian A. Sullivan) and Houghton Library (Susan Alpert); Massachusetts Historical Society, Boston (Peter Drummey); Edith Wharton Restoration, Lenox, MA (Scott Marshall); Development, Alumni and Publications Office, Middlesex School, Concord, MA (Hope Sage, Judith W. Sheldon); St. Albans School Library, Washington (Mark Hillsamer); Columbia Historical Society, Washington (Jack D. Brewer); Israel Humanitarian Foundation, New York (Nicole Shapiro); Museum of Modern Art Film Study Center, New York (Charles Silver, Eileen Bowser, Mary Corliss); Centre National de la Cinématographie, Bois d'Arcy, France; British Broadcasting Corporation (Jeff Walden); Rockford (IL) College (Mary P. Pryor); UCLA Film and Television Archive (Howard W. Hays); Margaret Herrick Library, Academy of Motion Picture Arts and Sciences, Beverly Hills, CA; National Archives, Laguna Niguel, CA (Fred Klose); British Film Institute, London (Jane Hockings); Paramount Pictures, Hollywood, CA (Alan J. Bailey, Debra Rosen); Connecticut

Historical Society, Hartford; Fairfield (CT) University Library; Chowder and Marching Club, Washington; The Spanish Institute, New York; Committee of Foreign Affairs, Congress of the United States (Helen C. Mattas); Connecticut Department of Transportation (G. Larry Larned); Westport Public Library and Westport (CT) Historical Society; Pequot Library, Southport, CT; Bridgeport (CT) Public Library; Fairfield (CT) Public Library; Amateur Comedy Club, New York (John Shannon); Women's National Republican Club, New York (Sheila Armstrong, Lila Prounis); New York Public Library for the Performing Arts; F Street Club, Washington (Richard Casiano); Bibliothèque Nationale Suisse, Bern (Andreas Berz); Junior Achievement, Inc.; Nahant (MA) Historical Society (Calantha D. Sears); Hartford Collection, Hartford Public Library (Janice Mathews); and Congressional Research Service (Marilyn L. Nelson).

I incorporate material from personal interviews and correspondence with the following individuals: Tadeusz Adamowski, Mary J. Adorno, Meade Alcorn, David B. Aldrich, Robert Allen, John Alsop, George W. Anderson, Jr., John G. B. Andrew, Mathilda, Duchess of Argyll, Jean Pierre Aumont, Letitia Baldridge, Herbert E. Baldwin, Milton Barall, Betty Beale, Cobina Wright Beaudette, Julie Belaga, Ralph Bellamy, Joan Bennett, Edward O. Berkman, Florence Berkman, A. J. Drexel Biddle 3rd, James F. Bingham, Shirley Temple Black, Robert L. Bliss, Nicholas Bobrinskoy, Tania Bobrinskoy, Mary P. Bolton, John W. Boyd, Gioia Marconi Braga, D. Chadwick Braggiotti, and Mario Braggiotti.

Rama Braggiotti, Charles Breveton, B. V. Brooks, Clarence J. Brown, Jr., Vanessa Brown, Herbert Brownell, Dora Brunner, Lee Bryan, Helen B. Burns, Prescott S. Bush, Jr., Joaquín Calvo-Sotelo, Benita Braggiotti Carey, Regine Carr, Antonio Carrigues, Diana Churchill, Marcella Cisney, John Cocchi, Ruth Steinkraus Cohen, Molly C. Minot Cook, John Coolidge, Jean Patrice Courtaud, Royal E. Cowles, John W. Crowley, Elizabeth G. Curren, Dorothy Currier, Elizabeth Cushman, Anne H. Cutler, Roger Damio, Glenn R. Davis, Shelby Cullom Davis, Soledad de Castiella, René de Chambrun, John L. DeForest, Olivia de Havilland, Jane Randolph del Amo, Oscar de la Renta, Antonio de Oyarzabal, Beatrice Lodge de Oyarzabal, Juan de Oyarzabal, Matilda de Oyarzabal, Kit de Pinto Cuello, Miguel Primo de Rivera, Helena Lodge de Streel, Jean-Paul de Streel, Duchess de Sueca, Thomas Dewart, Paul Dietrich, Joan Dohanos, Stevan Dohanos, Peggy Donovan, Stanley Donovan, Gerald D. Dorman, Marie M. Dowling, Henry A. Dudley, Jonathan Dugan, Richard A. Dugstad, Angier Biddle Duke, Peter Finley Dunne, Jr., Elizabeth Eames, Kay Young Eason, John L. Ellinger, Marge Chain Ellinger, William D. Eppes, John L. Ericson, Emlen P. Etting, Gloria Braggiotti Etting, Frank J. Fahrenkopf, Jr., Douglas Fairbanks, Jr., Edwige Feuillère, C. Richard Ficks, Gary F.

Filosa, Robert H. Finch, Kevin Fitzpatrick, Barbara T. Eisenhower Foltz, Micol Fontana, George E. Ford, Gerald R. Ford, Philip Francoeur, Walter Frese, Eleanor Gabrielsen, Dorothy Gamble, William A. Gaston, Jr., Anne-Marie Gauer, Albert Gelardin, Lawrence M. Gilman, Esther Bemis Goodwin, Nicholas Gossweiler, George K. Graeber, Lee Graham, Jacqueline Green, John Green, Fritz Grunebaum, and Kay Halle.

Irene Halligan, Yvonne Hamilton, Alice Kelley Harlow, Arthur Brooks Harlow, H. Patterson Harris, Josephine E. Harris, Christina Hawkins, Allene Gaty Hatch, Cecilia G. B. Hill, Roger Hilsman, Stella Holtzman Henig, Katharine Hepburn, Charles Higham, Verna Hillie, Mildred S. Hilson, Janet Annenberg Hooker, Charles S. House, Jane Pickens Hoving, Frances Howard, John A. Howard, Halsey DeW. Howe, Elizabeth L. Hughes, Owen Read Hutchinson, Sally Curtis Iselin, Louise Russell Jackson, George Blake Johnson, Charles H. Joseph, Jr., Walter Judd, John J. Karol, Thomas H. Kean, Deane Keller, Chester Kerr, Eleanor King, August W. Kissner, Miles Kreuger, John Kriendler, Erich Krohn, Elizabeth Kuhner, Richard Lamparski, Joey Lampl, Muriel Angelus Lavalle, Katharine Wylie Lawrence, Clare Eames LeCorbeiller, Henry Lee, Douglas Leigh, Elsie Leigh, Landa Braggiotti Leute, William R. Leute, Hans-Adam, Prince of Liechtenstein, Marie, Princess of Liechtenstein, George Cabot Lodge, Henry S. Lodge, Henry S. Lodge, Jr., Pat Loomis, Caroline Oveson Lovelace, A. C. Lyles, Joseph F. McEvoy, Patrick McGilligan, Barbara Barondess MacLean, Allen Manning, Harriet Manning, Lily Lodge Marcus, Stanley Marcus, Edward W. Marshall, Marjorie Martin, Augustus P. Means, Thomas P. Melady, Carol Merrill-Mirsky, King Michael of Romania, Robert Michel, Leland Miles, William J. Miller, Olive Montgomery, George S. Moore, Edmund Morris, Robert Morris, Sylvia Jukes Morris, Charles T. Morrissey, Robert Mosher, Kevin Muldoon, George Murphy, Jack Davis Neal, Sr., William L. Nichols, Paul H. Nitze, Jack Noel, Assia Noris, Garrison Norton, Fred G. Nunes, Victoria Horne Oakie, Edmund O'Brien, Cavin O'Connor, Herbert S. Okun, Marcel Ophuls, and Frank Oram.

Egidio Ortona, Tere Pascone, Iva S. V. Patcevitch, J. H. Cameron Peake, Robert L. Peterson, Emily Lodge Pingeon, Anson C. Piper, W. R. Bruce Porter, Enrique Quintana, Maxwell Rabb, Trudy Rabin, Edwina H. Rager, Allen Raymond, Jr., Carla Rea, Michael Rea, Jesús Luque Recio, Joseph Verner Reed, Robinson Risner, María Rodríquez, Aline, Countess of Romanones, Archibald B. Roosevelt, Rita Ross, Martha Rountree, Eve Blickensderfer Sacksteder, Frederick H. Sacksteder, Leon Sarin, Eugene A. Scalise, Sr., Mary Jane Schang, Robert C. Schnitzer, William W. Scranton, Cabot Sedgwick, Hans Sellhofer, Ken Sephton, Bill Shine, George P. Shultz, William F. Siering, Jr., Delia Silva, Alfred R. Simson, Veronica

Cinelli Simson, Katharine A. H. Smith, Peter B. Smith, Richard Joyce Smith, Douglas Soutar, Hamilton Southworth, William B. Sowash, John Spaeth, Verna F. Spaeth, Mansfield D. Sprague, Cordelia G. Stagg, Frederick Stagg, Charles F. Stanwood, Virginia Steiger, Peter Stephaich, Donald Stewart, Adam Stolpen, Robert Strausz-Hupé, Tad Tharp, Rosamond Higgins Thompson, Henry F. Tiarks, Nancy Todd, Geoffrey Toone, Faye Towne, Barbara Ulrich, Annette L. Veler, Evelyn Venable, Robert Vieux, Jean-Philippe Vurpillot, Vernon A. Walters, G. Harold Welch, Benjamin Welles, C. Martin Wilbur, Paul W. Williams, Kate Winter, Henry Woodbridge, George L. Woodford, Joan Stafford Wright, Pauline Young, Jack Zaiman, and Donald F. Zezima.

Many others helped with suggestions, insights, and resources, particularly Congressman Christopher Shays, Leonard Guttridge, Walter Renschler, Alexandria Crump, Carmine Di Arpino, Gus Johnson, Caroline Hutton, Gerald A. DeLuca, Jeremy McKeon, Gordon C. Wilcox, Sam Sherman, Greg Miles, Tad Tharp, Thomas McKee, and Jan and Bryant Northcutt. I am indebted to Casey Ribicoff for granting permission to quote from the interviews of Abraham Ribicoff at the Oral History Research Office, Columbia University, and to John L. DeForest for allowing me to include portions of his unique sixty-four-year diary in the narrative.

I owe special thanks to Ann Rossell for her kindness and confidence at the very beginning of this project. The ongoing support and interest of Harriet Manning made this task doable. The considerate and considerable hospitality of Carolyn and Roger Mansell in Palo Alo, Antonia and Paco Millan in Marbella, and Beatrice and Antonio de Oyarzabal in Madrid and Washington eased the many long days of research.

The abiding hands-on concern and enthusiasm of Richard H. Gentile and Wally Woods undoubtedly carried the Lodge story to publication. My wife, Katharine, devoted countless hours to preparing the pages of the manuscript and always believed it was the book John Lodge would have wanted.

Research aide Kimberly Genova contributed significantly to the initial phase of the research, and Ildara Klee added greatly to the final presentation. Reviews of the text by Gary L. Rose, Paul Siff, and William B. Kennedy provided welcomed editorial direction and focus. I am especially grateful to Michelle Quinn and Sidney Gottlieb of the Sacred Heart University Press and to Sacred Heart University President Anthony J. Cernera.

Illustrations, unless otherwise credited, have been provided from the collections of Francesca Braggiotti Lodge and of the author.

CHAPTER 1

An Illustrious Lineage

I f it was John Lodge's fate to deliver his last speech in a women's club, it also seemed a curious coincidence that the site of his birth would one day become a similar gathering place for ladies. Lodge first saw the light of day in what would become the well-trod ladies room of the F Street Club in Washington, D.C. This dwelling, known as the Alexander Ray house, was converted to a club for society women thirty years after John's birth on October 20, 1903.[1] His mother's old bedroom fitted perfectly the need for a powder room.

"It struck many as an appropriate setting for the birth of a future movie heartthrob," Francesca Lodge recalled. "John actually remembered very little of the house at 1925 F Street which his parents rented. But he was quite pleased that the place, located close to the White House and in the midst of many government buildings, was so well-preserved and well-regarded."

The comfortable Greek Revival townhouse provided only temporary living quarters for John, his older brother Cabot, and his parents George and Elizabeth Davis Lodge. They were away from Washington for most of each summer, and 1903 was no different. They vacationed at Nahant on the Atlantic coast north of Boston. About six weeks after their return to Washington, Mrs. Lodge gave birth to her second son in an upstairs front bedroom overlooking the horse-drawn streetcar line. The baby was named John Davis for his maternal grandfather, Judge John Davis of the United States Court of Claims, who had recently died.

By the time young John had learned to walk, the design of a new and permanent house in Washington's elegant residential district to the northwest was underway. After some three years of paying rent, the Lodges had sought their own home, one planned and constructed to their wishes and needs. This large Georgian-style house designed by George at

2346 Massachusetts Avenue was completed in 1906. The four-story dwelling with a shady rear garden overlooking Rock Creek Park was a belated wedding gift from George's father, Senator Henry Cabot Lodge, whose Washington address, 1765 Massachusetts Avenue, also stood as a reminder of the Lodges' New England roots. There had been a Lodge on the Washington scene since the late nineteenth century, and there would be one for much of the twentieth.

Senator Lodge combined a keen and scholarly interest in American history with a determination to hold public office. Born in Boston in 1850, he graduated from Harvard and then enrolled in its law school. While a law student, he wrote for the *North American Review*, serving as its assistant editor under Professor Henry Adams until accepting a position as lecturer on American history at Harvard in 1876. That year he began the first of eight books of American biography and history.

In 1881, at the age of thirty-one, Henry Cabot Lodge ran on the Republican ticket for the Massachusetts legislature and won. Five years later, he was elected to the U.S. Congress. In 1892, despite a Democratic sweep led by President Grover Cleveland, the scholar-politician entered the Senate. He would be re-elected five more times, rising to a position of leadership and power within the Republican ranks and gaining the respect and confidence of its future Party leader, President Theodore Roosevelt.

In 1871, Lodge's marriage joined together two distinguished New England families who were already distantly related. During his last years at Harvard, Henry had met a cousin, Anna Cabot Mills Davis, the sister of his pre-college tutor. Her father, Admiral Charles Henry Davis, had studied at Harvard in the 1820s before embarking on a naval career. A fleet captain in the Civil War, he played a major role in the Union victory at Port Royal. He later took command of the country's South American squadron. When his wife joined him in Brazil, they left their 18-year-old daughter Anna—called Nannie by family and friends—with relatives in Boston. Lodge's mother, a Cabot by birth, invited her for an extended visit at the family's summer house at Nahant, and she accepted.

After a summer-long courtship, Henry and Nannie became secretly engaged. Two years later, on June 29, 1871, the day after his graduation from Harvard, they were married in Cambridge. Twenty-one-year-old Henry Cabot Lodge entered a life of scholarly achievement and public service with the unswerving loyalty and devotion of his wife. All who knew Nannie described her as a woman of rare charm and unusual intellect.

Some forty years later, these two descendants of Pilgrim and Puritan settlers, Brahmin to the core, might have been among the prototypes that inspired a bit of local doggerel. This taunt, of a Boston increasingly alien to the heirs of her founders, was delivered by Irishman John Collins Bossidy at a Holy Cross College alumni dinner in 1909. It remains an oft-repeated view of old Boston.

And this is good old Boston,
The home of the bean and the cod,
Where the Lowells talk only to Cabots,
And the Cabots talk only to God.

John Lodge disliked hearing that Cabot-to-God verse. "It dogged his political and social life without letup," Francesca remembered. "That rhyme really pulled at his coattails." As it did his grandfather's. Yet it hardly lacked veracity in the eyes of many.

Journalist Emma DeLong Mills observed Henry Cabot Lodge at the peak of his political power in the U.S. Senate in 1919. "Aristocratic, nervous—he twisted a rubber band in his fingers all during the discussion (on the World War I peace treaty). . . . An absolute autocrat, I should judge him to be and by his impatience when others of his party spoke, one who likes to manage every detail himself."[2]

Long after, John Lodge, too, spoke of the Senator's bearing as well as his affinity for hard work and commitment to public service: "My grandfather was accused of being cold and distant. He was a reserved, thoughtful man, sincere in his self-sacrifice for his constituents and his country. He was a wealthy man, who could have elected to lead a life of leisure. Instead of that, he chose to work ten hours a day. He wrote a brilliant life of Alexander Hamilton, among other things."[3]

John's father, George Cabot Lodge, grew up in this fertile scholarly environment. Born October 10, 1873, he was soon called "Ba-by" by his sister Constance, older by eighteen months. The name stayed with him and was soon transformed into "Bay."

Constance, Bay, and a younger brother, John Ellerton Lodge, reaped the rich harvest of five generations of entrepreneurial ancestors. Early in the eighteenth century, English-born immigrant John Cabot had wed a Salem, Massachusetts merchant's daughter named Anna Orne and soon amassed a fortune in the rum and molasses trade. Two of their sons, Joseph and Francis, inherited his mercantile shrewdness. As privateers in the service of the English during the French and Indian War, the brothers multiplied their father's wealth. Joseph Cabot's seventh son, George, continued to add to the family coffers.

After studying at Harvard, young George Cabot was sent to sea in the 1770s and quickly earned a reputation as an aggressive trader and merchant prince. He accumulated a fortune as a ship owner who traded in everything from slaves to opium. He married a first cousin, Elizabeth Higginson, then entered state politics shortly before the American Revolution ended. Elected Senator from Massachusetts in 1789, he endorsed Alexander Hamilton's economic policies and influenced the programs of the Federalist party.

In 1842, George's granddaughter Anna Cabot married John Ellerton Lodge, the son of Liverpool merchant Giles Lodge, who in the early 1790s had fled a slave uprising in Santo Domingo and took refuge on an American schooner bound for Boston. There he founded the American branch of the Lodges. This first American John Lodge compounded both his father's and his wife's wealth through seagoing exploits in the China Trade. Their only son, the future senator, and, in turn, his offspring were thus assured a great measure of financial independence.

From both sides of this remarkable family, young Bay Lodge learned of its merchants, soldiers, sea captains and senators. As with the education of many of these forebears, his courses followed a curriculum based on the time-tested classics and humanities. Bay studied at the Noble school in Boston and, after his father went to Congress, at the Emerson Institute in Washington.

The doors of Harvard opened to this dashing, tall-standing scion of old Boston. Bay entered with the class of 1895. His first two years' work was mediocre enough to place him on probation. By his junior year, courses in philosophy and French literature stimulated his interest in college lessons and turned him around academically. Nonetheless, overshadowed by his father's reputation as "the scholar in politics," he suffered periodic depression.[4]

In his final year, he began to write poetry. He mailed many poems home, seeking his father's approbation. The Senator encouraged Bay's literary bent. He even showed his son's rudimentary efforts to Theodore Roosevelt, himself Harvard '80 and recent author of *The Winning of the West*. Roosevelt took an enthusiastic interest in Lodge's writings. Roosevelt's success in pressuring magazine editors to critique as well as accept Bay's poems undoubtedly advanced his career.

In the summer of 1895, twenty-one-year-old Bay and his parents traveled to Europe. The Continent was very familiar to these urbane Yankees. An annual trip abroad was *de rigueur*. For the first time, their itinerary included Spain. The poverty and primitive conditions apparently appalled Bay. He never went back. By a twist of fate, some sixty-five years later, Spain would become a well-loved second home to his son John and native land to many of his descendants.

Free of any monetary cares, Bay settled in Paris for the study of French literature. Harvard pal Joseph Stickney welcomed him to the

Sorbonne, and they savored the Bohemian life that artists and writers had sought along the Left Bank since pre-French Revolution days. In his letters home, Bay expressed the belief that, for him, a literary career seemed tied to an academic post. Then he began to wonder whether a commitment to poetry would isolate him from the snug mainstream of a life to which he had been quite accustomed. An emotional conflict between a drive to write epic poetry and a need to prove he could earn a living of some sort intensified. This inner turmoil brought Bay to the brink of a nervous breakdown.

Bay's biographer John Crowley contends that this clash between words and action, between poetry and making money, ultimately between the world of art and the world of Boston society, was to pervade both his work and his life: "Although he tried desperately to resolve the tensions, he would choose finally to abandon action, money-making, and Boston altogether."[5]

In the spring of 1896, Lodge decided to forego his work for an advanced degree at the Sorbonne and to return home. Perhaps the acceptance of several sonnets by *Scribner's* and *Harper's* magazines influenced the move. Lodge's hoped-for appointment as an instructor at Harvard that fall failed to materialize. With his father's consent, he returned to Europe to continue his studies. This trip would take him to Berlin to learn German and to investigate Teutonic philosophy.

When Bay came home in 1897, he carried the manuscript of what would become his first book, *The Song of the Wave and Other Poems*. His father agreed to underwrite its publication, indicating that his work showed promise. Reviewers generally acknowledged its strong rhythmic power within a context of highly extravagant expression and tangled syntax. But overall, his efforts were marred by immaturity, haste, and unevenness. The volume sold poorly, and the Senator hardly recouped his expenses. Unable to find a university teaching post to his liking or to make a start toward a livelihood from writing, twenty-three-year-old Bay accepted an offer from his father. He would act as private secretary to the Senator.

Bay began a dual existence in Washington: office chores during the day, writing poetry at night. "Although he did not neglect his secretarial duties," Crowley records, "he dispatched them with little enthusiasm; and the existence of manuscript poems on Senate stationery suggests that his night's work intruded upon his daytime activities."[6]

Theodore Roosevelt, who had recently left the post of New York City Police Commissioner and assumed the position as Assistant Secretary of the Navy, often invited him to stop by his office and talk about "the aspects of life in general." Lodge also met New York-born novelist Edith

Wharton, who shared his dislike of the "philistine-plutocrat atmosphere" of high society. She delighted in his exuberant good health and joyous physical life, and noted his "deep eyes full of laughter and visions."[7] The future Pulitzer Prize-winning author of *Ethan Frome*, she encouraged his poetic efforts, while to herself recognizing his artistic deficiencies: "He grew up in a hot-house of intensive culture, and was one of the most complete examples I have ever known of the young genius before whom an adoring family unites in smoothing the way. This kept him out of the struggle of life, and consequently out of its experiences, and in the end his intellectual precocity was combined with a boyishness of spirit at once delightful and pathetic."[8]

When thirty-nine-year-old Teddy Roosevelt resigned his post at the Navy Department at the outbreak of the Spanish-American War and organized a regiment of volunteer cavalrymen called the "Rough Riders," George Lodge sought military service. He signed on as a naval gunnery cadet, albeit under the watchful eye of his maternal uncle, Captain Charles Henry Davis, Jr., commander of the USS *Dixie*. In combat, Bay seemed to have felt a true sense of accomplishment, perhaps for the first time in his life. In June 1898, he participated in attacks on Cuban blockhouses and defenses with the zest of a sea warrior. "We engaged a battery at a place called Trinidad," he wrote his mother in an unpoetic, straightforward account, "and yesterday we engaged the same battery, a gunboat in the harbor, and a gunboat that came out to us, and used them up pretty badly. So you see I am in it. Nothing very serious so far, but we still have been under fire and have killed a good many Spaniards."[9]

Bay relished the adventure aboard ship. "It's a great business to be here & see the wheels go round & be a wheel oneself even if not a very big one."[10] Although he won a promotion to ensign at the end of the war, he rejected a naval career. In retrospect, a number of the Lodges and Davises felt that young Bay's happiest days were with the Navy; years later, his son John viewed his naval duty as the most exhilarating and satisfying of all his careers. But for Bay, his single-minded passion for poetry overrode all else.

In the midst of this rededication to literature, Bay Lodge met a beautiful and intelligent Washington debutante named Matilda Elizabeth Frelinghuysen Davis. She came from a family distinguished by generations of public servants, including Senator Theodore Frelinghuysen of New Jersey, Governor Matthew Griswold of Connecticut, and Senator John Davis of Massachusetts. Her mother, Sarah Frelinghuysen, had reigned as one of Washington's most popular belles when her father Frederick T. Frelinghuysen served as a New Jersey Senator from 1865 to 1877 and later as Secretary of State in the administration of Chester A. Arthur. Her social position remained secure as the wife of John Davis, a leading Washington lawyer and judge, and, after his death in the early 1900s, as the wife of Brigadier General Charles L. McCawley.

Bessie—her shortened surname among family and friends—was of a serious nature. She had tried to become an Army nurse during the Spanish-American War, but her parents refused to allow her to face the hardships of such a life. Bessie found much pleasure in reading and seemed the ideal partner for the impassioned Bay. He now intensified his efforts to succeed at his craft, inspired by the encouragement and admiration of Bessie. As much as possible, she immersed herself in his inner world of poetry. "She moves in the dusk of my mind," he acknowledged, "like a bell with the sweetness of singing."[11]

Senator Lodge heartily approved of his prospective daughter-in-law. But the Davises took a dim view of a poet in their family. Bay tried to allay their apprehension by trying to achieve a measure of commercial success by writing several novels and plays. His labors proved unsuccessful. Judge and Mrs. Davis planned for their daughter a very large wedding in September 1900. Bessie and Bay, however, felt uncomfortable over the very thought of the extravagant preparations and ceremony. He persuaded Bessie to elope. She proved a willing conspirator. For weeks, it seems, she had worried about the effect of the wedding celebration on her father's declining health and had tired of hearing her mother's frequent complaints about the bother and expense of the affair.

On August 18, 1900, Bessie and her personal maid secretly met Bay at the Church of the Advent in Boston. There was no maid of honor or best man for the brief ceremony. Only later did they discover that Bay's brother John had arrived at the church with the organist and quietly watched from a side aisle. For many, it seemed a scandalous way to begin a marriage. But not to Theodore Roosevelt. He noted the occasion in a letter to Senator Lodge: "Bay really has a touch of genius in him, and we cannot hold genius to the lines to which we hold commonplace people." In reply, Lodge noted, "Whatever the manner of his getting married, he has made a most fortunate choice, in my opinion, and I hope it will develop him."[12]

Bay and Bessie sailed to Europe for an extended honeymoon in Paris, where the husband-poet resumed his writing. The interlude lasted a year. In September 1901, they returned to Washington with the prospect of more commonplace domestic responsibilities added to the unrelenting drive toward literary recognition.

CHAPTER 2

A Young Francophile

B ack in Washington, Bay took a more dispassionate and philosophical view of his work. He wrote to his father's Harvard classmate and his own close confidant, Dr. William Sturgis Bigelow. "I suppose in time all this will count and the world will appreciate my surpassing genius; just at present it doesn't seem to care a damn for me or my works. . . . Fortunately I am getting very calm about publishing and about the world generally."[1]

His world took on a new dimension in 1902. At the Senator's large house on Nahant's Cliff Street on the eastern tip of a rocky peninsula jutting into Boston Bay, the Lodges awaited the arrival of their first child. Early in the summer, on July 5, Bessie gave birth to a son. Named Henry Cabot Lodge for his grandfather, he later added a "Jr." and like his namesake was known as Cabot by family and colleagues.

Bay and Bessie soon moved to a nearby summer cottage at Forty Steps Beach. An old-fashioned stone house, it had once belonged to his grandparents, John and Anna Lodge. The Lodges' circle of influential and highly literate friends at Nahant and beyond widened in these years to include playwright Langdon Mitchell, diplomat Cecil Spring Rice, and lawyer Walter Berry. Novelist Edith Wharton invited them for long weekends at her country place, The Mount, in Lenox, Massachusetts, and for New Year's Eve get-togethers at her home in Washington. She always thought Bay's charm and personality outshone his poetry and admired his living every moment to the full.

Bay next turned to writing a three-act blank-verse drama taken from the biblical stories of Adam, Eve, Cain, and Abel. He labored month after month on this epic of family disintegration. Entitled *Cain*, it met with mixed reactions. Reviewers praised his literary energy and passion, but again noted a certain immaturity.

In his later years, John Lodge spoke poignantly of Bay's writings. "I am bound to say that my father's poetry reaches me in a very deep way and always has. I have a great sense of identity with his verse and with his aspirations. I do not know whether or not this is in part a subconscious congenital impulse born of my filial feeling for a man I hardly remember. I do not think so. Of course, it is quite probable that being his son I share some of his tastes and possibly even a part of his temperament."[2]

In the fall of 1903, some sixteen months after the birth of Cabot, younger son John joined his brother in the nursery. That year, three of the country's important future industries took fledgling steps. Henry Ford formed his own automobile company, pointing toward the mass production of low-priced cars. The Wright brothers made the first flight of a heavier-than-air manned plane, focusing attention on the potential use of the sky for travel. And Edwin Porter produced the first truly dramatic motion picture, the twelve-minute-long "Great Train Robbery," paving the way for countless hours of mass entertainment (and roles for the likes of John Lodge some thirty years later).

The year 1903 was also auspicious for the occupant of the White House. President Theodore Roosevelt completed a treaty with the new republic of Panama—an event John Lodge would officially help celebrate fifty years later. Bay asked Roosevelt to serve as John's godfather. The President was such a frequent visitor to the Senator's Washington home on Massachusetts Avenue that Lodge even built a special door opening on a rear garden so that Roosevelt could enter unobserved. The two families shared festive occasions, especially Christmas dinner when the President carved and served a large roast goose or turkey.

A sister, Helena, born in 1905, joined her brothers as the youngest child of the Lodges. Nonetheless, Bessie continued to dress Cabot and John in little girls' clothes as was the fashion at the turn of the century. So close in age, the brothers were dressed alike and virtually raised as twins. The Lodge children shared luxurious, almost regal, surroundings. There were nurses and cooks, and later governesses and tutors, to watch over and teach them. Servants, from maids to chauffeurs, eased their way in a setting of natural formality. There was never any profligate spending, but rather a solid affluence. Almost every day, Mrs. Lodge read to her children a story from the Old Testament or a tale of Dickens, Scott, Thackeray, or Poe. At tea time and around the dinner table, they acquired a basic knowledge of French from the conversation of their parents. Their nannies usually were French or German, adding to their grasp of other languages.

When their grandfather visited, his vast knowledge of many subjects fascinated the young Lodges. They eagerly anticipated his readings aloud, often from a book of short stories or essays. They never forgot the

Senator's account of how *his* grandfather, Henry Cabot, hid under the dining room sideboard when George Washington came to Beverly, Massachusetts, to have breakfast with Henry's father, a Federalist leader and U.S. Senator.

In 1907, Bay began a monumental blank-verse drama based on the Hercules legend. *Herakles*, he felt, would be his *magnum opus*—an accomplishment only a select few would ever see or understand. He perhaps wondered whether he would live to complete this play. He had contracted malaria, possibly during the Spanish-American war, and his doctors discovered a weak heart, no doubt from an undiagnosed case of rheumatic fever years before. By 1909, Lodge seemed to have aged well beyond his thirty-five years.[3] The anticipation of a summer holiday on Tuckernuck Island, off the Massachusetts island of Nantucket, filled Bay with renewed energy and heightened spirits. On the morning of their father's and grandfather's departure from Nahant to Tuckernuck, Cabot, John, and Helena stood by the door as Bay ran down the stairs. He turned to speak to the governess and the maid, then bid his children good-bye.

Bay and his father settled easily into the serene routine on Tuckernuck. They read, sailed, swam, and talked. But on August 19, Bay ate some clams, and during the night he suffered severe intestinal pains and nausea. By the following evening, the Senator recognized the signs of a serious illness, even appendicitis, and walked across the island to telephone a doctor on Nantucket. The next day, a physician arrived, followed by a specialist from the mainland.

Within an hour after the specialist examined Bay, he called to the Senator. "Come quickly downstairs. There's been a sudden failure."[4] At his bedside, Lodge lifted up Bay and held him. But in less than a minute, he died in his father's arms. "You will know the lonely agony of that moment for me," Lodge wrote family friend Dr. William S. Bigelow. "I cannot write of it even without wanting to cry out as I did then."[5]

A port-mortem examination revealed a very serious heart condition, aggravated by over-activity and acute indigestion. The Lodges held a memorial service in Boston. A few days later at the beach at Nahant, Bessie and Bay's brother John rowed off from the shore. The heavy-hearted widow held her poet-husband's ashes sealed in a Greek urn Joe Stickney had given them as a wedding present nine years earlier. Following Bay's wishes, she cast the container into the dark sea.

With the death of their father, Cabot, John, and Helena faced a break in the secure pattern of their structured and unruffled lives. Their mother gradually reverted to the more conventional modes and manners from which her husband had partly rebelled. John Lodge remembered his mother telling him "in a gentle, loving way" that their father was gone, and he felt a sense of immense desolation. Bessie Lodge would raise her children with devotion, love, and courage, even if it meant withdrawing somewhat from life. She left to others—the Senator, Roosevelt, Edith Wharton, and Bay's first biographer, Henry Adams—to uphold and advance Bay's literary standing. In any event, his books went out of print after a dozen or so years, his reputation faded, his place in American literature ignored.[6]

Educating the three Lodge children was foremost in Bessie's mind. She repeatedly said, "Always keep your sights high." They continued to live in Washington and spend summers in Massachusetts. Cabot and John enrolled that fall in Miss Ward's classes in the comparatively rural northwestern area of the capital. Cabot, because he was the oldest and bore the Senator's name, received more attention, partly, too, because he was so bright and eager and companionable. Little Johnny, only a year behind his brother, scrambled to keep up with the dutiful heir apparent to the Senator. Now fatherless, John not infrequently felt left out and unwanted when his grandfather took charge.

Uncle John Lodge was probably the nearest thing his nephews had to a father. He taught them to sail and fish, encouraged their interest in music and art, and showed them magical tricks he had learned as a child. He called John "Brown" because of his brown hair and brown eyes and Cabot "Little Boy Blue" because of his blue eyes and fair complexion.

Uncle John had struggled against chronic ill health as a young man and seemed always overshadowed by Bay's brilliance and flair. In his sophomore year at Harvard, his eyesight failed. He dropped out for treatment. Doctors corrected the disability, and he went on to finish his studies abroad. He developed scholarly interests in art, music, and literature. He wrote sonnets and odes, and painted and played several musical instruments. In the early 1900s, he began the study of Oriental languages and cultures, and received an appointment as curator of The Department of Asiatic Art at the Boston Museum of Fine Arts. In 1920 he was asked to become chairman of the committee on Oriental art for the Smithsonian Institution, which had just accepted the magnificent Oriental art collection of Charles L. Freer. John Ellerton Lodge soon became director of the Freer Gallery, skillfully selecting, acquiring and exhibiting thousands of porcelains, paintings, bronzes and ceramics. Aside from remarkable linguistic and curatorial abilities—it is said he helped break the Japanese code shortly before World War II—John often hid his feelings behind a biting sarcasm and an acid sense of humor. Married but without children of his own, he adored Bay's offspring. He exhibited a special concern over John who, nevertheless, often wished that his grandfather would take his hand.

Above all, it was Bessie Lodge who ultimately had the greatest influence in shaping John's and all her children's character and intellect. Possessed with a depth of wisdom, she never lost control of their destinies. "My mother was the one who gave us our standards, our motivations, our general deportment and our style of life," John always pointed out. "She made our childhood a bright, happy adventure. My grandfather was influential, but essentially my brother, my sister and I were brought up by our mother."[7]

Bessie taught her children not to think about themselves. If one became preoccupied with some selfish interest, she would direct that child to something else to think about. "She never punished us," John once remarked. "If she so much as frowned at anything we did, we'd be conscience-stricken not to cause her any pain, and we wouldn't do that again. She didn't care how many things got broken, but the one thing she couldn't tolerate was not telling the truth."

Their religious training, musical appreciation, and literary exposure dominated her life. The songs of Gilbert and Sullivan were as familiar to them as the Bible. The study of English and French classics were part of everyday activity. Helena recalls lying with her brothers on rugs on the grass at Nahant while her mother read aloud about Jacob and Rachel in the King James version of the Old Testament. John loved books, but for Christmas he usually asked for household pets, such as canaries and doves. A letter to Santa Claus at age eight requested "a big wooden chest to put things in and some candy—maple sugar and marshmallows—and some money."

After two years at Miss Ward's classes, Cabot and John entered St. Albans as day students. Founded as an Episcopal school stressing the education and training of choir boys for the Washington Cathedral, it enrolled some 130 boys in grades 4 through 12. Both entered the same class in the Lower School, although Cabot was more than a year older. A very good student, Cabot excelled in all subjects save arithmetic. Uncle John referred to him as "the wise one" because he was so solemn and studious. Nonetheless, by age nine, he had developed a nervous stutter.

John achieved high grades, completing his first year at St. Albans with an academic average of 93. But Bessie came to realize that a change would benefit all of them. Bay had always stressed the importance of living abroad and acquiring an international outlook and a second language. She decided to live in Paris and put her sons in French schools. Perhaps she felt that would revive her spirits. Besides, they could rent the house in Washington for a goodly sum and live more economically in Europe. Word of her decision initially upset the Senator and Nannie. But they recognized her desire for a measure of independence and the educational advantages for the children. The senior Lodges planned to visit during vacations.

Bessie and her children sailed for France in November 1912. Edith Wharton, who had settled in Paris shortly before Bay's death, had encouraged Bessie to return to the French capital. She greeted the Lodges as their railroad train pulled into the Gare St. Lazare station and hurried them off to rooms she had found at the Hotel de Tremoille. Cabot and John were soon sent off to a boarding school in the suburb of St. Cloud. Suddenly tossed into the midst of hostile French schoolboys who talked so fast in an unfamiliar accent that the Lodges could hardly understand a word, they were bewildered and homesick. Bessie realized she had made a mistake. They were too young to be separated from their family. She rented a comfortable apartment and sent the boys to a day school run by a Monsieur Gory at 18 Rue Matignon, near the Champs-Elysées.

"The Lodge boys—now known among their peers as Henri and Jean—soon learned to speak, even think in French," Francesca Lodge later noted, "and they loved the language. John had an advantage he wished every American learning the French language could have." Many years later, in a talk to the Federation of Franco-American Clubs in Connecticut while he was Governor, Lodge expounded on this advantage: "I learned French from French friends and teachers. For in learning French, I also came into direct contact with the wonderful culture of France. I learned the traditions of France, the history of France, and I came to know its magnificent literature, its poetry and novels and drama. I learned, too, the virtues of the French mind, its classic wit, its shrewd deductive powers, its capacity for penetrating thought and precise expression."[8] Lodge was on his way to becoming a lifelong Francophile and an expert linguist.

Sports, too, were important at École Gory. John and Cabot learned swimming, fencing, and gymnastics. The gym instructor also taught a form of self-defense called "boxe française," or savate, in which the feet are used. "They teach you how to box in this school," John wrote to Grandmother (Gamuzzy) Lodge just before his tenth birthday in October 1913. "You work so much harder in France than in America."[9]

Monsieur Gory was proud of his two American students, who stood near the head of their class. John cultivated an interest in opera and plays. "There were some parts where I almost cried," he explained to Gamuzzy after seeing "Michel Strogoff." "For instance, when they put out his eyes. And others where I laughed myself to death. . . . When the Englishman came in and said: 'Je concheils a toi de ne pas toucher cet homme,' and when the Frenchman carried him on his back."[10]

Life in Paris uplifted Bessie's spirits. She recaptured some of the happiness of her days with Bay not so long before. Edith Wharton moved to an apartment on the Rue de Varenne and often invited Bessie and the children to tea or lunch. Henry Adams, whose brother Brooks had married Nannie's sister, Evelyn Davis, had a large house on the Bois de Boulogne. John, Cabot, and Helena periodically saw Adams, whom they called Uncle Dordy. He had spent much of his youth traveling about the United States and Europe. Uncle Dordy fascinated them with his stories of the wonders of the Continent, especially his account of the 1895 trip through Europe with their grandfather and father. The old writer's tales charmed the youngsters and stirred their own curiosity to explore the Old World.

For their first summer in France, Bessie Lodge rented a seaside house at Paris Plage, a Normandy resort. On Bastille Day, July 14, 1913, everyone dressed in costumes for a carnival. John chose the military outfit of a Zouave, feeling very dashing and important. Cabot dressed as a *spahi*, looking very much like a young Algerian cavalryman. The carefree, fun-filled months away from Paris passed quickly for the boys. Monsieur Gory's school opened for the fall term all too soon.

The rigorous academic routine challenged and motivated the two brothers from America and taught them how to study and concentrate. "By American standards," Cabot wrote sixty years later, "we were required to work very hard all morning and all afternoon until supper time, except for a thirty-minute airing in the park." They were not without mischief. Such pranks as dropping bags of water to the street from their apartment balcony gained them the appellation "les enfants terribles de Madame Lodge."[11]

In 1914 the Lodges again anticipated a long holiday at the end of school. In mid-May they packed for Dieppe on the English Channel, where Bessie would join her Aunt Lucy Frelinghuysen. Mrs. Wharton opened her picturesque manor house at nearby Offrannville and entertained the Lodges and a growing circle of expatriates. The unencumbered peaceful years ended that summer. In far-off Sarajevo, a Serbian nationalist, out to avenge the oppression of his countrymen, gunned down Archduke Francis Ferdinand as he motored through the city. Ironically, the heir to the throne of Austria-Hungary had hoped his visit would signal the beginning of more autonomy for the Slavic people in the Balkans. Most European powers quickly mobilized when Austria demanded reparations from Serbia, which rejected the idea and broke diplomatic relations. With the European equilibrium tumbling, war broke out first between Germany and Russia. Then on August 3, the Kaiser also declared war on France and the following day invaded Belgium. The streets of Dieppe were lined with farewell scenes as young Frenchmen reported to military duty. In the village square, farmers brought together their horses for use by the army.

Each animal was branded with a number on a hoof so that it might be returned to its owner.

The Senator and Nannie had already arrived in England for a late summer visit. Their daughter Constance and her husband Augustus P. Gardner, a Massachusetts Congressman, were with them. They immediately realized the dangers facing their family across the Channel. Gardner hurried over from London to persuade Bessie to leave France. She agreed to go to England, a safer place, although it already had declared war on Germany. She packed at once. "We left Dieppe in two taxicabs," John recalled of the eighty-kilometer flight to the nearest seaport. "I had to leave my birds behind, and I was weeping. . . . Uncle Gussie filled the cabs with gasoline cans so we could make Le Havre. We got on the first boat out. I'll never forget, as we left the dock, the people ashore were waving and singing the 'Marseillaise.' "[12]

On the night of August 5, they sailed from Le Havre to Southampton. When they reached the Lodges in London, Bessie rented a small flat on Half Moon Street near St. James Park. But the entire family soon decided to return to the United States. The Senator booked passage on the *Olympic*. John's most vivid memory of the voyage centered upon two celebrities aboard ship. One night Cabot and John crept out of their bunks and hid behind a pillar in the ship's ballroom to watch a dancing couple. Fascinated by their twirls in perfect time to the waltz music, John wondered if he would ever be as tall and grown up and graceful as Vernon Castle to lead a pretty young lady like Irene Castle across a dance floor in such a romantic setting.

"Senator Lodge had been concerned about his grandchildren's long absence from the United States," Francesca remembered. "He thought it would make them too foreign and unaccustomed to the New World. The boys were approaching an age when an American boarding school was to be considered. If they remained in Europe for another year or two, the Senator believed at that time, Cabot and John would become strangers in their own country. And almost aliens to their old friends."

Both Lodges re-entered St. Albans School in 1914. By the end of the first term, their grades fell far short of their earlier high level. Cabot's top mark was an 85 in Latin; John's, an 81 in science. A close pal, James J. Wadsworth, the son of New York Senator James W. Wadsworth, remembered them as well-imbued with European ideas, not to mention being out of touch with Yankee ways of self-defense. In a fight one day, John knocked down his unsuspecting opponent with a fast "savate" kick to the head which would have pleased Monsieur Gory. Wadsworth, who became Cabot's deputy at the United Nations in the 1950s, recalled the scorn John encountered: "He was, of course, just as brave and just as nimble, and just as good as any American boy; but oh my! He didn't fight fair because he used his feet."[13] Totally bilingual, the Lodges could easily break into French. And their English often bore a Gallic trope. "The Americans automatically assumed they were putting on airs, which of course they were not at all," concluded Wadsworth. "They were perfectly normal kids."[14]

Back in Washington, Cabot and John became aware of the major role their grandfather played in the Senate as spokesman on the tariff, national defense, and other key issues. When he invited them on walks, he talked about the momentous events in Europe that were pushing America into a position of world leadership and an overseas war. He encouraged his family to bone up on history by using his enormous library of some 15,000 books—a collection housed in a large high-ceilinged family room with an upper gallery of shelves bulging with volume after volume. The Senator frequently worked at a desk there while the family and guests sipped tea or read. "When some remark caught his attention," Cabot recorded in his memoirs, "he would stop work at his desk and join us, taking out a book of essays, or poetry or a volume of Shakespeare to prove his point. I remember his often standing with a book in his hand, reading some passages and obtaining our complete attention."[15]

Prominent visitors dropped in at 1765 Massachusetts Avenue. French and English ambassadors and diplomats from other lands came by. As chairman of the influential Senate Foreign Relations Committee, the Senator was privy to many high-level international concerns. John remembered hiding in the parlor to overhear a *tête-à-tête* between his grandfather and the French Prime Minister.

At home Cabot and John shared a bedroom, and at school they studied side by side. A high degree of competitiveness developed between the two, and John, less mature, suffered emotionally as a result. Especially so when his grandfather singled out Cabot for special attention and praise. Physically, John developed a nervous tic. When overcome by stress, he uncontrollably batted his eyes.

Boarding school was the next step in the education of the Lodge boys. They would soon leave Washington again, and this time deepen their New England roots.

CHAPTER 3

In Class and On Stage

A character in the novel *We Happy Few* by Helen Howe observes that "You must admit the boys are taught their three R's." "Yes—Respectability, Republicanism and Ritual," replies another. "You know as well as I do that the boys all come from the same social, economic, and even geographical background. They are reared for one aim—business success."[1] Howe describes a fictional New England preparatory school. Called St. Cuthbert's and situated in Constable, Massachusetts, it bore a similarity to a boy's school in Massachusetts that she knew well and where her cousin, Reginald Howe, Jr., was a housemaster.[2]

Both Mrs. Lodge and the Senator agreed upon a St. Cuthbert's-type school. They chose one in Concord, an intellectual center and once the home of Emerson, Thoreau, Hawthorne, and the Alcotts. Middlesex School, founded in the early 1900s, shared the same point of view as a number of well-established English-model boarding schools for young boys, such as Groton, St. Paul's, and St. Mark's. It differed chiefly from those institutions in that it had no ties to Episcopal doctrine, or to any church for that matter. Middlesex was a non-denominational school, a factor that Bessie Lodge believed would have attracted and pleased Bay.

Started by Frederick Winsor (whose sister founded Miss Winsor's School in Boston), Middlesex had flourished in large part because of its bonds to Harvard and the patronage of College President Charles W. Eliot. The 350-acre rural campus became a veritable "feeder" school for nearby Cambridge. Year after year, virtually an entire class moved on to Harvard, which was Winsor's alma mater; at graduation only two or three enrolled elsewhere, usually Princeton or Yale.

The acceptance of the Lodge boys into the ranks of "the happy few" was not automatic, even for the grandchildren of a Massachusetts political nabob. Winsor informed their mother that he already had a dozen or so applications on his waiting list: "It does not look very hopeful for your two boys. If you would be willing, however, to have them share a room, it would add distinctly to their chances."[3] The Senator spoke up in no uncertain terms. "I want them educated in Massachusetts, and I am particularly anxious that they should prepare at your school, as their mother has now decided that she would like to send them there. . . . There will be no difficulty about their occupying one room. . . . I cannot believe they are not better prepared than most boys. I trust that you will be able to find places for them."[4]

As the spring term ended, Winsor still discouraged the Lodges; they were unsure of their admittance, even after Bessie Lodge and Nannie made a special visit to the campus. Winsor greeted them, but audaciously suggested they also travel outside New England. Nonetheless, he showed them quarters in a neighboring farmhouse where the boys might possibly be housed if accepted by Middlesex. "I must tell you," Bessie wrote the next day, "that as the boys have never been north of Washington for the winter, I could not let them room in the farmhouse. I am afraid to introduce them to New England cold in a wooden house & oblige them to walk so far in all weather."[5]

In early July 1915, Winsor finally sent word to Mrs. Lodge that her sons would be admitted—and housed in warm quarters. A condition on acceptance was passing several entrance exams. Cabot and John immediately began tutoring lessons under the aegis of a Yale instructor, Frederick J. Manning (who would become professor of history at Swarthmore College and the husband of President William Howard Taft's daughter, Helen). Both long deficient in mathematics and weak in geography, the Lodges studied diligently and passed their exams. Eleven-year-old John, according to Manning, was less able to concentrate and was in sad need of the orderly discipline of a good boarding school. He was somewhat rebellious, and "had to write his answers under constant compulsion."[6]

The very week that Cabot and John were preparing to leave for Concord, tragedy struck at home. Nannie Lodge died suddenly from a heart ailment. To those closest to her, it seemed as if she had never fully recovered from the loss of Bay six years earlier. "If I have been of any use in the world, if I have attained any small measure of success, to her I owe it as to her I owe the happiness which life has brought me in the years now gone forever," the Senator wrote in a sketch of her life.[7] Privately published in 1918 with a dedication to the Lodge grandchildren, the book included many of the hundreds of letters of recollection and sympathy the family had received.

The boys went off to Middlesex wearing mourning bands on their sleeves. There, they joined some 150 other young men in a rigorous academic and athletic environment. Both did well at the start. Their proficiency in French gave them a decided edge, and John easily scored a grade of 99 in French. At the end of the December term, Cabot and John ranked first and second, respectively, in their seventh grade class of seventeen boys.[8] By February John replaced Cabot in first place with an average of 83 and remained head of his class until falling to fourth in June. A half-century later, the French teacher, Luis A. Baralt, remembered the Lodge boys as "very neatly dressed (both alike) perfect little New England gentlemen, polite and eager."[9]

Outside of class, it was a different story. Although quite shy, John was full of boundless mischief and was often late for lessons and untidy. Cabot, too, was something of a showoff. His friends began calling him "Cab-Horse." Their classmate Finley Peter Dunne remembered them well: "There was a lot of teasing, some of it in very doubtful taste, about their famous grandfather, which Cabot tossed off nonchalantly, but which seemed to bother John, who did not have his brother's capacity with the quip. During that year, John developed a nervous affliction, in which his eyelids fluttered spasmodically."[10]

Both Lodges got into serious trouble for "breaking into" the town library to return a borrowed book after the building had closed. They also found themselves incurring the form of punishment called "rounds" for such "careless offenses" as lateness to class, absence from study periods, and the like. A round consisted of a lap around the three-quarter-mile elliptical driveway circling the center of the campus. John chalked up over 160 rounds during his first year, and Cabot walked off nearly as many.

A more agreeable activity for the brothers that first year was participation in a school production of *HMS Pinafore*. John, a high soprano, sang the leading female part, Josephine. Cabot played Buttercup. John always considered this Gilbert and Sullivan operetta his theatrical debut. Their mother traveled from Washington to see the production, and later reported the event in detail to the Senator. He replied to her: "I acted a great deal when I was in college and liked it and did well at it which gives me a peculiar interest in their success. I am especially pleased that they sang so well—something I could never do at all. . . . John must have been quite lovely. I can imagine how handsome he must have looked with his big, black eyes."[11] John continued in female roles in *The Mikado* and *The Pirates of Penzance*, and played men's parts in other student shows. Clearly, he ended the year on an academic, as well as a theatrical, high note. John's higher scholastic standing rankled Cabot, and he felt the classroom competition should end. He pleaded with his mother to be allowed to skip a grade and leave John in the class below. A summer of tutoring would assure his jump ahead. She agreed, feeling, as well, that John was advancing too fast for a twelve-year-old.

"John was terribly upset over Cabot's gain," Francesca explained. "He felt unrewarded for his classroom performance. But his admiration for his brother never wavered. On the other hand, the breakup affected his motivation and nerves." To console John, his mother permitted him to wear long trousers, beginning in the fall semester.

During their 1916 Christmas holiday in Washington, the Senator reviewed their progress. John ranked first in his class; his brother, too, stood high academically. Their grandfather Lodge, however, was distressed to learn that Middlesex did not offer Greek as a regular course of study. He wrote Winsor to express his dismay over this omission. Winsor acquiesced. Having no Greek instructor on campus, Winsor made arrangements to bring one from Boston by train three times a week.

Enthusiasm over ancient languages paled that winter as the United States severed diplomatic relations with Germany after it had announced full-scale resumption of submarine warfare against all countries, belligerent or neutral. Senator Lodge called for an end of partisanship in the world crisis and backed President Woodrow Wilson in preparations for war. Cabot especially felt that all his grandfather's causes were his own. On April 3, 1917, when front-page headlines heralded Wilson's war message, he was alarmed at an inside story telling about a near riot at his grandfather's office, where pacifists gathered to harangue him. The encounter ended in fisticuffs. Called "a damned coward" by the leader of the anti-war group, the Senator punched him squarely on the jaw.[12]

With Americans on the battlefields of Europe, their Uncle Augustus Gardner resigned from Congress to take up service in the Army, becoming the first member of either House to leave for military duty. Major Gardner at his own request transferred from the Adjutant General's staff to an infantry battalion so that he could be a line officer and go to France, even dropping in rank to do so. Since the outbreak of war in Europe in 1914, he had advocated the cause of military preparedness and defense. "You can't improvise a battleship or a submarine or a torpedo or a sailor after a war breaks out," he had declared in a well-received speech called "Wake Up, America!"[13]

In field training for overseas duty in early 1918, fifty-two-year-old Uncle Gussie contracted pneumonia during an extremely cold January. The eight-term former Congressman died in a Georgia military hospital six days later. His nephews never forgot his early call for adequate national defense and his departure from Congress for military service. "To his country he gave his life just as if he had fallen on the field of battle," the Senator wrote them, "and as long as you live you must always think of this and try to live up to the high ideal of life and service which he has left to you."[14]

Housemaster Reginald Howe, who would soon leave Concord to start the Belmont Hill School, commented on the brothers' general attitude at the end of the 1917-18 term: "Both boys . . . adopt for some unknown reason at times, a special privileged point of view that is very inexcusable. This has cropped up with Cabot in the past in his relations with the school servants, and does with John occasionally in little ways. John's report under the circumstances is, I think, quite satisfactory. He failed only one examination."[15]

Henry Woodbridge, who enrolled at Middlesex at age twelve in September 1918, remembered his first meeting with John while on the roadway working off "rounds" for tardiness and unprepared lessons: "John was very friendly to me, a newcomer three years younger. He was popular on campus, more so than Cabot, who was arrogant and did not quite fit in. He wasn't good in athletics either. John had a very bad nervous twitch. I guess his family thought he might be headed for a nervous breakdown of some sort that term."[16]

At the end of the first semester, John had built up 132 rounds, failed geometry, and barely passed Latin and English. He stood eighteenthth in a class of twenty-five. His highest grade was 83 in French; his general average stood at 69. "Physically the boy has never seemed to me better," reported Howe to Mrs. Lodge. But his attitude continually displeased the faculty. "I have appealed to him in every way possible, and he has assured me that he would try, but the flesh has been very weak. He has fallen off in rank . . . eleven places since last June's report." Bessie decided that her fifteen-year-old son needed plenty of outdoor exercise and building up in a mild climate. She realized that his health took priority over studies. "I hope sincerely that he will do well in his new school," concluded Howe, "and that he may return to us perhaps for a final year of work. I have grown very fond of John and shall miss him."[17]

In early 1919, John boarded a westbound train for a refreshingly different environment and routine. The final destination of the four-day journey was Arizona. The Evans School in the small western town of Mesa offered a program designed to build individual self-reliance and confidence. Teddy Roosevelt's sons had attended Evans, as had the offspring of other prominent Easterners. Founded in 1902 by H. David Evans, a Cambridge-educated linguist and sportsman, the school met the needs of those who found it necessary to take a rest from their regular preparatory or college courses and yet did not wish to lose entirely the thread of their studies. Situated on a desert ranch, Evans combined life in the open with a measure of university-geared instruction. Mornings and most evenings were devoted to study; afternoons were completely turned over to outdoor pursuits.[18]

At first, John had expressed little enthusiasm about living alone—every Evans schoolboy did—in a 12 x 14-foot cabin, furnished with stove, table, bed, and washbowl. But he soon adjusted well. Each of the twenty-five or so students made his own bed, chopped wood for fuel, and cared for a horse. "Mine was a small horse by the name of Dixie," John recalled fifty years later. "He was proud-cut and full of vim and vinegar."[19]

Twice during the winter, trips on horseback of a week's duration took the boys to the foothills of the Pinal Mountains, where they set up camp in the wilderness, cooked meals from the back of a wagon, and slept on the ground. There were but few rules, and those were based on common sense. Headmaster Evans firmly believed that "life in the West, with its vision, distance and colour, could kindle a boy's imagination, and leave him that ethereal spark which might at any time burst into flame."

"The change in climate and academic pace, along with individual instruction, benefitted John," Francesca recalled. "His overall health improved, and his nervous twitch subsided. He also avoided an influenza epidemic of gigantic proportions raging throughout much of the country." Former Middlesex schoolmate Frederic Coudert wrote John in January 1919 to report that the flu was devastating: "It is very bad in Boston, & I should not be a bit surprised if school was in quarantine. . . . I got the flu the day after you left & am still in the house getting over it. My sister got it Tuesday & has contracted pneumonia, but has passed the crisis yesterday."[20] That month John learned of the death of his illustrious godfather, Teddy Roosevelt, who was still grieving the loss of his son Quentin in combat a few months before the war ended. On February 9, 1919, Bessie wrote: "Gampa [Senator Lodge] delivered the Eulogy on T.R. today in the Senate. Be sure to read it in the paper."[21]

Evans issued monthly progress reports on every student. John steadily improved. At the end of his first full year in Arizona, the headmaster wrote of good grades in all five courses (Latin, French, German, algebra, and geometry). He also expressed approval of Lodge's cabin "housekeeping" and care of his horse, both on the trail and in the stable. John's overall conduct merited a "variable: generally good."[22]

While learning to ride and handle horses challenged students, other sports were not overlooked; the Evans ranch included a baseball field, a swimming pool, and several tennis courts. For entertainment, the students welcomed excursions to the main street of Mesa for movie shows with Wallace Reid, Tom Mix, Charlie Chaplin, Lillian Gish, and Pearl White. During his summer vacation, John continued to build himself up. He worked outdoors at Nahant under his grandfather's head gardener. Content to be close to nature, he thought about becoming a forester.

Bessie wrote frequently with words of encouragement and advice: "As you grow stronger your neck will not bother you," she emphasized. "You know that the great point is to get rid of that twitch & I am sure that you yourself want to & much realize how all important it is."[23] While overcoming his nervous tic and building up his self-assurance, John had grown to a height of six feet. Back East, an equally tall Cabot entered his final term at Middlesex. In June 1920, he graduated eighth in his class of nineteen and passed the entrance exams for Harvard.

John remained anxious to go back to Middlesex and pick up his place in his original class. Although Evans provided personal tutoring, students often got carried away by the outdoor life and neglected their studies. Mrs. Lodge suggested to John that he request a list of books from Concord and try to keep up with its curriculum. In any event, he would have to pass certain examinations to be readmitted into the class of 1921. John studied harder than usual, passing the tests in French, German, and math with an average of 77. He rejoined his old classmates in the fall, the start of a difficult academic year. John failed several courses, spent many hours with a tutor, and at least once faced probation. Happily, his "rounds" dwindled to a mere handful, and in June, with a general average in the 60s—the passing mark was 60—he managed to receive a diploma. In retrospect, his academic record as a teenager could only be called erratic.[24] Once again, John feverishly boned up on English, history, Latin, and physics, spending three weeks with a tutor.

That summer John visited Europe, where he and Cabot worked for the privately funded Committee for Devastated France. Slowly recovering from four years of war, the country sought volunteers to help run camps for boys whose fathers had been killed or whose homes were destroyed. One of the jobs the Lodge brothers undertook at a French Boy Scout camp required transporting supplies in a Model T truck. John often took the wheel of the vehicle, which had a tendency to jackknife. Cabot's biographer, William J. Miller, describes the two brothers in the truck: "John, you're not very good at driving, you know," Cabot warned. Just then John turned the wheels too sharply, and the truck jackknifed right through the window of a cafe. The owner came out shouting, "That's the way Americans are! When they want a drink, they drive right into the cafe in their car!"[25]

Passing his entrance exams, Lodge joined eighteen of his Middlesex class of twenty-three students entering Harvard that September. The Harvard *Crimson* offered the 856 incoming students a panacea for the next four years: "Would you make the most of college?" it asked. "Then keep busy—avoid idle ways as you would the plague and idle friends as your worst enemies. It does not matter what keeps you busy—studies, athletics, competitions, self-support, social service—as long as it has some purpose."

This post-war idealism would soon meld into the hedonistic spirit of the 1920s.[26]

At Cambridge, John fell into an already close-knit circle of chums. Most were from Middlesex, and included Finley Dunne, Thomas Howard, John Ricketson, and Thomas Nickerson. He shared a room in Gore Hall with Blake Johnson, a pal from Nahant. "He differed from most of us by being very 'straight' about sex and such things, about which we were inclined to be somewhat raucous," Finley Dunne stated years later. "But there was nothing epicene about John, then or ever. We ended up liking him; I certainly did."[27]

Lodge and a dozen members of his class joined the Fox Club in their sophomore year. Cabot already was a member of this social club housed in a large clubhouse on Boylston Street near Harvard Square. Although Harvard would soon adopt the house plan and strive for a new sort of classless undergraduate society whereby housemasters and faculty became better known and more accessible among the students, eating clubs clearly defined a person and prescribed the social *modus operandi*. As Fox men (and Lodges from Boston's North Shore), both John and Cabot enjoyed a busy extracurricular life that frequently entailed theater openings, debutante balls, sailing parties, symphony galas, and athletic victory celebrations. "An undergrad was judged by invitations stuck on his dorm room mirror."[28]

John drank very moderately, which was not the case of his fellow club members. "This, in spite of the fact that the steward Richard Evans provided us with any amount of gin, bourbon and Scotch—at a price of course," roommate Blake Johnson pointed out. He added that "As far as I know, John had no time for girls while in college."[29]

John spent an average amount of time toiling over studies but rarely to the detriment of other pursuits. A party always perked up when he arrived, according to his classmate Hamilton "Bud" Eames: "John was the slowest character alive—always late for everything, and teased about it. He would grin and agree."[30] "John was an average student with many interests and social activities," recalled Paul W. Williams, the son of a New Bedford Baptist minister. Williams, a scholarship student who became a leading New York attorney and judge, remembered John's joining the Glee Club and being elected to the prestigious Signet Society: "He developed an interest, too, in public speaking and debating as I did. But I really got to know John later as a fellow law student at Harvard."[31]

At the end of his freshman year, John put aside his books for nearly two months of manual labor at Dr. Wilfred Grenfell's medical outposts in Newfoundland and Labrador. In the 1890s, this English physician and missionary had founded hospitals, orphanages, and other social services in

Canadian coastal villages. Young men such as Lodge came each July and August to volunteer their time constructing buildings, unloading supplies from boats, carrying logs, and shoveling coal. Cabot had enjoyed the experience in 1920. John now pitched in, working in a hospital and building an orphanage.

During his sophomore year, John enrolled in courses in fine arts, French, geography, and geology, and—to fulfill major requirements—studies in history and government. As did most of his class, he maintained the proverbial "gentleman's C" grade average. French as usual gave rise to his highest mark, a B. Periodic term papers on such subjects as Washington Irving, the British acquisition of Cyprus, Walt Whitman, and Harding and the election of 1920 awakened his innate writing talent. His essay on Oliver Wendell Holmes, Sr., as a satirist received an A and the praise of English Department Professor Kenneth Murdock.

From time to time, he contributed a letter to the pages of the *Crimson*. In February of his sophomore year, he commented on the postwar reparations and the European financial crisis in a long and perceptive analysis: "Let us hope that our sporting instinct in this case (France's demands for reparations) will not push us to actions which would cause unlimited trouble in the future. . . . Let us endeavor to help Europe in such a way that no discord will arise in the allied camp. In this we have failed so far; and it behooves us rather to prevent the impending disaster than to peacefully stay at home and prepare for it. Should Europe sink beneath the sea," he concluded, "would our first cry be, 'what of our banks?' "[32]

Aside from an interest in international relations, John found great pleasure in undergraduate theatrical activities, as did Cabot. Both joined the Cercle Français, a group that presented three or four classical French plays each year. In 1923 John was elected president of the Cercle, and under the coaching of Ernest Perrin, a professor of French diction, immediately proceeded to play major roles in a number of rarely seen comedies and dramas by Labiche, Murger, Theuriet, and Busson. A revival of Molière's *Tartuffe*, an ambitious and difficult task, won praise from undergraduates and Boston Francophiles.

John's interest in the theater soon embraced musical comedy, dominated at Harvard by the popular Hasty Pudding Club productions. To perform in its 1923 show, John took singing lessons and proved to be as good a singer as an actor. In the spring of his junior year, he was cast as the leading man (playing three characters opposite other undergrads in female roles) in *Who's Who*, written by Joe de Ganahl '25 and William Lindsay White '24, son of the journalist William Allen White of Emporia, Kansas. The show carried a professional touch from the staging by Lou

Silvers, the Tin-Pan-Alley composer of "April Showers" and musical director for Al Jolson. Broadway's Sammy Lee directed the dancing numbers. After the Cambridge and New York performances, Lodge apparently was offered both a leading part in a Broadway musical and a role in a Boston production of *Mademoiselle Modiste*.

The *Crimson* critic, P. W. Hollister, called *Who's Who* a Pudding show "for the most part fresh as no Broadway show will ever be, inspired, perspiring, untiring, and at times downright comical." He singled out Lodge for praise: "In this home of the bean and the cod, where Lodges may play with the Moynahans and Cassidys, it is with pleasure that the honors of the evening are split three ways: between J. S. Moynahan, A. B. Cassidy and Lodge. Moynahan's feet, as usual; Cassidy's height and lines; Lodge's general excellence."[33]

At Harvard, John also studied in George Pierce Baker's flourishing theater workshop. After appearances in several plays directed by Professor Baker, John received an offer from the Theater Guild of Boston of a singing part in a one-act play called "The Daughter of the Sun God," replete with primitive Indian songs and Gregorian chants. He declined the role.[34] In November 1924, Baker left Harvard for Yale, which had received a large gift from philanthropist Edward Harkness for the building of a university theater and the development of a full-scale drama program. The professor felt Cambridge had made no attempt to provide proper physical facilities nor endowment for that area of the humanities. John, together with many other Harvard men, complained that the university was negligent in letting Baker go, especially to its closest Ivy League rival.

Lodge's interest in amateur theatrics continued during school vacations. For two summers, 1923 and 1924, he signed up as a counselor at Camp Pasquaney in Bristol, New Hampshire. The boys' camp chiefly needed him to run a program of plays in the absence of Ernest Watson, a Dartmouth professor long associated with Pasquaney's little theater endeavors. "In 1923, I was a young 14-year-old camper," remembered Charles F. Stanwood, later director of the camp. "He directed plays I was in. In the theater he was a strict and somewhat impatient taskmaster, inspiring our fear when we had not learned our lines, and filling us with awe when he occasionally spoke our lines and acted our parts to show us how we should proceed."[35]

John's responsibilities centered around a major production and two short plays, a schedule originally fostered by camp founder Edward Simpson Wilson, a knowledgeable and keen student of the theater. Lodge drew his talent from a camp of boys from families such as the Biddles, Colgates, Paysons, and De Rhams. His charges included a young Kentuckian named Thruston Morton, a future U.S. Senator and Chairman of the Republican National Committee. John set lofty criteria for the young thespians. In the 1924 Pasquaney yearbook, he wrote; "Drama flourished. . . . We aimed high, higher than is the custom in institutions of this type. . . . Besides the keen enjoyment derived from the Theater, we have also benefitted in knowledge and appreciation of the drama."

Apart from the camp's stage, John led hiking parties in the mountains, patrolled the lake waterfront, played tennis, and organized canoe trips. Pasquaney counselor John Spaeth, Jr., always remembered a boating adventure with Lodge and a dozen campers on Cliff Isle. The boys cruised to the island in a motor launch which towed a caravan of three canoes stacked with clothes and bedding. When the launch pulled up to the camp site, Spaeth asked John to untie the first canoe and pull it alongside the boat. Instead, he stepped into the canoe and lost his balance, causing all three canoes to capsize or tip over . . . and dump all their gear into the lake. When Lodge became Governor of Connecticut, Spaeth, by then Dean of the Faculty at Wesleyan University, wrote him a congratulatory letter. He ended it by saying he had confidence that the State's new chief executive had by now "learned how to keep his ship on an even keel."[36]

By the summer of 1923, brother Cabot had completed Harvard in three years. His grandfather urged him to take a newspaper job, believing it a valuable and stimulating preparation for launching a political career. He joined the *Boston Transcript* as a cub reporter. But at the end of his first six months as a journalist, Cabot decided to cash in on his grandfather's long-promised gift of a trip to Europe. Before he left, the Senator took him to see President Coolidge. "This young man finished Harvard in three years, but I had to bribe him to do it," he announced. For his trip, Coolidge gave him a "To whom it may concern" letter of introduction.[37]

After Cabot left Cambridge for newspaper assignments and travels far and near, the paths of the brothers crossed and joined less frequently. Before they went their different ways, the Lodge boys had cut a wide and enviable swath, becoming the spark of many carefree parties and the object of affection for many girlish hearts. And at Harvard, their circle of friends had opened to include a magnetic family of talented and energetic young people who had recently settled in Boston after an uncommon upbringing in Europe.

And so the world of Francesca Braggiotti began to intertwine with that of John.

CHAPTER 4

Francesca

In Italy they were known as "those crazy Americans"; in Boston, "those crazy Italians."[1] The Braggiotti clan—Pa and his attractive, unpredictable brood of eight children—left behind a large and cheery villa near Florence to begin life anew in America. It was 1919. World War I had ended, and the country was about to enter a dynamically liberating decade. Thousands of miles away in Arizona, John Lodge dreamed of his Massachusetts school days and longed to return.

Although their Braggiotti name bore the sound of ancient Tuscany, they were really old Bostonian under the skin. Their recently deceased mother, the comely, statuesque Lily Schlesinger, had been born in Massachusetts, studied voice in France, and concertized on both sides of the Atlantic. Her husband, Isidore Braggiotti, too, was a transplanted New England-bred musician. Together, they brought up four girls and four boys in a carefree, uninhibited atmosphere that raised eyebrows even among the unselfconscious Italians.

Isidore had left Boston for Europe before the turn of the century to pursue an overriding interest in music. His father, François Braggiotti, was of Venetian descent but had settled in Smyrna. There, he ran an export business dealing in Oriental rugs, figs, and attar of roses. He traveled frequently to the United States and eventually became an American citizen. In Boston he met and married Martha Chadwick of Beacon Street. Their son was brought up in Paris and New England. He was half Italian and looked Italian.

Isidore had a pleasing singing voice and a broad knowledge of music. He was often invited to participate in musical programs. One day he attended a soiree at the Paris house of Sebastian Schlesinger, a retired American businessman and an accomplished amateur composer. As Isidore handed his hat and cane to the butler, he heard a young woman singing one of Schumann's lieder. The mezzo-soprano voice was that of Schlesinger's daughter Lily. Two weeks after this meeting in 1900, they were married. They spent their honeymoon at Niagara Falls and in Boston, and then journeyed back to Europe to a villa in Florence.

They chose a centuries-old cream-colored stucco villa with green blinds brightening all the windows. Situated in Montughi, on the outskirts of Florence, it stood amid olive and cypress trees, orchards and gardens, and was reached by a half-hour carriage ride from the center of the city. The Braggiottis immediately proceeded to convert a large patio into a two-storied glass-ceilinged music room. This private auditorium centered around two concert grand pianos and a cluster of blue and gold sofas and chairs. It was circled by a balcony with a blue majolica balustrade and an upper wall border of sculptured heads of Wagner, Bizet, Verdi and other composers. This costly renovation was a wedding gift from Sebastian Schlesinger, and as a tribute to him, his bust joined the row of musical luminaries.

Of German-Jewish background, Sebastian had settled in the United States, served as a soldier in the Civil War, and made a sizable fortune in the import and export of steel. In Boston, where he acted as the German Consul, he married Countess Berthe de Pourtales, a member of a large and aristocratic French-Swiss family. Their daughter Lily was born in Nahant, not far from the summer home of the grandparents of her future son-in-law John Lodge.

Lily and Isidore's music room was the focal point of artistic activity in the Braggiotti household, and to a great extent in all of Florence. Both parents taught singing to a selected number of pupils, a vocation for which they were well-qualified and suited. Students from all over Europe and America came to the villa to enroll at their school.

Weekly Saturday musicales with performances by pupils and visiting artists—from time to time they included pianists Paderewski and Harold Bauer, soprano Emma Eames, cellist Pablo Casals, and tenor Beniamino Gigli—attracted many guests. The programs never failed to present an instrumental or vocal selection by one or more of the little Braggiottis: Berta, Francesca, Stiano, Mario, Marta, Gloria, Rama, and Chadwick.

"Ma stressed upon us that she expected each of us to be an expert in some field," Francesca once explained to John. "The important thing was to decide what it would be and then do it well. Some of us had beautiful voices, but no one chose singing as an eventual vocation. We had heard so much singing that we sort of rebelled. At first I studied the piano. But I soon chose dancing lessons because it was the only thing I could do better than my brothers."

At the age of nine, during a visit to grandfather "Nonno" Schlesinger in Nice, she first performed on a stage as part of a ballet at the Monte

Carlo Opera house. Dance would become one of her greatest pleasures. Formal education meant little to her. They were taught French, English, and German languages as well as art and history by their parents and by a round of nurses and governesses—a signorina, a fraulein, an Irish-English woman, and a mademoiselle. From time to time, Francesca and one or more of her sisters and brothers studied other subjects at a nearby Catholic school. They periodically spent a number of months on visits to Berlin and Paris. "I was in Paris during the time Cabot and John were living there as young boys," Francesca recalled. "But our paths never crossed."

The outbreak of hostilities in Europe in 1914 began to change the Braggiottis' unfettered existence. Italy declared war on Germany, causing a severe drop in the enrollment of vocal students at the villa. The departure of a number of tenant farmers into military service, along with some of the sixteen servants, interrupted the smooth-running routine. A potential source of income was lost when the Braggiottis failed to take charge of a large feudal estate in Silesia, near Warsaw, left to them by Grandmother de Pourtales. As the war intensified, many large villas surrounding Florence were converted into hospitals and rest homes for wounded soldiers. In these makeshift quarters, Francesca and Berta toiled day after day caring for battle-torn troops. They sewed linen sacks to hang on each soldier's cot to safeguard belongings and wrote letters for the sick, blind, and dying. And occasionally they bolstered morale by singing folk songs and dancing between the beds.

Weary and exhausted by their volunteer work, midway through the war the Braggiottis journeyed to sunny Nice to visit Nonno. Long walks along the Promenade des Anglais, rides in open carriages along the coastal roads, and daily shopping excursions were a happy change from the ordeal of a homeland at war. Then, suddenly, seventy-nine-year-old Nonno Schlesinger died one morning in January 1917. It signaled the approaching end of a glorious epoch. Sebastian Schlesinger's affairs were complicated by assets in America and a domicile abroad. Isidore wanted to go to Boston to help settle the estate, but German submarines were then attacking all transatlantic ships. The plan never was carried out as hoped for. Lily developed cancer, and soon after the end of the war, she died at age forty-seven. Her grieving husband lost all interest in running the villa, the scene of unforgettably happy times when delightful music constantly echoed through its many rooms. At that point, although with very little money in hand, he and Francesca decided to move to the United States.

Francesca packed for days, closed up the house, and gathered together Pa and her sisters and brothers for the long trip. At the French port of Boulogne-sur-Mer, they boarded the SS *New Amsterdam*, bound for the United States. In late November 1919, in the midst of a snowfall and after a stormy crossing, the ship docked in Hoboken, New Jersey. On the deck, clustered around Pa, a nursemaid named Julia, forty trunks of belongings, two dogs, and a cage of birds, were the Braggiotti children. They ranged in age from eighteen-year-old Berta down to six-year-old Chadwick.

In spite of a dock strike, Pa managed to move the mountain of luggage off the pier. He shipped all forty trunks to Brookline, Massachusetts, where his cousin, Jessie Whitney, had rented a house for his family. In Boston their train was met by a raft of Braggiotti and Schlesinger cousins. It was dark by the time they reached their new home at 78 Upland Road. To the older children, it looked like a wooden box after the marble halls they had known in Italy. They joined the rest of their extended family in the dining room. The table was set, with a half of grapefruit on each plate and beside it a glass of milk. The young Braggiottis had never seen grapefruit before and had never drunk milk with their meals in Europe. It was just the beginning of many new experiences and adjustments.

The two oldest children, Berta, born in 1901, and Francesca, born in 1902, had all but ended their schooling. They stayed at home to help Pa run the house and his new voice studio. They soon pitched in when he started a singing class in Maine with twenty-six pupils. He had once promised soprano Emma Eames that if he ever came back to the United States, he would go there in summer to train vocal students.

Schooled in ballet in Florence and Nice, with a keen interest in the then-emerging "interpretative," or modern, dance, Berta and Francesca began devising routines for the entertainment of their admiring family and a growing circle of enraptured friends. The ongoing support and encouragement of Mrs. Barthold Schlesinger, widow of their great-uncle, opened many doors for the captivating and graceful Braggiotti sisters. A dance exhibition before the city's grande dame, Mrs. Jack Gardner, at her fabled, art-filled Fenway Court home helped to build interest in their performances. Before too long, the sisters were welcomed as members of the Vincent Club, an exclusive women's club in Boston. Each year the club produced a musical revue to raise money for St. Vincent's Hospital. Berta and Francesca joined the cast of the show, the first to be presented before an audience of both men and women. With this change, a problem arose. Would the ladies be allowed to expose bare legs? In 1920 the city fathers of Boston considered uncovered limbs a sign of immorality.

Francesca and Berta, however, refused to go on with rehearsals unless they were permitted to dance stockingless and in bare feet. A meeting between the mayor and the club was arranged. He was given a chance to judge the "respectability" of the dance as well as to inspect the costumes to see if they might be offensive to Bostonians. "We charmed the mayor," Francesca pointed out. "He agreed to our appearances without shoes. Our performance became the talk of Boston, and soon we were asked to dance at other charity events."

A Vincent Club member who had seen them in the annual revue asked Francesca to consider giving dancing lessons to her younger daughter. The Braggiotti dance class opened with a group of a dozen or so girls in a large upstairs hall in the Brookline Firehouse. "Many a time we were shaken out of our nymph-like world of floating veils and moonlight sonatas by the shriek of sirens below our studio," recalled Gloria, who with Marta, often joined the aggregation to learn the basic steps and positions of the classical dance.[2]

Whenever they had the time and money to study, Francesca and Berta took advantage of professional dance instruction. In 1921, they enrolled for a three-week course in New York with Luigi Albertieri, ballet master of the Metropolitan Opera Company and Covent Garden.

The sisters' teaching continued to attract attention and pupils. Francesca taught girls crippled with polio and added lessons for boys and men, including Harvard undergrads. Founders of other schools, including the well-known tap dancer Ned Weyburn in New York, came to Boston to learn about the Braggiotti classes and courses. Periodic school recitals and special charity appearances brought the sisters much personal publicity and popularity in and about Boston. They were in demand, socially as well as professionally. Engagements or private parties in New York and Newport followed. "I spent a number of summers in New York in the 1920s in different dance courses and usually lived in a 5th or 6th floor walk-up," Francesca explained. "I got to know a number of young dancers and actresses. Helen Hayes was one of them."

In the summer of 1922, Francesca and Berta received a call from the managers of B. F. Keith's Theatre. Would they like to appear as a dance team in vaudeville? Keith's bookers thought a society girl act would be a novel addition to the usual array of animals, jugglers, puppets, gymnasts, magicians, and comics. They signed for a week's run in the heart of downtown Boston. The carefully rehearsed and mounted act—it featured a shimmery gold drop curtain and striking red carpet stretched across the stage—captivated theatre audiences.

At every performance a mannish-looking matron in a brown suit plodded down the aisle to sit near the stage. But at the end of the Braggiotti act, she would quickly leave. Enamoured with Francesca, this fan was Amy Lowell, cigar-smoking poet, polyphonic prose writer, and individualistic member of the old Boston clan that seemingly only spoke to the Cabots. Before the end of the run, and in response to the "dancer of silver shadows," Lowell wrote a poem "To Francesca Braggiotti, After Seeing Her Dance 'Fragrance.' "[3] Lowell sent a copy of the verse to

Francesca. Her acknowledgment began a friendship. She visited the Lowell house in Brookline frequently as a dinner guest after a long, tiring day of dance. They'd sit by the fire and talk about faraway places like China and about Amy's forthcoming book, a biography of Keats.

That year, 1922, the Braggiotti sisters were ecstatic over a chance to study dancing with Ruth St. Denis and Ted Shawn at their school in Peterborough, New Hampshire. St. Denis, a New Jersey farm girl, had embarked on a career in the 1890s as a dancer skilled in high kicks, splits, rollovers, and other feats. After a series of uneventful engagements with producer David Belasco, she set about creating a style of modern dance through innovative movements of the body and exploitation of forgotten principles of tribal gesture, breath rhythms, and torso articulation. She stressed Oriental themes and trappings—bare feet, bare waist, bells and glittering costumes.

Ruth St. Denis's popularity grew with her continuing creativeness. In 1914 she married Ted Shawn, who became her dance partner and co-founder of the Denishawn school. Their approach and execution of the free-flowing interpretive dance intrigued Francesca. She could hardly wait to be immersed in their avant-garde school, which was beginning to change the course of dance, of costuming, of staging, and she soon revamped their own school using the Denishawn method.

Francesca also took an interest in acting. She and her sisters were drawn into a theatrical undertaking at Harvard not long after they met Edgar Scott, president of the college's Cercle Français. The undergraduate players needed young ladies with a thorough speaking knowledge of French to appear in its French-language productions. Because Pa's studio—actually a separate wing on the Brookline house—was so large, many rehearsals of the Cercle plays took place there.

Among the club's most active members were John and Cabot Lodge. At a casting session during the first term of John's sophomore year, Francesca was introduced to both boys. Her friends had spoken of these two attractive and well-traveled brothers. And sharply dressed. They stood out in striped trousers, a dark jacket over a hard bosom shirt, and gray vest and spats.

Because of Francesca's and Berta's facility at speaking French, along with an obvious stage presence, they easily won roles in the Cercle plays. Few productions over the next three or four years lacked a Braggiotti in the cast. Even teenage Gloria played ingenue parts, and one year eleven-year-old Rama appeared. Rehearsals at the Braggiottis were so much fun that a number of the Cercle members regularly gathered at 78 Upland Road for a good time. The Lodges joined in on many Sundays for impromptu musicals, dancing, games, and general roughhousing.

Professional artists and students alike filled the music room week after week. English actress Lady Diana Manners visited when her play *The Miracle* came to Boston. Harvard freshman Emlen Etting, who spent hours sketching his theatrical friends, often stopped by. He had been a roommate of Mario in boarding school. Isidore Braggiotti welcomed everyone, believing that if real love existed in a family, people were drawn and reacted to it. "You'll never see a crowd in the house of an unhappy family," he pointed out.[4]

John was attracted to this free-spirited, bohemian atmosphere generated by Isidore and his eight animated and personable offspring—said to have been the inspiration for Margaret Kennedy's *The Constant Nymph*, a story of a father and his large family of sensitive, freedom-loving children and first published as a novel in 1924. Lodge joined right in, raising his voice in jaunty song and loud debate. He liked to be the center of attention, even to the point of providing a bit of impromptu comedy relief in such free-for-alls. Cabot's presence was felt too, yet in an imperious and more restrained manner. The brothers took every opportunity to stop by the house in Brookline or the dance studio, recently relocated to Berkeley Street in Boston.

John and Cabot were amazed and amused by Francesca and her family. And Cabot was soon smitten. By Christmas 1922, he was Francesca's steady beau, and they began seeing each other nearly every day. In her diary, beginning in January 1923, Francesca briefly jotted down her impressions of each day's highlights. "At studio 11 A.M.," she wrote on January 2. "Cabot called me up from Back Bay station. Just back from Washington. Started out new dance for Boston Opera. I felt so weak. Just up from flu. No inspiration. . . . Cabot met me at studio 3:30. We had a cozy evening together at 78 [Upland Road] by the fire. Charmant! I weaken." Two days later, she recorded: "Studio all morning, mostly working on our new dance. We are getting more busy every day. The School is a great success—120 pupils now. I love it. It has opened doors to endless opportunities in my life. I am begetting a terrific mental problem between my duty & my desire. Love for art or love for love? . . . Cabot called me up at 10."

The dancing school attracted many ambitious and eager youngsters, and Francesca was busy teaching into most evenings. "John Lodge & Alexander [Sandy] Hamilton came to the studio," she noted. At the end of the work day, Cabot usually appeared. "He is sympathetic about everything. Vero simpatico!" she concluded.

A Braggiotti Sunday soirée in early January honored Shakespearean actor Walter Hampden, who was passing through Boston on tour. "Many interesting people," wrote Francesca. "Cabot, John & Sandy Hamilton stayed on. We dined at the Country Club & I walked home. The evening was gorgeous. The country covered with snow. Cabot seems to understand me. Can it really be? I am trying to know him."

Cabot often came from classes in Cambridge to spend as little as a half hour in Brookline. Or he'd send a large armful of roses. Sometimes he would borrow a car and pick up Francesca for shopping, a concert, or just a long ride. No matter how busy and exhausted, she found time to see him. They spent many hours talking in the music room. "I was crazy about Cabot," she admitted. "You couldn't avoid it. He was very attractive, intelligent, well-mannered and thoughtful."

By early spring, there were rumors around Boston of a forthcoming engagement between the handsome and bright Harvard undergraduate and the popular and accomplished Boston dancer. Then an accident changed the path of their courtship. During a rehearsal for a vigorous Russian dance routine, Francesca heard a loud snapping sound and stumbled onto the floor. The troupe stopped and rushed to her side. Taken to a doctor's office, she feared the worst. The physician examined her leg and reported torn ligaments in her knee, a serious mishap for a dancer. He prescribed total rest for at least two weeks.

Francesca spent several days in bed, but with a student recital in final rehearsals, she felt the need to work at the studio. She struggled back and forth to the school on crutches, directing from a chaise lounge. In the process, she aggravated her condition. Cabot remained a frequent caller. He traveled by streetcar to Brookline; other times his friends, Dr. and Mrs. Henry Sears, loaned their car and chauffeur for the drive from Cambridge. Emily Sears, their debutante daughter, had participated in plays of the Cercle Français, and they all adored Francesca. After his visits to Francesca, Cabot occasionally accepted the invitation of Dr. and Mrs. Sears to dine at their home. The irrepressibly witty and naturally unassuming Emily was usually included.

During the weeks of confinement at home, Francesca realized that any serious relationship with Cabot, especially marriage, was not in their best interests. He had his sights set on a political career, if not in his twenties, then later on after a period of apprenticeship in journalism and world travel. She had built a thriving dancing school, helped by her sisters, and welcomed frequent opportunities to perform on the professional stage, both locally and in other parts of the country. Broadway would soon beckon, perhaps even Hollywood. It would be no idyllic match if a politically ambitious Lodge and a theatrically-bound Braggiotti linked up as man and wife. Besides, many of Cabot's friends and relatives voiced disdain over the very idea of such a marriage. Cabot knew where his chums stood. "Hold on!" they continuously repeated whenever they thought he was close to putting a ring on Francesca's finger. Although terribly fond of him, and perhaps truly in love, she looked down the road—bumpy at best, she concluded. She surmised that Cabot needed a girl like Emily Sears, a young woman of position, polish and means.

With a clear and focused look at the future, Francesca gradually encouraged Cabot to see more of Emily. He would soon finish Harvard and begin work on a newspaper. Francesca with an injured knee faced a long period of recuperation and rehabilitation. She decided to go abroad and seek the best European doctors. There, she found no significant relief from the chronic discomfort, in spite of a regimen prescribed by physicians and therapists in Switzerland and Italy.

At one point, she entered a clinic in Bologna, whose staff placed her legs in a heavy plaster cast. "I have seen nothing but walls, beds, plaster casts and doctors," she complained in a letter home. She felt like a prisoner in a far-off feudal tower. One day, her aunt, Berthe Merol, came from Paris to see her, and for no apparent reason accused her of having an affair with an Italian doctor at the clinic. Francesca could take no more. She asked a friend from Genoa and a sympathetic nurse to smuggle her out of the sanitarium. One night they came and secretly guided her to a car that took them to a boat bound for America. Once aboard, the ship's doctor agreed to cut off part of the cumbersome cast so that she could massage and exercise the weakened muscles. In Boston she slowly picked up her work at the studio. A dancer's stock-in-trade are legs in tip-top shape, Francesca bore in mind. Without that, a performer faces bleak prospects. Her workaday future and family destiny depended on her recovery and return to center stage. Love and personal happiness would have to remain in the wings.

But that would change when John, not Cabot, re-entered her life.

CHAPTER 5

Stage-Door Johnny

J ohn Lodge returned to Cambridge for his senior year in September
1924. Many classmates had just toured Europe, vacationed in the
West, or worked at a summer resort. Now back at Harvard, they were
"masters" of the strategy of lining up classes so that they would not have
to rise much before 9 A.M. nor trammel with lectures after 1 P.M.
Enrollment rose to 3,000 undergrads. Scholastic standards, too, were on the
rise. But athletically, Harvard fell into a slump. That fall, on the football
field, rivals Yale and Princeton topped the Crimson.

John's thoughts turned more and more to graduation and his future
plans. Brother Cabot, after many months of overseas travel and newspaper
interviews with Italy's Mussolini, France's Poincaré, Austria's Michael
Hainisch, and other heads of state, had returned to Boston in time to cover
the Republican National Convention for the *Boston Transcript*. During his
stay in Paris, he saw a great deal of Emily Sears, who was touring Europe
with her parents and sister Jean.

The Republican Convention in Cleveland turned out to be somewhat
humiliating, if not for Senator Lodge, at least for Cabot. His grandfather
found himself reduced to an ordinary delegate without any speaking
assignments or committee posts. He was just part of the crowd. Coolidge,
in becoming President upon the sudden death of Harding in 1923, had
assumed the political leadership of the party. He still remembered
Senator's Lodge's high-handed manner toward him, a fellow Massachusetts
Republican whom Lodge viewed as a parochial politician.[1]

Cabot was indignant at the obvious disregard of the once-powerful
Party chief, but his grandfather brushed it aside. He had lived through too
many political battles to worry over the slight. Whatever the outward
changes and differences in the course of one's life, good manners, he
reminded Cabot, must always prevail. Senator Lodge turned to

Shakespeare and spent most evenings in bed reading. He returned to
Nahant for the remainder of the summer and spent hours every day
working on a book on the recent debate in the U.S. Senate on the new
League of Nations.

Lodge had approved the League idea in 1919. But to many observers,
he was unwilling to devote himself to positive action toward creating a
workable peace-keeping body. Antipathy toward both President Wilson
and the postwar Republican Party leadership kept the Senator away from
whole-hearted cooperation and compromise. Lodge did offer limiting
conditions to the covenant in the treaty establishing the League. These
reservations, part and parcel of America's commitment to the League,
made clear that the United States was under no obligation to come to the
defense of League member states without the approval of Congress. This
Lodge-rendered qualification virtually killed America's membership in the
world body. Years later, both Lodge brothers would claim their
grandfather was ahead of his time. This proviso, they pointed out, was a
key article of the United Nations charter in the 1940s—a document the
United States signed in the closing days of the Second World War.

Lodge labored over his manuscript in spite of physical discomfort from
a prostate condition. The illness was his first since the autumn of 1922,
when a combination of throat and digestive troubles prevented him from
taking an active part in the closing weeks of his Senatorial campaign
against Boston banker William A. Gaston. In that election, he defeated his
opponent by the narrow margin of 7,000 votes. In late summer, Lodge
welcomed John back from his camp job, pleased to hear of his theatrical
accomplishments at Pasquaney. He suggested that they talk about his
career plans during a school holiday in Washington later in the term. But
on November 9, he was stricken by a cerebral hemorrhage and died that
evening. A funeral at Christ Church in Cambridge brought together state
and national leaders, including Secretary of State Charles Evans Hughes,
Massachusetts Governor Channing Cox, and Secretary of War John W.
Weeks. As the cortège moved past Harvard and through the gates of Mt.
Auburn Cemetery, it passed the graves of a veritable panoply of old New
England's foremost citizens—Oliver Wendell Holmes, Sr., Henry
Wadsworth Longfellow, Edward Everett, Asa Gray, Julia Ward Howe,
Louis Agassiz, Francis Parkman, and Charles Sumner. Lodge had known
many of them during his seventy-four years.

The funeral procession came to a stop near a Gothic chapel-like
brownstone crypt set in a hillside on the bank of a small lake. Guarded by
two tall American elms, this mausoleum with an "L" carved in script
above the entrance held a dozen family members. After the final
benediction, John Lodge headed to Brattle Street and Harvard Square. He

surely wondered how his life would change without Grandfather directing the affairs of the family. What lay in store for him in 1925 and beyond? For one thing, his days in the Cercle Français were growing short. And he was losing track of many friends, especially the Braggiottis. For Francesca, matters at home left little time for her to even think about the Cercle and the Lodge boys. Suddenly they seemed a world apart.

Illness struck the Brookline household. Young Marta Braggiotti, an excellent student and promising athlete at the nearby high school, developed tuberculosis. Various family members chipped in to pay for her care at Saranac and other TB sanitariums. But Francesca ultimately bore much of the expense, some $500 a month. "Coming from an environment of health, activity, joyous shouts and public applause," John once wrote to Francesca after visiting Marta, "it must have been harder for her than for most to relapse with any resignation into the monotonous routine of the life which she has to lead here."[2]

The Braggiotti dance studio expanded into larger quarters and required a full-time manager and more teachers. Teenage Gloria soon devoted all her spare time to the school and dancing. She handled many of the children's classes and filled in for her sisters when they were called away for interpretive dancing roles with the San Carlos and German Wagner opera companies in Boston and with the New York Philharmonic in a performance of Ruth St. Denis' new ballet "Le temps" at Lewisohn Stadium. These jobs also provided money for the musical education of Mario Braggiotti. An undeniable wizard at a piano keyboard, he had left home to study at the Paris Conservatory.

All the Braggiottis felt the pinch of limited finances. Pa, as usual, was unable to cope with the situation; moreover, he added to the problem. Day after day, he headed for the Somerset Club to play cards. A compulsive gambler, he ran up large debts among his well-heeled confrères. Completely broke and in debt, Isidore could no longer face his friends. Humbled and embarrassed, he wanted to leave Boston.

This turn of events could not have happened at a more inopportune moment. Francesca and Berta had been offered a contract with the Shuberts for a musical in New York. When told by Francesca of this opportunity, her father nearly cried. "But Mumi, who's going to look after the children and the house?" The sisters realized if their family was going to stay together and get on its feet, they had to stay close to home.

"Pa, nonetheless, remained depressed," Francesca explained. "One day, he suggested a move of his studio to California. He'd try for better luck there. I agreed and helped him pack his trunks of clothes and music. Together, we boarded a train for Los Angeles. I found for him a small house with room for a studio. I placed advertisements in local papers that soon attracted a number of students." Francesca soon returned to Brookline as head of the family, a role not unfamiliar to her since the days in Florence.

John Lodge seemed fascinated by the acting jobs of his friends. Stiano Braggiotti, for example, two years younger than Francesca, was on his own starting a career as an actor in New York. The final months at Harvard were passing by quickly, but a theatrical career after graduation was out of the question. He had an offer of a post in the diplomatic corps as secretary to an ambassador assigned to South America. He also considered entering the U.S. Navy. His family dismissed both ideas, believing graduate school would serve him better. Mrs. Lodge suggested a year of pre-law preparation in Europe. She discussed the superiority of courses in the traditional English centers of learning, Cambridge and Oxford. But French friends of Bay apparently pointed out that the French way of setting forth issues was so different from the Anglo-Saxon method (and Harvard's) that it would give John a greater breadth of education. Exposure to the intellectual life in Paris, they claimed, would be a tremendous advantage. His mother agreed.[3]

Before starting classes in Paris, John joined Bud Eames and their buddy Keeny Gordon for a bicycle trip through Germany. They pedaled from Cologne to Nuremberg, regularly fortified by tankards of German beer and plates of würst. On an impulse, the trio auctioned off their bikes in the middle of Nuremberg's main square. With his handful of Deutschmarks, John boarded a train to Italy, where he caught up with his mother and sister. They spent weeks in southern France, at Hendaye, and from time to time crossed the Spanish border to Irún and Loyola. It was John's first view of a land he one day would know so well.

John enrolled in the Ècole de Droit at the University of Paris and moved into a pension for students on rue Notre-Dame-du-Champs. He audited courses, compiling within a year some 500 semester hours. His fluency in French gained him access to tutoring groups with Gaston Duveau, the Secretaire de l'Ordre des Avocats, and a Professor Drouin, an authority on the history and philosophy of the law. Lodge developed a keen awareness of the political affairs of postwar Europe by reading the city's newspapers and listening to legislative debates. Happily, he did not have to take the examinations required of the French law students. That alone gave him free time to enjoy the student huddles at favorite Left Bank hangouts and artist gatherings in cozy Montparnasse cafés. By the end of his year in Paris, Lodge had acquired an unusual grasp of law and philosophy, a stimulating exercise that would place him in good stance as a clear-thinking and skilled writer, speechmaker, and debater.

When school ended in 1926, he quickly hurried back to Massachusetts for a Lodge wedding. In early July, he served as best man to Cabot at his marriage to Emily Sears, old Boston's foremost society gathering of the year. At the end of the summer, John collapsed and was rushed to a hospital in Bar Harbor, Maine, where doctors performed an emergency appendectomy, but he recovered in time to begin his first year of studies at Harvard Law School in the fall.

While the atmosphere at college had been lighthearted and relatively untaxing, Harvard law demanded the complete attention and stamina of its students. Led by Dean Roscoe Pound, the faculty taught by the case method, interfused with the Socratic approach to education. Thus, the important thing was to know what questions to ask. Answers to problems were often queries to be decided *de novo*. "The teacher is the midwife between the student and the great imponderable cloud of knowledge which hangs over the world," Lodge once said of the way of teaching at Harvard.[4]

As a law student, Lodge worked diligently with singleness of purpose. Yet he ended his first year with an average of 58, passing all exams but Property I. That area of the law stymied John. He repeated the course twice before receiving an acceptable grade. And Property II, an advanced and very demanding course given by Professor Joseph "Gentleman Joe" Warren, so troubled him that he asked his classmate Paul Williams to help. "After each lecture, we studied together, discussed the cases, analyzed the issues, and prepared for the next day," Williams recalled. "I worked with John virtually every day. He wasn't one to duck a hard problem."[5]

Yet Lodge's interest in the theater remained constant. He advised the Cercle Français on its selection of plays and reviewed its annual production—Molière's *L'Avare*—for the *Crimson*. And in the spring of 1927, he listened to a series of lectures on the movies at the newly expanded Harvard Business School just across the Charles River. Harvard alumnus Joseph P. Kennedy, then president of FBO Pictures, persuaded his alma mater to put up money for the symposium, then arranged for the visit of film industry leaders Adolph Zukor, Jessie L. Lasky, Cecil B. DeMille, Marcus Loew, William Fox, Will Hays, Harry Warner, and others to speak on campus. Seeking a statesman-like role in Hollywood, Kennedy had inaugurated the series, noting that the oldest of American universities now recognized the youngest of industries, hitherto an academically neglected enterprise.[6] John later purchased a copy of the printed text of the lectures, *The Story of the Films*, from Boston's Old Corner Book Store and read about the fascinating growth and future of the movies. With talking pictures now being introduced, he wondered if there could be a place for him before the camera or maybe in a studio office. But by June 1927, his thoughts again were on Europe and a vacation with his mother and sister. They sailed on the SS *Suffren* and spent a month in Brittany.

Before John left, he renewed his friendship with Francesca. She told him of her latest plans—a career in Hollywood. Berta and Gloria, she explained, would supervise the dance classes. Pa, after a year or more in Los Angeles, missed Mumi and first-hand news of home. "I decided to live at his bungalow and make the rounds of nearby film studios and hopefully land some well-paying assignments."

Not long after her arrival, director Alexander Korda asked her to test for the leading role in *The Private Life of Helen of Troy*. The results impressed Korda, who had just arrived in America from Europe, where he had completed a string of successful pictures. He invited her to his private "house" right off the set to discuss the script. Once inside, he urged her to select any of the luxurious gowns or furs in the bedroom closets. Once she signed a contract, it was made clear, she would settle in as his girlfriend as well as his star. Almost fooled by the setup, Francesca decided differently.

Later that year Francesca secured a small role in Samuel Goldwyn's *The Devil Dancer*, a melodrama starring Clive Brook and Anna May Wong. She also coached dancer Gilda Gray and a group of girls for a sinuous Oriental dance for this silent movie, which was poorly received. After five months, Francesca had only a handful of bit and extra parts and modeling jobs to her credit. More memorable were a date with Charlie Chaplin at the première of his film *The Circus* and a weekend with William Randolph Hearst and Marion Davies at the fabled Hearst Castle.

Back in Boston, Gloria worked very hard to fill in for Francesca, as did Berta. As winter approached, Berta complained of headaches and excessive fatigue, and grew very weak. The doctors thought her appendix might be the cause. John came by to see Berta often and consulted with her physicians. He arranged for her to enter a hospital and in the process became indispensable to those Braggiottis remaining in Brookline.

When Francesca heard about Berta's illness, she was torn between a powerful urge to return home and a desire to continue her career in Hollywood. But Berta's hospitalization decided her choice. She and Pa rushed back to Brookline. Twenty-six-year-old Berta, too weak from several operations for intestinal obstruction and adhesions, died a week after their arrival.[7] John made all the funeral arrangements, standing solidly beside Francesca, helping and comforting her and all the family. Pa returned to California, not wanting to live in Brookline ever again. Francesca gave up her hopes for work in the movies.

Francesca's return to Boston in February 1928 renewed her close ties with Lodge, now a second-year law student. A chronic "stage-door

Johnny," he stopped by the studio or house several times a week. The ambitious dancer and the percipient student had been pals for nearly six years in various situations and moods, from unmitigated jollity to heavy grief. "John was crazy about the kind of life I led," Francesca observed. "He wanted to experiment, break away from his structured existence, and partake of the opportunities around him. He wished to be part of the theater. He wasn't particularly interested in politics at that time. And a law career seemed a stopgap. Years before, I had had long talks with Cabot about John and what he should do. Cabot was very narrow-minded, pegging his brother as a future lawyer, banker or teacher. John, so bright and popular, made Cabot a bit jealous."

In the spring of 1928, "love caressed me with its wing," John confessed in a poem to Francesca. During one of their habitual polemic discussions—so heated it segued into an argument—John reiterated his admiration and love. Unexpectedly, this fearful row ended in a secret and unofficial engagement. But Francesca still told herself: "How dare he do such a thing when he knows his family doesn't approve of me!"

Long letters, interspersed with hastily written notes—his often in French and signed "Jeannot"—passed between Brookline and Cambridge. "Without your love, everything would seem dull & futile," John wrote. "With it, the world seems to lie before me like a land of dreams."[8] Francesca cautiously looked to the future. She refused to pursue their relationship until she met Mrs. Lodge. She knew the importance of convincing his mother of the strengthening bonds between John and herself.

"I do hope you & Mother will have a talk together," John advised. "Mother is, at present, in a loss as to what to think & I should like to have the situation made clear to her."[9] The Lodges seemingly protested, not because of the Braggiottis' unusual lifestyle and lack of money, but because of the apparent strain of TB as a "family malady" and the Jewish background of grandfather Schlesinger. Furthermore, Francesca's well-publicized appearances in vaudeville, not infrequently between performing dogs and baggy-pants comedians, hardly made a strong case in her behalf.

The turmoil of a meeting between the Lodges and Francesca drove John into a state of physical and nervous exhaustion. He even became vexed over the arty and mildly suggestive publicity pictures Francesca recently posed for to promote her studio and her stage appearances. He wanted them destroyed. John looked upon such publicity in connection with a show business career with disfavor.

In a verbose and prosaic letter, John spelled out the do's and don'ts for the future. "I do not want you to give up your dancing career. You can be nice to people, without letting them touch you any more than to shake hands. I should like no one to touch you, I mean men." After six pages of a long analysis of their relationship, he warmed up. "They are not sacrifices, but pleasures and joys. Tell me, my darling, that you feel as I do about love. Read this letter with the utmost care and you will realize that I am a true idealist. . . . The manifestations of love are pleasing to see. I can't help having mine in spite of the fact that I am an intensely reserved person about it."[10]

Francesca describes the initial meeting with Mrs. Lodge and Helena as "an absolute disaster." She could gauge their feelings about the imagined tabloid headlines: "Blueblood Brahmin Gets Engaged to Barefoot Italian Dancer." Mrs. Lodge, depressed and desperate, told her son that "people who are in love make one feel it." She was convinced of John's love for Francesca but not of her love for him. "I am distressed at her distress," he reported to Francesca, "and also at having possibly to distress you, but you can with your strength & imagination cure this situation. I leave to you the means to do it. It will be another wonderful expression of your love for me."[11]

John's manifestation of love for Francesca—and for show business—brought about a decisive move. When classes ended for the summer, and after a short stay with family in Bar Harbor and a visit to Marta at Saranac, he traveled to Los Angeles to look for work as a movie actor. The première of *The Jazz Singer* in late 1927 had evoked wild enthusiasm over the potential of talking pictures. Producers of the Al Jolson blockbuster, Warner Bros., commenced the shooting of "talkies" in addition to its silent movie roster. By mid-May of the following year, virtually every Hollywood studio had geared up for sound. Highly praised for his undergraduate performances in the college theater, John felt he might get a foothold in pictures. He often remarked that he was merely "the ham in the Lodge sandwich." An ex-classmate at Harvard, Donald Loker, had quit Cambridge and gone to California to make movies. As Don Terry, he was completing his first picture, *Me, Gangster* at Fox. And Sandy Hamilton, too, had left Harvard to produce a movie for First National Pictures.

On the train to Hollywood, where he had arranged to stay with Francesca's father, John wrote to Francesca several times a day. "I am thinking of you incessantly. I put away my typewriter to write to you. It seems like such a cold instrument of communication." His first trip West since his school days at Mesa, the journey recalled that period. "It has been eight years since I was out in this part of the world, & yet I feel quite at home in this country. It is much like Arizona & brings back memories galore of the two years I spent there." California rekindled a "delicious sense of freedom."[12] John made the rounds of the studios, using letters of introduction from friends back East and from Isidore, whose singing studio was prospering because of the start-up of the "talkies," a novelty for fans long conditioned to voiceless pictures. He also joined the cluster of extras hoping to be singled out for work, perhaps a bit part, maybe a featured role.

To Francesca, he wrote: "It might be that I remain out West (strictly, *entre nous*) if I find that I can secure a satisfactory position in Hollywood. I might remain there, go to Leland Stanford Law School or to night school & take my degree & possibly my bar exams there. In that case we might get married earlier, perhaps soon after you come out." He anticipated a singular partnership with Francesca: "We are both so interested in life & in so many phases and manifestations of it that any idea which one of us expresses finds an interested mind and a vibrant note in the other."[13] This alliance, John realized, would also make her family his. He remembered the words of his grandfather: "Your grandmother, when she married, made her family mine—a great and very precious gift, for her father and mother, her sisters and brothers, were all unusual people, and their loyalty and devotion for me has been one of the best of my life's possessions."[14]

But John Lodge failed to break into the movies that summer. The experience, nevertheless, would pay off in the future. On July 30, he reported a meeting in the front office. The boss was a "hardboiled but pleasant enough fellow who immediately suggested that I stick to the law, remarking that in the movies no intelligence was required. . . . He asked me what my wardrobe consisted of. I now regret not having brought my cutaway and top hat. . . . I must devise some plan for calling attention to myself & find out whether or not this is my line."[15]

Brushing the stardust aside, John journeyed back East for his final year. There would be little time together with Francesca that fall. She planned to take Berta's remains back to Italy for burial. John studied the sailing schedules and booked accommodations. As she had done on other voyages to Europe, Francesca arranged to perform nightly in the ship's lounge in exchange for free passage.

In the interim, John convinced his mother of the merits of his marriage to Francesca. Perhaps Mrs. Lodge remembered some of the wedding obstacles that were faced and overcome with Bay. Maybe, too, she thought of a second marriage she almost entered into in Paris with a Frenchman. She had fallen in love with Jean du Breuil de St. Germain. But as he was Catholic, the Lodge family—especially Bessie's father-in-law who provided an allowance for household expenses, albeit meager—opposed the match and threatened to take away her children if she wed du Breuil. Bessie broke off the courtship and never saw him again (he was killed a few years later in the war).[16]

Mrs. Lodge did become, in the years ahead, a warm and loving ally of her daughter-in-law. Later, during John's campaign for Congress, someone at a rally asked campaign worker John L. Ellinger what had caused all the applause from an adjoining room. "Francesca Lodge just cut a mean rug; she danced a tarantella," he replied. "Sir, I beg your pardon," Mrs. Lodge interjected, after overhearing Ellinger's remark. "I picked up what you said and I must tell you that there isn't anything 'mean' about Francesca Lodge. I should know for I am her mother-in-law!" Ellinger immediately explained that the swing-era expression "to cut a mean rug" was a popular slang phrase describing a wonderful dancing performance, nothing more.[17]

On Saturday, December 22, 1928—the day Francesca arrived back from Italy—her engagement to John Lodge was front-page news. As predicted by the future bride, both newsboys and loudspeakers along Boston streets shouted this headline. They set a marriage date for early summer. But there still were hurdles to clear before that first step as wedded partners.

CHAPTER 6

Marriage, the Law, and Greasepaint

"At high noon today in the Church of the Advent, the picturesque Francesca Braggiotti forsakes her nationally heralded terpsichorean name and exchanges vows with John Davis Lodge." So wrote the society reporter of the *Boston Evening American* on Saturday, July 6, 1929 under an eye-catching headline spread across six columns. "And the socially invested," the writer assured her readers, "attend to see given into the safekeeping of the grandson of the late Senator Henry Cabot Lodge, the most glorified society girl of the day." At its culmination, the Lodge-Braggiotti wedding took on the trappings of a grand social event. But in the weeks and months leading to the nuptial day, the principal parties faced innumerable anxious moments and made a number of earnest decisions. Shortly after their engagement was made known, both Francesca and John decided that Boston would not be their future home. Although Francesca had built up a thriving school with an enrollment of over 1,000 pupils with an annual return of some $25,000, and John had made sundry friends and potential business contacts from nearly fifteen years of schooling in the area, both sought a different cosmopolitan setting to begin their marriage.

The decision saddened Francesca for it meant leaving her successful dance studio. With one sister dead and another seriously ill, only Gloria remained to run the school. She, too, had her sights set on a career outside of Boston, hoping to settle in New York. When the school manager, Edith Ferguson, showed interest in continuing the classes, they sold the studio to her and the teaching staff. The family's ties with the Braggiotti-Denishawn School of Dancing ended that June, not long after a large-scale recital of students and teachers, highlighted by an aptly entitled finale called "Souvenir." Danced by Francesca in a Worth gown once worn by her grandmother, it ended in a final bow with Gloria and the entire ensemble of several hundred performers.

The proceeds from the sale of the school helped pay for the education of both Rama, a freshman at Harvard that fall, and Chad, a scholarship student at Andover. The money also provided for the special care of Marta, who planned to recuperate in the bracing desert air of the Southwest. But money was still needed for the wedding day and the long-planned, extensive honeymoon trip to Europe—practically *de rigueur* for a Lodge. To help out, Francesca signed a well-paying contract that spring to dance nightly at a club in Boston. Nearly all John's relatives voiced dismay over the booking. Only John Ellerton Lodge spoke up in her behalf. He admired her artistic ability and unequivocal pluck, and her natural charm and engaging personality. To show his support for her enterprising effort, he came every evening to the nightclub to watch her performances from a small table off to the side. After she danced, he'd invite her to sit with him. At a quick glance, the lean, distinguished-looking gentleman could easily have been taken for playwright Eugene O'Neill.

Uncle John actually wrote a letter to his family, saying how lucky John was to have a girl like Francesca. Years before, he himself had caused a minor scandal by eloping with a household nurse. He married Mary Connolly in the sacristy of a Roman Catholic church in 1911. Self-effacing and unassuming, Mary became the ideal companion for the extraordinarily gifted, yet chronically ill, scholar. Washington hostess Mrs. Winthrop Chanler described her as "a lovely and loveable woman of gracious silences."

John, too, stopped by the nightclub whenever possible. One evening, after seeing her perform a sultry Oriental dance, he asked: "Cesca, do you think you could cover a bit more of your bare stomach? Perhaps with a belt?" She added a string of beads in a strategic spot, realizing her costume was still somewhat daring for the times.

Concern over Francesca's club act—not to mention cramming for final examinations—caused John to lose a good deal of weight, along with tufts of hair from atop his head. His worried state led to a case of ulcers. His grade average of 62 seemingly delayed the actual receipt of his law degree for two years, until June 1931.[1] Francesca wondered whether he would have the strength to get through the wedding festivities. At least there were no religious differences to contend with. Baptized years earlier in Florence by an Anglican priest, Francesca welcomed Episcopal Bishop Charles Slattery (and a son-in-law of Senator Lodge's old classmate Bishop William Lawrence) to officiate at the marriage.

Law school chum Paul Williams, who served as one of the eleven ushers at the ceremony, remembered the weekend: "After the Friday evening rehearsal, there was an ushers' dinner at the Hasty Pudding Club-house, complete with vintage champagne, notwithstanding Prohibition.

After much singing and many toasts, we all piled into taxicabs to continue the party at the Egyptian Room of Boston's Hotel Brunswick where Leo Reisman and his orchestra played. Eddy Duchin, already building a big following of his own, was the pianist."[2]

The next morning, the street in front of the church was jammed so tightly with people eager for a glimpse of the bride that two traffic policemen had difficulty in clearing a space large enough for the bridal limousine to draw up alongside the entrance. Long before its arrival, John was so anxious for the ceremony to begin that he insisted on standing up in front of the church altar at the very beginning of the organ prelude. Paul Williams finally persuaded him to sit down until he heard the first strains of "The Wedding March."

Francesca wore a Florentine medieval-styled gown of white satin and a court train banded with old lace that belonged to Grandmother de Pourtales. Maid of honor Gloria Braggiotti wore a yellow chiffon dress and a hat of yellow horsehair trimmed with cornflower blue ribbon. Three young dance students acted as flower girls. Brothers Stiano, who was preparing for his Broadway début, and Mario served as ushers. Mario had traveled from London, where he and his partner Jacques Fray had been a two-piano team in the orchestra pit for the musical comedy *Funny Face* co-starring Fred and Adele Astaire. Their friend George Gershwin, whom they first met in Paris while he was composing *An American in Paris*, had engaged the keyboard performers for the London run of his popular show. Mario incurred the wrath of Astaire by leaving the musical to sail back to Boston for his sister's marriage, an event he was determined not to miss.

Cabot, the best man, stood beside John at the altar rail. Only days before, he and Emily had returned to Boston from a seven-month trip around the world. He would soon join the *New York Herald Tribune* as an editorial writer. When John had told his brother of his engagement to his former girlfriend, Cabot indicated that the Cabot Lodges would see little of the John Lodges in the future. Nonetheless, to all the wedding guests, the brothers seemed as close as ever. At the reception at Upland Road, music reverberated through the house as Mario played the old family piano and Pa and Stiano sang. John joined in on several choruses of "O, sole mio." Even Cabot sang along.

That evening the newlyweds left for New York to board a ship bound for Europe. They struck fellow passengers as a couple out of the pages of an F. Scott Fitzgerald story—attractive, self-assured, graceful, and perhaps a bit exotic and mysterious. Every night they danced for hours in the ship's salon to the delight of onlookers who considered them a professional dance team and requested at least one solo number before the music stopped. None would have guessed that the wife had fallen victim to seasickness and the husband remained restricted to a bland ulcer-healing diet.

From the beginning of their marriage, they decided that neither would be seen alone in nightclubs or similar gathering places with a member of the opposite sex. That decision would squelch any groundless gossip or idle rumors—a wise move, they believed, for anyone in the public eye. But in some ways they flirted with unconventionality. "When we visited Italy," Francesca recalled, "I introduced John to my old beaux and we went out together." Apparently John did an about-face from their courtship days. "John," Francesca added, "encouraged me to dance with other men, and that surprised these European-bred gentlemen who believed a young wife only danced with her husband. 'You watch out,' I'd say. 'You're always throwing me into the arms of admirers.' Oddly enough, he only acted jealous when our children or our dogs got too close or received too much attention."

In Paris they went horseback riding in the Bois du Boulogne with friends from John's student days. On one particular outing, Francesca rode ahead with several others while John remained to the rear at a slower pace. Suddenly, he came galloping up beside Cesca. A dashing and ardent husband is that John Lodge, thought the Frenchmen. "C'est charmant," one of the horsemen observed. "John can't be apart from Francesca for more than a minute." But John had other thoughts on his mind. "Cesca, you unpacked the wrong underdrawers! These are too tight for riding."

In September, John and Francesca returned home just in time for the marriage of sister Helena Lodge to Edouard de Streel, First Secretary of the Belgian Embassy in Washington. The brief ceremony at Mrs. Lodge's home on Massachusetts Avenue was performed by the Rev. James H. Ryan, rector of Catholic University. An informal reception followed, and the de Streels quickly left for a honeymoon in Europe.

The Lodges moved into an apartment at 103 East 86th Street overlooking Park Avenue. On September 30, John opened an account at Morgan Guaranty Bank and the next morning started work as an associate at the large and influential law firm of Cravath, de Gersdorff, Swaine & Wood at 50 Broad Street in the heart of New York's financial district. Tracing its beginnings back to 1819, the firm had long attracted an impressive list of corporate and individual clients. To serve them and a number of high-level government agencies, both foreign and domestic, it recruited its young associates chiefly from Columbia, Harvard, and Yale.

Before graduation, John's Harvard pal Paul Williams, with a letter of recommendation from Dean Pound, had secured an interview at Cravath and accepted their job offer. The position provided an opportunity to learn to handle corporate reorganizations. John, too, sought a meeting at

Cravath. Francesca had previously danced at parties given by senior partner Carl de Gersdorff and remembered his interest in the arts. She contacted him, putting in a good word for John, which led to a position for him at the firm at a salary of $2,000 a year.

Both John and Paul Williams quickly discovered that Cravath lived up to its reputation as a "sweatshop." They toiled long hours, often late into the evening and on Saturdays. The two frequently left Broad Street at the same time, occasionally walking from downtown to upper Park Avenue, a hike of some five miles. They usually discussed the day's legal tasks and news of their Harvard classmates. Francesca periodically invited bachelor Williams to stay for dinner. During the first months of marriage and last weeks of 1929, the young husband and fledgling lawyer expressed anxiety over two approaching events: preparations for the bar exam and parenthood. Both would take more time and concentration than he could have predicted or thought possible.

At his office, Lodge immersed himself in a variety of matters to help prepare for the bar: wills, estates, accountings, mortgages, contracts, leases and bankruptcies. He prepared briefs, court papers, and motions, and gained a reputation as an industrious and well-liked worker. He enrolled in Harold R. Medina's bar exam course, not long after Francesca gave birth to their daughter on April 12, 1930. They chose the name Lily de Pourtales Lodge for the chubby brown-eyed baby.

That summer John rented a house in Locust Valley on Long Island, an area where a number of the Cravath partners lived. Paul D. Cravath, who single-handedly dominated the firm, took a special interest in his new associate. Lodge occasionally handled and expedited personal affairs for this astute, hard-working senior partner, a member of the firm since the turn of the century. Cravath was starting to ease up on his office duties. He was becoming a frequent world traveler and taking on an important role in charity and cultural affairs of the city.

John had no regrets about leaving Boston for New York. Manhattan throbbed to a faster, more exciting beat, and that alone made him happy. The Lodges quickly made new friends from among the conspicuous movers and shakers of the city, and renewed ties with family and schoolmates as well as with theater and dance acquaintances of the recent past. John enjoyed being with an array of interesting and interested people, including Marc Connelly, the Otto Kahns, Anne Morgan, Walter Damrosch, the Theodore Steinways, Heywood Broun, the John Throckmortons, Ruth Draper, Osgood Perkins, the Juan Trippes, John Mason Brown, the Gifford Pinchots, Catharine Dale Owen, the Gordon Knox Bells, Carl Brandt, the Douglas Ellimans, Rosamond Pinchot, Frederic Coudert, the Gerish Millikens, and Richard Aldrich.

John readily accepted the attention his name and his career generated. With his strong personality and commanding presence, he often dominated a group, impressing most, overawing some. Articulate, outspoken, opinionated—and *au courant* with events, personalities and issues of the day—he evidenced a talent to get along with all kinds and to absorb differing philosophies and points of view. And with Francesca at his side, he was discovering new worlds.

John's life seemed little affected by the dramatic turn of events on Wall Street, rapid, momentous occurrences that pushed the Jazz Age into times past. The stock market suffered such a resounding fall in prices in late October of 1929 that it was called a "crash." The value of the Lodge brokerage account dropped significantly. Before the end of the year, there had been a modest recovery, providing a measure of hope that the losses would be temporary. But during his first weeks of fatherhood that spring, stock prices took another sharp nosedive across the board, and the entire economy felt the repercussions.

John quickly lost another sizable chunk of his stock holdings and much of his cash savings, not to mention the default on a personal loan of some $5,000. Lodge's share of the income from his grandfather's well-invested $1.5-million-dollar estate, however, provided a much appreciated cushion of five or six thousand dollars a year. Francesca, who had stayed clear of the fervent stock-buying spree, ended up with more ready cash than her comparatively well-to-do husband. At age twenty-one, she had put aside an inheritance of some $20,000 from her grandfather in a Boston bank, and along with some small savings accounts, it remained an available and safe resource. Better off than the vast majority of people facing the deepening depression, John and Francesca nonetheless could not have predicted the undeniable downturn in their lot.

As a new associate at Cravath, John spent hours every day doing rote review of case documents. A good deal of the paperwork seemed meaningless, if not boring. A bright moment in his career came when he passed his New York State bar exam in substantive law on October 29, 1930. However, he required reexamination in the procedural part: pleading, practice, and evidence. A cram course to pass these remaining sections filled his evenings. More and more, he looked upon his work as too narrow and confining. He envied Harvard classmate and theatrical manager Dick Aldrich's exciting forays into the arts, in contrast to his rather mundane law work.[3]

By the fall of 1930, unemployment was soaring. President Hoover's oft-repeated words of encouragement, "Prosperity is just around the corner," fell on deaf ears. That year, though many New Yorkers watched the construction of two architectural marvels—the world's tallest structure, the Empire State Building, and the interstate link spanning the Hudson River, the George Washington Bridge—the city staggered and stagnated under Mayor Jimmy Walker, who would soon face charges of inefficiency, neglect, and incompetency.

When Lily was six months old, Francesca felt the need to keep busy and make some money. John worked night after night at his law office, often to nearly midnight. By returning to the stage, she would fill her lonely evenings and earn some ready cash. Besides, Pa's voice studio had felt the pinch of hard times, and he was again in debt. So on November 5, Francesca made her Broadway début in *The Vanderbilt Revue*, a two-act, twenty-nine-scene show featuring Lulu McConnell, Joe Penner, and Evelyn Hoey, with music by Fray and Braggiotti. Her brief but striking tarantella, followed by a tango by Charlotte Ayers, were, in the words of the *Times* critic, "the high spots in an otherwise painfully orthodox and old school first-act ending." Francesca received $150 a week from the show (in which John had invested).

Then on March 22, 1931, she starred in *Dance Variations*, a benefit for the New York Infirmary at the Martin Beck Theatre. Joining her were singer Nina Koshetz, Gloria (who had recently appeared in a New York production of *Lysistrata*), and Mario and his partner Jacques Fray (who were preparing for a program of jazz and songs with Maurice Chevalier at Carnegie Hall). Two weeks later, Francesca entertained patrons at the opening of a new supper club called Très Gai at the Park Central Hotel on West 55th Street. By mid-summer she was in rehearsal for the melodrama *Three Times The Hour*. The first play written by Valentine Davies, this early offering of the 1931-32 season had a cast of twenty-six characters, including a banker's high-spirited mistress, played by Francesca. When she expressed doubts over the role, producer Antoinette Perry said, "Don't worry. You'll be a hit just walking across the stage in a black, tight-fitting dress." Panned by the critics, the show ran only two weeks.

Though John voiced little objection over his wife's return to show business, he would have preferred to be the family's sole breadwinner. "Francesca has not had her share of good times as far as money is concerned," he wrote to his father-in-law, "and I would like, if possible, to give her a sense of security for the future."[4] Francesca, too, would have preferred to carry out her philosophy that it takes two to make one career—in this case, John's legal vocation. But she had no abiding interest in the law or the life of a lawyer's wife. With time weighing heavily on her hands and others needing her support, she did not hesitate to look for work on Broadway.

Lodge anticipated each summer weekend when he could go off to the Long Island countryside to swim and play tennis at the Atlantic Beach

Club or Piping Rock. There, on the outskirts of Hempstead, the three Lodges occupied a weather-beaten cottage on the old farm property of Arthur Brisbane, editor-in-chief of the *Daily Mirror*. In exchange for its use, they painted the entire dwelling a luminous bright blue. They decided the old farmhouse in the middle of nowhere needed a distinctive, contemporary facelift. "Then we planted sunflowers all around it," Francesca recalled. "On Sundays, lines of cars often passed by to look at the colorful results."

One of John's most satisfying assignments that year involved a new Metropolitan Opera star. The foreign-born diva arrived in New York from Paris without knowing more than a handful of English words. So opera patron Paul Cravath sent John to act as translator for the attractive soprano, Lily Pons. His duties included spelling out in French the details of her contracts. Later he would be called by Paramount Pictures to step in and perform similar tasks when Pons signed for movie roles.

It was one of his last assignments for Cravath. Lodge wanted to work for a small law firm, one less regimented, high-powered, and corporate-oriented. Paul Cravath sympathized with John, who also expressed a wish to participate in outside interests to a greater extent. Cravath recognized the problem of what he called mapping out a program of life. "As I look back over my own life," the seventy-year-old lawyer wrote to Lodge, "I am inclined to think I made a mistake in allowing it to be completely absorbed in professional work which, while interesting, was not always inspiring. If I could live my life over again with the aid of my present accumulation of experience, I would try to be less completely a slave to work, and not postpone until old age many of the interests and activities which I now find contribute so much to the pleasure and satisfaction of life."[5]

Lodge left 15 Broad Street on August 21, 1931 with Cravath's blessing. He joined a low-keyed two-man law office at 50 Broadway, an arrangement which also offered a chance for greater income. The senior partner was a highly extroverted Texan, Richard A. Knight. John now filled his briefcase with papers on law cases involving mortgage, arrears, personal bankruptcies, and broken marriages. He helped one Harvard classmate obtain a divorce. For another friend, he prepared a will and testamentary trusts. He pursued a well-known young actor for payment of a long-overdue promissory note. He saved an Irish acquaintance from imminent deportation. But international matters, especially those using his linguistic skills, pleased him the most.

After seven months with the flamboyant and unpredictable Richard Knight, John set up his own small practice in an adjoining office. Knight had been a bit too erratic for Lodge's liking. A half-dozen years later, John wasn't too surprised to see a *Life* magazine picture of his onetime law partner standing on his head at the entrance of the Metropolitan Opera House. In top hat with tails flying, Knight had just cartwheeled through the Met lounge and caused a disturbance as he skipped down the aisle to an orchestra seat. Expelled by the police, Knight obliged eager photographers with a handstand. Before he died in the 1940s, he had kidnapped his own child from his wife and eventually was disbarred.

John's break from the high-pressured atmosphere of Broad Street allowed him to try his hand in some extracurricular endeavors, sideline activities Cravath ruled out. The New York Young Republican Club sought Lodge's aid in the 1931 campaign of Herbert Brownell, a candidate for the State Assembly. Brownell had settled in Manhattan after working his way through the University of Nebraska and graduating from Yale Law School in 1927, where he was editor-in-chief of the *Law Journal*. Another young lawyer, Thomas E. Dewey, served as Brownell's campaign manager.

Dewey sought Lodge's participation in the fight against the city's Democratic incumbents. The future New York governor also suggested that John might persuade Cabot, at the *New York Herald Tribune*, to give editorial support to the candidacy of Brownell. But Cabot stayed clear of the political imbroglio in New York that year.[6] Brownell lost the race by a narrow margin but won election in 1932 and served five years in the State Legislature. During the 1931 campaign, John delivered his first political speech, an address at the Valley Stream Republican Club in support of Long Island Congressman Robert Low Bacon. John had had a brief taste of politics on a grassroots level and in the process had made friends with a handful of rising young Republican leaders.

The lure of the greasepaint again entered into his life. Actor-director Gene Lockhart, who had recently performed with Francesca at the Très Gai Club, invited John to play the leading role in an Amateur Comedy Club production (and six performances) of Noel Coward's *The Young Idea*. Francesca joined the cast too.

By 1932 silent films at Broadway theaters had completely disappeared, replaced by the talkies, and few screen stars surpassed Greta Garbo in popularity. The Swedish actress had made the transition to sound with Metro-Goldwyn-Mayer's *Anna Christie*. Her husky, alluring accent made her an even bigger box office attraction than she had been before the movies talked. With a major hit on their hands, MGM rushed the charismatic Garbo into new roles. The only drawback with a sound track, the studio realized, was the loss of receipts from foreign audiences. And one of the largest overseas markets for Garbo pictures had always been Italy. With a half-dozen Garbo films on American screens, MGM wondered how these pictures could best maintain her tremendous appeal among Italian fans. Finding that subtitles drew comparatively small audiences, the studio decided to dub the sound track in Italian.

MGM tested dozens of voices for the "Italian" Garbo, but not one measured up for her personal approval. The studio began to look around the country, with little success. MGM concluded that most Italian women had unsuitable accents to speak for their star. Carlo Beuf, head of MGM's foreign department and a friend of Francesca, urged her to take a test in a New York recording studio. She read several pages of Garbo's dialogue in Italian. Both the actress and MGM liked what they heard. They offered Francesca a six-month contract in Hollywood to dub a half-dozen films, beginning with *Mata Hari*. She accepted the well-paying proposal. John accompanied her to California and stayed several weeks before returning East.

On March 19, 1932, the day they left New York, Francesca wrote in her notebook: "It nearly broke my heart to leave cunning little Lily. . . . if it weren't that my beloved Jeannot [John] were with me & that I was going to see Marta & Papa. . . . I couldn't have done it. Instead of getting stronger about sentiment within, I am, as I grow older, getting more & more sensitive." Five days later, on the morning of March 24, their train pulled into Los Angeles Station. Pa was there. It had been three years since they had seen him. "He is thin & quite older," Francesca wrote, "but the same cheerful optimistic dear & entertaining." The Lodges stayed at his house on South Lafayette Park Place, less than two miles from downtown Los Angeles.

Francesca reported for work at MGM's synchronizing studio. She spent long days in a dark room seated in front of a dimly lighted music stand. Hour after hour, she recorded dialogue in Italian as a Garbo film flashed on a screen. "It nearly ruined my eyes," she said of the experience. "I listened and listened to Garbo. She had her own rhythm and sort of 'embroidered' her words. Part of her great charm was the way she breathed. When *Mata Hari* reached Italian audiences, Garbo's line, 'Give me a cigarette,' caused a sensation and was repeated everywhere. Garbo told me she actually liked 'her voice' better in Italian."

John enjoyed being around the studios and movie people. On sunny days, he drove to the beach, acquiring a salubrious dark tan. Francesca joined him there on Sundays, and they rarely left the shore until sundown. After he returned to New York, he wrote Francesca: "I am sort of fed up with New York & would truly welcome a good job at a stated salary of good size. So don't think that I want to stay here because of the little money I have made. But I am counting on nothing from MGM, although, of course, I am hoping. . . . I think Hollywood is the place for us, & I don't want you to weaken."[7]

Obviously John had come home a bit starstruck. No doubt, he

wondered if he had made the wrong decision just a year earlier by turning down a request by silent screen actress Pola Negri that he consider playing her leading man in her first talkie.[8] He had met the Polish-born actress at a New York party as she prepared to return to the screen after losing the bulk of her fortune in the stock market crash. Basil Rathbone took the part in *A Woman Commands*, a picture that met an indifferent reception at the box office and ended Negri's American film career. But the Rathbone role might have launched a career for Lodge outside the law at a time when his job was in a slump not unlike that of many other fields.

Over ten million people were jobless by mid-1932, and thousands of World War I veterans were marching on Washington to demand payment of military service bonuses. New York was so deep in debt that its leading bankers were forced to loan the city $350 million. Half of Lodge's clients couldn't pay his fees. Francesca's MGM contract helped make up the slack as did the $1,000 she received for endorsing Pond's Cold Cream. Her endorsement was so unique and eye-catching that it spun off scores of lookalike ads featuring society ladies. And her prospects in Hollywood looked bright. Upon seeing her incredibly long blonde tresses one day at MGM, Douglas Fairbanks, Jr., tagged her "the girl who could sit on her hair."

John, however, spent a gloomy and unsettled summer apart from his wife. And from Lily, too. Lily went off to visit the Lorillard Spencers in Newport, then Cabot and Emily in Beverly, and lastly Grandmother Lodge in Washington. He counted the days until he'd be reunited with Francesca in Hollywood in late August.

On his second trip West that year, John took along work for a New York client. When he arrived in Los Angeles, Francesca had nearly completed dubbing Garbo's latest pictures, *As You Desire Me* and *Grand Hotel*. During a break, a friend on the lot asked her whether her husband played tennis.

"He plays well enough," she replied.

"Is he good enough to play in a tournament at Malibu to replace Gary Cooper, who's sick?"

"Sure. I'll ask him to get in touch with you."

Francesca told him of the invitation. "This is fantastic exposure for you. Who knows—it may change your life."

He moved onto the film colony courts—a dashing, well-tanned giant with a well-honed serve and a solid backhand. He was perhaps the only person on deck who was not connected in some way or another with the film industry. John won his match. His appearance generated numerous compliments both for his tennis stance and good looks. Afterwards, the Lodges went to a party given by Adeline "Ad" Schulberg, wife of B.P.

Schulberg, the head of production at Paramount and a talent agent in her own right. Ad told John that he ought to be in pictures, but he laughed it off. Others pointed to Lodge as a potential leading man along the lines of Clark Gable, and asked whether he'd be interested in making a test. He smiled, his large brown eyes shining on hearing such praise. But he backed off. Francesca was a bit run down from months of dubbing Garbo, he explained. They were off to Mexico to relax.

On their return to Hollywood, John found messages urging him to reconsider the suggestion. Schulberg again pressed him to take a screen test. He agreed to make one for Paramount on the day prior to his departure for home. "I took it more or less as an experiment," he explained later, "because I had been approached by theatrical agents before and advised I should become an actor. I wanted to lay the ghost once and for all by taking a test."[9]

John phoned his prep school and college classmate John Lee Mahin, now a busy Hollywood screenwriter. He had Jean Harlow's latest hit, *Red Dust*, on his growing list of credits. Mahin agreed to prepare a rough script, telling John that it wouldn't do any harm to go before the cameras. "You'd even have some fun."

"What should I do on camera?" John asked.

"Do something you're used to doing, like talking on the telephone."

Mahin concocted a scene with John, a lawyer alone at a desk making a phone call. When the improvised conversation ended, he would stand up, then merely walk away from the camera. John had always wondered how his back photographed; here was an amusing way to find out. Paramount director Erle Kenton shot the ten-minute scene. At the cry of "That's a take," Lodge was on his way back to Pa's to pack for the trip home.

The following morning, Ad Schulberg called. "It's in the bag." She told Lodge to go over to see the people at Paramount. "And you'd better unpack your trunk." Lodge saw the studio executives, who offered a contract for $75 a week. He laughed. "I'm just a lawyer on a lark. The test was just for fun. I have to get back for an important case set for trial." So, New York it was.

When the Lodges arrived at their 86th Street apartment, they spotted a large envelope from Paramount on the doorstep. It upped the offer, doubling the initial sum to more than he was making practicing law. Again, he turned it down, not realizing what a clever ploy it turned out to be. Finally, another urgent wire arrived. Paramount raised the offer to $275 a week, an amount substantially greater than John and most city lawyers could hope to earn in the best of times. The rewards now seemed really worth taking time out from the law.

"I cannot commit myself on advising John to leave the law for the movies," Francesca noted in her pocket diary. "It opens doors to a multitude of pros & cons." For days, they debated over leaving the city. "He is extremely able," she wrote. "I rather hate to see him leave it." After much deliberation, John Lodge decided on the adventure. "He has a lot of courage," concluded Francesca. "I admire him so."

On October 14, 1932, he signed a six-month contract. His work would begin in Hollywood two weeks later. Since his college days, acting had beckoned him. He had both pursued and resisted it. Putting aside his legal briefcase, he now wondered how Hollywood would handle his talent. His new career was about to launch him into unchartered waters on a voyage no Lodge had ever embarked upon.

CHAPTER 7

Personality in Pictures

On the very day Lodge made up his mind to close the door on his law practice, a new Paramount film called *Night After Night* opened to rave reviews. One of the comedy's leading players—by no means its star—was Mae West in her first screen appearance. Her irresistibly funny witticisms on men, sex, and society instantly caught the public fancy. They sparked an avalanche of glowing fan letters at the studio and led over 5,000 theater owners to re-book the picture. A new star joined the Hollywood galaxy. In the words of her leading man George Raft: "She stole everything but the cameras."

Her vampish wit and swagger struck audiences as someone they wanted more of. Paramount wasted little time in agreeing to West's demand that production begin on a version of her earlier stage success *Diamond Lil*. The story of a romance between a detective disguised as a Salvation Army captain and a woman of the underworld required a dark, handsome, straightforward lead to play against the blonde bombshell and her *double entendres*. After seeing a photograph of John Lodge, the young actor on his way from New York, West expressed interest in casting him in the part.

The Paramount publicity department lost no time capitalizing on the news of West's attention to the latest studio discovery. It sent out a story announcing the movie début of John Lodge in her next picture, now retitled *She Done Him Wrong*. Word of the "Lodge Goes West" press release reached John as he was preparing to wind up his legal work and pack for California. As he thought about the idea of sharing the screen with West, he began to wonder if he might end up with little or no say about his roles. Paramount, too, may have had second thoughts about signing an unproven commodity at an uncommonly high salary. The studio by the fall of 1932 was in deep financial trouble, building up a loss that would total $23 million by year-end. The lot was on the verge of bankruptcy.

Closer to home, John's decision to go West struck the Lodge family with alarm, although they could not have been too surprised. John had been flirting with films for a half-dozen years. Hearing the news, his mother told him it made no sense to abandon the law. "I have an anchor to leeward," he told her. "I can always return to the law." His brother criticized the whole idea of "going Hollywood" and wanted him to change his surname so as not to capitalize on, or taint, the Lodge political heritage. Indeed, that fall Cabot was seeking political office. As a candidate for the Massachusetts Legislature, Cabot saw no benefit voter-wise accruing from a brother headed for life in the cinema's fast lane. The studio had the final word. It recognized the publicity value of a famous old cognomen and rejected the thought of a name change. John himself felt no need to hide behind a screen alias. The five letters of his surname fit perfectly on any marquee.

John could take a measure of satisfaction from the thought once expressed by Senator Lodge. He had told his grandson that it was all right to be an actor as long as he was a good one. In his youth, the Senator proudly recalled, he had gained immense enjoyment from playing roles in Hasty Pudding shows. Old pages in photograph albums held pictures of him in female roles as Lady Macbeth and Fair Imogen at Harvard in the 1870s. At the time, he even paid Boston stage managers for the chance to act bit parts in operas.[1]

Life in the 103 East 86th Street apartment was about to be a closed chapter. "Good-bye to our little 'love nest,'" wrote Francesca on October 12. "We've been so happy here. Lily has learned how to walk in these rooms. I shall miss it often." Lily had also learned to talk during Francesca's interval at MGM. "I had not seen her for six months & to hear her talk fluently is astounding." She had grown, too, now weighing thirty-three pounds and standing three feet high. Her long black curls came close to her waist. And at age two and a half, she loved games and was giving her first press interview: for a baby magazine called *Babies Just Babies*, run by Eleanor Roosevelt, wife of the Democratic Presidential candidate.

On the eve of their departure for Los Angeles, Francesca celebrated her thirtieth birthday. "Life has passed by like a flash," she noted, "yet I feel to have gotten its very best, absorbed its greatest beauty, been blessed by God." The Lodges—and Lily's nurse Lila—sailed on the SS *Virginia* of the Panama Pacific Line. Their old Buick, rebuilt instead of being replaced, was loaded into the hull for the voyage via the Panama Canal.

The movie business seemed to reach out to them; on board was a Warner Brothers film crew shooting scenes with William "Stage" Boyd and Sheila Terry for a B picture called *The House on 56th Street*. When the ship docked at the port of Los Angeles, a cluster of newsmen, photographers, and movie fans anxiously awaited the appearance of the latest Paramount property. Francesca and Lily were told by Paramount to stay hidden in their stateroom; John would meet the press without a family in tow and give the impression that he was an unattached bachelor. "The studio did not want the public to know that the new handsome heartbreaker was already 'hooked,'" Francesca explained. Hurt yet proud of John, she felt like a worm hiding under a stone.

The Lodges loaded the Buick and drove to their new home, a modest-sized Spanish-style dwelling only seven minutes by car from Paramount at 348 North Highland Avenue in a middle-class Hollywood neighborhood. Pa had rented the furnished house for $160 a month. It offered a degree of privacy and looked out onto a large enclosed garden. The street reminded Francesca of Boston's Commonwealth Avenue with greenery and trees down the center.

John reported for work at the end of October. The Paramount front office eagerly showed him the publicity his contract had stirred up. The tales of his distinguished ancestors made news and provided a peg to introduce the newcomer to moviegoers. One particular headline caught his eye: "Scion of Boston Bluebloods to Play Opposite Belle of Broadway." It was pure "exploitation stuff." He realized that the studio had hired him as much for his social background as for his acting ability—perhaps even more. Besides, the thought of playing opposite the hard-boiled, sexy Mae West still troubled him.

"But you can't cast me in a leading role! I haven't had any experience in front of a camera."

"Experience?" they laughed. "Experience? What the hell has that got to do with it?"

John didn't want to get such an acting plum without working for it. He had left Boston to prove he could rise by his own efforts, not as the grandson of Senator Lodge of Massachusetts. Now in Hollywood, he wanted to continue to shed his ancestors and be a fellow making his own way and a good living for his wife and child. I must start in pictures slowly, thought Lodge. I must walk before I run. Let me study for two months, going over scripts with directors, observing technical aspects on various sets and watching scenes being filmed.

The Paramount executives were flabbergasted. No actor had ever turned down a big role for a small part. They shook their heads and backed off. John got his way, entering the movies as he had learned to walk, cautiously and slowly, one step at a time. Meanwhile Mae West proceeded to pick another tall, dark, and handsome Paramount contractee with a half-dozen undistinguished assignments to his credit. As her leading man in *She Done Him Wrong*, Cary Grant won instant acclaim and permanent stardom. The picture, which cost $260,000 to produce, eventually grossed over $3 million. When *Variety* announced the top box office pictures of 1933, it headed the list. Lodge later had misgivings over his well-intended refusal to enter films with West, a decision he paid dearly for in Hollywood.

Movie fans, alerted to the forthcoming new screen "find," wondered what the definable "something" was that Lodge had which all the trained and readily available actors in Hollywood did not have. Ad Schulberg was asked that question two weeks after Lodge arrived at Paramount. "I saw in him all the restraint and charm and intelligence Ronald Colman has," she replied. "He is not the blatant actor. There is a crying need in Hollywood for leading men of the 'gentleman' type. We are tired of seeing men in drawing room roles or portraying gentlemen adventurers who have the appearance of clerks. I feel strongly that Mr. Lodge will be a very important star. And I am never wrong. He always has had a yen for dramatics, and while he is not an actor, he has all the intelligence to interpret moods. Directors had rather work that way with a person who feels something working within. Mr. Lodge's tests were so splendid that I could have signed him to both Radio [RKO] and MGM."

Hollywood correspondent for the *Boston Daily Globe*, Mayme Ober Peak described Lodge's special appeal: "The slender, 6 ft. 2 in. broad-shouldered young man with irregular features is not exactly what you call 'Hollywood handsome.' His eyes are his best feature—the biggest, blackest, most penetrating eyes I have ever seen in a man's head. His cheeks and firm chin are cleft with dimples—when the latter are in play, you are reminded of Gable's famous knock-down and drag-out smile."

Outfitted in a double-breasted, gray business suit, John struck reporter Peak as if he had come to attend a business conference instead of a movie interview. He seemed a bit apprehensive over adjusting to the so-called glamorous celebrity life. "You see, I am just a normal man. You won't find anything flamboyant about me. Neither will Hollywood find me a Puritan. . . . This business presents something different every day. It is very colorful and has great charm. I have the feeling I should like it best from the executive or directing standpoint. Going in as an actor might give me the opportunity to learn the business from every angle."

Had he any interest in politics, the family business? he was asked. "There is plenty of time for me to go into politics. The field isn't very propitious now. There is so much organized graft, so much radio publicity which can glorify a man or tear down his principles overnight. California offers me more opportunity. New York is Democratic. I am a Republican. I should like it best to grow up with a pioneer country like this. . . . My legal experience will be more useful to me, however, in projecting my personality in pictures than in politics." Nonetheless, Peak concluded her long interview with prophetic words: "And I'm inclined to believe that after John Davis Lodge's name has been filled for the nonce over theater marquees, he will be passing bills in Washington as Senator Lodge from California."[2]

Lodge had pulled up stakes in the East to work hard at his new and challenging craft. He drove to the studio at 6:45 every morning, learning about makeup and wardrobe. He talked with studio experts in many fields, rehearsed with voice and dramatic coaches, and took part in tests with other newcomers who were being tried out. Paramount was turning out nearly 60 films a year, more than any other studio. Many, he observed, were society satires and drawing room dramas, not to mention the comic vehicles for the Marx Brothers, W. C. Fields, and Mae West. Its output often emphasized sexuality and eroticism, ingredients its individualistic directors—Lubitsch, DeMille, Mamoulian, von Sternberg—mixed to good effect. Yet the studio showed a lack of imagination in capitalizing on the acting talent under contract. Overall it pulled in many different sorts of performers but didn't really groom them. Paramount under B. P. Schulberg seemed more skilled at exploiting the backgrounds of new stars, such as Clara Bow and her unwanted slum child beginnings in Brooklyn. And he loaned them out to other filmmakers for far more than he was paying them.

Neither Paramount nor Hollywood had many genuine society types in their midst. Perhaps Katharine Hepburn, like Lodge a product of "old" New England, and Franchot Tone, a well-bred Ivy Leaguer, could point to similar pedigrees. Hollywood evidenced more sympathy for anyone who had fought his way up, starved, sweated, and wept, so long as he or she did it in rags. And socially, film folk could not make up their minds just how to deal with the grandson of Senator Lodge, who took no pains to be just himself, a plain Boston blueblood. John would have to work extra hard to change their minds.

Many fellow workers expressed disbelief that Clark Gable was still drawing a relatively modest salary as a star at MGM, while a novice like Lodge cashed a weekly check for $275. As "Gable's newest rival," John faced formidable male competition and perusal at Paramount from Gary Cooper, Randolph Scott, Cary Grant, Ray Milland, Kent Taylor, and Richard Arlen. The casting department soon considered Lodge for a contemplated picture called *Ruby Red*, then for a part in *The Lives of a Bengal Lancer*. They finally got him on screen in a Cary Grant-Nancy Carroll vehicle called *The Woman Accused*.

Lodge's first role—as a doctor who examines a murder victim played by Louis Calhern—was a very brief, but capably done, bit. Part of a cast of twenty players, he had no chance to make an impression. The majority of reviewers lost sight of him. "I couldn't find John Lodge, who is supposed to have a role in the story," wrote *New York Herald Tribune* critic Richard Watts, Jr.[3]

The Woman Accused was based on a *Liberty* magazine serial authored by ten different writers, including Rupert Hughes, Vina Delmar, Vicki Baum, Zane Grey, Irvin S. Cobb, and Polan Banks. Notwithstanding the array of literary talent, the overall results were shallow and disappointing. The melodrama lacked appeal, chiefly because Nancy Carroll, the woman accused, was acquitted of murder though she was in fact guilty. Only the last sequence had the audience cheering. For the finish, hero Cary Grant horsewhipped hired killer Jack LaRue, who in the process did a memorable bit of acting. In any event, the staging amid Art Deco settings was quite pleasing, and the photography and vocal recording (for still-rudimentary sound pictures) were excellent.

Long before *The Woman Accused* opened in March 1933, Lodge was assigned to another film, a rather gruesome and sadistic tale called *Murders in the Zoo*. Directed by Eddie Sutherland, this thriller opened with an irate jungle animal collector in the act of destroying his wife's lover by a bizarre means; he sews the fellow's lips together with thread and then leaves him to perish miserably among pythons and tigers. Lodge fared little better at the hands of the animal collector-husband, played by Lionel Atwill, a mainstay of horror pictures of the 1930s. Lodge, as the wife's latest lover, is invited to a formal dinner party at a city zoo. Caged wild animals overlook the festive gathering. Suddenly bitten by a mamba placed surreptitiously near his feet by the zealous Atwill, Lodge meets a quick yet painful death.[4] As a corpse, he stays in view for much of the picture's second reel.

One critic of these cheerless events wrote: "As for John Lodge, he was stiffer in his love scenes than as a corpse." At least the melodrama provided an opportunity for John to work with some of the studio's capable and popular stock players: comedian Charles Ruggles, romantic duo Gail Patrick and Randolph Scott, and screen siren Kathleen Burke (as the beleaguered wife), who had just gained attention as "The Panther Woman" in a Paramount feature. *Murders in the Zoo* received a big build-up, opening at New York's prestigious Paramount Theater.

Early in 1933, the studio decided to test John's mettle in a new setting. The front office wondered how rugged this tall, broad-shouldered Easterner really was. So they assigned him to a Western shot on location with long days of roughhouse scenes and rigorous riding. Let Lodge prove himself as a cowboy, they decided. "The studio sort of had the idea I had spent my life sitting in Louis XIV chairs, discussing poetry," John recounted later. "So they cast me as the villain in *Under The Tonto Rim*, a Zane Grey story directed by Henry Hathaway early in his career."[5] Hathaway and the crew did not realize that Lodge had, indeed, learned to ride and rough it on a ranch in Arizona years before. A little fun was expected when he mounted the spirited horse selected for him. But the tables were turned when, as a cattle rustler in large sombrero and high boots, he rode without the least difficulty or apprehension.

Hathaway pulled out all the stops in the last scene of the picture—a free-for-all-fight. Lodge was pushed, then dragged down several flights of stairs. He blocked punches, which, if they had landed, would have knocked him unconscious. The hero, a dumb cowpuncher played by Stuart Erwin, worked him over without letup. "Hathaway was pretty rough on everybody, but especially Lodge," recalled the picture's female lead Verna Hillie. "He insisted on feats dangerous and uncomfortable to his stars. He didn't care how bad it was for actors or animals. John was told a double would do the hazardous scenes. But he ended up pulled down a flight of stairs on his face. Another time Ervin refused to do a scene involving a stampede of cattle. So Hathaway had him fired from Paramount."[6] Luckily, John completed the picture nonplused and unscathed. Paramount released the bottom-of-the-bill Western in early April; few reviewers took notice of the proceedings with Erwin, Lodge, Hillie, Fuzzy Knight, Fred Kohler, and Raymond Hatton.

Outside of Los Angeles and Boston, the major dailies paid little heed to Lodge's movie-making. John had a ready-made coterie of fans in Massachusetts but few elsewhere. So Paramount insisted he provide "hometown" readers a recap of his experiences for the *Boston Advertiser*. He did not want to do it. But the studio pointed out that it would ghost the series if he didn't write it himself. So John agreed to record his impressions. "Hollywood, in my opinion, has been outrageously libeled, vilified and damned by those who seek notoriety at the expense of the good name of others," he noted. "I can say with some little authority that most of the stories about Hollywood are, at best, only half truths, luridly colored by distorted imaginations." Lodge found the people in the industry in general friendly, hardworking and extremely hospitable. "They are deeply interested in their work, and when they relax, they are as dignified as any group of artists or business people in the East. . . . For every minute of fleeting fame, there has been expended an hour of hard work and mental agony. For every dollar earned, there is a thousand dollars of worry spent."[7]

And Lodge had much to worry about that spring. Shortly after writing these words, he was summoned to the front office. Studio executives told him there were no assignments on tap. His six-month contract was up, and they would not exercise the option to continue the agreement. They had paid him a total of $7,150 since October at a time of a widespread economic slide, and the results hadn't caused much of a stir. Over half his salary was spent on professional expenses: agent commissions, photographs, publicity, makeup utensils, clipping services, trade ads, wardrobe, and secretarial and valet services. His trust fund income paid most of his day-to-day bills. Nonetheless, this Hollywood contract made his law earnings look like cigarette money. "I, like many others, am sitting on quicksand these days as the movies are going through very bad times," he wrote his mother on April 13, 1933. "Who knows what I shall be doing next?"[8] To pass the time, he delivered a speech at a local Kiwanis Club dinner. His talk stressed the importance of "character" to do our duty in the midst of troubled times. He termed character a greater key to success and happiness than intellect.

After three minor pictures, even Lodge himself admitted he was somewhat stiff, although he described it as a natural, traditional reserve. The poise, polish, deep voice, and striking looks so clearly apparent in his screen test didn't register well in his films at Paramount. He failed to come across convincingly and seemed especially uncomfortable in love scenes. "His speech was fine," Verna Hillie remembered, "but he needed acting lessons. We both arrived at Paramount the same time, and did lots of screen tests with potential contractees and sometimes with each other. For one thing, he knew nothing about the art of kissing on camera. He just went overboard on several takes with French kisses."[9]

Oddly enough, John's dark, expressive eyes caused problems in close-ups. They projected a rather disagreeable and overpowering look. From certain angles, his visage became almost mean and villainous. He seemed headed for anti-hero parts as a heavy, even a gangster. His directors and cameramen agonized over his somewhat sinister, albeit sagacious, gaze.

A close friend viewed Lodge as "a man who could use English, cultured English, with a voice already perfectly trained oratorically. On top of that here was a man who knew what to do with a butler, who had the most magnificent background in America, also being physically as presentable as Clark Gable."[10] But as a departure, John tested for a muscular role not unlike Tarzan, a part Johnny Weismuller had just scored great success with at MGM. Paramount prepared a similar script of African adventure called *King of the Jungle*. To get John in shape for the tryout, Francesca prescribed daily muscle-building exercises. But the test results proved a letdown, and Olympic swimming champion Buster Crabbe, a more apt vine swinger, was chosen for the lead.

John thought he was through in pictures, not having established himself measurably in any way. It looked as if he'd have to go back to the law. In an attempt to rekindle interest at Paramount in his career, he asked friends back East to write the studio with words of praise for his performances and to ask to see him in bigger roles. Closer to home, he urged others to send letters to the editors of local papers and trade journals commenting on his innate ability to be an important American actor. It was his first experience in self-promotion, a skill that would be honed in other fields at other times.

Apart from the sound stage, John enjoyed continuing to meet a diverse cross-section of film workers. He found chatting with so many different types an education in itself: "One can learn almost as much from a year's stay in Hollywood as one could from ten years of foreign travel." He was hospitable to prop men, assistant directors, carpenters, chauffeurs, and publicists, if they met the only test that counted: genuineness. John believed he was becoming more tolerant, less opinionated, more philosophical, and more rational after six months in Hollywood.[11]

One of his best buddies was the scene-stealing comedian Jack Oakie. An established and versatile star at Paramount, he looked after Lodge, protecting him from opportunists. "They hit it off," Jack's widow Victoria Horne Oakie observed years later. "They'd talk, play the piano and sing half the night."[12]

The Lodges periodically attended major film premieres and occasionally ventured into nightclubs. They did not socialize with John's female co-stars; for that matter, they saw few of his fellow players off the set. Their circle of friends, who usually gathered for tennis or an evening of good conversation and parlor games, included Frederic March, Johnny Mack Brown, Ralph Bellamy, Fay Wray, Helen Hayes, Dorothy Parker, Gene Raymond, and Ivan Lebedeff.

One gossipy—perhaps spurious—story found its way East from Hollywood. The Lodges, it was reported, were not very popular there because Francesca was too exuberant: "It was told that in a game of Charades, Cesca had ridden into the room as Lady Godiva, sitting on the back of a gentleman on his hands and knees draped in a bear rug. She was clothed only in her gorgeous hair, which was thick and plentiful enough to conceal her figure modestly."[13] On the other hand, John struck many as too straight-laced. He resisted the advances of female and male co-stars, apparently never playing that Hollywood game. Moreover, his old-guard social attire—a morning coat, striped trousers, spats and walking stick—seemed clearly out of place and the butt of occasional jokes.

Lacking a studio affiliation or a contract in the late spring of 1933, Lodge had plenty of leisure to study, rest and play . . . and ponder his future. Francesca wasted no time filling her days, which were especially long when John's wake-up calls were set for dawn to accommodate location shooting schedules. She decided to work part-time. She helped to open a new Elizabeth Arden Beauty Salon on Wilshire Boulevard and promoted Pond's skin creams in advertisements featuring her in a striking gown designed by MGM's Adrian. That studio cast her as a courtesan for a brief suggestive scene with Lionel Barrymore in *Rasputin and the Empress*. But a law suit against MGM by a member of the surviving Russian royal family for defiling their image cut Francesca's work out of the picture. As a stand-in for Garbo, she danced the mazurka in MGM's *Anna Karenina*. She taught dancing at a nearby arts center and performed in neighborhood productions. Hearing of her choreographic talent, director George Cukor called upon her to handle the ballroom sequence for his latest picture at RKO. She went to the studio to teach the cast and extras how to perform old-fashioned waltzes and polkas for an important scene in the film version of Louisa May Alcott's classic *Little Women*. The picture starred Katharine Hepburn, who had recently made her screen bow in Cukor's *A Bill of Divorcement*. Soon after rehearsals began, Francesca made known the fact that John was at liberty. Cukor told her to bring him to the studio; he needed a technical expert on the manners and customs of old Concord, Massachusetts, the locale of the Alcott story. The director also wanted Lodge to work as a dialogue coach.

Not long after this backstage assignment began, John won a role in the picture as well, a solid but small part in a prestigious production. Cukor assigned him to the part of John Brooke, the tutor of the Lawrence boy, played by Douglass Montgomery. Lodge was an ideal addition to the large and distinguished cast: Hepburn, Montgomery, Joan Bennett, Jean Parker, Spring Byington, Edna May Oliver, Paul Lukas, and Frances Dee, who as Meg married Lodge in a picturesque outdoor wedding ceremony. Three-year-old Lily made her movie début in the picture, appearing among a group of youngsters in a schoolroom scene.

Little Women provided Lodge an opportunity to be part of a superbly crafted undertaking that accurately and painstakingly captured the life of a New England family during the Civil War era. Costumed in high-waisted gray trousers, congress gaiters, and a pleated and ruffled shirt, he moved comfortably into the plot. The Alcott story characters were people to whom Lodge related (and in a sense easily might have been related to). Enhanced by thick black sideburns, he fit into the period role with ease, sensing that portrayals of figures from long-gone days might once and for all gain him a secure footing in front of the cameras.

Photographed in the style of finely etched ferrotypes by cinematographer Henry Gerrard and underscored with musical themes created by composer Max Steiner, *Little Women* engendered interest in more costume pictures, as well as in more literary classics, for the screen.

A hit from the day it opened at New York's Radio City Music Hall, it amassed big profits for RKO and received Academy Award nominations for best picture and for director George Cukor. (Mae West's *She Done Him Wrong*, the film Lodge nearly made, also garnered a Best Picture nod.) *Cavalcade* won the top Oscar, but *Little Women* picked up honors for the best screenplay adaptation.

The widely acclaimed film boosted Katharine Hepburn's career, but did little for John Davis Lodge, who was billed twelfth in the credits. Nonetheless, Hepburn always remembered him as "a charming man, good actor."[14] With no screen prospects in sight, he began studying for the California bar exams. He concluded that he might practice law in the state. From time to time, he stopped by Paramount to pick up his mail and have lunch. It was there that he was "rediscovered" one day in the commissary. John and Francesca were midway through their meal when they felt the stares of a foreign-looking gent from a nearby table. They recognized the keen observer as director Josef von Sternberg. After they left the dining area and walked out the door toward the parking lot, they realized von Sternberg was following them. Francesca had a hunch; she whispered to John, "I bet he's sizing you up for something." Von Sternberg, the Svengali to Paramount's reigning exotic "import" Marlene Dietrich, stepped in front of the Lodges and introduced himself. "I've been searching for a particular face and presence to play the leading male role opposite Dietrich," he explained. "I have not found the ideal romantic actor who could handle this unusual part. But you have a certain aura and distinct bearing that might meet my requirements. Let me test you for this role. It's the Russian Count Alexei in *The Scarlet Empress*, a story of Catherine the Great."

He had searched for a performer with intelligence, someone who would avoid "an artificial characterization." Passing muster, John was re-signed by Paramount at $400 a week and taken under von Sternberg's wing for this full-scale costume epic. "The making of a film," von Sternberg once stated, "provides time for little else than outright manipulation of an actor's body and mind, and willing or not, this subject, this slavery, becomes part of his life."[15]

That fall Lodge again started work at Paramount. He quickly realized he still had much to learn about pictures. Von Sternberg demanded that John take less heed of the camera and not be uncomfortable when its lens focused exclusively on him. He coached John for close-ups, tense encounters that often caused John to stutter. He built up John's confidence, especially for the powerful, demanding love scenes with Dietrich. In the process, Lodge gained the respect of this meticulous director. And of Dietrich, too. She later wrote of her co-star in her autobiography *Marlene D.*: "Lodge conquered the hearts of all American women. He was *the* Russian hero, the romantic figure par excellence. John Lodge became our friend, and he won von Sternberg's unlimited respect."[16]

During the months of production, John revealed himself as an actor of force and fire. But playing opposite Marlene Dietrich day after day, he worried if the on-screen love-making opposite this alluring actress might carry over away from the cameras. She had the reputation of not letting go off the set. He insisted that Francesca come with him to the set to act as script coach and helpmate. Enamored of Dietrich, von Sternberg welcomed the move. Marlene got the message. Every day she paused in front of Francesca, said a quick good morning, briskly clicked her heels, and saluted.

Every single scene bore the imprint of von Sternberg. In his first movie, character actor Sam Jaffe won acclaim as the dissolute Czar Peter, as did screen veteran Louise Dresser as the meddling old Empress Elizabeth. Virtually every detail, every gesture, was masterminded by von Sternberg. "The tapestry of the Russia of Catharine the Great was evoked in all its grandeur, though it was a recreation and not a replica," he noted in his autobiography. "The story of the rise of a guileless young princess to a mocking and ruthless empress could not be dull."[17]

Production ended in December 1933. But the formidable tasks of editing and scoring took many months. John's best work in an American film, and ultimately his favorite role, remained in the can and unseen until the picture was finally released in September 1934. *The Scarlet Empress* heralded Lodge as a new and important leading man, notwithstanding being overshadowed in a carnival-like conglomeration of scenes, ranging from grandiose and grotesque to fantastic and erotic.

The *New York Herald Tribune* pondered over its heavy, brooding preoccupation with sex, symbols, and overemphasized settings: "The whole picture represents a soul conflict between Mr. von Sternberg's admiration for gargoyles and his determination to play his characteristic Svengali to Miss Dietrich's cinematic Trilby." The critic voiced misgivings over a Dietrich-Lodge love scene in a haystack—made excruciatingly difficult to film by John's allergy to straw—and concluded that Lodge was "a bit too monotonous as the great Catherine's first love."[18]

Time magazine ran a review with a photo of John as the dashing Russian Count complete with striking neck-length wig and roguish mustache. Their words gave him little encouragement: "Whatever talents as an actor Henry Cabot Lodge's grandson may have are set off to poor advantage by the picture. A tedious hyperbole in which Director Josef von Sternberg achieved the improbable feat of burying Marlene Dietrich in a welter of plaster-of-paris gargoyles and galloping Cossacks, it seems all the more inadequate by comparison with Elizabeth Bergner's *Catherine the Great*.[19]

It didn't enjoy much success in the United States, although the British press praised the film and Lodge. *The Scarlet Empress* a generation later gained recognition as a masterpiece of visual stylization and imaginative interpretation. Included in anthologies of major films and on lists of classic motion pictures, and shown in film museums and cinema workshops, it has often been described as one of the finest and most convincing costume pictures ever made in Hollywood. "It was thirty years ahead of its time," film historian John Kobal writes. "Every celluloid inch of this masterpiece marked it as a stone of the first water, enhanced by the superlative performance of the star."[20]

Yet all this later praise and acclaim did not benefit Lodge in 1933 or 1934. Now a leading man with star potential, he wanted to advance to star status. Back at Paramount once more, he waited and waited for the studio to find a suitable vehicle, perhaps another costume epic. By the laws of averages and common sense, he concluded, he should have been in considerable demand on screen.

Many mornings he was amused by Lily, who had the makings of a performer in her own right. She'd put on his hat and muffler and with his walking stick in hand, prance into the living room. "Where are you going?" he would ask. "I am going to the stu-di-o," she would say. John loved this routine, embellished by her keen observations of the mannerisms of von Sternberg, now a close family friend.

With little to do, the Lodges journeyed East in February 1934 for a leisurely vacation in Boston and Washington. After their return to California, John had no jobs waiting. It was an upsetting and anxious time for an actor with his biggest, and possibly best, work delayed in release.

After three months on the sidelines, John was given the role of an English actor (and the insane brother of Ray Milland) in *Menace*. Not at all an important picture at Paramount, it proved a better-than-average whodunit with a large and competent cast. "A rapid-fire mystery, suspenseful and jammed with thrills," noted the *New York Times*. "The acting—like the story—is better than that normally encountered in mystery films. Gertrude Michael and Paul Cavanaugh, last seen together in *The Notorious Sophie Lang*, are an excellent acting combination. The other bows may be shared by Henrietta Crosman, John Lodge and Halliwell Hobbes."[21] Hardly a starring role or a sympathetic one, it, nevertheless, registered with audiences, especially in England.

Lodge soon received an offer outside the studio gates. European producer Max Reinhardt had seen John in *The Scarlet Empress* and visualized him at once as Theseus for his forthcoming production of *A*

Midsummer Night's Dream at the Hollywood Bowl. In a radio interview at the time, Lodge explained that this role was one he had wanted to interpret since first reading the play as a young boy. "In recent years," he noted, "Shakespeare's plays have been presented as works of literature only, rather than as entertaining drama and have therefore not had the public appeal which is their due. Professor Reinhardt gives Shakespeare a human and modern treatment which brings the great Bard of Avon close to the many thousands who will throng to witness the Reinhardt production."[22]

Francesca had become very familiar with the requirements of working on the stage of the Hollywood Bowl. The year before, she fulfilled her great artistic wish: to lead a large *corps de ballet* in an outdoor performance of an interpretation of a Strauss waltz ("Tales from the Vienna Woods") played by a symphony orchestra (conducted by Bernardino Molinari). Reinhardt suggested that she alternate the role of Hippolyta, Queen of the Amazons, in *A Midsummer Night's Dream*, with Jacqueline de Wit. Moving onto the mammoth outdoor stage with three pairs of Russian wolfhounds in tow, she carried off her part with characteristic flair and presence. John's lines set the mood for the opening scene of the Shakespearean fantasy: "Now, fair Hippolyta, our nuptial hour draws on apace; four happy days bring in another moon: but, O, methinks, how slow this old moon wanes!"

Reinhardt had turned the stage into a sylvan glade and cast the fanciful creatures of the piece with Mickey Rooney (as Puck), Evelyn Venable, Sterling Holloway, Walter Connolly, William Henry, Julie Haydon, and William Farnum. A brand new star emerged from the production when Gloria Stuart as Hermia withdrew several days before the opening because the schedule of the film which she had been making at Warner Brothers during the rehearsal period ran longer than anticipated. An 18-year-old understudy about to enter college took her place. Olivia de Havilland never joined her freshman class at Mills College. Her highly praised performances led to a contract for a tour with the play to the San Francisco Opera House, and other northern California stages. Lodge, too, continued in his role, enhancing it, as one critic said, by his regal bearing and pronouncement. Yet when Warner Brothers decided on a movie version, it chose contract player Ian Hunter for Theseus, while only signing Olivia de Havilland and Mickey Rooney from the stage presentation.

Pa—Isidore Braggiotti—failed to attend opening night. He had suffered an attack of tonsillitis, which quickly developed into pneumonia. Isidore died on the eve of the Hollywood Bowl spectacular. His last year compressed moments of joy, pride, embarrassment, and turmoil. An old

Boston flame had followed him to California. A charming, well-meaning yet persistent widow with a fortune in railroad stocks, Edith Perkins Cunningham led him to the altar. Early in their marriage, the reluctant groom found that he couldn't stand another minute under the same roof with the overly solicitous Edith. The marriage soon broke up.

He lived to see all but one of his children making headway in life. Stiano was a mainstay on the Broadway stage; Gloria, a fashion editor of a New York newspaper; Rama, a cartoonist; Francesca, a dancer and actress; Chad, a Harvard student and campus baseball and tennis standout; Mario, a radio and concert performer (he had just completed a scene in Eddie Cantor's *Kid Millions*. Only Marta, struggling for a cure in Tucson, faced an unrewarding future (and a short one, as her tuberculosis proved terminal in early 1935).

Before the year ended, another tie to old Boston was severed. The *Social Register* dropped the John Davis Lodges. In its eyes, his work in movies clearly carried a social stigma. "I cannot see why anyone who has been absent as long as I should be included in such a record," John told a reporter. "I'd rather have my name in the Standard Casting Directory than in the *Boston Register*."[23] Joining Fred Astaire's wife, the socially prominent Phyllis Potter, on the 1935 "out" list, Lodge apparently never gave the expulsion another thought.

That fall the thriving Fox Film company took notice of Lodge, a stock performer who had done his best work in period costume. Producer Buddy DeSylva and director David Butler offered him a major role in a Reconstruction era story playing a Yankee married to the daughter (Evelyn Venable) of a crusty old Kentucky aristocrat (Lionel Barrymore). Most important, he portrayed the father of the reigning little star of all Hollywood and a national idol, Shirley Temple. As *The Little Colonel*, this pint-sized Duse routs the bitterness and false pride of her grandfather who has turned his back on his daughter and her Northern husband. In the end, Shirley keeps the family in harmony. "Shirley was so bright, so full of talent, so unspoiled," Evelyn Venable recalled. "For *The Little Colonel*, Shirley had a good supporting cast. John Lodge, the well-bred gentleman that he was, portrayed Shirley's father and my husband very convincingly."[24] Francesca remembers how closely Shirley's mother guided her progress both on and off the set: "Shirley's place in pictures was remarkable. The only criticism I heard stemmed from those who thought she shouldn't have been making more money than the President of the United States!"

John valued the opportunity to play with Lionel Barrymore, noting years later his friendliness and unfailing good humor. To Shirley, the veteran actor was irascible and plodding as he stumbled over lines constantly. Barrymore's forgetfulness prompted Shirley's help; she unfailingly learned everyone's lines and never hesitated to prompt a cast member, young or old. But it was Bill "Bojangles" Robinson as a Negro butler who with Shirley won the greatest applause. The screen's first interracial couple, Robinson and Shirley sang and tap-danced on a staircase in a scene that became an unforgettable moment in movie history and led to their re-teaming in two more films of the 1930s.

"The Little Colonel" premiered at Radio City Music Hall on March 21, 1935, and the audience applauded for a solid eleven seconds after Shirley's final scene in Barrymore's arms. A popular film ever since, it marked Shirley Temple's (and John Lodge's) début in Technicolor, as the end of the picture was shot using this still relatively experimental and costly color process.

At the completion of the Fox assignment, Lodge headed for New York and Washington to discuss possible stage roles in *The Old Maid* with his Fox co-star Evelyn Venable and in *Symphony* with actress Lois Moran and director Felix Weissberger, Reinhardt's assistant at the Hollywood Bowl. As Francesca was unable to accompany him when he went East, he wanted to avoid any suggestion that they were going separate ways. He sent out a press release explaining that his wife was performing in a theater dance presentation tied to the Los Angeles opening of Paramount's *Lives of a Bengal Lancer*. That alone was the only reason he was traveling alone.[25]

John's hoped-for Broadway début came to naught. He was back in Hollywood before spring. The opening of *The Little Colonel* rekindled interest by the press in this patrician actor. Fan magazine writer Nancy Smith described Lodge, again at liberty: "Tall, well over six feet. Straight as an arrow. Broad shoulders that are always thrown back squarely. Expressive eyes that look clear through you as he talks with the enthusiasm of a young college boy. A laugh that is effervescent. A smile that charms you. A voice that is soothing, yet which carries a distinct note of sincerity. A charming host."[26] Such descriptive praise seemed to go unnoticed by Hollywood casting offices. They only remembered criticism of his "stiffness" on screen. In fact, John carried in his pocket a particularly pointed review on this aspect of his demeanor and pulled it out often, mulling over the words and feeling further discouraged.

A production of Shakespeare's *King John* early in the summer got him back into acting. John played Philip in this rarely staged play at the Pasadena Playhouse. This part in a first-rate production highlighted his abilities to hold his own in a dramatization whose dialogue delved heavily into such matters as the inability of many politicians to distinguish between the public good and their own ambitions, the conflict between church and state, and the true meaning of patriotism. All were issues Lodge related to because of his keen interest in history and government.

A still unknown performer named John Carradine played an important role. The Lodges had befriended the gifted young actor, who literally had been living on the streets of Hollywood while seeking jobs. The cast also featured future Broadway star Judith Evelyn and child actor Gene Reynolds, as well as Francesca. As Constance, the mother of Arthur, pleading for the safety of her child, she revealed herself as a creditable Shakespearean actress. "Her intelligent reading and emotional interpretation brought the text completely to life," one observer wrote.[27]

Rehearsals and performances of *King John* occupied only a few weeks of summer. At home John again anxiously waited for new assignments.

CHAPTER 8

Britain's Clark Gable

L odge had last visited Europe in 1929. Since his wedding trip that year, economic malaise had fallen upon Britain and every country on the Continent, and military buildups pointed toward rising tensions on many borders. John followed overseas events closely. He took notice of the rise of Hitler and rearmament in Germany, the advance of Mussolini's army across the Mediterranean into Africa, the strength of the leftist movement within France, and the expansion of the imperial navy in Britain. With time on his hands, he longed to return and see first-hand the turbulent changes in the lands he knew well and was eager to get back to work or to travel. Both would unfold before him quite suddenly. His agent telephoned one morning to ask if he really spoke French as easily and fluently as he had claimed. A French film company was seeking an actor who could handle French and English versions of an important film. The Paris-based producers had seen Lodge in the eighteenth-century period piece *The Scarlet Empress*. Could he speak their language well enough to co-star in a similar costume epic, they wondered. John urged his agent to tell the French outfit to call him directly. The following day, Francesca answered the phone. "John," she exclaimed, "Paris is calling!"

A conversation in French instantly convinced director Maurice Tourneur that Lodge could hold his own with the likes of Pierre Fresnay, Jean Dubucourt, and Jean Max. He accepted the role as Grand Duke Frederic in the dual language version of *Koenigsmark*, based on the novel by Pierre Benoit. The internationally known actress Elissa Landi, reputedly an European aristocrat by birth if not actual royalty, already had agreed to star as Princess Aurore in this high-budget production which was nearing its shooting date. Lodge signed a ten-week contract for $500 a week plus $2,000 for travel expenses from California to Paris. In mid-July, he packed his bags and boarded an east-bound train. From New York, he sailed on the *Isle de France*, arriving in France just as pre-production began on August 1. Francesca remained in Hollywood, then joined him in the fall.

Lodge's character called for the wearing of a monocle, a bit of stage business befitting a scheming duke in a fictional European kingdom of the early 1900s. With determination and practice, Lodge made the eye piece a natural accessory, as much as the decorations on his Teutonic military uniform.

Koenigsmark opened in December 1935, with decidedly mixed reactions. *The Hollywood Reporter* noted its "bad continuity, labored dialogue and improbable story," but described John as "ultra-excellent" as the villain whose part in the murder of his brother is eventually exposed. The French version fared better critically and commercially, and played in Europe for the remainder of the decade.[1]

John's return to Paris, where he had spent several years as a youngster and later as a graduate student, did not go unnoticed. Edith Wharton, ever the gracious hostess, relished his visit. In her seventies, she continued to write and publish stories. At home, John would on occasion imitate Wharton's distinctive and rapidly-spoken French, adding a touch of her cultivated New York accent and mannerisms.

The American Club of Paris invited John to speak that fall. As a luncheon guest, he fascinated his audience with his comments on the differences between stage and screen techniques. He declared the cinema to be the first new art form to appear in centuries. But theater-goers, he explained, need not fear. The stage had not lost its appeal nor importance because of the newly arrived "illusionist art" called movies. In a personal aside, he felt certain in saying that he was the first American lawyer to play on the French screen (and perhaps the first American movie actor to play a major French-speaking role): "I know that reciprocity has been carried out in this matter, since among the many foreign stars welcomed to Hollywood there is Charles Boyer who studied law."[2]

News of Lodge's film work in France reached England before he completed *Koenigsmark*. British International Pictures (BIP) offered him a meaty role at its Elstree production complex near London. Brian Desmond Hurst, the proposed picture's technical expert in charge of action shots, suggested casting John in a fast-moving drama entitled *Ourselves Alone*, about the conflict between the Sinn Fein and the Royal Irish Constabulary in the early 1920s. Three days into the shooting, production chief Walter Mycroft liked what Desmond Hurst had caught on film and made him director. "John and Desmond Hurst got along like a house on fire," Francesca recalled. "He was fascinated with John's keen grasp of languages and history, and felt John was more British than American."

John initially agreed to play the part of Captain Wiltshire, an English intelligence officer; British actor John Loder was assigned the role of Inspector Hannay, who is determined to capture the notorious rebel leader, Michael O'Dea. Both Hannay and Wiltshire are in love with O'Dea's sister, Maureen, played by Antoinette Cellier.

But after a week or so of filming, Desmond Hurst felt John identified more with the Irish character, so he switched Lodge and Loder into each other's roles. The move proved auspicious. Lodge played the single-minded Irishman to much acclaim in a drama not unlike Hollywood's version of the rebellion, *The Informer*, released earlier that year. *Ourselves Alone* ends with a prophetic observation spoken by Lodge after he has shot O'Dea and then realizes Loder and Cellier are in love: "You've seen a miracle in Ireland. Two out of three people will be happy."

For Lodge, the picture at last confirmed his talent as a major dramatic actor. He dominated every scene and was hailed as an impressive performer. And for the first time his name appeared above a film title on marquees. He was a bona fide star, and was called in England "the actor Hollywood neglected." His performance stamped him as a major discovery throughout the British Isles. John Lodge, the actor, had arrived.[3]

Off the sound stage, John and John Loder became good friends. The tall, squared-jawed actor with a name so similar to Lodge's had graduated from the Royal Military Academy and actually served in France in the war and in Ireland. Soon the two began getting each other's fan mail and calls. Writers and later film historians periodically confused the two Johns, although Loder's career continued well into the 1960s on both sides of the Atlantic.

Perhaps one of the finest accolades of Lodge's dramatic persona came from a member of the cast of *Ourselves Alone*. Ballad singer Cavin O'Connor performed several period songs in a scene in an Irish pub. He assumed John was as British as Loder. Only later when Lodge became a U.S. ambassador did O'Connor realize Lodge hailed from the States.[4] Others on the set believed him to be Canadian. And one studio director once remarked to John, "Don't keep saying you're an American. Come on, admit it. You're one of us."

Lodge had planned a long holiday after his second overseas film, but BIP and Desmond Hurst quickly assigned him to another role. *The Tenth Man*, adapted from a play by Somerset Maugham, gave him the lead as a ruthless yet charming industrialist who serves in Parliament. He overextends his financial position and illegally manipulates trust funds. Meanwhile, he wins a closely fought re-election contest. Before his downfall, his character boasts, "I'm a crook and a good one." In spite of a bleak ending—the suicide of Lodge's character—this psychological melodrama of high finance and politics found a receptive audience.

John's performance, which entailed campaign speeches as the beleaguered MP, surpassed his earlier work with Desmond Hurst and co-star Antoinette Cellier (playing his estranged wife). Billed as Britain's Clark Gable and "The New Star Sensation," he imparted poise and charm to a rather unpleasant character, with hardly a trace of an American accent. "John Lodge squares his shoulders manfully to an uncompromising part," a critic wrote, "and hammers its nature home with a vigor that suggests an unbridled lust for power."[5]

By summer, John's screen accomplishments earned him a long-planned vacation. The Lodges decided to forego a conventional holiday on the Riviera or along the Rhine. Instead, they chose the distant and little-known Brioni in the Adriatic Sea. Picturesque and peaceful, this island off the coast of Yugoslavia offered sunny days of relaxation with hours of walking barefoot on expansive beaches and bicycling through unspoiled villages.

One day while cycling, they heard a voice in Italian call out to Francesca, "Is that all your own hair?" Replied John in perfect English, "It sure is." The stranger, a tall, friendly Italian, had just come ashore from a large sailing vessel anchored in the bay. They chatted a bit, then introduced themselves. The yachtsman gave his name, Amide, and then invited John and Francesca to come aboard his boat *Amrita*. Only when the crew addressed him in terms befitting royalty did they realize that Amide was Amedeo, the Duke of Aosta and the nephew of Italy's King Victor Emmanuel, and in his own right one of his country's outstanding military leaders and aviators. His wife was Princess Anna of France.

"The Duke talked about his hope to become the Italian Ambassador to America," Francesca remembered. "But a year later Mussolini appointed him Viceroy of Ethiopia. He was a giant of a man—nearly seven feet tall—and well-liked by people of every station. During World War II, as a general in the Italian forces fighting the Allies, he was captured by British troops in Africa. He died in a prison camp from tuberculosis at the young age of 43. We lost a dear friend from those carefree pre-war days."

In a letter to sister Gloria, Francesca described the holiday as "the most exciting, exhilarating and thrilling summer of my life." To close their vacation, the Lodges journeyed to the Salzburg Festival to hear a perfor-mance of Beethoven's *Fidelio* conducted by Toscanini.[6]

John reported back at Elstree for his third starring role under the direction of Brian Desmond Hurst. *Sensation*, based on a short-lived play called *Murder Gang*, told of the adventure, triumphs, and misfortunes of a group of British crime reporters who descend upon a village to cover a murder story. An intriguing and highly dramatic story not without a bit of humor and a touch of romance, *Sensation* turned out to be an uncommonly good film. Lodge played an aggressive, self-assured Fleet Street newsman, and Margaret Vyner portrayed his oft-neglected fiancée. A capable supporting cast, including Diana Churchill, Joan Marion, Billy Shine, Felix Aylmer, and Francis Lister, added to the plot. John even found an opportunity to utilize his singing voice when the reporters gather around a piano for a drinking song after an arduous day on the beat.

Lodge added to his laurels with *Sensation*. "When one considers the acting," *London Star* critic Richard Haestier noted, "honors are easy for John Lodge, who has one of those semi-tough, smart roles for which he is so eminently suitable. He does a nice piece of work."[7]

With John busy on BIP sound stages, Francesca and Lily, who had rejoined her parents in mid-1936, sailed back to America, where she reentered grade school in Washington. Plans were made for Grandmother Lodge to bring her to Europe the following spring. Francesca returned to Britain on the SS *Rex* shortly after Election Day. The family was still celebrating Cabot Lodge's hard-fought Senatorial victory in Massachusetts. The only Republican to unseat a Democrat in the U.S. Senate in the overwhelming Roosevelt landslide of 1936, he quickly entered into a position of leadership within his party.

John looked to 1937 as another year of continued screen success in England and perhaps a role or two on the Continent. He now had fan clubs in England and literally had been mobbed on several occasions by admirers who tore off bits of clothing as souvenirs. Francesca, too, found studio work. She choreographed dance numbers for a musical called *Glamorous Nights*, and the Roma Film Company summoned her to Italy for a possible screen role. Their lives suddenly seemed somewhat disjointed and gypsy-like as they hopped in different directions, from London to Paris to Rome, in pursuit of movie jobs.

Francesca's Italian friends from her youth included Count Galeazzo Ciano, now son-in-law of Fascist dictator Mussolini. Ciano, Italy's foreign minister, remembered Francesca from her school days when he had helped her pass exams. Often his family had vacationed near the Braggiottis on the Italian coast near Genoa. Ciano, in 1937, sought her help to inaugurate filmmaking at Italy's new studio, Cinecittà, the largest in Europe. With sixteen sound stages, it was the showplace of Italian cinema, a veritable Hollywood on the Tiber on the outskirts of Rome. The film center was close to Mussolini's heart. He sought to raise Italian films to international preeminence. He chose his son Vittorio to produce and distribute pictures, and to place Italy on an equal footing with the United States in the movie business.[8] Father and son demanded a production that would remind Italians and the world of the glories of Imperial Rome and reinforce the theme of an Italian-African empire. They seized upon a colossal epic called *Scipione l'Africano*—an historical spectacle commemorating the victory of Scipio over the Carthaginians of North Africa in 202 B.C.

Francesca's work as the Italian "voice" of Garbo, as well as her Tuscan roots and widely recognized accomplishments as an interpretative dancer, rated her high on the list of potential Italian cinema stars. Two years earlier, in 1935, filmmakers in Rome had wanted her to play a lead in a patriotic epic, but the Italian invasion of Ethiopia led to such tension between Italy and England—where John had just begun his career—that she turned down the opportunity so as not to embarrass him. By late 1936, Il Duce's military forays into Africa had eased, and Francesca traveled from London to visit friends in Italy. One of them borrowed some of her photos and, unknown to her, took the pictures to director Carmine Gallone.

Francesca signed for the role as the Queen of Carthage. She transformed her waist-long blond hair into dozens of small braids that fit under a dark wig. Exotic costumes accented her Salomé-like dances for scenes within her Carthaginian palace. She joined co-stars Isa Miranda, Annibale Nichi, and Memo Benassi and hundreds and hundreds of extras for the Cecil B. DeMille-inspired epic. Nonetheless, the film sagged as it tried to emulate Hollywood. One sharp-eyed critic noticed wristwatches on the arms of extras in a Roman crowd scene and telephone poles in the background of another. "Undramatic and stilted," wrote most reviewers.

It did play briefly in the States, mainly at a few art houses. The *New York Times* compared it to the last act of *Aida*. The paper gave its highest praise to Francesca: "Miss Braggiotti is superbly undulant: a welcome feminine relief from the masculine speechmaking, chest-beatings and careful insertions of false daggers into operatic chests on the various battlefields outside her various boudoirs."[9]

The film entered the recently organized Venice Film Festival and won top honors. Francesca accepted the prize for Vittorio Mussolini and Cinecittà. An opening was planned in Germany that year. Hitler, it seems, wanted to meet Francesca and invited her to represent his fascist neighbor in Berlin. Hitler and Mussolini were on very friendly terms; the former insisted on unrestricted German rearmament and the dissolution of the Versailles Treaty. Yet not until October 1937 would they meet and vow mutual aid if attacked. Francesca weighed the pros and cons of appearing as the highly visible guest of the Third Reich. John sized up the situation without hesitation. He wanted no part of Hitler's hospitality. It could bring repercussions. Francesca agreed. Years later, as he entered his first political race, John reminded her of the wise decision to stay clear of the German Fuehrer. Without a doubt, a Lodge career in politics would never have gotten off the ground in the post-war decade if the filmmaking Lodges had crossed over into that Axis land in 1937 or 1938.

In early 1937, when John's picture at BIP shut down for a week, he headed for Rome to visit Francesca at Cinecittà. Producers there asked him to consider a role in an Italian movie. A new linguistic challenge, it intrigued Lodge. But first he had to fulfill an assignment at Elstree, in a picture that would prove to be one of his best-remembered British films.

The Bulldog Drummond novels by "Sapper" (pen name for Herman Cyril McNeile) had been the basis for fast-paced detective movies both in England and the United States. Britisher Ronald Colman had made his well-acclaimed talking picture début in Hollywood as Bulldog. In England Ralph Richardson among several other actors played the popular sleuth until Lodge won the role in the latest adventure called *Bulldog Drummond at Bay*. Dorothy Mackaill and Victor Jory played key parts. Elstree's *Bulldog*, although not a prestige picture, did rank as first-class entertainment of its type. The Lodge "Bulldog" revealed a rough and tumble side of his acting talent. He becomes involved with a dangerous gang of international crooks and profiteers who are deviously gathering arms and weapons in the "sacred cause of peace." In particular, they seek a highly advanced radio-controlled airplane, kidnapping and torturing its inventor. Bulldog Drummond comes to his aid against the ringleader's henchmen.

While shooting a scene in a railway car, director Norman Lee called action—and got it. Lodge's punch to the jaw of bad guy Hugh Miller floored him. "The realism would have been all right," Lee recalled, "but instead of going on with the scene according to the script, John politely bent over Miller and asked, 'Have I hurt you, old man?' "[10]

One of the screen's better Bulldog Drummonds—British actor Ray Milland and Canadian-born Walter Pidgeon also portrayed the detective—Lodge brought a certain gentlemanly flair to the resourceful fellow with a knack for getting into and out of tight corners. Film historian William Everson wrote of his interpretation: "There was an aggressiveness in his speed and an arrogance in his bearing."[11]

John completed *Bulldog* in March 1937, then rushed off to Rome. Both Francesca and John were exhausted from months before the camera, and soon caught the grippe. They decided to rest in the mountains at Cortina. But John's flu turned to jaundice, and he spent two weeks in bed. Meanwhile, Francesca was offered several more film roles in Italy. She opted for a picture in Rome that provided the male lead for John. Their only film together, *Stasera alle Undice*, did not bolster his state of health.

John understood Italian fairly well, but had rarely spoken this language. However, with his wife's daily coaching, he memorized his lines, and delivered them to the director's satisfaction. Francesca had double duty: "My concern with John's dialogue and his acting shifted my own efforts as co-star to secondary level in this story of gangsters on the run. I wasn't pleased with the results on screen. I decided then and there not to work with John again in a foreign language film." Francesca's voice had problems of its own. So closely identified with Garbo's in Italy, it gave the studio second thoughts about future leads for her. Actually, much of her dialogue was dubbed by an Italian actress. Besides, her earnings could not leave the country. A bank balance of some $15,000 in lire had to be spent in Italy. Friends urged them to buy expensive clothes, paintings, and jewels. Francesca had a better idea. She picked out an expensive automobile, a sporty Lancia Landa convertible with a special push-button automatic device to raise and lower the top. One of the first cars to have such a mechanism, it attracted small crowds at every crossroads on the journey from Rome to London. The vehicle replaced the modest English Ford that John had purchased in 1935 for £42.

John's mother came to Europe that spring, and he joined her in Brussels, where Helena Lodge and her family lived. Barely recovered from his jaundice, he contracted the mumps and remained in bed for another ten days. ("No definite after-effects," he pointed out on a life insurance application five years later.) Mrs. Lodge worried about her son's health and vagabond banging about in hot hotels and rented quarters: "a nerve-racking life for any man of refinement," she reminded him. She begged John to settle down in his own home in England and forego work in Italy and France. Seven-year-old Lily had rejoined her parents, and Mrs. Lodge hoped his British studio work would not allow jobs outside London. "Oh, Johnny, what is money compared to health & a quiet mind!" she exclaimed. "You have every opportunity for this in Elstree it seems to me—besides which it is more dignified to have a home even if it is in a foreign land. Hiring other people's homes for two months does not seem very satisfactory."[12] The Lodges took her advice, at least to a degree. They signed a year's lease for a comfortable country home northwest of London and near Elstree. The antique-filled Victorian dwelling called "Oakfields" in the village of Mill Hill would become home for the longest period of any of their European sojourns.

Settled at Mill Hill, John reported for work on his next assignment, an ambitious project for Gainsborough Pictures directed by Carol Reed. Titled *Bank Holiday* (and in the United States, *Three on a Weekend*) it was inspired by MGM's Oscar-winning hit "Grand Hotel." Much of the story is set at a seaside resort over several days in August. The British locale provided its own distinctive atmosphere, rich in minor characterizations.

Teamed with Margaret Lockwood, probably the most accomplished English actress Lodge ever worked with in films, John played a soft-spoken yet nerve-racked gentleman whose wife dies in childbirth at the very beginning of the picture. Lockwood, a nurse, becomes strongly attached to him before setting off on a holiday at the seashore with her boyfriend (Hugh Williams). The rest of the story develops her growing realization that she cares deeply for Lodge and her fears that he may take his life before she returns to London.

Bank Holiday succeeds best as a realistic depiction of characters and situations involving a beauty contest participant, a Cockney couple with three rambunctious youngsters, a romance-hungry typist, and dozens of blue-collar Londoners on holiday at the seashore. The plot alternates between the cheerfully lightweight and the grossly sentimental. Intermingled with a measure of suspense, these were elements that Carol Reed would refine and amplify in his future films, notably *The Stars Look Down, Odd Man Out,* and *The Third Man.* "The direction has a nervous vigor," concluded the *Liverpool Post* film critic, "and this is emphasized by the presence of John Lodge. . . . The acting is good. . . . John Lodge has not a great deal to do, but, as usual, whenever he appears, he electrifies the screen."[13]

Brian Desmond Hurst soon told Lodge that he planned a major film on Lawrence of Arabia with John as the lead. There were also discussions of a possible play on the London stage. One unique appearance did unfold. John's agent Jack Dunfee lined up an interview before a television camera. On October 2, 1937, John and Francesca were guests of Leslie Mitchell, host of *Round the Film Studios,* telecast from John's dressing room at Pinewood Studios. The BBC program, one of the very early regular features beamed to the thousand or so viewers in and about London in this pioneering period of television, led to a second appearance.[14]

Dunfee urged John to go on the BBC's *Picture Parade.* "I am afraid there is no fee," he explained, "and all they are prepared to do is send a car . . . and when necessary, an expense account of 2 guineas. However, the important point is the publicity angle. . . . Television is now in its infancy and we think that those who are in early will reap the benefits later on."[15] John went before the live TV camera again. He and actor Anthony Ireland and director Paul Stein chatted on the set of *Just Like a Woman* at Elstree.

Along with adventuresome forays into a new and largely experimental medium, John and Francesca were building up an inventory of unusual, often humorous, experiences. When introduced to Mrs. Patrick Campbell, the London theater's mercurial grand dame, she looked them over, then remarked, "Oh, how boring. You mean you're married and removed from the hurly burly of the chaise lounge."

John always remembered a railroad trip to Brussels. A passenger in his compartment had overheard him speaking English, then perfect French, a bit of Italian, and even some German. The observer, convinced that Lodge was a foreign spy, reported the multi-language conversations to a customs official. Lodge's passport was quickly examined. How could an American speak these European languages so well, the official pondered. He stopped the train at a small depot and turned John over to the local police. Detained for hours, Lodge finally convinced the gendarmes that he was not a foreign agent, merely a multilingual American actor living abroad.

John's portrayal of Bulldog Drummond and the grieving husband in *Bank Holiday* placed him among the most popular English-speaking film stars. In a year-end *Fame Magazine* poll, he ranked twelfth among the top twenty performers in the country. Only two other Americans joined him: Paul Robeson and Arthur Tracy. (Three British musical comedy favorites headed the list: Gracie Fields, George Formby, and Jessie Matthews.) John looked ahead into 1938 to more continually challenging roles. Francesca, too, viewed 1938 as a special year in a familial way. She had dropped her screen work to have a baby. Beatrice Anna Cabot Lodge was born in London on May 2. Eight years younger than Lily, she brought back a semblance of domesticity that the Lodges seemed to have lacked since leaving Hollywood. Because of the age difference, Francesca jokingly referred to Lily and Beatrice as "my two only children."

The year 1938 would prove John's most active on screen. He had completed the comedy thriller *Just Like a Woman* before Beatrice's birth. Playing a jeweler's agent commissioned to find a string of black pearls, he is outwitted by a rival buyer, portrayed by American actress—and the lead in Paramount's *Menace* in 1934—Gertrude Michael. The picture proved that he was adept in lighter roles as well as the heavier fare in which producers had usually cast him.

Pearls also figured prominently in John's next film, a seagoing yarn called *Queer Cargo*. As a tramp steamer captain, Lodge is smuggling pearls to Singapore when the crew mutinies and demands the gems. The ship is soon seized by the pirates whose leader Lodge had saved from a sea disaster years before. After the intervention of a British destroyer, Lodge seemingly gives the pirate captain the pearls. The picture was not well received at the box-office.

Next came *Lightning Conductor* at Pinewood Studios, the third of John's five films in 1938. He gave a solid yet unsympathetic interpretation in the part of a thief who steals secret air defense plans. To avoid discovery, he quickly slips them into a bus conductor's (Gordon Harker) pocket. A comic spy story, it offered suspense and laughs as Lodge attempts to retrieve them, lastly in a forest where a swarm of bees attack.

Midyear, he returned to Elstree for what would prove his last assignment in England. *Premiere* reunited him with his very first British

director, Walter Summers, and his co-star from *Lightning Conductor*, Judy
Kelly. The backstage murder of a highly disliked impresario on the
opening night of a Parisian musical comedy occupied Lodge in this
seventy-one-minute whodunit. As French police inspector Bonnard, he
tracks down various suspects during the course of the show and gets his
man just in time to return to his seat before the final curtain. *Premiere*
mixed drama, music, suspense, and comedy, and even a dash of romance,
all to good advantage. (For its run in the States in 1940, it was retitled *One
Night in Paris*.)

Francesca offered career advice and encouragement in the midst of
John's busiest year of acting, as she had from his first step onto a movie
set: "Nothing must interfere with the progress of your career and I am
willing to make all sacrifices. Other things are secondary, except health.
One must not be rash as this work is full of pitfalls whether the artist is
to blame or not. Yet again . . . we must take chances." She believed a
London theater appearance would enhance John's standing: "I feel that
acting a good part in a well-organized West End production serves a useful
purpose whether the play be popular or not, and as you are a movie star,
you can afford to be less than a startling success in your first play."[16] And
in another short note, she suggested that he keep his eyebrows up: "Don't
squint your eyes in close-ups." For thinning hair, she devised a new regime:
"Wash it with plain soap and water every morning as you would shave."

By 1938 Bessie Lodge had come to accept her son's profession, and
even made special efforts to see his pictures when they played in the
United States. She occasionally traveled to New York to view them at one
of the small uptown art theaters, such as the Little Carnegie, Trans-Lux,
or 55th Street Playhouse. Moreover, she was becoming a perceptive movie
fan and outspoken critic. After seeing *Bank Holiday* twice, she dashed off
a letter: "If I had liked it better, I would have gone again tomorrow, but
the play is not good enough for you. You are excellent—could not be
better. After you, I thought much the best actor was the policeman, then
the man who robbed the bank. . . . Apart from the charming policeman
& the ocean and the thunderstorm & of course, you, the play seemed to
have no merit. Probably Miss Lockwood is more interesting in better
roles. She is attractive & graceful. . . . The Irish play ("Ourselves Alone")
& "Koenigsmark" were so good that I am sorry to see you in this.
However, you can't always choose; I realize that. I am glad the critics do
not agree with me. . . . I was surprised at the frequency with which the
actors preface their remarks by 'Listen'—a term only used here by the
lower classes."[17]

A month later, after seeing a number of Hollywood releases, Mrs.
Lodge again revealed a growing affinity toward the cinema. "It is

interesting that the English appreciate you so much, because it seems to me that they send good actors over here—men like Rathbone, Rains and Laughton. If these men were appreciated in Hollywood, why didn't they appreciate John," she wondered.[18] She critically appraised John's so-called counterpart, "I saw Clark Gable for the first time the other day. He acted with Colbert in *It Happened One Night*. I thought he was good, but his diction is too common for the leading role in *Gone With The Wind*. That man was a cultivated southern gentleman in spite of his cynicism, whereas Gable speaks Amurrican. Perhaps he will learn to speak correctly for this part."[19]

Mrs. Lodge wondered whether her son might want to return to Hollywood. The near-outbreak of war in Europe over the Sudetenland stunned much of the world. With Hitler on the march, many British actors in Hollywood were notified that they might have to leave the States on short notice. "I wanted you to know about this at once," she wrote on September 13, 1938, "so that you could keep in touch with the situation."[20]

Francesca remained in close contact with John's Hollywood agent. That year Paramount wanted John to return for the lead in a Sylvia Sidney picture directed by Dudley Murphy. The studio offered a minimum guarantee of $5,000 for five weeks' work. "First feature billing . . . first class transportation both ways," the studio wired. The deal fell through when the producers were unable to obtain distribution approval. Not long after, Paramount cabled information on a Claudette Colbert picture. But by then John was busy on sound stages in Paris.

The actor Hollywood overlooked truly had little or no overriding desire to return to California. Movie moguls there had done very little with his potential; the English, in contrast, had immediately capitalized on his screen presence. Perhaps the British accepted polished and aloof players more than American audiences. With his correctly spoken English, they forgot he was an American. Moreover, they reacted favorably to a performer who came across as both a regular fellow and an intellect when the part called for it.

John's British pictures in the United States rarely moved beyond city art theaters into regional movie houses. And overall, American critics were largely unimpressed with his European work, which caused only tepid reaction when imported into his native land. John came to prefer movie-making in Europe. There it was possible to see how the rest of the world moved and not be tied to a studio every waking minute. "In France," he observed, "when an actor is cast for a part in a screen show, he simply fills his professional obligations the way any businessman does and forgets the whole thing for the rest of the day. He is able to live his family and domestic life, go out into the world and see what goes on, maintaining his personal, non-professional contacts, and in general, conduct his existence on a civilized basis. In Europe, it isn't a super profession; it's merely a technical or professional way to making a living."[21]

John, however, overlooked the toll that acting was taking on his health. Following bouts of jaundice and the mumps, he ended up in a London hospital with ulcers. His Hartley Street physician attributed his discomfort to "swallowed air," common in patients with hyperacidity and hyperactivity, and specially common in high-strung persons: "Getting heated-up mentally will make you swallow air, and will also aggravate the hyperacidity and hypermotility. Your very nervous and mental make-up, which enable you to do the creative work that you do, impose certain penalties upon the vegetative nervous system. School yourself to be philosophical. Do not allow yourself to be bothered by matters which, as you will realise later, are of no real importance," this physician urged in a list of ten good health guidelines. More practical doctors on the scene hooked John up to a stomach pump. His mother, too, advised: "Knock out cocktails and champagne."[22]

John recovered, and soon headed for Paris and screen parts in his adopted country. Motion picture activity in France flourished. Called an era of "réalisme poétique" and led by such directors as René Clair, Jean Renoir, Abel Gance, and Marcel Pagnol, French cinema attracted a talented and dedicated array of actors, writers, and technicians. Internationally acclaimed works such as *Sous les toits de Paris*, *À nous la liberté*, *L'Atlantide*, *La Grande Illusion*, and *Le Paradis Perdu*, brought unprecedented attention to the small studios in and around Paris. And French performers became favorites of moviegoers around the world: Jean Gabin, Louis Jouvert, Arletty, Harry Bauer, Danielle Darrieux, Fernandel, Michel Simon, Annabella, and John's latest leading lady, the glamorous Vivienne Romance.

L'Esclave Blanche cast John as a visionary Turkish patriot who in 1910 tries to introduce the benefits of Western European countries into a pre-democratic Turkey. His young French wife, played by Romance, braves prejudice and strange social customs, including the slave-like demeanor of Turkish women. Lodge gains the ear of the Sultan in order to initiate some important reforms in his court. Lodge's enemies prevail, sending him a second wife whom he is forced to accept. Romance attempts to flee the country, is arrested, then released, and finally joins her husband in exile.

Directed by Marc Sorkin, the story wavered between two themes, romance and emancipation. The romance angle dominates, while the subplots lack suspense and imagination. The picture did not measure up to the genre of the highly original, often cynical, French films of the period. When *The Pascha's Wives* (its American title) opened with English subtitles in New York several years later, the *Times* called it "unaccented and monotonous . . . too sluggish even to come to a climax."[23] Yet in Paris it played for more than six weeks at the prestigious 5,200-seat Gaumont Palace.

War clouds and mobilization in late 1938 little affected the movie business on the Continent. But in England the business fell into a lull because of several studio reorganizations and amalgamations. Lodge prepared for a new film along the lines of *Bulldog Drummond*, but this project died for lack of financial backing. So, with temporary quarters at the Hotel Lincoln in Paris, John turned toward Rome and his second Italian film.

Believed to be the only major American actor of the 1930s ever to have made films in the Italian language, John relished another opportunity to appear before the cameras at Cinecittà. Despite the dismemberment of Czechoslovakia by Hitler and premonitory signs of more Axis power plays, he was reassured by the Munich Pact and Prime Minister Neville Chamberlain's affirmation of "peace for our time" that fall, and so moved on with his career as usual.

Batticuore (*Heartbeat*) provided him with a number of charming love scenes opposite Assia Noris. He plays an aristocratic Englishman-diplomat who encounters an attractive, school-trained Parisian pickpocket. She is coerced into practicing her trade at an embassy party. At this reception, John in white tie and tails is perfectly cast as he dances and romances Noris. Lodge, who rarely felt truly comfortable in love scenes, appears more self-assured in *Batticuore*. And, as an English lord speaking Italian in a French setting, John moves effortlessly through the fairy-tale story, which ends happily (a departure from most Lodge pictures) with a wedding of the co-stars.

Nearly sixty years later, Assia Noris vividly recalled her work with John in *Batticuore*: "The filming took place smoothly and without problems. The audio in Italian films was in 'presa diretta,' and there was no dubbing as in the practice nowadays. John had no problems with the language. The fact that he was interpreting the role of a foreign diplomat made the accent very realistic and plausible. The film was very well received by the public and had considerable success."[24]

Francesca predicted more such roles for John and an occasional picture for herself. "We are such gypsies and do so many things," she wrote to sister Gloria in Philadelphia. Earlier that year, Gloria Braggiotti had wed longtime family friend and artist, Emlen Etting. Francesca voiced her pleasure over her new brother-in-law and reminded Gloria that one person can only be part of a whole and "therefore never complete unless sharing. Old maids devote themselves to cats, etc., but are never happy as there is no return to what they give & they therefore bring down their lives to the level of cats."[25]

In February 1939, on a break from assignments, John and Francesca boarded a ship for a short visit to the United States; it was his first in three and a half years. He decided to take a look at acting opportunities in California and to see his family in Washington.

In two years, Senator Cabot Lodge had assumed an influential role in the Republican Party and on Capitol Hill. His aged grandmother, the once-indefatigable Sarah Frelinghuysen of the post-Civil War decades, was ill. She required day and night nurses, increasing her sizable household staff to ten employees. Mrs. Lodge regularly went back and forth between her home and her mother's, spending hours each day overseeing her care.

John spent hours at the Senate observing Cabot in sessions of the special committee on unemployment and relief. Francesca introduced nine-month-old Beatrice to the Lodges, including her older Lodge cousins, George and Henry. Francesca visited The White House, lunching with FDR's daughter-in-law Betsy Cushing Roosevelt, a Braggiotti family friend. During the Lodges' visit, John's grandmother died, and Bessie soon came into a share of the old Frelinghuysen holdings. After the large estate was settled in late 1940, she turned over a sizable portion to her three children. John received nearly $100,000 in stocks and bonds that he added to his growing portfolio at the Morgan Bank.

John's trip to Los Angeles generated some interest. Director John Stahl at Universal wondered whether Lodge could play opposite Irene Dunne. But before his Hollywood agent Harry Edington could arrange a test, the studio signed another actor. The business hadn't changed one iota on the West Coast, John thought. It soured him toward any expectations of starring roles in his own country. He mulled over his future in Europe and even considered returning to the practice of law. A friend from Cravath, Colin Ives, suggested going into business, perhaps starting his own: "It has always seemed to me that law is a little too pettifogging as far as your talent is concerned. Multitudes of people with much less ability than you have can be successful lawyers but only a few have such broad abilities and it would seem a shame to waste them solely on the law."[26]

There was not more time to pursue the matter; John was due back in Paris for an important picture, a French sequel to the widely acclaimed *Mayerling*, the ill-fated romantic saga between the Hapsburg crown prince and his mistress, touchingly played by Charles Boyer and Danielle Darrieux. By July, all four Lodges had settled into a rented country house in Montmorency, near Paris. John relished his role as the Hapsburg heir, Franz Ferdinand, in the story of the star-crossed marriage with Countess Sophie Chotek. (Some forty-five years later, diplomat Lodge became friends with Franz Ferdinand's grandnephew, the Prince of Lichtenstein, and joked about being his "old uncle.") "John's picture is promising to be a knockout," wrote Francesca to her sister Gloria Etting. "It is his 21st & perhaps his 'coming of age' in the movies. Every actor or actress needs about 20 pictures to learn on!" She noted their tenth wedding anniversary. "Time has passed so quickly . . . so happily that I can't believe it's true."[27]

Nationalistic fervor among European politicians and statesmen spilled over onto movie sets in the wake of the Munich crisis and mobilization. Francesca warned John to "never mention that one has worked in Italy or spent time in Germany"—both fascist regimes were now joined together against France and England—"And never wear any colors faintly reminiscent of Italy as that is interpreted as a deliberate affront." John took her words to heart as he traveled to the south of France for location shots on the episode that led to World War I.

The film, *From Mayerling to Sarajevo*, was director Max Ophuls' idea, recalled French actress and co-star Edwige Feuillère: "It was based on a story by Curt Zuckmayer, an Austrian refugee, and adapted for the screen by Curt Alexandre. I had just finished a picture with Ophuls called *San Lendemain*, and welcomed the next role as the Archduke's wife; it was a vivid recreation of a part of European history. Ophuls cast virtually every role from members of the prestigious Comédie Française. Lodge was the only non-French player in the entire picture. He spoke French easily, and played the Archduke with remarkable ease, and photographed strikingly well. But as an actor, he remained shy."[28]

Lodge became intrigued with the character of Franz Ferdinand. Here was a well-intentioned gentleman whose only wish—to live in peace with his wife and children—could become the pretext for a war. To prepare for the role, John contacted relatives and friends of the couple.

The production moved into the town of Romans sur Yserses, fifty miles south of Lyons, to recreate the state visit of the Hapsburgs to Sarajevo. A former French ambassador, hired to advise the producers on period customs and protocol, asked Ophuls, "Aren't you afraid to make this picture? Aren't you tempting the fates by such a vivid re-enactment?"[29] Tensions off-camera were indeed growing. By late August, the cameras rolled on the great tragedy of 1914. From day to day, men who were hired as extras for street crowd scenes kept disappearing. Ophuls realized that they were being called to duty in the French army.

Back at Montmorency, Francesca began to plan a drive in the Lancia to Romans to bring John back at the end of that week's shooting. As she packed, concern grew over a possible confrontation between Germany and France. One night she watched French armed troops march by. The situation seemed very bad, especially when local police came by crying "lumière," demanding all light be extinguished to reduce enemy bombing targets. Francesca filled the Lancia's gas tank and several extra containers. She turned on the radio for news, hearing word that French children would be evacuated from Paris. She decided to cancel her visit to John.

Meanwhile, on location, Ophuls lined up cameras for the crucial scene depicting the assassination of the Hapsburgs. Midway through the shooting, news spread like wildfire of the imminent invasion of Poland by Hitler. Cast and crew, already decimated by military call-ups of the past week, rushed off for the latest word on the crisis. Ophuls soon heard of the full mobilization of France. Germany had already demanded that France and Britain each end its military alliance with Poland. Ophuls immediately broke off filming and sent everyone home. Still in makeup and costume, John commandeered an auto and rushed north to join his family.

Francesca had paused during the gathering tidings of war to pen a letter to Gloria on August 27: "We are on the eve of the world's greatest catastrophe & I write you from our little house outside of Paris from where we might have to flee within a few hour's notice. By tomorrow we shall know if we can sail & probably if there will be war! There is a stampede home. John has still two more weeks' work on his picture. All is such a mess, but our troubles do not compare, and disappear in thin mist when I see the tragedies that surround us. Two million men are under arms here today! The good-byes, etc. are heart-breaking. . . . We shall try to stick it out to the last."[30]

The U.S. Embassy shortly ordered all Americans to leave France. Then, on September 1, German troops stormed across the Polish border, triggering a declaration by France and England. The Lodges piled their belongings into their car and set out for Le Havre, hoping to board a ship to America. Nine-year-old Lily remembered the urgency of the task, the loading of suitcases, and the bewildered look of people carrying their possessions and leading their children and animals to safety. At Le Havre the Lodges encountered thousands of Americans vying for space on the few remaining ships bound for the United States. While waiting for word of a departure, John found a room in a private dwelling near the port. Lacking beds, it was little more than a shelter from the predicted German bombing raid. "It was nightmarish," Francesca remembered. "We faced frequent air-raid alerts and had to evacuate to high ground outside of Le Havre."

On September 11, 1939, the day the German army moved into Warsaw, the Lodges boarded the SS *Washington*, a passenger liner with accommodations for 1,000 passengers. The ship's captain agreed to carry an additional 700 people. They poured onto the liner to escape the expected enemy attack. In the mob stood novelist Thomas Mann, violinist Fritz Kreisler, impresario Sol Hurok, actor Robert Montgomery, and tennis stars Bill Tilden and Don Budge. Ambassador Joseph Kennedy pulled strings to detour the ship to Southampton, where his wife Rose and three of their children—Eunice, Kathleen, and Bobby—boarded the overloaded vessel.

John secured space in a cabin for his family, but he bunked in the ship's gym with New York drama critic Richard Watts. Hundreds were herded into other public rooms and assigned a cot. Even the post office became sleeping quarters, and in the empty swimming pool, Bob Montgomery joined eighteen other refugees. To save water, bathing, now a privilege, was carried out at pre-set times.[31] Francesca became seasick, and to protect Beatrice from getting lost in the crowded passageways, she placed a collar around her and tethered her to a deck chair. Inquisitive Lily ventured all over the SS *Washington*; at set times, she met her parents at a clock in a nearby lounge.

After six and a half days at sea, the ship steamed into New York Harbor. Even the Lancia awaited them on the dock after they passed through customs. Exactly twenty-five years earlier, John and his mother, brother, sister, and Lodge grandparents, had hurriedly driven to the French coast to escape a German invasion. And now in the summer of 1939, John Lodge the actor had reenacted the historic moment that triggered the First World War. Suddenly propelled through time from 1914 to the end of another era, he looked beyond the steamship pier to glimpse the Statue of Liberty. It was time, he decided, for more important tasks than acting out the past if he were to help safeguard and defend his precious homeland.

CHAPTER 9

Watch on the Rhine

L odge was thankful to be out of harm's way. But after seven years in other parts of the world, he felt New York for him had lost its initial allure and one-time fascination. Transcending local encompassments, he publicly admitted he liked English clothes, French food, Italian autos, and Southern California climate. Yet, he realized, Manhattan offered the best situation to pursue opportunities to re-establish his American acting career and perhaps build a base even for new endeavors. Within weeks of his arrival, a radio station asked him to broadcast his own personal view of the world predicament. Over WQXR, in a statesman-like talk called "American Solidarity in Crisis," he described himself as a refugee within his own country.

All owed a debt of gratitude to America, he declared, "whether longtime citizens, returning natives or recent immigrants. It is time to sound a clarion call for solidarity in this country. Our greatest protection against attacks on our democratic way of life lies in the common sense, integrity and solidarity of our people." Without a "national character," he explained, "we cannot hope to defend ourselves against the onslaughts which propaganda of all kinds will make on our emotions, our prejudices and our sympathies. It has been said that the questions of war and peace for the United States depend on our strength." "Our military strength," he continued, "we leave in the hands of our government and they delegate its development to that body of army, navy and aviation experts who are most competent to deal with it. Our economic strength involves—to be sure—the united efforts of every member of our vast community. It, too, however, in its directives must be placed in the hands of specialists. But our moral strength is the business of every man, woman and child in this country who calls himself an American citizen."[1]

His acting career seemed on hold as he was drawn toward taking an active and commanding part in his country's defense. His well-stated commitment to a strong and united America needed to be put into action. Brother Cabot had long been in the Army Reserves as a cavalry officer, and through his senatorial rank was known to many top Army commanders. But John preferred the Navy. He immediately applied for a job in U.S. Naval Intelligence, backing his request with a handful of recommendations from high-level friends, including former Under Secretary of State William R. Castle (and father-in-law of his one-time stockbroker Alan Winslow). The Navy reviewed his request for an appointment with favor, but he failed the color perception test because of an inability to distinguish between blue and green hues. However, this shortcoming was waived. That winter Lodge was commissioned a lieutenant in the Naval Reserve and assigned as an inactive volunteer for Special Services, namely intelligence duties.

Meanwhile, from France came an urgent plea. The producers of the incomplete *Sarajevo* needed him back in France to shoot several key scenes. Without them, the picture could not be released. Lodge suggested that the work be finished in the United States with co-star Edwige Feuillère. He explained that the State Department had been very stringent in granting U.S. citizens permission for European travel. "For the smaller parts, many French-speaking actors could be obtained in New York," he added.[2] As it turned out, Lodge received an okay from Washington to return to Paris. On December 28, 1939, he sailed on the *Conte di Savoia* through submarine-infested waters for France and some ten days of hurried filming. "I was struck by the outward calm and lack of change in the French capital," he wrote. "Indeed, the war seemed on 'hold' as I moved about Paris. Yes, there were uniforms everywhere, but the average man in the street appeared to have lost the nervousness that was so apparent throughout the spring and summer of 1939. The brusqueness, which had unpleasantly characterized the manners of government officials, had given way to a gentle politeness and a sympathetic exchange of conversation. Among the military, boredom prevailed as the so-called 'phony' war had not led to action on the Western front. Nightclubs, theatres and movies attracted the usual crowds. Only an eleven o'clock curfew and a partial blackout of street lights stood in contrast to pre-war Parisian nightlife."[3]

At the film studio, there were challenges of a different nature. Lack of heat, inadequate interior lighting, and fewer technicians tested the mettle of everyone. Moreover, the unit's expert cameraman, an anti-Nazi German seeking French citizenship, had been arrested in Germany and sent to a concentration camp. Money to finish the picture was scarce, but spirits were high and the job got done.[4] In mid-January, Lodge booked passage back to New York.

From Mayerling to Sarajevo opened in Paris on May 1, 1940. In spite of a rather abrupt ending which utilized stock newsreel shots to tie the tale together, filmgoers reacted favorably, and the film drew audiences. Then, in early June, Nazi planes filled the skies over Paris. German troops soon marched into the city, beginning a four-year occupation. Ophuls' picture clearly sympathized with the old Hapsburg regime and vividly depicted the outbreak of the First World War. The Axis invaders immediately closed the movie theater and seized the film. It was banned throughout France, and every available print was burned.

Producer Eugene Tuscherer managed to smuggle out a copy from the projection booth of a Brussels theater and deliver it to New York by plane from Lisbon. Tuscherer, a Czech who upon the Nazi invasion had fled to southern France, sought to recruit Lodge as a partner in a reworked *Sarajevo*. Would he join with him to create an English version of the picture in Hollywood? "Feuillère could be brought to America and coached to improve her English," he stated. "The previously shot scenes depicting Vienna and Sarajevo could be used in the American version." But as the war enveloped more of Europe and interest dimmed in a reconstructed production of the long-ago story of Franz Ferdinand, the plan fell apart. Having fled to Cannes, Tuscherer seemed to have used the remake idea as a ploy to secure an American visa through Lodge's contacts.[5]

In October 1940, nearly six months after its European opening, Lodge's latest film (with English subtitles) had its American premiere in New York. A gala benefit organized by Francesca and several dozen social leaders, it raised funds for a mobile canteen and an ambulance for Red Cross relief work in London. Audiences compared the picture with the haunting, poetic *Mayerling* of 1937, and it came up short. The Ophuls sequel, in contrast, told the piteous account of two hapless lovers headed to a portentous end beyond their control. The picture left viewers with no sense of fulfillment or exaltation.

"Considering the fact that this picture was made in France during the tense months of last winter," noted *New York Times* critic Bosley Crowther, "it has been done with surprising effectiveness. True, it hit tedious stretches, there is too much emphasis upon court details and the direction of Max Ophuls is occasionally listless or ponderous. But Edwige Feuillère creates an altogether lovely and sensitive Countess Sophia. John Lodge plays Francis Ferdinand with a slightly monotonous but compelling masculinity and other members of the cast are uniformly good."[6]

The destiny of Lodge's picture was as ill-fated as the Hapsburg story itself. The film ran briefly in New York and Canada; few theatres booked the historical saga now overshadowed by the new wave of European upheavals. The inauspicious outcome lowered Lodge's interest in further screen projects. By the spring of 1940, he had already turned to the stage and accepted the post of president of the New York Theater Guild. There were plans to revive *Peter Ibbetson* with both Lodges and Douglass Montgomery in the title role. But director Constance Collier failed to raise the needed funds of some $20,000.

While John waited for the call to active duty, he and Francesca were re-teamed as players in summer stock productions. A light Viennese comedy called *Caprice* opened at the Bass Rocks Theater in Gloucester, Massachusetts. John gave a creditable performance as a suave, handsome bachelor; Francesca was vivacious and charming as his love interest in roles originally played on Broadway by the Lunts. For a week's run, Lodge received $50 plus five percent of the box-office gross. Later that month, John alone appeared with the South Shore Players at Cohasset in Philip Barry's *Tomorrow and Tomorrow* with Violet Hemming and Staats Cotsworth.

In early August, the Lodges traveled to the Ogunquit Playhouse on the Maine coast for an ambitious staging of Jean Giraudoux's comedy *Amphitryon 38*. The play, adapted into English by S. N. Behrman, dealt with the Greek god Jupiter and his infatuation for a beautiful woman on earth. Michael Strange, a former wife of John Barrymore, poet, and would-be actress, played the lead, Alkmena, with a singularly flat and matter-of-fact approach. Francesca in a supporting role did justice to the lovelorn Leda. The best of the cast, noted the Boston papers, was John. "Mr. Lodge was perfectly suited for the role of the tall, handsome head of the gods, Jupiter, and he played it with fitting gusto, virility and zest," concluded the *Boston Globe* critic.[7]

Anxious to spend weekends out of New York, the Lodges scouted various country locales. With two Braggiotti brothers happily settled in Connecticut, John and Francesca looked for a place in Fairfield County. Westport, a commuters' town on Long Island Sound, attracted them. Its well-established community of artists and performers and its summer theater made it an apt choice. In May 1940, they rented a cottage on the grounds of the Longshore Country Club, where they made frequent use of its tennis courts and beach. The following year, they rented a house in nearby Southport, a large dwelling on prestigious Sasco Hill overlooking a small golf course and a picturesque harbor. During the week, they continued to live in a New York apartment on East 96th Street.

New York producers had looked Lodge over during his summer stock assignments. They liked what they saw. In the fall of 1940, John was headed for Broadway. On September 25, he signed a contract at $300 per week with the Shubert brothers as "the roving lover" and opera talent scout in a musical adaptation of the 1930 comedy *Tonight or Never*.[8] Revamped with operetta-like songs by prolific Viennese composer Robert

Stolz, sumptuously staged, and retitled *Night of Love*, the production gave Lodge an opportunity to sing. In the company of former Metropolitan Opera soprano Helen Gleason as the love-seeking prima donna, and joined by singers with trained voices, Marguerite Namara and Martha Errolle, Lodge held his own. Yet at times his baritone voice was not always equal to the demands made upon it by Stolz and his lyricist Rowland Leigh.

The show opened at the Shubert Theater in New Haven, then continued on a pre-Broadway tour to Washington, Philadelphia, Chicago, and other cities. Between out-of-town engagements, John in a letter acknowledged Cabot's words of praise for his performance in *Sarajevo*, then added a few words about *Night of Love*. "I am in New York for a few days, preparatory to returning to Montreal where the show opens next Monday to run for a week. We then play Toronto for one week, and open in New York on January 6th. I expect the show and everyone in it to be crucified by the New York critics. However, I intend at the moment to remain with the show."[9]

As John predicted, the press panned the proceedings, calling the vehicle plodding and lackluster. It offered a number of easily forgettable songs—"Tonight or Never," "Without You" and "I'm Thinking of You." Yet Lodge proved satisfactory as the well-tailored, ingratiating "kept young man with a polish not entirely confined to his shoes." In fact, his feet stopped the show. A clever but brief tap dance by Lodge brought down the house. Overall, John and his fellow players suffered through a distinct lack of dramatic invention and a first act which contained a tiresome load of hoary old jokes. *Night of Love* fizzled out after three nights on Broadway.[10]

During much of 1940, playwright Lillian Hellman toiled over a new script about the overriding fascist threat to world peace. Her previous play, *The Little Foxes*, had focused on a family of villains and victims; her latest drama was a statement of concern of the Nazi peril, centering on a noble character who acts to oppose and destroy evil. The people of *Watch on the Rhine*, with the exception of a conniving reprobate, were decent and admirable, in contrast to those of *The Little Foxes* who were full of hate and greed. Hellman's *Watch on the Rhine* was a timely and powerful message to an America on the brink of war. As soon as producer Herman Shumlin read the script early in 1941, he immediately made plans to bring it to Broadway.

With the failure of the Shubert production, Lodge again was at liberty. Shumlin, who also decided to direct Hellman's play, auditioned John for the supporting role as David Farrelly, the son of a wealthy and cosmopolitan widow living in a large country house near Washington. The story takes place in the spring of 1940 in the Farrelly drawing room and centers upon the return of a daughter and her family after many years in

Europe, where she and her husband had been active in the anti-Nazi underground. Lodge plays a thrity-nine-year old lawyer whose placid existence is jolted into reality as events unfold among his mother's house guests, who include a penniless, blackmailing Rumanian count and his young American wife. John's youth in a similar Washington setting and his initial career as an attorney were a true-to-life frame of reference. The role seemed tailor-made. A natural extension of his past existence, he took on the character of David with an untheatrical demeanor.

Lodge was surrounded by a superb cast in this propitious drama. Lucille Watson played his mother, and Mady Christians, his sister. In the male lead, Paul Lukas was a brilliant choice as the anti-fascist German. George Coulouris handled the opportunist and repulsive count with skill. As the Farrelly grandchildren, Eric Roberts, Anne Blyth, and Peter Fernández were very effective. A carefully selected group of talented players, they acted with exceptional teamwork and assurance.

On April 1, opening night telegrams piled up on John's dressing room table at the Martin Beck Theater. His *Scarlet Empress* cohort Sam Jaffe wrote: "Glad to see you came out from behind those gargoyles and into legit." From Mario Braggiotti: "We know your success will be no April Fool. Love & Luck & Merde." Mary Sargent penned an apt message: "May your watch never run down."

The press reviews were exceptionally good the next day. "The enjoyment you take in these people and the sympathy you have for their ordeal depend largely upon the high quality of the acting," wrote Brooks Atkinson of the *New York Times*. "It is a play of pith and moment, and the theater may be proud of it." Of Lodge he noted: "In his outbursts of anger, John Lodge is merely strident as a brother, and also alarmingly Bostonian for an old Washington family, but when he is under control he acts with decision."[11] Most reviewers singled out Lodge as admirably cast and personable and effective as the son who rises from the ever present shadow of his long deceased father to meet dire emergency on his own initiative.

Watch on the Rhine ran on Broadway for 378 performances. In later years, it came to be regarded as one of Lillian Hellman's most overrated dramas. "Out of the context of the period," Hellman biographer William Wright writes, "it seemed breathlessly jingoistic and too elementary in its good guys-bad guys delineations. If it now appears a heavy-handed morality play, it was a lucid dramatization of the heavy-handed moral dilemma facing America at that time: Was a confrontation with fascism inevitable and at what point?"[12] The point seemed close. By July 1941, the German blitzkrieg had carried Axis occupation to France, Belgium, Norway, Denmark, Yugoslavia and Greece. And Russia was the next target.

Less than a month after it opened, the New York Drama Critics Circle awarded *Watch on the Rhine* top honors as the best American play of the season. At the Circle's annual dinner at the Algonquin Hotel, Lodge and the cast appeared in a scene which was also broadcast over NBC. With his run-of-the-show contract, John was assured of a long engagement and steady employment well into the next season.

Lodge's on-stage dilemma spilled into reality during the rehearsals and out-of-town run of the Hellman play. Friends of Max Ophuls contacted John for help in getting the German-born Jew a visa and a job in America. Ophuls, his wife, and their thirteen-year-old son Marcel had fled to Aix-en-Provence in unoccupied France. Max's uncle wrote John from Los Angeles to ask whether he would use his connections in Washington to try to expedite the case. John contacted Maxwell Rabb, an aide of Cabot. "Mr. Ophuls is in real danger due to the anti-Hitler propaganda he broadcast in Paris previous to the German invasion," Lodge explained. He urged Rabb, who in the 1980s would serve in the Reagan Administration as Ambassador to Italy, to alert the State Department and prepare the necessary paperwork to grant visas for the Ophuls family. That summer they escaped from a beleaguered Europe. In New York, a grateful Ophuls came backstage to thank John for his efforts in saving him from certain death at the hands of the Nazis. Max Ophuls journeyed on to Hollywood, where he reestablished his career as a leading director.[13]

John's contract for *Watch on the Rhine* brought him a salary of $12,000 for 1941, more money than he had earned as an actor since 1938. Francesca contributed to their income that year by co-starring with former silent screen star Ramón Navarro in a summer stock production of *Tovarich* at the Bass Rocks Theater. With a solid foothold in the theater, the Lodges looked around to buy a home in the suburbs for weekends and the summer. After renting for two years in Westport and Southport, they found all they desired in country living in a secluded house on Westport's Easton Road. Bounded on three sides by the Aspetuck River, the property included two waterfalls, a small island, and extensive gardens. The house itself consisted of four bedrooms, a solarium, two recreation rooms, as well as living and dining rooms and a kitchen. Outside there was plenty of space for kennels and stables. Early in 1942, they purchased this recently built clapboard dwelling and its nine and one-half acres for $36,000. Plans were made to move that summer and to add a caretaker's cottage and tool house.

In a letter to his mother, John described the property and the thought of owning a house for the very first time: "It is very practical & fresh & new & clean & sweet. It's a wonderful feeling to own my own bit of land and my own roof. I am not getting a mortgage but am paying for it all outright. . . . I can't wait to show you my place when we are all cozily settled there, baby and all." John planned to move in at the end of June as the Lodges, indeed, were expecting their third child in mid-June.[14]

In the midst of their house-hunting that winter, Japanese planes attacked U.S. forces at Pearl Harbor, propelling America into the war that Europe had been fighting for two years. On December 11, Congress voted to declare war on Japan's Axis partners, Italy and Germany, "to insure a world victory of the forces of justice and righteousness over the forces of savagery and barbarism." John knew it was only a matter of time before he would be summoned to active duty in the Navy. He added a rider to his contract with producer Shumlin that he was subject to call at any time without notice.

Although the country was now at war, the Roosevelt Administration continued the tradition of selecting an outstanding play of each season and presenting it before the President as a benefit for the research fund to cure infantile paralysis. *Watch on the Rhine* was chosen for 1942, and on January 25 the entire production journeyed to the capital for a command performance at the National Theater. Few in the audience actually expected President Roosevelt to leave the White House during that turbulent time. Since the war began in December, he had only left the Executive Mansion to address Congress and attend church. To the surprise and delight of those participating in this special Presidential birthday event, Roosevelt entered a theater box with his secretary Grace Tully, Federal Security Administrator Paul McNutt, Assistant Federal Housing Administrator Raymond Cahill, and the wives of Archibald MacLeish and Henry Morgenthau. The unexpected sight of the wartime leader added drama to the on-stage indictment by Hellman of Nazi atrocities. Roosevelt's presence, it was noted, brought forth the largest force of protective agents ever mustered for a presidential appearance.[15]

After the performance, Roosevelt acted as host at a supper party at the White House for the entire company of *Watch on the Rhine*. A large excavation on the front lawn surprised many guests who, when they asked, were told by security guards that it was the beginning of a tunnel for a bomb shelter. "The White House," recalled actress Lucille Watson, "seemed to be in darkness because of the heavy blackout curtains at all the windows. Inside, there were machine guns in the corridors. All this *did* affect the gaiety of the occasion but did not dim the brilliance of the people who sat at the President's table at supper. . . . He was at his most charming, like a father entertaining his children, with a flow of amusing and interesting anecdotes."[16]

Before the meal, each member of the cast was presented to FDR. When Lodge was introduced, Roosevelt greeted him warmly: "Well, hello, John. I remember you. Do you remember me?" This was one of the very few occasions in his life when Lodge was completely tongue-tied.

Watch on the Rhine ended its run on February 21, after forty-seven weeks on Broadway. It immediately went on tour as far west as Chicago. Lodge continued with the show. When the play reached Boston in mid-March, he accepted an invitation to speak at a businessmen's luncheon sponsored by the Advertising Club of Boston and the *Boston Post*. He shared the podium with Massachusetts Governor Leverett Saltonstall and U.S. Senator David I. Walsh. Before a gathering of 1,200 Bostonians, Lodge expressed the conviction that the theater in wartime must be kept alive: "It has a very important function for stimulation and relaxation."[17]

Before the play left Broadway, Lillian Hellman and Shumlin sold the movie rights to Warner Brothers for $150,000, a considerable sum at the time. The studio's leading actress, Bette Davis, sought the part of the Farrelly daughter, and won this secondary role in the screen adaptation by Dashiell Hammett. Recreating their original stage roles were Paul Lukas, Lucille Watson, George Coulouris, and Eric Roberts. Lodge, too, seemed headed to join them at Warner Bros.[18]

For months a pregnant Francesca had been tired and nervous, and somewhat anemic. John counted the weeks until he could leave the play's long tour. After nearly 450 performances on Broadway and on the road, he had grown weary of *Watch on the Rhine*. Then, while he was in Chicago, thirty-nine-year old Francesca on May 19 gave birth at Harkness Pavillion in New York to a daughter. It was readily apparent that Edith Frances Lodge was retarded. It was days before John, heartsick and exhausted, could leave the show and go to New York and Francesca's bedside. Baby Edith was soon brought to Villa Lodge in Westport, where she required special care. Only family and closest friends were aware of their tragedy. The baby would become the "unknown daughter" of the Lodges. John apparently wanted to raise the child at home, adding special caregivers, but the shortage of domestic help in wartime soon ruled this out. Both Francesca and John decided against placing Edith in an institution, a prevalent practice of the time. Before long, they found a nearby foster home for the child. The greatest sadness of their marriage, the matter became a subject never referred to by the Lodges.

After fifteen unbroken months on stage, John firmed up his plans for wartime service. At age thirty-eight, with four dependents, he clearly could have avoided military duty. Moreover, the Navy now had second thoughts about giving the go-ahead to an officer with color perception deficiencies and an occasional "nervous stomach." But he dismissed the idea of not serving in uniform. Finally, after many appeals, he was reexamined. His physical defects were waived, and on August 13, he was assigned to active duty.

In view of his linguistic abilities, he thought a liaison assignment with the French Navy or the British Navy overseas would best utilize his skills.

That summer, as the war entered its ninth month, Lt. John Lodge, having played many film roles in the uniform of a military officer, reported for duty in the Special Events Section of the Third Naval District Public Relations Office. Lodge's foreign language skills were given short shrift by the Navy: it was Lodge the actor, Lodge the public speaker, that they quickly capitalized on.

CHAPTER 10

A Military Bearing

Lodge's superior officer, Lt. Thomas W. Dewart, welcomed him to the Naval District headquarters at 90 Church Street. Dewart had joined the Navy's public relations unit in 1941, leaving a high-level job at the *New York Sun*, a newspaper managed by his family. Lodge was the newest member in an office that in little more than six months had grown from a handful of naval personnel to over thirty-five officers. By the time John arrived, demands for more extensive press, radio, and photographic coverage of the role of the Navy increased daily.

Taking one look at Lodge's background, Dewart and the District Public Information Officer, Lt. Comdr. Edmund S. DeLong, immediately assigned him to special events. His major duties revolved around telling the American people about the Navy's wartime role—in essence, public appearances at fund-raising rallies, war bond drives, and defense plant ceremonies. These speech-making chores struck John as a natural extension of his stage and movie assignments, only now he was preparing most of the text and not repeating the words of a scriptwriter. Besides, he had an opportunity to weave his own views and philosophy into the overall context of these official morale-building messages.

Lodge and the tenacious Tom Dewart hit it off immediately. They worked closely together on a new program to recognize industrial plants for exceptional production achievements, known as the "E" Awards. In the course of duty, hardly a day passed without a prank or a session of zesty insults between the two. To some observers, they acted like immature schoolboys. But for John, the office hijinks provided a playful release from the constraints of military procedure and a harmless outlet for his innate sense of humor and biting wit. Dewart later remembered with nostalgic glee the office pranks, especially the time Lodge shoved him into an upright clothes locker and shut it tight.

"Wait a minute, Lodge. I'm your CO," he recalled saying to John from inside the locker. "You're going to get a court martial if you're not careful."

Junior officers and civilian employees paused in their work to observe the latest Lodge-Dewart shenanigans.

"You better let me out of here," Dewart demanded.

"Boss, you've got to say it nicer than that."

"Please, Lodge, let me out."

"You've got to do better," John insisted.

Back and forth it went, until Dewart said, "Dear John, will you please open the locker door?" At those words, Lodge opened it, and the two buddies went off to lunch at a nearby restaurant of John's choice.[1]

At award ceremonies and rallies, Lodge in his dark blue uniform impressed all who saw and heard him. His military bearing came easily. Perhaps some of it rubbed off from three years in the Massachusetts National Guard while a Harvard undergraduate. Unquestionably, his movie roles as uniformed officers and noblemen gave him extra poise and confidence. He went over big with defense plant workers when he called them "soldiers of production," praising their determination to provide the fighting men with the tools they needed for victory. He spoke forcefully, with great sincerity and enthusiasm. Many war industry leaders commented on the "punch" he gave those gatherings, inspiring workers to boost production of materials for the Navy. The president of the Kollmorgen Optical Corporation in Brooklyn, for one, singled out Lodge for praise after an "E" award plant presentation: "He acted as master of ceremonies in a manner which completely won the hearts of his audience and helped very materially in imparting to the occasion its true meaning of practical patriotism."[2]

By the end of 1942, he was speaking on several set topics, "The Challenge on the Home Front" and "Essential Aspects of Total War," to resounding acclaim before Rotary Club luncheons, high school assemblies, defense plant rallies, American Legion meetings, and Red Cross fund drives. And he often accompanied Naval war heroes to communities where they related combat experiences before industrial, civic, and fraternal groups. On one such trip in upstate New York, Lodge traveled with two young veterans back from Guadalcanal and Malta. They spoke to over 5,000 aluminum workers on assembly lines, in pot rooms, and in mills—even from a truck platform out on a construction job.

A quick study, Lodge had an immediate grasp of an audience and could say in a few words and with tact and grace just what it took to have his listeners with him. "This war is not the exclusive property of the Armed Forces," he said at a labor-recruiting drive. "It is a total war. It is our war. . . . The victory, when it is won, will be your victory."[3]

John's acting credits and family ties were sometimes highlighted in regional newspapers; a former movie star in a small town generated extra coverage, as did a brother of a leading U.S. Senator. During the winter of 1942-43, John traveled extensively throughout New York, Connecticut, and New Jersey, participating in a half-dozen ceremonies and rallies nearly every week. Many events were coordinated by his Harvard classmate and now a Naval lieutenant, Richard Aldrich, also assigned to the same office.

Now and then, his audience was bigger than a few thousand plant workers. On the coast-to-coast radio series *Stage Door Canteen*, produced by the American Theatre Wing in New York, he congratulated the *Canteen* for their work in entertaining large numbers of enlisted men on leave who visited the recreational center every day. "You may be sure that the Navy extends to Stage Door Canteen—in spirit—its coveted "E" for Excellence," he said to master of ceremonies Bert Lytell on the CBS broadcast.

Hearing firsthand the exploits of battle-tested heroes, he wanted to be near the fighting front. So early in 1943, Lodge applied for overseas duty. His request was granted that spring, and in April he said good-bye to Francesca and their children. In New York, he boarded an LST as a military passenger in a convoy of fifty-four ships. On the third day out, his vessel experienced engine problems. Efforts to repair it at sea failed. The craft left the convoy and with auxiliary power limped back to port at a speed of some five knots, unprotected by destroyers and loaded with 800 tons of TNT and lethal gas. Later, his political opponents investigated the incident in an attempt to twist it into an example of Washington "pull" that brought "combat-shy" Lodge back home. They found no grist for their mill.

Back in New York, he transferred to another ship, and in early May boarded the destroyer USS *Doyle* as a junior officer of the deck. Operations and intelligence officer Robert Morris recalled Lodge's agitation one night when a nearby merchant marine ship against orders cruised with its lights ablaze. "He felt strongly about rules and regulations," said Morris.[4]

In June, Lodge landed in Algiers and joined the staff of Vice Admiral H. Kent Hewitt, who had been ordered to establish and command the U.S. Eighth Fleet in the Mediterranean. Earlier, in November 1942, Hewitt had led amphibious forces for Operation TORCH and successfully conducted U.S. landings in Morocco, but at a cost. The U.S. forces had sunk twenty-eight French ships and killed over 1800 officers and men of the French Navy in their futile stand against the Allies. And the French remained bitterly divided between the Axis-backed Vichy government of Marshall Pétain and the Free French led by General Charles de Gaulle.[5] Hewitt was now planning the American invasion of Sicily. Meanwhile, he had to deal with the Free French Navy, at their headquarters in North Africa. The

Admiral sought a French-speaking officer to act as ongoing liaison with the French high command. Although he would have preferred a commander or a captain to fill the post, he overlooked Lodge's lower rank, sized up his linguistic skills, and gave him the nod. John chiefly assisted with the rearmament and supply of the small Free French Navy, which had completely broken away from the Vichy government in France.

Not long after his arrival in North Africa, John wrote a long letter to his cousin Matilda Frelinghuysen in New Jersey. He expressed the belief that America was too optimistic over the progress of the Allies. Such optimism did not exist in Algiers, he noted: "The job looks long & hard & costly & the fighting front apparently looks far better from home than the home front does from here. We can however hope, fervently, that the optimism at home will prove to have been justified."[6]

Lodge told of a pleasant meeting with the brilliant and prolific French writer André Gide. They talked of Paris, the war, de Gaulle, even Edith Wharton. To Lodge, Gide seemed part of France's past: "I hesitate to think what the future of France may be. Inadequate diet over a period of years, millions of prisoners, destruction of their cities & the general sapping of their morale will, I'm afraid, preclude the possibility of any sudden rehabilitation. France is, when all is said & done, 'la grande victime.' "[7]

Cousin Matilda's letters were eagerly welcomed that summer. As yet, mail from Francesca had not reached John. He worried about problems at home, recalling Cabot's remark to them on his departure, "Never give a man overseas bad news." It was later discovered that an incorrect post office code number had shunted her letters to another overseas location.

The long-awaited invasion of Sicily by American and British forces (Operation HUSKY) brought Lodge closer to the combat zone. An extra duty involved press censorship of the invasion, an assignment which came about when he voiced the opinion that the Navy lacked the public recognition other branches had been receiving. Amphibious landings on Sicily on July 10, 1943 proved the Allies had the capabilities to strike the enemy on his own soil. In total darkness and heavy surf, General Patton's Seventh Army moved from landing craft onto the shore. The Italian defenders were completely caught off guard by the assault and never recovered. Thousands surrendered, and the U.S. casualties were a great deal fewer than anticipated. The entire conquest of the island took only thirty-eight days. The operation succeeded in opening up Mediterranean Sea routes and advancing Allied bomber bases closer toward central Germany.

Meanwhile, as liaison officer, Lodge came face to face with strong feelings of resentment by the French Navy toward its American partner. Even by the summer of 1943, the French did not believe that America and Britain could defeat Germany. They regarded a Europe controlled by the

Fascists with considerably more favor than a Europe controlled by the Communists. Although the French Navy very much desired the liberation of France, they generally regarded Americans and British allies with suspicion and distrust. That outlook affected Lodge personally. At one point, French intelligence officers viewed him as some kind of spy in the employ of Germany. His spoken French was just too perfect for any real American. A report supposedly was even prepared to discredit him. He quickly squelched any such suspicions, chiefly because of a special diplomatic assignment.

His linguistic skill and indubitable tact landed him a very unusual task for a mere lieutenant. Admiral Hewitt ordered him to Casablanca to meet Vice Admiral Ronarch'h, commander of the French Navy. Wary of American motives in the Mediterranean, the French admiral sought to safeguard his country's future. Nicknamed "le robuste," he turned out not to be the big bad wolf described to Lodge by others. "He is a square-headed Breton, large of frame and energetic of manner," John later wrote of the naval leader. "He is unquestionably a man of unimpeachable integrity and thoroughly upright character. He is possessed of a most competent and contagious sense of humor and is a wholly delightful companion."[8]

Lodge broke the ice. The admiral spoke openly, almost without discretion, of his views on French political trends and on his attitude toward America and Britain. "Now don't you dare tell me that America has come here to liberate France," Ronarch'h finally exclaimed, waving an admonitory finger in front of Lodge. "You have come here in your own interests."

"We Americans," Lodge answered, "love America as much as you French love France. We have the best interests of America at heart and we hope very much we are not fighting a war which might be counter to our own interests. If it was *not* counter to our own interests to land in North Africa, Sir, it must, therefore, be *in* our interests. It is *our* interest to liberate France, but it is also in the interests of France."

"We Americans love France," Lodge pointed out. "It is our hope that you will learn to love America and Americans. Our interests are really identical. We must not allow our traditional, sentimental and eminently fruitful friendship to be vitiated by any such spurious suggestions that they are not. We have everything to gain by close collaboration and friendship."[9]

The two-day mission, the first test of his diplomatic skills, may have persuaded the French naval leaders in Africa to cooperate more closely and openly with its allies. Soon Americans were playing a preponderant part in supplying and equipping the existing French fleet. U.S. communications equipment, radar, clothing, fuel oil, ammunition, and other supplies passed to their ships. In addition, U.S. naval personnel trained the French, truly becoming cooperative partners in the war against Germany and Italy.

Lodge assumed another VIP mission in North Africa that summer. Admiral Hewitt assigned him to a group of U.S. Senators on a world-circling tour of war installations. "We have come from America to get a picture of the war in the various theatres," said Senators Richard Russell, James Mead, Ralph Brewster, Albert Chandler and Henry Cabot Lodge in a joint statement. "We shall take this picture back to the American people who have a consuming interest in the progress of the war—and in the problems of the peace."[10]

Cabot Lodge had been elected to a second term in November 1942. Although to his friends he had expressed a preference to serve with his old Army unit, he stood for re-election. As a member of the Military Affairs Committee, as well as a reserve officer, he was told by colleagues he could be of tremendous value to the Senate. He soon joined the Congressional fact-finding group on a 41,000 mile trip to inspect far-flung war areas. The first stop, England, led to meetings with Churchill, Lord Mountbatten, and King George VI, as well as to scores of conversations with GIs at military posts. In Morocco, Cabot expressed surprise to find John there as an aide for his visit. But the admirals recognized the value of familial ties to high-ranking legislators, especially those on military affairs committees.

Entertainers from pre-war days sometimes crossed John's path in the most unusual circumstances. In Marrakesh, John and fellow officer Henry A. Dudley scouted extra billets for Allied officers. One day they pulled up to the entrance of one of the luxurious palaces of the Sultan's family. John knocked on the door. It opened, and to his surprise, there stood the glamorous Josephine Baker of the Folies Bergère. Delighted to see an old acquaintance from Paris and a fellow American, she threw her arms around John and welcomed him and Dudley into the sumptuous dwelling. Baker, a house guest recuperating from a respiratory illness and a rigorous tour of camps from Morocco to Egypt, helped convince the country's ruling family of the need for more military quarters in Marrakesh.[11]

And from Hollywood, dashing actor Douglas Fairbanks, Jr., Lieutenant, junior grade, served with John in Algiers. He later led a commando outfit near Salerno.[12] Young French film star Jean Pierre Aumont, aide-de-camp of General Rosset, later came upon John in the Vosges section of France. Novelist John Steinbeck, a Mediterranean war correspondent, also visited John's ship during the invasion of Italy.

Back home, Francesca gave much of her time to raising money for Navy relief activities. Just before the attack on Pearl Harbor, she had organized on the lawn of their rented Southport home a children's fair with a version of A Midsummer Night's Dream danced by Fairfield,

Connecticut youngsters. Proceeds from the gathering, called "Goods for Our Gobs," provided shore-to-ship gift packages for seamen.

Francesca also spent many hours working at the Stage Door Canteen in New York alongside actresses Lillian and Dorothy Gish, Helen Hayes, Katharine Cornell, and Gertrude Lawrence, who was married to Dick Aldrich. In Westport she started a victory garden and managed to produce a bumper vegetable crop. With gas rationed to four gallons a week, she saved part of her allocation by hitching up her daughters' pony and cart and carrying them miles across town to school.

The quick fall of Sicily into Allied hands put into motion plans to invade the so-called toe and heel of Italy's boot. Operation AVALANCHE, with Salerno as the target, commenced in force. On September 6, 1943, Lodge boarded Admiral Hewitt's flagship, USS *Ancon*, a converted Panama Pacific liner. As she steamed out of Algiers, she was flanked on her bow by several destroyers and joined by a growing flotilla of invasion craft. For the undertaking, Hewitt assigned Lodge an additional job: naval historian. His notes provide a vivid account of the invasion, which stood out in stark contrast to the earlier and more easily fought battle to take Sicily:

> September 6: Barrage balloons over convoy glistening in the morning sun. USS *Philadelphia* is in the lead. Our position is 3rd in the Port Column. The *Duchess of Bedford* is on our starboard beam. Khaki-clad troops can be seen jamming decks. Convoy doing 12 knots.
>
> September 8: An enemy submarine is known to be patrolling on our track. Enemy air attack probable. . . . The hills of North Africa appear dimly behind in a haze. . . . AVALANCHE opens up a possibility of Italy falling of its own weight. Never since Hannibal attempted to cross the Alps has there been such an attempt.[13]

On September 8, as attack forces approached Salerno, some thirty miles south of Naples, General Eisenhower announced an armistice with Italy. "In justice to the Italians," writes naval historian Samuel Eliot Morison in his multi-volume account of World War II, "the armistice had to be announced before we landed on their soil, but it was singularly ill-timed with reference to embarked troops. These, naturally assuming that they were to have a walk-over at Salerno, proceeded to relax, mentally and otherwise. Senior officers tried to undo the mischief by warning the men by loudspeakers that they would still have to fight Germans. . . . The general impression seemed to be that the war was over. We were landing in Italy and the Italians had quit, hadn't they?"[14]

This step did not change invasion plans. The Allies knew the Italian garrison at Salerno Bay had been replaced by crack German troops. An estimated eighteen German divisions were believed now in Italy. A day later, in the pre-dawn hours, the convoy reached the Gulf of Salerno. It prepared to land troops on the beachhead without any shore bombardment in order to achieve surprise. As the sun rose directly over the mountains behind the Salerno plains, the enemy waited. The Axis troops opened fire. A crisscross of heavy cannon firings pelted the Americans. Allied ships retaliated and shelled the heavily defended coastline. John caught a sight of HMS *Abercrombie*. She suffered a hit, then listed to port. Small ships stood by for rescue. It was later discovered that the hard-hitting vessel had struck a mine. But she reached an even keel by counterflooding, then managed to steam to safety at Palermo.[15]

Lodge's journal continues:

2116 hours September 9: Landing barge afire . . . port quarter . . . distance about 800 yards . . . cause unknown.
2135 hours: General Quarters. Planes overhead . . . Flares dropped on port bow.[16]

German gunners hit many soldiers in landing craft as they waited to storm the beaches. The Luftwaffe bombed and strafed the shore on a scale never before or since equaled in a Mediterranean battle. A thousand GIs were wiped out as they struggled to gain a foothold on enemy territory. Lodge concluded: "Those two or three days were just murderous."[17]

Overhead, planes circled low and fired at Lodge as he prepared to go ashore. He jumped on top of a pile of bedding rolls and twisted them over his body. At the same instant, a half-dozen men fell onto the heap of mattresses, and John felt their weight. Shells whistled and exploded in every direction as he waited for the attack to subside. Unharmed, he and his unit soon landed on the beach. John hit the ground often. One particular dive filled his mouth with wet sand. All in all, a minor inconvenience, he thought.

Later, Lodge came upon some Italian soldiers. These troops, when hearing of the armistice with the Allies, quickly surrendered. Lodge, with his speaking knowledge of Italian, had exclaimed "Amici, amici" through a portable loudspeaker. He readily won their confidence. They helped unload supplies from the landing craft, eager to be a part of the American side. Many Italians spoke to John about relatives in the United States, declaring they never wanted to fight America.

The following day, John returned to the *Ancon* in expectation of a second wave of fire by the Germans. He wrote: "By evening we pulled out to try to avoid the enemy attacks. It was good to be under way and the cool breezes seemed to lift not only the breathless humid heat of the September sirocco but also the strain of the last few days."[18]

Forty hours later, on September 13, the Germans struck again. The situation took a turn for the worse; tentative plans were made to withdraw forces already on land. At the peak of the Axis retaliation, John from the deck of his ship witnessed a brutal attack. A German plane some 20,000 feet above his vessel detached a radio-controlled glider bomb, a new device and apparently the first such rocket dropped since the war began. Lodge was sure it was headed for his ship. But it changed course and hit the USS *Savannah*, 200 yards off starboard beam. A direct hit, the missile killed over 275 men. As the wounded struggled in the sea, small craft went to their rescue and picked up survivors. The blast blew a large hole in the *Savannah*'s bottom and opened a seam in her side. She kept on an even keel by shifting fuel oil and retreated to Malta for repairs. The vessel's dead were later taken to the beach, sprinkled with gasoline, and cremated. A horrible sight, it remained vividly etched in John's memories of the war.

The Allies beat back the furious attack. Lodge returned to the beach and billets in Salerno. "It was good to hear Italian spoken and to look out on the peaceful parched hills in the September sun," he recorded.[19] With the capture of Salerno by the American Fifth Army, the troops moved toward Naples in bitter fighting. German tanks and planes continued to attack at every opportunity. On October 1, Naples fell to the Allies, and the march to Rome pressed on.

Back in Algiers that month, Lodge received special orders to act as counsel in a general court martial. His legal training had not been overlooked by the Navy. John's "client" was a young enlisted man from Kansas City. The case involved a group of off-duty sailors in Algiers who after drinking too much went to a brothel. The brothel keeper apparently didn't deliver the "goods" as promised. The inebriated gang dragged him to an open balcony, then held the helpless fellow by his heels. Someone shouted, "Throw him in the street!" Several of the sailors let go of his feet, and he fell head-first from the third story, suffering fatal injuries.[20] Lodge tried his best to get an acquittal for the seaman who had apparently played a subordinate part in the misadventure. The Naval court, however, saw it otherwise, and sentenced him to three years in the Portsmouth Navy Yard prison in New Hampshire. John was crestfallen by the verdict of manslaughter; he had become close to the young defendant. He wrote the boy's family, urging them not to admonish their son too severely: "What he needs from you is not a scolding but a vote of confidence, a pat on the back, and your expressions of affection. He had been tried in battle and not found wanting, and he is now being tried even more severely."[21]

At John's urging, the Kansas lad put aside his bitterness, and became a model prisoner, very grateful to his counselor for all his efforts. From prison, the seaman wrote Lodge that there was a chance his sentence would be reduced. He hoped to be restored to active duty, even after his bad conduct discharge. "I am almost sure they will send me back to duty by fall. So things aren't so bad after all," he concluded. "Maybe I will be able to repay you someday. You were swell to us. And I promise you we will never forget it."[22]

Lodge's liaison work with the French Navy continued into 1944; that winter he was assigned to the staff of Rear Admiral Lyal A. Davidson at Oran to prepare French cruisers for combat and, in turn, a landing in southern France. In a letter to Cabot that winter, John shared his views of Mediterranean operations. "We have no naval attaché yet and the liaison is officially not a U.S. but a UK concern though I do my best along those lines with all the authority of 2 stripes. Chains of command and operational echelons to the contrary notwithstanding."[23]

Turning to broader policies, Lodge believed America, as a partner in battle, should accept other responsibilities which come with fighting a war overseas: "Is it inevitable that a policy of national self-interest is not also a policy which will tend to preserve peace? Is it impossible that what is good for the U.S. should also be good for the world? I do not believe so. In fact I believe that precisely the reverse might very well be true if we can learn to administer the power which we accumulate with an eye on the interests of others. After all a *good* bargain is one which is beneficial to both parties. We are adept at good bargains at home, but we seem incapable of extending our efforts to territory liberated in considerable part as a result of our own great endeavor."[24]

By the time Cabot received his brother's letter of January 26, he had resigned from the Senate to serve in England as assistant chief of staff in the new armored divisions of General Willis D. Crittenberger. Not long after he landed at XIX Corps headquarters, he took off for Algiers with the General for a meeting with allied forces. Again, the two brothers shared a brief reunion. From North Africa, Cabot flew to Naples to establish headquarters to plan for missions into northern Italy.

But in mid-April, Cabot became ill. It seemed like an upset stomach due to a meal of spicy chili. Possible dysentery, the doctors thought, or perhaps the recurrence of ulcers once suffered in his undergraduate days. Cabot soon became so sick that he was rushed to a military hospital in Naples. There, the chief of surgery, an old Harvard classmate named Richard Chute, took charge. A study of x-rays of his intestines indicated the presence of an ulcer; the condition blocked the passage of food. General Crittenberger and Cabot's doctors decided to send him home for surgery at once. General Jacob Devers, the senior Army Commander in the Mediterranean theatre, placed his military plane at Cabot's disposal, and it took off with him, a doctor, and a nurse. The party made a brief refueling stop at Casablanca. John met the plane and comforted his sick brother.

Cabot arrived at Walter Reed Hospital some forty hours later. According to some reports at the time, he was near death. Specialists hurriedly conferred, then stopped the intravenous feedings and other treatment. They ruled out an operation. Solid American food was ordered. A hearty steak was placed before Cabot. He perked up and nibbled at his favorite dish. After a brief convalescence, he returned to Naples, where his unit had begun to advance northward. Cabot's collapse greatly upset John, and he followed the course of his illness and recovery closely. "I have never admired Cabot more than on this occasion," John wrote General Crittenberger on May 4, 1944. "He had every reason to be deeply disappointed and to be irritable and difficult. Instead, he was cheerful, optimistic, and completely under control. He met the challenge as just another obstacle in the race which he is determined to run."[25]

At the completion of a full year overseas in May 1944, John Lodge received a promotion to the rank of lieutenant commander. On June 6, with a vast invasion force at Normandy, the Allies carried out their long-planned liberation of France. Later that summer, John attended a meeting between Secretary of the Navy James Forrestal and Commander-in-Chief of the Free French, General Charles de Gaulle. John soon learned of the plans to invade southern France on August 15, a decision that placed Lodge aboard a liberty ship under the command of the naval advanced bases unit.[26]

The Seventh U.S. Army and French First Army established fortifications on shore, east of Marseilles, without much German resistance. Lodge moved to a new station on the Mediterranean, Toulon, as Senior U.S. Navy Liaison Officer with the French Naval District Headquarters (Préfecture Maritime). His assistant, a recent Williams College graduate (and later its Professor of Romance Languages), Anson C. Piper, remembered their association. They shared a large, high-ceilinged office in the once-elegant Grand Hotel de Toulon, which the French Navy had taken over following the German withdrawal. Their work involved constant and almost exclusive contact with their French counterparts, handling convoy routing, mine sweeping, mine disposal, harbor clearance, transfer of ships, employment of civilians, and requisition of buildings and vehicles.

Lodge had a good rapport with the French, according to Piper. He was particularly kind to his French subordinates, especially his civilian driver and their secretary, "without whom our duties would have been even more difficult than they actually were." Young Piper enjoyed his four months of work with Lodge: "He never lost his 'cool;' he never required the impossible; and he was always a gentleman."[27]

That summer John journeyed to Rome. He saw little outward change from his last visit in 1938 during the Munich crisis, except for a multitude of uniforms and the fact that life was no longer as pleasant and carefree. "The Grand Hotel has retained its erstwhile E. Phillips Oppenheim flavor, although gastronomically speaking, the opportunities are neither as varied nor as satisfying as before," he wrote to his cronies back at 90 Church Street. "The Italians have retained their appreciation of the amenities of life and it is my devout hope that Rome may regain her pre-war standing among the European flesh-pots."[28]

The U.S. presidential election returned Roosevelt to the Oval Office for an unprecedented fourth term. Lodge felt that the servicemen overseas were little interested in American politics and generally out of touch with the campaign. "I am rather fearful that this gap that I speak of will be a source of considerable dissension and trouble in the post-war period," he observed to a fellow naval officer already back home in Philadelphia.[29]

With his job at Toulon apparently accomplished, John got orders to return to the States. En route to England, he obtained permission to pass through Brussels to see his brother-in-law Edouard de Streel and, in turn, bring Helena (in Washington with Mrs. Lodge for the duration) firsthand news of the situation in Belgium.

On the morning of December 30, 1944, Francesca, Lily, and Beatrice were waiting at home for a taxi to take them to a train bound for Philadelphia and Washington. The phone rang. Francesca answered it. To her surprise and amazement, the caller was John. He was in a phone booth at the Westport station. He had flown across the Atlantic, stopping at the Azores and Bermuda before landing in New York in the early hours of that morning. Twenty minutes later, a cab pulled into the driveway, depositing a jubilant passenger with several days' growth of beard and an armful of gear and uniforms. John had missed the Christmas holiday but was united with his family in time to celebrate New Year's Eve. And best of all, he was home on a thirty-day leave.

A month later, he rejoined the Special Events section of the Naval Public Relations office in downtown Manhattan. Another round of speaking dates at incentive rallies, "E" award ceremonies, war bond drives, and Red Cross gatherings occupied Lodge as victory in Europe approached. That spring he traveled to dozens of plants producing war materials; many were in his home state. He was greeted warmly at such industrial sites as the Dictaphone Corporation in Bridgeport, American

Brass Company in Waterbury, Chance Vought Aircraft in Stratford, and Andover Kent Aviation in Middletown.

He now took interest in the commercial affairs of Connecticut beyond just public speaking at its defense works. For a business friend in New York, keen on acquiring a Connecticut factory and hiring local employees, he tapped his new acquaintances in the state for information on available plants. The war in Europe ended in May 1945. That month he delivered the graduation address before the last Navy V-12 Unit at Wesleyan University. His engagements began to move beyond morale boosting. He served as toastmaster at his Harvard class dinner. Other groups, such as the Elementary Principals Association, sought him out as a speaker on such topics as compulsory military training.

Much wider exposure stemmed from radio appearances. On May 3, over WHN in New York, he talked about the close friendship between American and French forces, and the liberation of France on *The Navy Reports* series: "The principles on which this great military achievement were founded must not be forgotten with the cessation of hostilities. They must not be confined to the United States and French navies. They must be extended to our relations with all foreign powers. . . . The world has, through its machines, reached the status of a large but integrated community. This state of affairs is fraught with danger; it is however also pregnant with a mighty challenge."[30] Program M.C. Barry Wood introduced Lodge and congratulated him on his recent decoration: the Legion of Honor conferred by General Charles de Gaulle, "a fitting reward for his many months of work as American Liaison Officer with the French fleet." He also received the Croix de Guerre with Palm that year for his exemplary performance with the French forces.

On Memorial Day, he addressed radio listeners from a NBC microphone at Rockefeller Center. Although the Germans had surrendered a few weeks earlier, he reminded all of the unfinished task in the Pacific. "When, like the proverbial ostrich, we have stuck our heads deep in the sand of peacetime pursuits, the enemy may strike again," he intoned. "We cannot win the peace unless we first win the war, and we cannot win a total war without a total victory. We have a solemn compact with our fighting men."[31]

John tried to secure an assignment in the Pacific. He sought a liaison job with the French Navy, but learned that the U.S. Navy had no clear-cut relationship there with that fleet. "While it is very pleasant to be living at home and although I am very happy in my work," he wrote Cabot, "I hope to get a glimpse of the Pacific business before it is over." He also looked to France and a government post, perhaps with the tribunal set up for the trials of war criminals.

The war with Japan ended abruptly that summer with the dropping of atomic bombs at Hiroshima and Nagasaki. Although Lodge was due for discharge after three years' active service, he requested a postponement. He wished to remain in uniform to participate in the largest Navy Day celebration in U.S. history. Then, in November, he was offered the post of Naval Intelligence Officer in Rome, but turned it down.

Instead, the Lodges leased a furnished apartment for one year at 829 Park Avenue at an annual rental of $3,000, and John made plans to leave the Navy by 1946. "If in the future, I can be of any use to the Navy in any capacity," he wrote to a fellow officer in Washington, "I hope very much that they will consider me among the most available reserve officers."[32] In the years ahead, he always proudly declared that he was particularly happy *not* to have missed service in the Navy in World War II. And summer after summer for the next twenty years, he returned to the fleet for Reserve assignments, which he often described as some of the most exhilarating of all his broad experiences.

Having composed a talk called "The Challenge of Peace" at the close of hostilities, he began delivering this clarion call to more and more attentive civic and community groups in and about New York. "Our faith is freedom," he stated. "We must keep that faith. In order to keep that faith we must discharge our responsibilities. That is the real challenge of the peace—a challenge to the American people to discharge their peacetime responsibilities as citizens in order that the nation's fighting men shall not be called on again to do their relentless duty in another formidable war."[33]

In the months ahead, this speech would take Lt. Cmdr. John Lodge to other podiums and forums, and eventually to platforms that added a new dimension to his life—politics.

CHAPTER 11

Politics: The Family Business

"We are in our beloved little home 'Villa Lodge' in Westport," wrote Francesca in her pocket diary on New Year's Day, 1946. "Once more all together after years of separations & heartaches. . . . Christmas was so happy. Beatrice believes in Santa & put the bread cookie & water by the fireplace just as we used to in Florence." The Lodges celebrated New Year's Eve quietly with a bottle of champagne in front of a glowing fire in the living room fireplace. From a nearby radio, background sounds of merry-making at Times Square added to the low-keyed occasion. John and Francesca looked ahead to the first full year of peace since 1941. John had begun thinking about postwar jobs and looking into career possibilities.

He mulled over his future in the theater and films. Both areas had lost a great deal of their fascination. "Mouthing the words of others did not seem very much of a challenge anymore," Francesca later recalled. Besides, his Hollywood films—and there was only *The Scarlet Empress* he considered a co-starring vehicle—had been forgotten. And his European pictures never received widespread U.S. bookings. Many roles were built around unsympathetic characters, and a few were downright villains. From another standpoint, after a six-year absence from the screen, John had aged. Soon he would be relegated to featured billing and eventually character roles. Down the road, he didn't want to become another secondary stock player. He considered his idol and old friend Walter Hampden one of the few matinee favorites who had aged well and continued as a great actor. All in all, acting struck Lodge as too narrow for the panoramic experience he now sought. Two days before Christmas 1945, he completed his last acting assignment. He recreated his role as Professor Brooke in a radio adaptation of *Little Women* for *The Theater Guild on the Air*. Katharine Hepburn as Jo starred on the coast-to-coast broadcast at the Vanderbilt Theater in New York. Sponsor U.S. Steel Corporation paid John $150 for his work.

The practice of law appealed even less to Lodge. After all the years away from contracts and torts, he had no desire to jump back into that profession. Writing, however, definitely attracted John. During his 20 months overseas, he recorded his thoughts and convictions. His notes on the challenge of war, he acknowledged, came about as much out of loneliness and boredom as from high excitement over the adventure.

In a foreword of what he hoped would begin a book, he explained: "These thoughts grew out of heated debates with friends under the low arch of Quonset huts; they emerged from listless conversations high on the flag bridge as our ship skidded noiselessly through the dense shadows of an early Mediterranean morning; they developed as a result of the shattering impact which war must have on the heart and mind of any feeling, thinking adult."[1]

He called his collection of essays *There is a Tide*, and showed it to friends in the publishing field. Lodge's manuscript generated curiosity, but publishers were seeking first-hand stories of combat and not soldierly philosophy. His literary acquaintances, in turn, suggested a career in academia. Hadn't intellectual curiosity been a Lodge family trait for generations? He replied conclusively: "I don't want to be buried on a campus in any shape or form." That ended any further discussion of university teaching or administrative work.[2]

John did not rule out a job in government service or business. He took his time in making a decision in those areas. He had the wherewithal to move slowly and cautiously. During the war years, his investments had grown. His financial advisor at Morgan Bank had recommended the purchase of a number of high-growth stocks, including IBM. John's income increased accordingly. With this cushion, he could afford to pursue activities that were less remunerative but public service related.

So in January he accepted the post as director of business relations for the American Economic Foundation. A non-profit, non-partisan organization in New York, it had among its activities a weekly syndicated "debate in print" column and the radio series *Wake Up, America*. Started in 1939 by insurance and oil-refining executive Fred G. Clark, the Foundation provided a forum for well-informed, intelligent discussion of economic issues and problems. John's Harvard roommate Bud Eames had recently joined Clark's staff as moderator of the weekly radio broadcasts. When John came by for an interview, office workers had been amused by the two old school chums' boisterous and intensely friendly greetings.

Lodge researched and lectured on economic and governmental subjects. He registered with the American Speakers and Writers Bureau and was listed in the *Public Relations Directory and Yearbook*, steps that brought him additional speaking engagements. Increasingly, his talks turned to the difficulties of keeping the world at peace. As a veteran back from the war, he felt the urgency to speak out. Personally, he also felt a growing drive to move into the political arena and make his opinions more widely known. "He strongly believed that it was not enough to take off your military uniform, sit back, stay out of politics, and then 'let George do it,'" Francesca explained. He expressed his desire to become politically active to Cabot, just out of the Army and preparing a campaign to regain his Senate seat. Cabot clearly vetoed the idea of a sibling in politics. "Let there be no nepotism in our family," he emphasized.[3] John wondered why Cabot reacted so strongly against another Lodge in public service. A contemporary of both John and Cabot at Harvard caustically compared the two brothers many years later: "John was basically an actor through all his activities—a ham, a performer. And not very bright or original. Cabot was intelligent and clever, yet could be mean and cold-hearted. He only spoke to those who could aid his work."[4]

In any event, a small circle of potential political backers grew just from listening to John talk informally about America's postwar role and its free enterprise system. A radio writer and concert manager named Olive Montgomery heard John's message firsthand one afternoon when she hitched a ride with the Lodges from New York to Westport. John presented a persuasive explanation of what sound economics meant to the country's survival.

"You ought to tell people what you've just told me," Olive urged. "My friend Suzanne Silvercruys Stevenson is making speeches at Grange meetings in Fairfield to help build support for her nomination for Congress. That is, if the seat comes up for grabs. John, why don't you run for office, too?"

"I don't know if people really want me."

"People don't want you, unless they *know* you. Tell them what's on your mind."

"If you can arrange some local appearances, Olive, I'd like to do it."[5]

Olive Montgomery sold the idea of Lodge as a speaker to a Greenwich luncheon club. Within a week, response to the program caused the group to re-schedule it in the evening. Still more interest switched it to a bigger hall that could accommodate guests from three neighboring communities. On the night of his talk, two hundred listeners came away pleased with what John had said.

More and more Republicans liked his message. Fairfield County's political boss, William Brennan, sized up Lodge as a potential asset to the Party team and invited him to speak at the Connecticut Young Republicans Convention in Hartford that spring. An insurance man in Stamford with close ties to the State Comptroller, who controlled state insurance patronage, Brennan expected John to be subservient to him. But it was not to be.

A particular concern of John's was the persistent hold of one political party over the executive and legislative branches of government. With the Democrats in control of the White House and Congress since 1933, Lodge stressed the pitfalls of what lay ahead in a one-party country. He read D. W. Brogan's recently published treatise *The Free State* and agreed with its author. If one party was so dominant and free of any real fear of defeat, it would dull its sense of responsibility to almost nothing. And if the other party had no hope of success, it may as well have its verbal fling, promise heaven and threaten hell, without having to face the reality of governing. He studied, underlined, and marked many passages of Brogan's book. He doubly underscored one line: "All statesmen in a free society must be politicians."[6]

As a politician, John fell short. He had never held any elective office at any level. A carpetbagger in the eyes of many, he had spent, in total, less than a year in Connecticut. But Lodge felt his careers in law and acting afforded a disciplined and empathic approach to the public arena. John's wartime friend Henry Dudley once remarked, "90 percent of politics is acting and a political life parallels an actor's life. Both have to take it on the chin along with the applause."[7] A quick study with deep-rooted experience in speechmaking as well as in writing, he had a tested facility in dealing with reporters and interviewers. Indeed, he had an impressive stage presence: he was undeniably a tall, attractive, and articulate contender, able to hold people's attention. Moreover, Lodge, the Naval officer, had proudly served his country well. If not a front-page combat hero, he certainly had stormed the beaches and dodged bullets. And the name "Lodge" itself carried an aura of unselfish duty and steadfast patriotism.

Early in 1946, Congresswoman Clare Boothe Luce expressed a lack of enthusiasm over running for a third term from Fairfield County's Fourth District. Acclaimed Broadway playwright, globe-trotting journalist, and glamorous wife of Time-Life publisher Henry Luce, she had been elected as a Republican to the House of Representatives during the war. Earlier, the seat had been held for one term by her stepfather, Dr. Albert Austin, a physician. His political success stemmed in large measure from a young, second-generation Italian American named Albert Morano, who managed his campaign in 1938 and then became his office clerk. Morano pictured the ambitious, self-assured stepdaughter as a viable candidate some day. Upon Dr. Austin's death, fourteen months after his defeat in 1940 by Democrat LeRoy Downs, Morano urged Luce to enter the 1942 Congressional race. Although not personally confident of victory, she ran, winning by a narrow margin of some 7,000 votes out of more than 134,000 cast. Eager to return to Washington, Al Morano gladly accepted her offer to serve as administrative assistant.

Luce joined the Military Affairs Committee, a group of extraordinary importance in wartime. An outspoken, nimble, and highly visible opponent of many Roosevelt administration policies, she relished delving into the fascinating realm of foreign relations. But her independence of mind, her refusal to conform to Party lines, and her freewheeling junkets made her appear unpredictable, if not unreliable. Even fellow Republicans stood at arm's length. Reporters followed her every move. A legislator with her calculated wit and narcissistic beauty attracted frequent press coverage. And she appeared on all sorts of celebrity lists and polls, including a national public opinion survey that voted her legs the most beautiful in America after Marlene Dietrich's.

Luce ran again in 1944. Her Democratic opponent was a woman. Twenty-nine-year-old Bridgeport attorney Margaret Connors engaged her in a heated, fiercely fought campaign. A number of influential pro-Roosevelt public figures outside of politics (Clifton Fadiman, Orson Welles, Dorothy Parker) loudly and forcefully opposed Clare. The election outcome was in question down to the wire. When the votes were counted, Clare Boothe Luce managed a slim two-thousand-vote victory.

By 1946 two personal events in Luce's life changed her outlook. Her only child, a daughter, died in an automobile accident shortly before graduation from Stanford University. In her grief, she realized she had no real faith and gradually turned to Catholicism. She was converted by Bishop Fulton Sheen and confirmed at St. Patrick's Cathedral in February 1946. A few days before, she indicated her wish not to seek re-election to the House. There were, she realized, a substantial number of Catholics in her district. Many people would say that political motives inspired her spiritual decision.[8] More significant, her vote-getting strength had ebbed. Some of Luce's closest friends later concluded that she quit more out of boredom. She was ready for something new, they claim, and anticipated "the next chapter" of her life.

The name of John Lodge as a successor to the extraordinary Luce entered into conversations among many Republicans. The press, too, mentioned Lodge as Congressional timber. Then a speech by John placed him among the front-runners for Luce's seat. For the first peacetime Memorial Day ceremony in five years, the town fathers of New Canaan asked John Lodge to deliver the main address. Wearing a full-dress white Naval uniform with his war decorations, Lt. Cmdr. Lodge stood out in the line of march down Main Street to the village cemetery. There, he was introduced as speaker by Robert S. Ogden, Jr., an executive with the *New Yorker* magazine and a prominent New Canaan resident.

John's opening words intrigued the large crowd: "Eleven months and four days ago the diplomats of the United Nations brought forth in this universe a new world, conceived in liberty and dedicated to the proposition that all nations are created equal." The style and phrases carried a familiar ring. Lodge, it was realized, had skillfully borrowed the opening of Lincoln's memorable Gettysburg Address to remind his listeners of another momentous political event, the founding of the United Nations organization in 1945. "Now we are engaged in a great war of words testing whether that world or any world so conceived and so dedicated can long endure."[9]

By his introductory tact, Lodge won the complete attention of the marchers and onlookers that morning. They eagerly awaited the rest of his message. The real challenge of peace was for Americans to discharge their peacetime responsibilities as concerned citizens, he pointed out, in order that the nation's fighting men shall not be called on again in another war. The core of his address was Lodge's well-honed "challenge of the peace" theme. But he now paid greater attention to the UN and the need to make it a true world federation. He mentioned the elimination of the veto power in the Security Council, limitation and inspection of the production of scientific weapons, and establishment of an international police force. To cope with the great problems of peacetime, Lodge looked to citizens of vision: "This then is our first responsibility: to pick good people to guide us through the confusion and despair of the post-war crisis."[10]

Many in the crowd cheered and shouted in support of John's inspiring words, delivered against a backdrop of American flags. In the audience were several political kingpins. That evening the New Canaan Town Committee chairman Charles K. Dickson and one or two other County Republican leaders telephoned John. After John's clarion call for men of vision, they now insisted that he position himself for the House nomination. Lodge, they concluded, was a bona fide Republican, war veteran and local resident who had something to say and knew how to say it.

Francesca and John discussed a possible race. "I didn't know enough about politics to give real strength to a decision to run or not to run," she later said. "We went over the dangers of politics—the good and the bad. I asked, 'Are you tough-skinned enough to stand it?' It was a gamble—a new adventure on the hard road of challenges and choices." And remembering their films in Italy, she and John realized there was much prejudice against anyone who had ever associated in any way, artistic or otherwise, with the Mussolini regime.

That summer John made his move and jumped with both feet onto the bandwagon, speaking before groups in many of the county's twenty-three towns. "I believe the Government should operate the traffic signals, but not attempt to drive the automobiles," he emphasized with a strong back-to-basics outlook. "The fight all over the world is between those who believe in the people as the source of the more abundant life."[11]

The backing of Clare Boothe Luce was important, almost crucial to any candidate seeking the party nomination. The mercurial, indecisive Congresswoman did not publicly reveal her choice. She first urged Colonel Truman Smith, a retired career officer and veteran of both World Wars, to run. They had met through *Bridgeport Post* publisher George Waldo and occasionally dined together in Washington during the war. Then she let it be known that she officially had to back her aspiring administrative aide Al Morano. When he failed to build much enthusiasm among local GOP workers, Clare leaned toward Lodge. Thus far, her devout followers still hoped she would change her mind and run again.[12]

When Lodge received the endorsement of the Westport Republican Town Committee, it moved Luce to switch her allegiance wholeheartedly to him. The hometown nod also helped to lessen the outcries of carpetbagger against John and the rumors that he had not lived in the state long enough to take part in its political life. Connecticut Yankees viewed newcomers warily, he recognized, and it was a contemptuous political adage in the state that a person had to live there twenty years before even gaining the right to vote. John met the carpetbagger tag head on. He termed it a slur on the loyalty of all naturalized citizens who came from foreign lands to make their homes in Connecticut: "Surely those Americans who came from Italy, from Poland, from Ireland and from other foreign countries are entitled to exercise their franchise as citizens of this state, and just as surely those citizens of Connecticut who came from other states in the Union should not be subject to any prejudice or examination."

Fairfield had grown accustomed to a charismatic celebrity as their Representative, and Lodge, with his show business background and patrician aura, would continue that distinction. Clare wrote plays; John acted in them. Clare summoned John and Francesca to her home in Greenwich. They needed encouragement and advice, she believed. "Get acquainted with the area and local issues that bother the average citizen," she said. "When you ride the commuters' trains to New York, John, tell everybody you would like to be the next Congressman, because you know for sure Mrs. Luce is not going to run. And let them tell you what they would expect of the next Congressman. And remember to ask questions, questions, questions," she told both Lodges. "And smile, smile, smile. Sam Rayburn once told me that the four rules for a candidate are: 'explain nothing, deny everything, demand proof, and give the opposition hell.' I've never been able to follow them, but maybe you can."[13] John pasted these rules on his shaving mirror and read them every morning during the campaign. Before the Lodges left Clare, she secured John's promise: if ever the Fourth District seat became vacant in the future, he had to support Al Morano for Congress.

Two weeks later, in mid-September, Republicans gathered for the District nominating convention. On the eve of the meeting in Greenwich, Morano publicly withdrew from the contest and threw his support to Lodge. Col. Smith and Suzanne Silvercruys Stevenson remained the only opposition. The following day, they, too, bowed out. Lodge was chosen by acclamation. In a brief acceptance speech, he hoped that the Republican Party did not adhere to a stand-pat reactionary philosophy: "The main purpose of the Republican Party must be to protect the interests of minority groups while protecting the majority from minority control. Republicanism must be a dynamic timely political philosophy if it is to survive." He urged the GOP to provide leadership in international relations and to make bona fide and valid accommodations of government to modern needs: "We must unite and destroy the sinister forces which are attempting to get a strangle hold on America. We must unite and smash communism and corruption in America."[14]

John joined eight other Connecticut war veterans running for Congressional seats and major state offices, exactly one-third of the twenty-seven top Republican and Democratic candidates. His opponent for the House seat was a formidable young man. Thirty-four-year-old West Pointer Colonel Henry A. Mucci had returned home to Bridgeport with rows of battle ribbons. Commander of an Army Ranger battalion which rescued over 500 American soldiers held by the Japanese behind enemy lines for almost three years at Cabanatuan in the Philippines, he was a widely acclaimed hero. The rescued combatants included the tattered remnants of the grueling Bataan Death March of some 15,000 prisoners.[15] Career officer Mucci earlier had been posted near Pearl Harbor when the Japanese attacked. In June 1945, Mucci received a hero's welcome and parade in Bridgeport. The Democrats quickly sized up Mucci as a charismatic candidate for Luce's House seat. Both Mucci and Lodge soon faced the major postwar issues—housing shortages, unemployment, veterans' benefits, labor legislation, European relief.

State assemblyman Oscar Peterson managed John's campaign. Bill Brennan, Luce's campaign strategist, had apparently sought that post, even after he had tried to derail the Lodge nomination shortly before the District Convention in Greenwich.[16] Off to a strong beginning, with noontime factory gate rallies at local plants, Lodge even picked up an endorsement by labor, who invariably backed Democrats. A local official of the UEW-CIO, Charles DeJulius declared over the radio: "Mr. Lodge stands squarely for free labor which is the bulwark of opposition to a socialized state."[17] DeJulius might have added that Lodge, as an actor, was himself a member of the American Federation of Labor. Lodge pledged not to support any kind of restrictive legislation, such as anti-strike bills. John even put his own shoulder to the wheel as a laborer and affirmed his commitment to more housing. He pitched in with 100 Westport neighbors one day to convert GI barracks to temporary apartments for veterans. The barn-raising volunteers included artist and magazine illustrator Stevan Dohanos, who backed John wholeheartedly and built up support for him among his fellow Hungarians in southwestern Connecticut. He later designed a striking Congressional campaign symbol: a bull's eye target with an arrow piercing the center, and then added the catchy line, "You can't miss with Lodge."

John's campaign took on a new histrionic twist one day. He and his opponent met as co-speakers at an Italian-American community hall on Columbus Day weekend. Col. Mucci in military uniform spoke first to the assembled crowd of first- and second-generation Italians. Many had only a rudimentary knowledge of English. He related how his mother had come from Italy with only $18 in her pocket. No, he wasn't born with a silver spoon in his mouth, the attractive war hero reminded everyone: "But we Americans of Italian extraction built the railroads, the skyscrapers, the highways."

When it came time for John to speak, he praised Mucci's war record. Dressed in a dark blue business suit, he looked at his opponent while praising his military accomplishments. "I could see he was somewhat baffled by this," Lodge recalled years later. "He was new at politics, and so was I. But I perhaps had been exposed to it more, and he felt that the game was for me to say nothing but unpleasant things about my opponent." John then turned to Mucci with an apology. He wanted to speak a few words in Italian: "I'd like to say something in my wife's native tongue." John shifted from English to the language he loved to delve into. He explained in fluent Italian that Italy was his wife's native land which he, too, had known since boyhood. "We spent our honeymoon there, and together made several Italian films in the capital. I feel half Italian!", he exclaimed. "My two daughters are half Italian."[18]

As John concluded his remarks, Francesca entered the room. She had been at a nearby Italian festival and wore a colorful folk costume. When the audience spotted her, they began clapping their hands in a rhythmic beat and singing a tarantella. Then they shouted to her to sing. She agreed but only if everyone joined in on the Trieste Song, a sentimental tone whose refrain—"Italy of my heart, you're coming to liberate us"—carried highly charged political undertones about an occupied city. The audience's enthusiasm buoyed Francesca. The crowd then turned to Mucci for a response in Italian. But the fellow, despite his Italian ancestry, could barely speak a handful of words.[19]

The Lodge team immediately capitalized on their linguistic advantage. For the rest of the campaign, whenever groups of Italian-Americans were on John's itinerary, he spoke in Italian and a costumed Francesca sang. To add a colorful climax to a rally, she often danced the tarantella. Not reticent about organizing backers for John's bid for office, Francesca utilized her experience from a recent county-wide campaign to build the first postwar season of audience subscriptions at the Westport Country Playhouse. She served as chairman there for the next eight summers.

A team on stage and in films, the Lodges emerged as quasi-political partners. "We were not the holding-hands type in public," Francesca explained, "but our togetherness was deep and complete in private. Public behavior was important; protocol was necessary. The fun was being able to talk over everything and everybody on all levels using expressions from four languages. John taught me a lot about complex international relations, while I made him realize the importance of the mentality of the 'man on the street,' which I always said was mine!"

Unsophisticated politically at the outset, Francesca acted as her husband's critic and goad. And she was willing to do the numerous and varied tasks that only aides of most politicians would perform. Francesca also counterbalanced John's chronic pompousness and inflexibility. "She smoothed off or burnished his rough edges," observed University of Bridgeport President Leland Miles. "She had the ability to move easily among people of every background, of every strata of society, while John always struck me as a bit of an elitist."[20]

Connecticut's Fourth District traditionally favored Republicans, but the thrice-wounded Colonel Mucci was such a local hero that his popularity spilled over among many groups of voters. But the party in power, the Democrats, were held chiefly responsible for a rising rate of inflation fueled by labor demands for higher wages and more fringe benefits. The unrest led to a series of crippling nation-wide strikes by auto workers, telephone employees, steel workers, and maritime groups. Truman, who had succeeded Roosevelt as President in 1945, was blamed for widespread high prices, clothing and appliances scarcities, and housing shortages. It all worked in the Republicans', and Lodge's, favor. By November, John's chances were viewed as exceedingly good.

In a last ditch attempt to alarm voters in his hometown the day before election, Lodge opponents stuffed in every mailbox an anonymous note:

If you are old enough to remember World War I, you will remember the name LODGE.

It will go down in world history as a wrecker of world peace.
That name is directly responsible for World War II.
Do you want to see your son get into World War III?
Then for the sake of World Peace don't take a chance on another
LODGE.[21]

The ghost of John's grandfather had been disparagingly resurrected to scare people who had forgotten or didn't remember old Senator Lodge and the League of Nations debate. Westport answered back by giving John Lodge a resounding 3,066 votes. Mucci and a perennial Socialist Party runner picked up a total of 843 votes. The rest of Fairfield County followed suit. In his first bid for office, Lodge received a plurality of 35,617 votes. The outcome: Lodge, 93,505 and Mucci, 57,888. John carried every town in the district except Bridgeport, where he lost by only 776 votes. Republican candidates made a clean sweep. The Connecticut GOP won all six Congressional seats, ousting four Democratic incumbents. It gained control of the State legislature, captured the governorship, and secured a Senate seat.

Lodge got unofficial word of his election while listening to the returns at home with a group of party workers. Lodge received a phone call. "You're in!" shouted Clare Boothe Luce over the line. "You lost by 500 votes in Bridgeport which means you'll win the county by at least 25,000 or 30,000."[22]

The Lodges and their guests hurried out the door, jumped into automobiles, and sped off to Lodge headquarters at Bridgeport's Barnum Hotel. Scores of supporters and well-wishers greeted them. When official word came through of John's victory and after Mucci conceded, a spontaneous torch-light parade took shape on the street, the first Republican victory celebration in the city since the early 1930s.

All New England, except Rhode Island, came under Republican control in a landslide described by one veteran Democrat as a people's mandate for "sweeping change in national affairs." In Massachusetts the Republicans showed their greatest strength since the days of Calvin Coolidge. David Walsh, a Senator for over twenty-five years, toppled under an avalanche of votes for Cabot Lodge. A new contingent of young Republicans, along with a handful of able Democrats, won seats in the Eightieth Congress, now controlled by the GOP. Many of the 144 new Representatives were veterans of World War II and eager to shape the Republican Party's revival: Jacob Javits, victor in Manhattan's 21st District; William F. Knowland, thirty-eight-year-old ex-GI from California; Joseph McCarthy, anti-New Deal politician from Wisconsin; Richard Nixon, young lawyer based in southern California; Thruston Morton, recently discharged Naval commander in Kentucky. The new Democratic members included another personable war hero: John F. Kennedy of Boston.

After the election, John and Francesca left for a well-earned period of rest in the sun on Florida beaches. En route they stopped in Harrisburg, Pennsylvania for Lodge to address the annual convention of the State's Council of Republican Women. He reiterated the new Republican thrust: "The Republican party is the party of true liberalism; it is the party of progress, of intellectual ferment—the party of freedom. We are the young Turks, the insurgents."[23]

The Lodges visited his mother in Washington. Proud of having two sons elected to Congress, the last brother team there since William and John Bankhead of Alabama, she characteristically wanted no "fuss" made on her behalf. Apparently, both sons were scheduled to be sworn in at the same time but in different locations. She hoped things would work out so she could watch each take his oath of office. Luckily, a procedural snarl delayed the Senate oath-taking to the day after the House swearing-in. Mrs. Lodge had just given up her large Massachusetts Avenue home. By 1945 she had found it impossible to find adequate domestic help. She had moved to a three-bedroom apartment in the Wardman Tower, an imposing wing of the adjacent Wardman Park Hotel near Connecticut Avenue.

Magazine publishers and society editors rushed to be the first to feature the Lodge brothers on their pages. Two political offspring with matinee-idol looks married to attractive women of stature and flair, these journalists exclaimed, had the ideal ingredients for full-blown coverage. But Cabot would have no part of any "brother act" or family group stories. And Bessie Lodge refused to be drawn in. She, for one, hadn't been photographed in ten years, even in a snapshot by her family, and so would remain completely in the background as Mrs. George Cabot Lodge, private citizen.

John Lodge brought his undeniable dramatic gifts to the political arena. The actor and the political orator, he came to believe, were one of the same species. Journalist Robert E. Rogers once said: "Scratch an actor and you find an orator. Scratch an orator and you find a disappointed actor." To Lodge, the sister state of the drama was public life, namely politics.[24] Impeccably dressed and groomed, Lodge was skilled at making "entrances" and adept at greeting people. "When John Lodge said hello to you," recalls public relations consultant and former White House social secretary Letitia Baldridge, "you really knew you had been said 'hello' to—even if he didn't remember your name or have a clue who you were." On the campaign trail and off, Lodge and his wife put their best foot forward. No matter what the occasion or where they might be, it was to them always akin to the excitement of a Broadway opening night.[25]

In 1946, Congressman-elect Lodge blazed a trail for future actors and entertainers seeking to enter Washington politics and government service. A few had served as honorary mayors of film-star communities. But none seriously considered a race for high elective office. With or without makeup, performers struck many as vain, egocentric, shallow, and empty-headed. "Actors were thought too ignorant for politics," Lodge concluded twenty years later, "but they have no monopoly on ignorance."[26] Gradually, other movie performers gained a place in government. In the mid-1960s, film actor and dancer George Murphy won election to the Senate. Shirley Temple, his (and Lodge's) juvenile co-star sought, albeit unsuccessfully, a Congressional seat, and served as a UN delegate and ambassador. In the 1980s, voters elected television actors Ben Jones and Fred Grandy to the House. A decade later, singer-comedian Sonny Bono followed in their footsteps. Tennessee Republican Fred Thompson, like Lodge a lawyer and a film actor, won election to the Senate in 1994. Four years later, wrestler, actor, and sports show host Jesse (The Body) Ventura won the governorship of Minnesota as a third-party candidate. And Ronald Reagan, a co-star with both George Murphy and Shirley Temple, moved from California movie sets to its Governor's office, then on to the White House. Once and for all, he demonstrated that an actor can be a good politician and a national leader.[27]

Both Reagan and Lodge emphasized the fact that acting prepared them for the criticism that comes to any politician, no matter how popular. They had endured a lot of negative reviews and experienced public criticism years before facing it as candidates and elected officials. With a performer's background, Lodge concluded, a political figure had the training and finesse to transform statements and speeches into dynamic, attention-holding pronouncements. At the very least, an actor-turned-politician could give conviction to what he was saying.[28] To the distinguished actor Edward G. Robinson, Lodge once remarked, "I love my part; you are dedicated to yours. Yet we seek the same spirit and the same goals: to make men happier and wiser and better."[29]

John Davis Lodge, formerly of Hollywood and Broadway, took his seat in Congress on January 3, 1947, and the curtain rose on a new act.

CHAPTER 12

Challenge of the Hour

The 1946 national elections reflected a broad lack of confidence in the leadership of President Harry Truman and the Democratic Party. The end of the war and the death of Roosevelt had diminished the strength of the Democratic Party, and the Republicans gained control of both the House of Representatives and the Senate. Not since 1930 had the GOP been the majority party in Congress. With it went key posts on important, far-reaching committees. And the Republican sweep brought an unusual honor for freshman Congressman John Lodge. He secured a coveted membership on the House Foreign Affairs Committee at a time when peace settlements, world reconstruction, and cold war resistance held center stage on a day-to-day basis.

John settled easily into the life and routine of a Congressman. He appointed former Connecticut House member and probate judge Raymond Watt as his executive secretary. He wisely took the advice of his friend, Washington lawyer Robert Jackson, and wrote a personal letter of thanks to each contributor to his campaign and kept reference cards on these supporters. John insisted his staff answer all mail within three days. Moreover, he read all his replies in draft, frequently covering them with corrective notes before a retyping. His office realized he was a stickler for definite form and perfect prose. Robert Jackson also pointed out the value of returning to Connecticut each weekend to maintain close contact with constituents. "This is particularly valuable during one's first term, although your first real battle will probably come in 1950," observed Jackson. "If you can repeat your striking majority in 1948, who knows what may happen in 1950 when Brien McMahon's term as Senator ends?"[1]

During John's first month on Capitol Hill, piles of mail, on topics such as rent control, income taxes, and education appropriations, overworked his staff, still busy organizing his new quarters. And in that

January, some 100 visitors stopped at his office on one form of business or another. His first legislation was the introduction of private bills to stop the deportation of three aliens who had been gainfully employed in the country for over twenty years. They qualified for immediate citizenship. His humanitarian concerns also led to a letter to Dean Acheson, then acting Secretary of State, protesting the move of Hungarians and Czechoslovakians by Russia into Communist-controlled slave labor camps behind the Iron Curtain. John requested a full investigation and report. And he addressed the House for the first time in a tribute to popular opera singer Grace Moore, a resident of his district who had died in a European plane crash.

In February, on the occasion of Washington's Birthday, John read Washington's Farewell Address before the House, having been chosen for this honor by Speaker Joseph Martin of Massachusetts (and a onetime campaign manager for his grandfather Lodge). He spoke about entering the family field of politics on the CBS radio series *We, the People*, prompting one Connecticut columnist to describe his voice as "the best we've heard since our immortal FDR."[2]

When President Truman called for the containment of Soviet expansion and the pledge of U.S. economic and military resources to aid Greece and Turkey, Lodge backed him. The bold, far-reaching Truman Doctrine, a commitment to arrest the spread of Communism, passed both houses that spring, followed by an initial appropriation of $400 million to bolster the two beleaguered nations. A firm believer in a bipartisan approach to foreign matters, he addressed the House to urge expansion of the State Department's information and education program abroad. "If this legislation is not passed by the House," Lodge stated, "our failure will have repercussions far beyond the details of the bill which are under attack. It will be interpreted abroad as further evidence of isolationism."[3]

On domestic issues, he followed the Republican position. He favored extension of rent control and a reduction in individual income taxes. The latter, he observed, would furnish incentives for business expansion and for the creation of new businesses by young veterans. John voted for the Taft-Hartley labor bill. "I voted for the bill because it guarantees to every union member the right completely to control his own union for his own benefit and because it protects the public against strikes in vital industries which threaten health, safety and the general welfare," he reported at the time.[4] Lodge made friends in his state's aircraft industry when he journeyed to Hartford to address the Connecticut Air Power Conference on the "Need for Aviation Expansion."

A cautious speaker, Lodge labored long and hard with his public talks. He worked for hours on a single passage; his statements were always the result of protracted delineation and devastating dissection. And he never missed a major vote in the House. Furthermore, his participation through interminable Foreign Affairs hearings gave him the well-deserved reputation as a highly conscientious member. A few home-based constituents took a narrow view. They expressed displeasure with his overriding involvement with foreign matters while seemingly paying only grudging attention to domestic affairs and ignoring some of their local problems.

As the first session of the 80th Congress neared adjournment, he went on record as favoring a number of humanitarian, monetary, and voter-franchise proposals: U.S. participation in the International Refugee Organization, the admission of Hawaii as a state, pension increases to Spanish and Civil war veterans and their dependents, restructured presidential succession (and a limit of the president's length of service to eight years), creation of the National Science Foundation, abolishment of the poll tax as a requirement in voting, and increased annuities for retired Civil Service employees.

John managed an occasional break during those momentous initial months as a Congressman. In June he addressed a special group back home: Lily's graduating class at Rosemary Hall, a private girls' school in Greenwich. After attending some ten different schools in as many years, Lily at fourteen had finally been able to put down some roots at one school. At Rosemary Hall, she excelled in her studies. Only in dance class did she not measure up, according to her mother, who taught dancing there and in return received a reduction in her daughter's tuition. "Lily's still the most awkward of all," she noted at the time, "but she's now on the Chapel Committee & that is nice."

In Washington, John, Francesca, and Beatrice settled into a second-floor apartment in the sprawling Wardman Park Hotel, adjacent to the building where Bessie Lodge lived. Nine-year-old Beatrice attended the Potomac School, a day school for girls. She spent afternoons after classes walking her dog and several puppies on the hotel grounds and observing a like ritual by many hotel inhabitants. The abundance of canine pets at the Wardman led the Lodges to call their new home "the Dogman Park Hotel."

On the very day Lodge spoke at Lily's high school graduation, Secretary of State George C. Marshall delivered the commencement address at Harvard. In his remarks, he outlined a comprehensive overseas plan against hunger, poverty, desperation, and chaos. "Its purpose should be the revival of a working economy in the world so as to permit the emergence of political and social conditions in which free institutions can exist." Marshall's proposal would occupy the agenda of Congress for many months to come. Even before the first session of the 80th Congress ended, it approved a $350 million emergency aid program for Italy, Hungary,

Austria, Greece, and China. Congress also spearheaded a conference based on the Secretary's proposal, which came to be called the Marshall Plan, to analyze the looming danger of a broad European economic collapse.

The U.S. aid program met pockets of opposition in the Republican Congress. Many isolationists believed that American goods would be removed from the domestic market for foreign consumption. Others predicted devastating inflationary spirals and an uncontrollable national debt. But Marshall pointed to the pending economic disaster and political upheaval in a handful of European nations unless more than stopgap aid was approved. Meanwhile, Congress, still debating the large-scale economic recovery program, prepared to adjourn for the summer. Before the members left the capital, President Truman initiated a first-hand appraisal by Congress of the expanding Communist threat and widespread economic turmoil. He urged a bipartisan group of Representatives and Senators to make on-the-spot inspections of Europe's plight and prospects. Ultimately, the joint Senate and House Smith-Mundt Committee undertook an extensive survey of twenty-two countries that year. Lodge was part of this group because of his membership on the Foreign Affairs Committee and on several sub-committees on national security and international law.

On September 18, 1947, John sailed for England on the *Queen Elizabeth* with four other Foreign Affairs members: Frances P. Bolton, Olin E. Teague, Chester E. Merrow, and Donald L. Jackson. Upon his arrival in London, John boarded a Navy plane for Prague. As it flew over Brussels, he radioed via the U.S. Embassy and Ambassador Alan G. Kirk a message of greetings to his sister Helena. As the plane headed East, John jotted down notes, short and roughly scrawled in a pocket pad: "This plane has one pilot and one radio man. I felt as though I were back in the Navy again. Reminds me of the war. As a matter of fact, the war is unfinished & the sooner we realize it the safer we shall be."[5]

Over Germany the weather became so hazardous that Lodge's plane was forced to land in Frankfurt. There, he switched to a C-47 provided by the Army. "Visibility zero as we approached Prague," he later recorded. "Morale of the boys here OK." At Vienna, Lodge noted that Austrian Minister Karl Gruber wanted all occupation troops of the Allies removed. Yet, John added, "He wants us to stay until the last Russian has left."

Hungary was his next stop. Budapest brought John unexpected secret agent-like intrigue. Lodge, now accompanied by Senator Alben Barkley, was met at the airport by U.S. Minister Selden Chapin and driven immediately to meet Hungarian President Zoltan Tildy ("Not a commie but a commie stooge," Lodge later wrote on September 26 in his pocket pad). Hungary's Foreign Office staff included a young liaison officer to the U.S. and British Allied Control Commission, Dr. Peter Stephaich. He was assigned to take Lodge by automobile to an official reception later that day. En route, the car broke down. Stephaich, a staunch anti-Communist, brusquely pushed John out of the vehicle and instructed the Hungarian driver: "You fix the car. I'll take this American gentleman to the dinner by taxi."

The problem with the auto gave Peter Stephaich a few hurried minutes to speak to Lodge without being overheard by any assigned drivers. "All our chauffeurs are secret police officers and can't be trusted," Stephaich whispered as they waited for a cab. "Your entire agenda is for show—a total fake. It's all arranged, complete with caviar and champagne, to give you Americans the impression that democracy is rapidly coming to Hungary. But it's just the opposite. The Soviets have overrun the country and are really in control."

"Why should I believe you?" asked John.

"Tomorrow, Mr. Lodge, we are going to see an ironworks. The man in charge will tell you in so many words that free enterprise prevails and all is fine and wonderful. Actually, many at the plant have been thrown into prison by the Communist regime. And the Russian grip is getting tighter. I know the speech well; I helped to write it. And it's all false."

Later, at the reception, Stephaich and Lodge managed a brief exchange of words: "If you ever need anything and run into a serious situation, Peter, let me know. I'll remember your name, and try to help you." John left word at the American Legation about Stephaich, who proved right about the rigged itinerary and the serious inroads by the Communists.

Later, as the Communist purges intensified during the winter of 1947-48, Peter passed a message to the U.S. Legation that he might need to flee Hungary. Would they help once he left the country? Then, on the eve of his marriage in Budapest, a friend from the Foreign Office informed Peter that he would be arrested the next morning. Without wasting a minute, he bolted the country with only the clothes on his back. He headed for Prague, where his brother was First Secretary at the Hungarian Embassy, then to Rome. Through Lodge's intervention, Peter, in order to gain admittance to the States, took a U.S. State Department exam as an "agricultural specialist." In America, his first job was milking cows in New Jersey. Lodge again helped Stephaich. He prepared special legislation to grant U.S. citizenship to the ex-diplomat. A few years later, at a dance in Philadelphia, Stephaich met Louise Hitchcock, daughter of the socially prominent and wealthy Peggy Mellon Hitchcock. They were married not long after.[6]

From Budapest, Lodge journeyed to Bucharest, capital of Romania. After a briefing by U.S. Minister Rudolf Schoenfeld, he visited the royal palace to see King Michael and his mother Queen Helen, the daughter of the late King Constantine of Greece. John had first met them before the war on the Adriatic island of Brioni. "The Queen & I had a good talk," Lodge jotted in his journal. "She is so brave & fine. Character, simplicity & real distinction. They are in danger. Had a long talk with the Maréchal de la Cour. The king must stay to the end—he is the people's only hope. But he must not stay too long." (Two months later Michael, the last reigning monarch in Eastern Europe, was forced by Soviet-backed Romanians to abdicate and leave his homeland.)

The next day, Lodge, who had been joined by Senator Carl Hatch of New Mexico and Congressman Walter Judd of Minnesota, landed at Sofia, Bulgaria. Briefings and a reception occupied the three legislators. But late that evening, they met alone. John had suggested that they make a stand for democracy in the totalitarian country. He urged the placing of a wreath on the new grave of Nikola Petkov, a patriot and peasant leader, hanged nine days earlier by the Communist-led Bulgarian government. "It would be a gesture of hope from freedom-loving Americans," he explained. "We would be acting as *individual* members of Congress in our visit to the grave site and *not* as representatives of the U.S. Government."[7] After a long and heated debate over the serious risk of incurring the wrath of Bulgarian officials, they agreed. A large green memorial wreath would be purchased with money out of their own pockets.

The next morning, Lodge, Hatch, and Judd surreptitiously lifted the wreath into a U.S. jeep. They followed it to the cemetery in another vehicle. With some difficulty, they found the unmarked grave of Petkov. Standing together, each stepped forward to say a few words in praise of the slain Bulgarian hero before they placed the wreath on the grave. They departed quickly for the airport and passage on a U.S. Air Transport Command flight to Istanbul. Once safely there, the U.S. Consulate, now aware of their act, announced the wreath-laying. The rest of the world soon read about the startling and dangerous gesture, and praised it.[8] The trio had risked injury, perhaps even imprisonment and death. When asked about it a few days later, in Turkey, Lodge declared, "We are as dispensable as anyone else."

Congressman Walter Judd, himself a courageous and dedicated humanitarian, legislator, and patriot, had warmly welcomed Lodge to a seat on the House Foreign Affairs Committee. John, he realized, had a unique affinity for Europe, not unlike his own attachment to China, where he had served as a tireless medical missionary before the war. And John understood the postwar problems overseas. "Lodge cared intensely about the issues of relief and reconstruction in Europe," Dr. Judd emphasized. "He knew the results of tyranny. Well-informed, intelligent and articulate, he crusaded on behalf of his convictions. Taking the stand in Sofia that Americans cared about patriots who died in the pursuit of their cause, Lodge also showed great courage."[9]

The Congressional fact-finding trip continued into October. At Istanbul, after a visit to Robert College, he noted that the institution, founded by Americans in the nineteenth century, played an important part in "Turkish rapprochement to Western culture, and paid enormous dividends." With that observation, perhaps he subconsciously skipped back into his 1939 French movie role as the old Sultan's adviser on Western ways. "We made a beginning with the U.S. Information Service," his notebook states. "If Turkey goes, the Middle East is gone as far as Suez. If Greece goes, Turkey is outflanked. We should help train Turkish and Greek Armies and Navies."

Lodge and Judd flew to Athens, then to Kavalla and Drama, where King Paul gave them an "amazing reception" and military briefing. The Greek King had the grace and dignity of his sister (and John's friend) Queen Helen of Romania, noted John. Paul reminded him of the tall and regal yet outgoing Duke of Aosta: "We drove with him in his Ford station wagon through cheering people. These people are unmistakably genuine in their enthusiasm. Their eyes light with joy. . . . They are going through so much in their battle vs. communism."

On his own, Congressman Lodge examined conditions in Italy, traveling by auto from Rome to Naples, Salerno, Milan, Turin, Trieste, and other cities. Meetings with Prime Minister De Gaspari and Cabinet ministers and an audience with Pope Pius XII gave him a firm and broad grasp of the perilous Italian situation. In the short run, it contained tremendous dangers. "If they don't get aid," he recorded, "Communist seizure is a threat." After brief stops in Warsaw, Berlin, Paris, Brussels, and London, Lodge sailed for home on the *Queen Mary*. By then he had been abroad for six arduous weeks.

President Truman had asked Congress to reconvene on November 17 to consider a request for stopgap aid of some $600 million to Europe. George Marshall had told him that Italy, France, and Austria could not survive beyond January 1948 without help. Lacking such immediate relief, Marshall's plan would be practically useless before Congress had a chance to consider and vote on it. In a special session of the House, Lodge spoke of a broad Communist surge, which, if successful, would take over Greece, Turkey, Italy, and the oil fields of the entire Middle East. He visualized a Communist coup in Italy in early 1948, "synchronized" with a general strike in France. He added that military and naval authorities in Europe had told him that Russia's armies could overrun all Europe in two weeks.[10]

John's grueling and eye-opening trip inspired a carefully thought-out address before the House. Called "The Challenge of the Hour," the talk on November 25, 1947 reminded his fellow legislators of the urgency to grapple with the problem on the basis of present realities. "It is sad that so soon after a terrible war we should be face to face with another great crisis," he declared in the most important and masterful address he ever delivered in Congress. "I say another, although in a sense the crisis is a continuing one. The age-old struggle for freedom is not yet won. It is hard for us after all the tragic losses in human life, the vast expenditure of national treasure, and the great Gethsemane through which we passed during the war years to find ourselves once more threatened with the dread menace of tyranny."[11]

The sixty-minute talk focused chiefly on Italy and its economic, political, and military weaknesses, and included an analysis of the need there for better and more effective U.S. Information Service cultural and information programs: "Let us make sure that these few remaining citadels of freedom do not become black and stinking hell holes of oppression languishing behind the 'iron curtain.' Let us meet the challenge of the hour. It is almost midnight in Europe. This is not time to grow tired. This is the time for action. The future is now. Mr. Speaker, this is the time for greatness."[12] Lodge's soul-stirring presentation of vital information and his earnest call for fast action influenced a positive vote on the Interim Aid Bill.

John's committee held public hearings with many Administration spokesmen and private citizens. The official record ultimately produced over 2,200 pages of testimony. The House group often worked around the clock to prepare its reports. Deputy to the assistant Secretary of State for economic affairs Paul H. Nitze, later senior arms control negotiator and adviser to several Presidents, recalls John's participation: "He was unconventionally right on the major issues, but uniformly wrong on the minor ones. He occasionally irritated committee members when he'd lecture them as if he were a professor and they, his students. All in all, the committee's report was the best analysis written on the Marshall Plan."[13]

The report concluded that non-Soviet Europe was now showing a genuine response to all realities of the proposed Marshall Plan. The recovery plan, it noted, depended upon certain political conditions, namely, the apparent limits to Communist expansion, the apparent willingness of European countries to collaborate to an unprecedented degree, and a willingness in Europe, collectively and in each country, to put its house in order. On April 2, 1948, both the House and Senate approved the Marshall Plan for the recovery of Europe. In the words of Lodge's confrère, Congressman Judd, the 80th Congress "turned the United States around, from a predominantly isolationistic country to one working as hard to keep the peace as it had to win the war."[14]

In a short time, Lodge had made many friends on both sides of the aisle as well as with the press. Much of his social life in Washington was spent in diplomatic circles where he and Francesca were frequent and welcome guests. They enjoyed being with foreign dignitaries and linked to affairs of world importance. He astounded many observers by switching from a broad New England accent to a flood of faultless French in order to explain American politics to a diplomat or foreign journalist.

The well-being of Europe had few advocates with greater vigor or enthusiasm than Congressman John Lodge. And of all the countries there, Italy was closest to John's heart. Hadn't the many Italian-Americans in Fairfield rallied to his side in the 1946 election? Didn't his attractive Italian-born wife win his heart as well as the admiration of many ethnic group voters in his district? Hadn't the music, dance, climate, and the very *joie de vivre* of old Italy fascinated him since his youth? The shaky state of affairs of that land in the tumultuous postwar years energized Lodge, and he sought to shield it from harm. It was a role he played well, to much acclaim and lasting gratitude, and it would occupy his days from the very beginning of his entrance into the halls of Congress to his leave-taking four years later.

In one particular speech, he vigorously attacked the Italian Peace Treaty. He urged that the treaty—and the peace accords with Hungary, Bulgaria, and Romania—be denounced, since Soviet Russia, a party to the agreement, had not abided by its terms since it was signed in January 1947. The agreement restricted Italy's armed forces, prescribed payment of over $350 million in reparations, and renounced her claims to former colonies. It was in the best interest of both the United States and Italy, he concluded, to object to the pact in view of the Soviets' continual attempts to interfere in Italy's internal affairs through bribery, intimidation, corruption, and coercion.[15]

In Congress he also sponsored legislation for the turning over of twenty-nine ships to Italy and backed a joint resolution providing for the return of some $15 million of Italian property in the United States. Later in the year, he wrote President Truman a letter to urge a stop to the scheduled withdrawal of U.S. troops from Italy. Lodge felt an American military presence would assure lines of communication and preserve the legality of the Italian government. He viewed the fall of Italy as an "immense loss in a strategic and material sense," one that would make the Vatican "a prisoner of the Reds."[16] Lodge also introduced a bill to increase U.S. immigration quotas for Italy, a successful measure that utilized the unused quotas of the past ten years. And in a speech on the floor of the House, he demanded that Russia return some 60,000 Italian prisoners.

Lodge also urged a review of the position of the United States if the anti-democratic forces prevailed in the upcoming Italian elections. The

White House, however, failed to react to his growing concern about the possibility of a Communist victory in the spring of 1948 and the loss of the country as a partner in the free world. But Francesca came up with an idea of her own. She initiated a country-wide campaign among Italian-Americans, urging them to write relatives in Italy and persuade them to vote against Communism. Over 10,000 people did so, including, of course, many Italians in Connecticut.

Not content with letters and cards alone, Francesca took to the air. She broadcast pleas in Italian over short-wave and recorded messages on discs for stations overseas; many were played in bars and cafés because many Italians lacked radios. It was the first election in which women had the right to vote, and Francesca believed that they would be the real balance of power. "Hold out," she declared. "Vote against Communist control. A Communist dictatorship will bring havoc to your country." Francesca next arranged for Italian-born Americans to record anti-Communist messages for short-wave broadcasts to Italy. With the cooperation of the World Wide Broadcasting Foundation, scores of Americans spoke directly to people in their old homeland. No more effective way to sell the advantages of democracy and free enterprise had ever been so personally conveyed. Italians voted overwhelmingly for democracy, and Premier De Gasperi's Christian Democratic Party won 48 percent of the vote.

As a member of the Foreign Affairs Committee, John was off again to Europe in 1948 at the request of chairman Charles Eaton. Once more, Italy was on the agenda for on-the-spot investigations, meetings with Premier De Gasperi and his Ministers of National Defense and Interior, conferences with U.S. Ambassador James Dunn and the local head of the Economic Cooperation Administration, and consultations with military leaders. On his return, John concluded that Italy's two chief problems were overpopulation along with a concurrent need for emigration and the ongoing threat of Communism. He encouraged a type of military lend-lease. "Peace is a product of strength," he emphasized, "while war is very often the derivative of weakness."[17]

Perhaps he was proudest of his part in bringing Italy into the North Atlantic Treaty Organization. An outgrowth of the Truman Doctrine and the Marshall Plan, the NATO alliance supported the principle of collective resistance and integrated defenses. When the treaty came to the Senate for ratification, word reached its chief proponent, Senator Arthur Vandenberg, and other key figures that France would not adhere to the agreement unless Italy was also a member. France, it seems, regarded Italy as the indispensable buffer between France and the whole communist world. Vandenberg was very reluctant to bring in the former Axis enemy and a country not on the Atlantic Coast. Yet his consent was crucial to muster a two-thirds vote for the treaty. John was approached, *sub rosa*, by his good friend Egidio Ortona, a junior secretary in the Italian Embassy, to help get his country into NATO. "John, unless you can do something about it, Italy will probably not be a member of the organization," said Ortona. For over a year, the two had shared their views on Italy and its participation in a Western alliance, sometimes when riding together by car, other times on horseback along Potomac trails.

John understood the tremendous influence his brother had over Vandenberg, who could tip the scales toward approval. John immediately called Cabot, a member of the Senate Foreign Relations Committee, and invited him and Emily to his Wardman Park apartment that evening "on a matter of the greatest urgency." They came, and John explained to Cabot why Italy should be in NATO.

"You listened patiently," John wrote in a letter to Cabot 35 years later, "and I could see that my arguments were having an effect in spite of Senator Vandenberg's argument that Italy is not an Atlantic nation. Indeed, they had such an effect that you transmitted your view to Senator Vandenberg. . . . He had such confidence in your judgment and such general admiration for you personally, that I believed your word in this matter was the decisive element. . . . I remember this so well because it was one incident in which you and I were able to collaborate most successfully. I found that a most satisfying experience."[18]

John's emotional advocacy of Italy's membership in NATO influenced his brother. Cabot, however, credits the role of General Alfred Gruenther, who was then deputy chief of staff for war plans and operations, as showing how crucial Italy was to the whole NATO concept. "To my mind, General Gruenther made an extremely strong case," Cabot recalled in a sheaf of unpublished recollections he called "Some Random Memories." "I was already leaning in favor of including Italy. After this presentation, I no longer had any doubts. After Gruenther and Gross [Assistant Secretary of State Ernest Gross] had left, I went looking for Senator Vandenberg and found him in the marble room in the Capitol, next to the Senate Chamber. I gave him the argument for the admission of Italy."

The next day the Foreign Relations Committee met, and before it was called to order, Vandenberg wrote a few words on a piece of paper, crumpled it up into a ball, and threw it across the table at Cabot. He opened it and read the words: "Italy will be in."[19] When the news of the Senate leader's about-face was received, France agreed to sign and NATO came into existence. Italy stood among the charter members in 1949. Cabot gave no official or unofficial credit to brother John for his role in the global turn of events. But Ortona, who would become Italian

Ambassador to the UN and the United States, acknowledged John's contribution in his memoirs. "In John Lodge," he writes, "were present all the components needed to make him an effective and active propagandist for Italian interest in the American Congress. . . . I worked with Lodge so that he would immediately put pressure on his brother."[20]

Time and again, John declared that the people of Italy represented a vital bulwark in the free world's defenses against communist imperialism. Most of Lodge's contributions to the postwar rebuilding and security of Italy were carried out in the halls of Congress; Francesca, however, took a grass-roots approach in helping her homeland. During a visit there with John in the fall of 1947, she saw thousands of crippled, orphaned, and hungry children. She immediately organized a campaign to raise money to aid Italian youngsters.

Francesca had learned about their needs from a modest, hardworking Irish priest, John Patrick Carroll-Abbing, at a child welfare center near Rome. Called Boys' Town of Italy, it had survived the last cruel winter of the war through gifts of food and clothing from American soldiers and their families. Things had been so desperate that the children were clothed only in rough wrapping paper held together by wire. Francesca lost no time in mustering emergency aid. She solicited funds throughout Connecticut for the construction of a dormitory and infirmary at Boys' Town. When Monsignor Carroll-Abbing wrote an account of the story of these beleaguered children called *A Chance to Live*, Lodge, then Governor, added these words about the genial priest in the book's foreword: "We find him deeply grateful that those who helped to meet the material wants of the children of Italy are now aiding him to minister to their minds and spirits. . . . Where some might have vilified and condemned, he has chosen to find essential goodness and promise."[21]

Lodge extended a warm and generous hand to war-torn Italy. The grateful nation remembered his support. In 1953 the Italian government made him a grand officer of "Al Merito della Republica" in recognition of his deep understanding of Italy's problems and for his effective contribution to the recovery and welfare of the Italian people. Lodge and George Marshall were among the first Americans designated for the award, one of Italy's highest honors. Ambassador Alberto Tarchiani presented the cross of this knighthood order at a ceremony and reception at the Italian Embassy in Washington.

Lodge's inter-cultural outlook focused on other lands in the late 1940s. The all-important Voice of America, he felt, broadcast too many weak and ambiguous pro-American programs. "The voice of America," he commented, "has been speaking with a frog in its throat." He was dismayed over the possibility that Congress might even consider discontinuing the entire overseas setup. At a luncheon at the Connecticut home of Elizabeth and Gordon Lamont, Lodge expressed concern. Mrs. Lamont spoke of another way of building understanding and friendship by Europeans for Americans. "Every day we throw away magazines and journals, even books," she declared. "This material shows pictures of our way of life, our freedom, our values of free enterprise. Couldn't we do something with this mountain of material? Why not send it overseas for foreigners to look at and perhaps read. What do you think, John?" "I believe it *could* serve as an invaluable way of communicating the American way of life," he concluded.

Lodge took up the idea with Senator Karl Mundt. The proposal was incorporated into the Smith-Mundt Act, also known as the U.S. Information and Educational Exchange Act of 1948. At Lodge's suggestion, Elizabeth Lamont wrote a summary on the organizational aspects of collection and distribution of discarded magazines and books. She received encouragement from General Lucius D. Clay, Military Governor of the U.S. Zone in Germany. With the backing of the Darien, Connecticut school superintendent, the local newspaper, Boy and Girl Scouts, and service clubs, U.S. magazines and books were collected. The Darien Book Aid Plan moved forward with the first shipment to Germany in January 1949.[22] For his help in Washington, especially lining up financial support for shipping the tons of material, Lodge became the Plan's patron saint. Soon the work of the Book Aid committee spread from Europe to North Africa, the Middle East, and Asia. By the 1990s, the independent person-to-person volunteer organization had distributed thousands of tons of good quality reading material to over 150 countries.

Lodge's record in Congress as "the man who gets things done" readily gained him renomination in 1948. His progressive leadership in foreign affairs and national defense, and, to a lesser extent, his views on such domestic concerns as high prices, housing, and taxes built up a strong following. But there were dissenters, and always would be. Called by some an overrated newcomer who relished the times a reporter, photographer, or influential person came within sight or sound, he shrugged the criticism aside. Even inveterate detractors had to admit that his Congressional record was not wholly discreditable, but then quickly added it was, of course, "decidedly undistinguished." Nonetheless, no one of substance in Democratic circles came forward to run against John Lodge. The task finally fell to an inexperienced yet well-educated New Englander with a background so similar to Lodge's that it bewildered and amused the citizens of Fairfield County. Moreover, it was a grudge match.

CHAPTER 13

Congressional Camaraderie

L odge's Democratic opponent, William Gaston, brought to the campaign of 1948 all the hoopla of vaudeville. A would-be playwright and dedicated playboy, the forty-nine-year-old rival had settled in Connecticut in 1939, just a year or so before Lodge. He, too, had ventured onto Wall Street after graduating from Harvard Law School and working in the District Attorney's office in Boston, his hometown. Like John, he attended Harvard College and served in the U.S. Navy (as an aviator in World War I). Moreover, Gaston knew both John and Francesca well before their marriage. Indeed, the dashing, albeit erratic, Brahmin had married Francesca's best friend, Rosamond Pinchot. The parallels between the Gastons and the Lodges did not end there. A Gaston opposing a Lodge in a political election was not new. Bill Gaston's father, a lawyer and banker, ran against John's grandfather for the U.S. Senate, losing by a small margin. "There is kind of a family feud on between me and Lodge," Gaston admitted to a reporter during the campaign. "I am out for revenge."[1]

If Gaston had earned any credibility as a viable candidate, it possibly stemmed from his efforts in the field of labor relations. He had served on the Textile Labor Relations Board when the National Recovery Administration of the New Deal was in its early stages.

Gaston lived chiefly from the income from a trust fund in a Boston bank, which, according to one member of his family, enabled him to pursue his principal interests in life: booze, broads, and boats.[2] On a political platform, he seemed affable with a pleasant speaking voice. Yet he generally evaded all factual material concerning issues and policies. Above all, he relished Lodge as his target. Gaston campaigned with nettling and undignified jingles and euphemisms making fun of his opponent's background, record, and demeanor.

John, on the other hand, wisely took the advice of Republican confrère Kenneth Bradley and refused to dignify Gaston's jabs and charges with any kind of a reply. When John declined to debate on the same platform, Gaston pugilistically pegged him "Dodging" Lodge, the "fugitive" candidate who ran away from face-to-face forums. Then he dubbed Lodge as the "flotsam and jetsam candidate who expects to ride in on the Republican tide."[3]

Turning to Lodge's family, the caustic Gaston declared: "In view of his very charming wife, his best asset, it would seem to me not inappropriate to dub him the petticoat candidate. In view of his distinguished senator grandfather and present senator brother, it would not seem inappropriate to dub him the coattail candidate."

John considered the great question of the 1948 presidential election to be whether the American people wanted to extend a "quarreling and disorderly" Democratic regime for another four years: "It is of utmost importance that we have an efficient and economical administration of the nation's affairs by government liberated from subversive Communist elements."[4]

On a platform, there was no denying that Lodge impressed most of the rank and file as a leader. An imposing, gregarious man whose dark eyes were alive with warmth and who talked with clipped accents, he would come into a room and take it over. If Lodge oft-times spoke predictable political rhetoric, his moving delivery did make a difference. Yet one or more of his backers periodically confronted him. Very worried over his demeanor, they'd say, "You've got to get away from this Harvard way of speaking and be more informal." So he'd try to project a bit of the personality of a good-time Charlie. Then, others would suggest he act less like a hail-fellow well met and be true to his Brahmin roots. They'd urge him to emulate his more subdued and statesman-like brother. He started declaiming in a somewhat pompous, overpowering, and almost bullying manner. And he'd end up losing a lot of his basic appeal and charm.

Once, when Lodge was haranguing a small, informal group of family and friends, Bud Eames, his old Harvard roommate, interrupted. "John, John, just a minute. I want to ask you a question. 'Do you buy your shirts like that, or do you stuff them yourself?' " "What? What?" questioned John. At first confused, he then realized the gist of Bud's deflating remark and laughed heartily over his overbearing discourse.[5]

Francesca often tried to bring him down a notch or two to the level of the man on the street. In 1948 she once again took an important part in the elections. She danced at rallies and sang and spoke in Italian. She handed out flyers. She wrote radio commercials for John with the themes "he knows the ropes" and "he's on the job for you." And she urged all women to vote, reminding them that 1,172,000 more women than men were of voting age in the country. The Republican presidential ticket of Thomas Dewey and Earl Warren benefitted from her sincere and energetic speech-making, too. On a national level, she joined party leaders in broadcasts aimed at changing the administration in Washington. "It's a good time to be alive, Republican and American," she concluded in her radio messages.

New York's Governor Dewey moved squarely to the forefront in his bid to oust Truman from the White House. Confidence in the President's leadership fell that year, and voters wanted a change, according to most polls. The self-assured Dewey rode high on a wave of widespread popularity and approval, and his party lined up solidly behind him. But the man from Missouri doggedly went to the grass-roots sections of the country and stated his case. Truman's whistle-stop "give 'em hell" crusade impressed the heartland. The stubbornness of the House refusal to support his programs of aid to housing and education led him to brand it the "no good, do nothing 80th Congress." The outcome of the election stumped all but a few of the experts and surprised many people. The feisty fellow who had succeeded Roosevelt walked off with a decisive victory in the greatest political upset of the century.

In Connecticut Dewey went against the tide and narrowly won the state. In the gubernatorial contest, Republican incumbent James C. Shannon and the candidate for Lieutenant Governor, Meade Alcorn, fell victims to Chester Bowles and running mate William Carroll by a slim margin of 2,285 votes. The Republicans also lost three of the state's six House seats. Among the winning Democrats was Abraham A. Ribicoff of Hartford. In the Fourth District, Lodge won a clear-cut victory over William Gaston, receiving a plurality of nearly 25,000 votes. When he returned to Washington for the opening session of the 81st Congress, he was now a member of the minority party. The Democrats had regained control, securing a majority of 93 in the House and 12 in the Senate.

John's popularity among his constituents and prominence beyond his district and state brought him many requests to speak throughout the country. In February 1949, he accepted speaking engagements in Indiana and Michigan. At Grand Rapids, at the request of fellow Congressman Gerald R. Ford, he gave the annual Lincoln Day dinner address. While there, Grand Rapids furniture manufacturers presented him with a dining room table made by local craftsmen.[6]

John's work on foreign affairs still required much attention. In April he addressed the house in support of legislation extending the Economic Cooperation Program. He witnessed the signing of the historic NATO pact, and a month later, he addressed a rally at Carnegie Hall sponsored by Common Cause, at which exiled leaders of every nation behind the Iron Curtain gathered to challenge Communism and pledge their unity to effect the liberation of their countries. In June he spoke to 1,800 guests at a fund-raising dinner of the New York State Republican Committee. His talk, "The Challenge to Lincoln's Party," urged "constructive alternates" to Democratic proposals. A week later, he flew to Salt Lake City to give the keynote talk at the National Convention of Young Republicans.

The House met during the summer of 1949. John proposed a bipartisan bill, known as the Lodge-Walter Amendment to the Mutual Defense Assistance Act, to provide $200 million in military aid to Chiang Kai-shek's pro-Western forces in China. The bill gave the administration the authority and funds for military assistance to those resisting Communism in the Far East. John met opposition; adversaries said the anti-Communists had lost the will to fight. "Certainly, we who urged them to make friends with the Reds can hardly blame those who no longer wish to fight them," Lodge replied. He pointed to Greek aid that proved successful in the Greek civil war. "It expresses our conviction that we cannot protect American national security by hunting with the hounds in Greece and running with the hare in China."[7]

The Truman Administration did not give the green light to the proposal of arms aid; almost every Republican voted for it, but only a few Democrats followed the example of co-sponsor Congressman Francis E. Walter. A bit later, the Senate authorized $75 million for mainland China. But the administration did not use the funds until mid-1950. By then, the Russians had sized up the situation and interpreted it as meaning that the United States would not make a real effort to help either China or Korea.

Two years later, after the Soviet-backed North Koreans had invaded South Korea, China had fallen to the Communists, and the United States had okayed arms and aid, Lodge recalled his incipient efforts. In a letter to Walter Judd, John recalled their efforts to save China from Communism and the Truman Administration's failure to act swiftly. "It would appear that they are about a year and a half late. The function of diplomacy, it has always seemed to me, is to anticipate trouble. Indeed, it might be said that diplomacy is successful insofar as troubles are prevented. The satisfaction which I might feel at this tragically late recognition of the realities of the situation in Asia is more than obliterated by the realization that had they heeded our pleas things might have been different."[8]

Turning to matters closer to home, Lodge supported a public housing bill providing for slum clearance and direct federal loans for privately owned low-income housing. It was a measure not unlike the legislation first introduced and passed by both houses in 1945. Yet, four years later, there was still a shortage of units. Many people with modest incomes continued to be priced out of the market, and others were unable to come up with an adequate down payment. Because private enterprise simply could not cope with the shortage of housing units, Lodge reluctantly favored federal intervention and voted for subsidized home-building. John remembered the House vote. Standing next to him was Noah Mason of Illinois, an elderly, short man with a very determined expression on his face. The public housing bill was carried by only four votes. "John, you ought to be ashamed of yourself," Mason lambasted. "You, a man who comes from an old American family with great dedication of public service. It really is dreadful that you should vote for this creeping socialism. What America needs is more men like Bob Taft!" "You jackass," snapped John, "this is Bob Taft's bill!"[9]

John also sought help in Congress for the problems facing industry in New England. He charged that Southern states, which received the lion's share of federal benefits, were using their government-supported economies to offer tax exemption inducements to New England firms to relocate in the South. He cited the government-sponsored move of United Aircraft's Chance Vought Division to Dallas, causing unemployment to some 8,000 Connecticut workers. "This can hardly be described as fair competition," he declared.

But his expertise in foreign matters took him away from regional problems by late summer. At the request of John Kee, chairman of the Foreign Affairs Committee, John left for Europe to observe European Recovery Plan operations in France and Italy and bring back data for legislative action. He visited the headquarters of Field Marshall Montgomery at Fontainebleau to ascertain what progress had been made on plans for the defense of Western Europe, and then made an extensive tour of Italian towns to check out ECA developments and progress in the battle against Communism. By September 22, he was back in Washington for the final weeks of the ten-month-long session of the 81st Congress and a vote in favor of Social Security amendments increasing benefit payments and extending coverage.

An imposing year of legislative meetings and debates, enactments and failures, 1949 spawned an unusual solidarity among the younger Republican members of the House. Many of these legislators had served in the war and took an overriding interest in a multi-billion-dollar Veterans' Pension bill backed by the American Legion. The Committee on Veterans' Affairs chairman, John Rankin, a Democrat, pushed the bill to a vote. To John and his circle of legislators, it had all the makings of a case of checkbook politics, backed by high-powered American Legion lobbyists. Congressman Glenn Davis of Wisconsin, then a member of the Committee, expressed concern about it to Donald Jackson of California.

They decided to call together a dozen or so of the other fledgling Republican members of the House to discuss strategy and tactics to oppose the bill, which already had the backing of GOP House leaders Joe Martin, Clarence Brown, and Charles Halleck. The first meeting was held in Don Jackson's office on a Wednesday afternoon at five o'clock. A heated yet productive discussion ensued. Attendees Richard Nixon, Charlie Potter, Norris Cotton, Kenneth Keating, Cale Boggs, Gerald Ford, and John Lodge emerged from the session united against the pensions. They planned a follow-up meeting on the following Wednesday.

"We were being treated by Joe Martin and Clarence Brown as just a bunch of warm bodies who gave the old bulls a majority," Glenn Davis later explained. "We were told how to vote and to keep our mouths shut. But most of us were vets with our own definite ideas and high ideals. This Wednesday group viewed the pension bill as bad legislation. Few of the Old Guard wanted to attack it. They didn't dare confront the large and powerful American Legion. But we stood up and helped to lick the bill—by just one vote."[10]

The opposition meetings congealed into weekly Wednesday afternoon gatherings. These young GOP lawmakers conferred on strategy for hearings, reports, bills, and amendments. Don Jackson referred to the group as the "Chowder and Marching Club," and the name stuck. Although no one has been able to determine the name's exact origin, Lodge might have tossed out the designation early on. In his first film, *The Woman Accused*, leading lady Nancy Carroll carries a banner with the words "The O'Brien Chowder and Marching Club."[11]

The Republican group quickly grew into an informal club with periodic social activities in members' offices, homes, and, as the group expanded, in downtown hotels and clubs, even in the White House. From that initial gathering in March 1949, the Chowder and Marching Club added a handful of Republican members from each new Congress. Forty years later, the aggregation had grown to over eighty past and present Congressmen, and had become a well-established and influential base of operations for young and not so young Republicans.

From the start, Lodge was an enthusiastic and loyal Club member. Glenn Davis remembered him as very likable, but initially very conscious of the fact he was a Lodge. The group decided to "humanize" John. Don Jackson arranged a dinner and movie party. Instead of a sneak preview of an unidentified new Hollywood film, he screened an old picture. The opening title and credits caught Lodge unaware. He and his colleagues viewed the vintage *Scarlet Empress* complete with the Dietrich-Lodge love-making in the hay. The good-hearted gathering gave John's friends a chance to razz him about his pre-House days of "heavy breathing" under klieg lights.[12] Many years later, in 1984, the Club again saluted charter member John Lodge. This time, at the Chowder and Marching's annual dinner, John, dressed in the members' traditional chef's hat and apron, became the recipient of the group's highest honor: a sommelier's chain, key, and taster. And there for the tribute were three U.S. Presidents: Nixon, Ford, and Reagan.

During his second term, Lodge spoke out as a progressive Republican. On *America's Town Meeting of the Air*, he debated the subject "What Should Be the Liberals' Program Now?," endeavoring, as the moderator George V. Denny, Jr., pointed out, "to find the true liberal among the speakers on tonight's program." Addressing his opening statement to Democratic Senator Paul H. Douglas, Lodge said that it was good to have divergent views within the two major parties. He continued: "I would not describe as liberal those Democratic politicians who oppose legislation on civil rights, on displaced persons, and on modification of the Taft-Hartley Law. But I do agree with your admonition that we should remember Lord Acton's formula that all power corrupts and absolute power corrupts absolutely. But Senator Douglas, we should also remember that the Democratic politicians have held great and increasing power in this country for many years." Then Lodge added: "The true liberal can find a spiritual home within the Republican party because it is, after all, the only political implement available to the American people in opposing the corruption of power to which you have so eloquently referred." A truly liberal program, Lodge concluded, must reflect the basic public interest and not destroy a free society which is the source of America's strength: "It is there that the real liberal must provide effective and constructive opposition."[13]

Early in 1950, Lodge criticized Administration efforts to silence Republicans in matters of foreign affairs in a speech before 1,100 members of the Women's National Republican Club in New York. A non-partisan supporter of foreign affairs legislation, Lodge declared that this position, however, should not deprive him or other Republicans of the "right to criticize or to disagree." He also urged Republicans to "carry the banner" on civil rights issues in the "best Republican tradition."[14]

That year Lodge took to the floor of the House to celebrate a milestone close to his family. On May 18, 1950, he noted the hundredth anniversary of his grandfather's birth. He spoke of Senator Lodge, President Wilson, and the Treaty of Versailles, and the misinformation that had been promulgated by historians as well as by the U.S. Government itself. "Indeed, ever since my grandfather's death some 25 years ago," John stated, "his name has been subjected to attack, vilification, and abuse based not upon the facts but upon . . . misinformation possessed by the Legislative Reference Service of the Library of Congress."[15]

John and his brother had been laboring to correct historical myths surrounding the opposition to the ratification of the Treaty of Versailles. The old Senator was not an "irreconcilable" nor part of "the little group of willful men" in the Senate, Lodge explained: "Unfortunately this lie has been widely believed and has in certain circles become a matter of historical acceptance. It is reasonable to suppose that those individuals who have spread this misinformation originally obtained it from the Library of Congress." Lodge set the record straight for the Library and urged its reference section directors to compile a balanced collection of works on Henry Cabot Lodge, Sr.[16] The Lodge brothers' public relations efforts on the old debate succeeded well. Even *Life* magazine shed new light on the matter in a well-illustrated layout with a text by Cabot. The article largely vindicated their grandfather's stand on the League issue.[17]

By the summer of 1950, John looked not to the past but to the immediate future. A gubernatorial convention in Hartford was taking him away from legislative debates in Washington. When it came time to move on to John's next challenge, his Capitol Hill colleagues expressed admiration for his accomplishments, his willingness to work hard, and his courage to persevere. Ohio's Frances Bolton went on record: "I do not know that there is anything finer that can be said of a man than that he is good to work with. You get to know him, you get to understand him, and then you are able to laugh with him, too."[18] Pointing to four years of close accord, Congressman Walter Judd described Lodge as a progressive conservative, like himself: "We were simpatico from the beginning of our friendship and collaboration."[19]

John relished opportunities for useful, far-reaching service as a Congressman—and the camaraderie, too. "There is," he concluded, "a basic sense of fellowship which suffuses all our doings and which in times of common stress and strain unites us in friendship."

CHAPTER 14

Affairs of State

T he Representative from Fairfield County stood quite apart from the ongoing infighting among his fellow Republicans back home. Lodge had successfully waged two congressional campaigns in his district and served his constituents well, but the thrust of his energies settled within the powerful Foreign Affairs Committee. After another term or so, he hoped that his high-profile position would gain him the post of committee chairman. Of course, he did not rule out a place in the Senate, the goal of many congressmen. Indeed, in 1950 there were the senatorial races in the making in Connecticut. And it was an election year for the governorship too.

By 1950 Connecticut had more people working, earning a greater income, and enjoying a higher standard of living than ever before. Although it had some 15,000 farms, Connecticut ranked as an industrial state. Over 400,000 factory workers within a population of two million people produced an estimated three to four billion dollars worth of goods (aircraft engines, silverware, firearms, clocks and watches, ball bearings, hats). During the war, an influx of workers came in, attracted by high-paying defense jobs. The majority stayed. Only a severe housing shortage and a need for more schools, hospitals, and roads curtailed the state's overall growth.

The third smallest state in area, Connecticut was governed from Hartford, its largest city (177,000 people). Pride in thriftiness kept taxes comparatively low. The state boasted of its charm and individuality. Many accomplished and prominent persons called Connecticut home; it had a higher percentage of names in *Who's Who* than any other state. And these newcomers generally thrived under the state motto "Qui Transtulit Sustinet" (He who transplanted us sustains us).

Politically, all was not well in the so-called "Land of Steady Habits." There was a crack in the traditionally solid stone wall of Connecticut

Republicanism. A split had developed between the old party leaders and the new, between upstate and down, between time-honored conservatism and forward-looking progressivism. And John Lodge found himself squarely in the middle of this struggle in his own party. One schism stemmed from the actions of the state's Republican figurehead.

In 1949 Democratic Governor Chester Bowles made a deal with Republican Senator Raymond Baldwin. The Senator and his wife Edith disliked living in Washington, and he wanted to resign. Senator Baldwin felt he could not repay his many social obligations properly to the likes of Saltonstall, Symington, and McMahon, all of whom had private means. He lived on his paycheck of $15,000 a year.[1] But he still wanted a job back home. If Baldwin gave up his seat on Capitol Hill to a Bowles-appointed Democrat, would Bowles, in turn, appoint him a judge of the Connecticut Supreme Court? Bowles agreed to the switch. In no time at all, Republican cries of "sellout" echoed from Greenwich to Norwich.

The senatorial post went to Bowles's former ad agency partner and onetime Assistant Secretary of State William Benton. The appointment came with strings; Benton would waste no time in building up a strong base from which to run for election the following year.[2] On the Republican side, there were at least a half-dozen contenders: retired General Leslie R. Groves, Congressman James T. Patterson, former Representative Clare Boothe Luce, investment banker Prescott Bush, three-term Congressman Joseph Talbot, and John Lodge. Governor Bowles's two-year term was ending, and the state also would vote for its first governor with a four-year term. Lodge wondered what his chances were for higher office in 1950. One day at an informal dinner party, he asked Kay Smith, wife of Col. Truman Smith: "Kay, which should I run for: the Senate or the Governorship?" "Tell me, John," she replied frankly, "from which position is it more advantageous for you to run for President?" John drew back and stared at her. "Something in his eyes conveyed the fact that I had touched an issue that he had been pondering over," Kay Smith always remembered.[3]

Lodge's presidential prospects evidently had been mentioned at home. Twelve-year-old Beatrice let her friends in on her father's future hopes. At John's twenty-fifth class reunion at Harvard that year, Beatrice joined offspring of his classmates at various activities to occupy their time. Someone asked her what her father did, and she replied, "He's the next Governor of Connecticut, and he's going to be the President of the United States." Ten-year-old Wendy Marcus of Dallas, daughter of Stanley Marcus, overheard her remark and piped up. "That's nothing. My father *is* President *now* of Neiman-Marcus."[4]

Lodge had been "discovered" and sent to Congress in large part by the staunch Republican Old Guard which was still engaged in a futile search for a way to bury the ghost of the New Deal. It was assumed that John would reflect the irremovable political attitude of his Fairfield sponsors. But clearly after the 1948 Democratic sweep, it became evident he had a mind of his own. He joined a resourceful rebel group which gave birth to the "radical" idea that the GOP would fare better if it got rid of its ultra-conservatism. Lodge more or less came to the conclusion that his rise on the national scene could come about by staying in Congress. It did not seem a good year for Connecticut Republicans running for higher office. He anticipated his third Congressional campaign. But his party had other ideas. Apparently an influential segment decided not to back Lodge for this contest. Many had had enough of his growing independence and theatrical flair as well as his comparative disinterest in grass-roots matters. GOP kingpins delivered the word: run for re-election to Congress without total party backing, or take on Governor Bowles with their support.[5]

Lodge weighed his chances against Chester Bowles. The incumbent in a short period had become a dynamic and highly visible administrator. He had started an advertising agency in New York five years after graduating from Yale in 1924. Benton & Bowles flourished, capitalizing on the growth of network radio and consumer magazines. By 1940 both Bowles and his partner William Benton had retired with a fortune to pursue other interests. The future governor, who kept a weekend home in Essex, entered public service as Connecticut's rationing administrator. In 1943 President Roosevelt named him head of the Office of Price Administration in Washington.

In 1946 he announced his candidacy for the Democratic nomination for governor, with support chiefly from trade union leaders, school teachers, and older low-income people. But he generated little backing from the state organization and its resourceful and undisputed leader John Bailey of Hartford (who had been with Lodge in the class of 1929 at Harvard Law School). Bowles lost out to Wesleyan University English professor Wilbert Snow. After the convention, Bailey moved into the Democratic State chairmanship. Snow went down in defeat against Republican James McConaughy, who initiated a broad program of needed postwar legislation.

Bowles devoted the next eighteen months to studying Connecticut's shortcomings in housing, education, health care, wages, and recreation. He spoke to innumerable clubs and groups, often meeting local Democratic leaders during his travels. Early in 1948, he again decided to seek the governorship. "I suspected that the sudden interest some key Connecticut politicians were also showing in my candidacy for Governor," he recalled in a political autobiography, "reflected their belief that the Democratic Party was headed for another disastrous defeat and that 1948, like 1946, was a good year to get rid of the remaining Rooseveltian liberals."[6]

With John Bailey's all-embracing support this time, Bowles won the nomination by acclamation. In his acceptance speech, he reviewed the many New Deal-type programs he would undertake if elected over Governor James Shannon (who had succeeded McConaughy upon his sudden death in March 1948). Bowles committed himself to tackle each and every problem of the Nutmeg State. With President Truman running far behind in the national polls, a Connecticut survey pointed to the overwhelming defeat of Bowles by some 220,000 votes, more than double the majority by which anyone had ever been defeated for public office in the state. According to the poll, citizens wanted a better organized and more efficient government, plus many of the programs Bowles proposed. In effect, the people said, "we don't want a Democratic Administration, but we want the things the Democrats stand for." Bowles was now convinced he would not win. The opposition described him as a "carpet-bagger" and "rich visiting yachtsman from New York." It played on his feelings that defeat lay ahead.

No one was more surprised than Bowles himself when he won. His margin of victory was slim, about 2,250 votes. When inauguration day arrived, the Republican-controlled House was in a mass huddle. Anyone becoming governor by so slight a margin might not, they cried, have been honestly elected. The House angled to continue Governor Shannon in office during a thorough investigation of that scant pro-Bowles margin. The House met great pressure to accept the election vote count. Nevertheless, Bowles' inauguration was delayed six hours.

Bowles's term as governor ranks as one of the stormiest of the century. The House constantly locked horns with him on almost every one of his proposals. He pushed a tax reform package that called for abolition of the sales tax and establishment of a personal income tax. That step made few friends on either side of the aisle. He met more success with construction programs for low-cost housing, mental hospitals, and schools. Yet the Republicans blocked or trimmed back practically all his public works plans. "This progression from Bowles' broad-scale legislative proposals to stalemate to explosion became the norm during the rest of Bowles' administration," writes Joseph Lieberman in his book on Connecticut politics, *The Legacy*. "At times more was accomplished, at times more exploded but the general trend continued. Always moving, always throwing off ideas, Governor Bowles managed to call five special sessions before it was time to face his second election day in November 1950."[7]

Six months earlier, in April 1950, John Lodge attended a dinner with 1,000 Republicans in Manchester, Connecticut. Would he make a move toward the nomination, they asked each other. "I have closed no doors," he replied to a question on his plans. "I hope to have the privilege of serving the'people of Connecticut in whatever capacity they may feel I can be most useful to them."[8]

Years later Francesca admitted that John knew very little about what was going on politically state-wide in Connecticut, who were their supporters, and whether they were honest: "I reminded John that the governorship was an administrative job, similar to corporate law, and not an area he particularly liked. He agreed, but he viewed the contest as a challenge, as were films and the Navy. He was civic-minded and loved Connecticut and its people. Nevertheless, I talked against it. He'd risk the near-certainty of a seat in Congress for a precarious run for governor. He jokingly said that if he lost that race, he could go back to the movies, and play old gentleman roles."

Vying for the governor's chair were two other Republicans: former Governor Shannon and Republican national committeeman Kenneth Bradley. Both lived in Fairfield. The County's Republican leader, William H. Brennan, now faced a choice of three local residents; a professional politician, he stayed neutral, at least publicly. An affluent Fairfield group controlled party finances and from such strength maneuvered to hand-pick a candidate from its area. The Hartford leadership, however, discounted urbane lawyer Bradley. Lodge seemed the easiest to handle, so they thought. Moreover, they viewed his chances to beat Bowles in a dim light. Lodge, the Fairfield Congressman, stood as a readily expendable scapegoat.

Having selected their underdog, they now had to get Lodge the nomination. For awhile, they met little opposition. A newspaper poll gave John a sizable surplus of delegates' votes. But a week or so before the convention, his strength started to drift away. Bradley, an avowed candidate, picked up votes. An upstate entrant, businessman William A. Purtell of Hartford, who had not even been a registered Republican until six months before, gained support. Pro-Lodge leaders were panicky the evening of June 14, when the convention opened in the Shubert Theatre, New Haven. John's three opponents sought to block him on the first ballot.

In the early morning of June 15, the situation looked so precarious for Lodge that party chiefs began to talk of a last-minute switch, naming ex-Congressman Joseph Talbot for governor and having John run for one of the Senate seats, probably against Senator Bill Benton. They called a meeting in a room at the Hotel Taft. But Lodge would have no part of the last-minute shift. Drawing himself up, throwing his head back in an imperious gesture, he informed them: "A friend of mine, who knows politics much better than I do, warned me against becoming a candidate. 'At four in the morning, in a hotel room,' he told me, 'you'll be counted out.' " Lodge the actor glanced at his watch. "It happens, gentlemen, to be just four A.M. I will not take the nomination for Senator."[9] John's steadfastness had just the right effect. Everyone in the room laughed. The group decided to go on with their original slate. John won the nomination later that day with 358 votes to Bradley's 134, Purtell's 99, and Shannon's 14.

A few hours after the nomination, a development came about at the convention which served as a warning that Lodge faced unfamiliar hurdles in state politics. The Republican who had rounded up many delegates' votes for Lodge and held the delegates in line was state Attorney General William Hadden, a candidate for re-election but not yet nominated. Just after Lodge's victory, he unwittingly became party to a political scheme. A cast off candidate, probably Bradley, convinced Lodge allies Bill Brennan and Clarence (Cappy) Baldwin, who was now state chairman, to turn against Hadden and hand George Conway, Republican majority leader in the state House, the nomination for attorney general. Lodge protested but couldn't save his friend.[10]

Years later, Lodge admitted he faced a power struggle that manifested itself at the convention and caused certain people to be dropped overboard: "I had nothing to do with it, absolutely, literally nothing. It's been supposed by some people that I did have something to do with it, because the nominee for governor very often has a lot to do with picking his running mates. In this case, it was all done by the state organization, including their picking me. It resulted in some bitter feeling, and had some eventual by-products which were very hard to handle because they caused a split in the party. This split in the party came before me and lasted far after me."[11]

From the stage of the Shubert Theatre, where he had performed a decade earlier as actor John Lodge, the intrepid candidate accepted his party's mantle with forthrightness and determination. "No political strings of any kind are attached to my candidacy," he stated. "I have but two obligations: First, to conduct an aggressive, hard-hitting, resourceful campaign in every corner of the state—a campaign based on principle rather than on expediency. I pledge myself to that end. And second, as Governor of this great state, to devote my time, my energy, and my faithfulness to the service of the people of Connecticut."[12]

John readily endorsed the party platform of increased benefits for labor, agriculture, education, public health, and the unemployed, and called for a broadened base of political participation. He also favored a reorganization plan to equalize representation in the Connecticut House to one member from each town, an equitable reapportionment in the Senate, and a dual-job ban for legislators who simultaneously held salaried positions in state judicial or administrative departments.

Two sad events in the wake of the convention influenced state politics and the election. Only days after John's acceptance speech, Republican strategist and Lodge backer Harold Mitchell died suddenly at home in Hartford, publicly reported as a heart attack but privately whispered as a suicide in the wake of his losing out as a party leader in the Hadden-Conway imbroglio. Gone was a force that might have united the party in the battles that loomed ahead. Brennan quickly became John's choice to fill out Mitchell's term as national committeeman until the National Convention in 1952.

Less than a week later, North Korean Communist troops marched southward, and suddenly Americans were fighting on that Asian peninsula. On June 30, at a Republican Club gathering in Teddy Roosevelt's old hometown, Oyster Bay, New York, John likened the Communist threat to an iceberg whose vast bulk lies unseen beneath the ocean's surface. He urged the Administration to resist Communist aggression everywhere and made it clear that there was no room for partisan politics in the field of foreign affairs.

The hostilities in Korea took John back to Washington. An emergency session of Congress charted the mobilization of America, including extension of the military draft. His familiarity with world affairs gained support for his bid for higher office. In July John suggested the convening of a special session of the Connecticut State Assembly to create a State Council of Defense. Not until August did he break away from Washington to campaign. John's greatest weakness soon came to the forefront: his lack of familiarity with overall state matters. Moreover, he was not well known in certain areas of Connecticut, especially the northern and eastern parts.

State Senator Charles S. House recalls the early part of the campaign: "We advised Lodge not to get into debates with Governor Bowles, who knew so much about Connecticut. We really weren't sure how knowledgeable John was with the ins and outs of the state. For example, the town of Mansfield includes the state mental institution, and we wondered the outcome if a voter asked him 'what are you going to do about Mansfield?' Lodge might have replied, 'Who's he? What's the matter with him?' "[13]

While John brought a tremendous stage presence to the campaign trail, his movie background was deemed a negative factor among many Yankee voters. Fairfield neighbors looked upon theatrical ties with little or no distrust; other parts of Connecticut were not so broadminded. In the land of the sedate, the self-righteous, and the simple virtue, it was said with some derision, you couldn't get ten votes if you had ever gone to a musical comedy or played poker with the shades up.[14]

John downplayed his acting career in press releases and official biographies. They merely referred to the post-Wall Street period of his life in these words: "subsequently he was employed by motion picture companies." The stress was on his military service and, of course, his record in Congress. In any event, John Bailey attacked Lodge by blasts in the form of a critic's review of a play or movie. He claimed Lodge's interest on certain issues was "out of character" or "heavy on tinsel."[15]

Bowles capitalized on his well-earned reputation as a wartime OPA leader. He deplored price boosts and proposed inflation cures. But from Hartford he didn't deliver. Lodge seized on this failed promise and built a case that Bowles was merely glib and totally inconsistent, and couldn't be relied upon to get things done. And so John's staff came up with the Lodge slogan: "A man you can believe."

John generally spoke in broad terms about the Republican platform, less about its specific planks. He had a natural inclination to make campaign issues seem either too deep or too shallow. He depicted the Republicans as "a bold and enlightened party." Apparently he taxed the patience of many political pros, who considered him their creation. He made it clear *he* was their savior.

Lodge repeatedly pinched the opposition's raw nerve. Bowles' membership in the Americans for Democratic Action (he was a founder and national officer) trapped the Governor. Lodge implied over and over that the liberal ADA was riddled with Communism and Bowles had leaned so far to the left that he was nearly in the camp of the Red menace. Bowles' platform rocked when the ADA urged the UN to withdraw recognition from Nationalist China and hand its seat to Red China.[16] Time and again, Lodge asked about the source of money to finance Bowles's many social programs. The tax revenues actually had dropped so low in 1951 that the state could not pay all its bills. The state's need to borrow month by month became another widely touted issue.

In early October, the two candidates met in a face-to-face debate under the sponsorship of the League of Women Voters. Lodge pulled himself out of bed to keep the date. He had a viral infection and fever of 102 degrees. The Windsor high school auditorium, jam-packed with 600 persons, grew hotter as each candidate clashed and blamed the other for every ill wind in the state.

Bowles raised the charge that State Treasurer Joseph Adorno had blackmailed him. Republican Adorno, he claimed, refused to pay state employees unless the Governor gave him authority to borrow from the banks during the summer low ebb of incoming tax income. Lodge knew Bowles had made a *faux pas*. He seized the moment and leaped to his feet: "I want to say that Joe Adorno, though just *accused* of blackmail, did not tell me about any such conference with the Governor."[17] The Democrats quickly realized that they had lost a sizable block of votes, especially among Adorno's fellow Italian-Americans.

Bowles struck back, calling Lodge a "Hollywood stranger" and "celluloid candidate." John retorted, describing Bowles as "opportunist," "free-spending," and "left-wing." The race made news far beyond the Nutmeg State. A former actor and an ex-adman were at each other's neck. And vying for a Senate seat stood a musically-minded Wall Street banker (Prescott Bush) and a tried and true Madison Avenue magnate (Bill Benton).

Francesca, too, stepped into the political fracas and at times played a soothing role. She actually launched her husband's gubernatorial campaign when he was forced to remain in Washington to attend to congressional duties. With unflagging vigor, she personally engineered the political train, kept it on track, running it on schedule, and picking up "passengers" until her husband was free of his Capitol Hill chores.

Some days Francesca traveled 300 miles, 16 to 18 hours non-stop. At home, bedlam prevailed. Clerk-stenographer William Siering and campaign manager Ray Watt had set up headquarters there. Telephones and door bells rang at all hours of the day and night. So constant was the noise that the Lodge dogs didn't bother to bark.

Once again on a Columbus Day, Francesca stole the show. To get to a rally in New Britain from a GOP dinner in Bridgeport, a distance of about fifty miles, she hailed a campaign sound truck. She needed a ride immediately, she explained. She had to arrive on time and hold the audience until John appeared. The driver agreed. In New Britain, she regaled an anxious crowd with stories of her childhood in Florence—and Christopher Columbus' in Genoa! "The campaign agenda was grueling," she admitted, "although exhilarating and exciting. I had all the fun; John, all the responsibilities."[18] One day, at a meeting at home between John and a political boss of questionable tactics, Francesca overheard the conversation. She sensed serious trouble if John agreed to ally himself with this particular fellow. She managed to warn him from an adjacent room by singing an Italian song with certain words conveying danger ahead.[19]

Periodically, the Lodges faced charges that they were catering and kowtowing to the Italians, Poles, French, Hungarians, and other nationalities. Attacks on Francesca and her gestures to get minority group votes spread. John answered back: "I feel it is just and honorable for one to love the land of his forebears. And I see nothing wrong in talking to people of any descent. They have their organizations, but they are first-rate Americans and naturally I have talked to them about things that would interest them. I cannot believe it divides the Poles, Hungarians or Jews to talk about problems they're interested in."[20]

The biggest rally of the campaign took place in the New Haven Arena. Over 7,000 exuberant Lodge supporters braved heavy rain to crowd into the hall and receive a welcome from the master of ceremonies, actor William Gaxton, who had been waging a one-man campaign to convince people of John's ability to run their state. That night Cabot made his only appearance in Connecticut to back his brother. His support seemed less than enthusiastic; his remarks, rather arch. "I have, of course, not come to Connecticut to tell you how to vote," he said, "because the citizens of this state are perfectly able to make up their minds for themselves without outside assistance. But I do hope that it will come as no surprise to any of you to hear me say that I would indeed be pleased to learn that, if you do happen to decide to vote Republican this year, that you had included a vote for my brother, the Republican candidate for Governor."[21]

A private statewide poll assured Bowles that he would carry Fairfield County, which no Democrat had since Governor Wilbur Cross in 1930, and, in turn, the rest of the state. This good news as a "shoo-in" had a debilitating effect on the Bowles campaign. "Since I seemed to be comfortably ahead, in all probability once the frenzy and the fury of the election were over," he recalled in his autobiography, "I would be the Governor for the next four years, no matter what I did during the campaign."[22]

On Election Day, more than 850,000 people turned out to vote in that off-year election—a greater than usual number, due in no small measure to political manipulator John Bailey's efforts among Democratic leaders to create widespread interest in keeping control of the governorship as well as both Senate seats. Bowles won by comfortable margins in the major cities, but as the evening progressed, the votes in the smaller towns and cities whittled away his lead. By 10:30 P.M., it was clear that Bowles had lost to Lodge. John's margin of victory reached 17,000. Senator MacMahon won easily over former Congressman Joe Talbot. Republican Al Morano, long eager to occupy Mrs. Luce's and John's seat in Congress, won in the Fourth District. In the nip and tuck contest between Benton and Bush, the outcome was too close to call.

On the Sunday before the election, Benton's people handed out leaflets in front of Catholic churches as worshippers left services. "Be sure to listen to Drew Pearson tonight at 6 P.M. for important news," the flyer announced. That night the influential radio commentator raised the question of Bush's ties to Planned Parenthood, anathema to many Catholics at the time. "It was a signal for Catholics to vote against Dad," Bush's son, Prescott, Jr., explains. "Actually my father's banking firm only handled the funds for the group. He had no involvement with Planned Parenthood policy; the money just came through his company. But he was a managing partner of Brown Brothers Harriman, and that was enough association to taint him in the eyes of many Catholics."[23] By midnight, Benton had beaten Prescott Bush by a narrow edge of 1,102 votes.

John had fought against a nationally known and powerful incumbent. "Bowles knew all about state government," Lodge admitted. "But he couldn't resist the temptation to take me on in the field of foreign affairs about which I had a considerable amount of current knowledge at that point. If he had challenged me in the field of state affairs, things might have come out differently."[24]

The overconfident Bowles in two short years had tried to do too much too quickly in "the land of steady habits." Bailey realized that Connecticut was not quite ready to march in the vanguard of progressive state governments. The GOP House had used every means to block his program. Bowles' defeat shattered his dream of winning his party's nomination for President in 1952; for all intents and purposes, it ended his political leadership. In 1951, Truman appointed Bowles as Ambassador to India. Seven years later, he was elected Congressman from Connecticut's Second District and served one term. Bitter and antagonistic toward Lodge, he never forgot that John torpedoed his political rise. Bowles viewed the opposition's campaign tactics as unethical mud-slinging and deplorable character assassinations. John took comfort in the words of nineteenth century essayist and biographer Thomas Carlyle: "No man lives without jostling and being jostled; in all ways he has to elbow himself through the world, giving and receiving offense."

A *New Haven Register* editorial pointed out that the election served definite notice that the people wanted, above all things, a Connecticut administration for Connecticut people: "It reveals at the same time the full extent of their opposition to an Administration that gave the State two years of bitter wrangling, of surrender to pressure group demands and all the costly cash appropriations, bond issues, borrowing and deficits that went with it." The paper also noted that the voters gave the new Republican governor a heavy majority in the lower house of the General Assembly and an almost even split in the State Senate of 17 to 19. The incoming administration, it added, would be faced with many trying problems—industrial, civic, economic, administrative, budgetary. "It is just as clear that these will offer no easy or ready-made blueprint for solution."[25]

The *Hartford Times* summed up John's status in the capital: "Mr. Lodge is unfamiliar with Connecticut and lacks experience in State affairs. We believe him to be a man of character and of excellent ability. His test will come when he has to show whether he proposes to stand upon his own feet and make his own decisions or let his party organization run the State."[26]

On election night, John delayed his appearance at GOP headquarters in Hartford, which had been full of apathy and gloom as Bowles carried the city by 24,000 votes. "I feel numb," Francesca remarked while waiting for the final tally. "I feel as though I'm having an operation without anesthesia." She expressed the thought that "kites rise against and not with the wind—maybe John's going to be a kite." Not until there was no doubt that he had been elected did John and his family emerge from their suite at the Hotel Bond. At that point, he made a triumphal entrance in the best tradition of the theatre. John, with Francesca and Lily and Beatrice dressed in red plaid mother-and-daughter dresses bedecked with tiny elephants, took full advantage of the "props" and "scenery." They made straight for a balcony. With arms up-flung in a victory salute, John and Francesca beamed down on the smiling upturned faces of rank-and-file supporters.

In the dizzy political swirl of the night and following day, hundreds of telegrams, letters, cards, and notes of congratulations reached the Lodges. Fifty-five Harvard classmates had contributed to his campaign in a drive spearheaded by Brooks Harlow, Mike Cowles, and Dick Aldrich. Their praise, along with a message from "all the foxes" of Harvard's Fox Club, thrilled John, as did his mother's wire: "Magnificent blessings on you both."

From his Lt. Gov. Edward N. Allen, John received personal regards—and a portent of trouble on the horizon. "Off the record," Allen added, "I'm beginning to think that we're liable to have more trouble with some of our Republican friends than we will have with the Democrats."[27]

Before Lodge's term in Congress ended, a special session of Congress on Red China's military presence in the Korean War was being discussed by the White House. John kept one ear tuned to Washington; the other, to Hartford. His top aides took a close pre-inauguration look at Connecticut's finances and discovered a multi-million dollar shortfall in revenues. They warned of the need for an emergency austerity program. The sudden deficit stymied Republican promises of new spending programs for education and medical care, and of no new taxes or tax increases.

As the Lodges prepared to move from Villa Lodge to the Governor's residence, a Hartford newspaper wondered whether naval reservist Lodge might be called back to active duty in Korea. The Navy gave an answer: as long as he was in office, a recall was most unlikely. And the *Bridgeport Herald* editorial staff selected Francesca as Woman of the Year (and Senator Brien McMahon as Man of the Year). A personality in her own right, the paper noted, she introduced something new to politics: "As scornful as more serious politicians may be of Mrs. Lodge's determined antics, she probably did more than any other one person to get her husband nominated and elected."[28]

At midday on January 3, 1951, Lodge arrived at the State House, accompanied by the colorful Governor's Horse Guards. A nineteen-gun salute startled their mounts. While horses jumped, legislators stood pat. The Democratic-controlled Senate—19 to 17—wrangled and then recessed all day in an atmosphere of bitter partisanship. It battled with the Republican-dominated House over the adoption of rules. Traditionally, the governor took office on the first day of the legislative session. The usual business of the General Assembly prior to the swearing-in was merely to organize itself and validate the election returns. The Senate now refused to agree with the House and to participate in the ceremonies.

Democratic kingpin John Bailey demanded a provision that would require a two-thirds vote of the Senate to suspend the rules. Republicans wanted a simple majority to take advantage of a possible switch of one or two Democrats to their ranks on a future vote. "To Bailey," records his biographer Joseph Lieberman, "this matter was of critical importance because the rules are suspended, especially at the end of a session, to bring bills out of committee and onto the floor for a vote. Since much of Bailey's leverage in the legislature was based on his ability to bottle up Republican measures in Senate committees, he was not willing to enable Republicans to overcome this obstacle by taking just one voter from Democratic ranks."[29]

The Republicans refused, so the opposition decided not to validate the votes which had elected Lodge. He had arrived at the capitol building at two P.M., ready to take over from Bowles. But hour after hour passed without any break in the political impasse. At four the House went into recess for ninety minutes. Meantime, John in cutaway and striped pants waited and paced.

The capitol corridors were filled with anxious and curious bystanders, all impatient at the logjam. Inaugural guests in evening clothes soon joined officials in business suits. During the legislative bickering, the Governor's Foot Guard played almost continuously. In the midst of the music, a passenger elevator stuck between floors. Fifteen men and women were rescued through a trap door in the top of the elevator. Cabot and Emily Lodge also waited for John's inauguration, but at nightfall they grew weary and left for Washington. Norman Allen, hungry twelve-year-old son of the Lieutenant Governor-elect, went off to the building's cafeteria. He brought back tea and the last bit of ice cream. Lodge's official celebration at the Hartford Club, postponed again and again, was called off at ten P.M.[30]

Throughout the waiting, Francesca felt helpless. It struck her as the opposite of a gala event. "On an opening night," she observed, "a performer feels the responsibility and gets into the spirit of giving. I want to move around and do something. But I find myself on the receiving end and not knowing exactly what I am going to receive."

John's advisers explained that the state constitution provided all officers be sworn in before a joint session of both Houses. Finally, Bailey said his party would not question the legality of "a one-house inauguration." A backhanded go-ahead. Shortly before midnight, after ten hours of feuding, the exasperated House Majority Leader Louis Shapiro made up his mind. One way or another, Lodge would be sworn in. Most Democrats refused to attend the ceremony. John, patiently waiting his cue in the wings, came center-stage. The biggest trouper of all, he took the situation in stride. He may have wondered whether his old Federalist Griswold forebears, Connecticut Governors Matthew and Roger Griswold, had met such turmoil in taking the oath of the state's highest office.

At 11:52 P.M., Chief Justice Allyn Brown, State Supreme Court of Errors, swore in the forty-seven-year-old John Lodge. Republican legislators and officials, together with their families, stood by as the end of a long and excruciating day drew near. John's inaugural address ironically stressed the need of the state to face the unpalatable task of separating the essential from the nonessential: "Harsh, unadorned necessity must rule our every decision. To adopt any less rigorous—any less realistic policy, would be a dangerous luxury." He voiced concern over a nation in peril because of the brutal Korean War and threatening Soviet imperialism. He viewed Connecticut's security at stake because of its aircraft and firearms production. As a famous arsenal of the nation, it brings, "not only opportunity, but also anxiety and hazard from Communists and saboteurs."[31]

Downstairs, in the huge columned entrance hall, a reception had been scheduled for the previous afternoon. The polished floor was now littered with cigarette butts, food wrappers and beverage containers. Six cushioned chairs, scattered about the room, were further reminders of plans gone amok. A week later, the Senate grudgingly validated the vote count. John Lodge officially took over as the seventy-fifth Governor of Connecticut.

The New York Times had a final word. In an editorial entitled "Connecticut Follies," it called the inaugural day proceedings childish: "The obvious assumption that this time the Democrats were taking revenge for what the Republicans did last time merely leads one to the conclusion that many members of both parties in the Connecticut legislature need a lesson in elementary patriotism."[32]

In the months ahead, John may have thought himself its teacher.

JOHN LODGE

A Photographic Record

John Lodge, Harvard '25.

The Lodges, circa 1906. Bessie with Helena, Bay with Cabot and John (right). *(Nahant Historical Society)*

Senator Henry Cabot Lodge, Sr.

John with his uncle, John Ellerton Lodge.

1925 F Street, Washington, John Lodge's birthplace in 1903.

Francesca and her brothers and sisters in Florence, 1914. Left to right: Berta, Francesca, Stiano, Mario, Marta, Gloria, Rama, Chadwick.

Camp Pasquaney counselors. John is second from left, second row.

Wedding day, July 6, 1929. Top row, left to right: Mario Braggiotti, Gloria Braggiotti, John, Isidore Braggiotti, Francesca, Cabot Lodge, and Stiano Braggiotti.

Katharine Hepburn as Jo waves to dancers Douglass Montgomery, Frances Dee, and John in the Oscar-nominated *Little Women* (1933). *(Museum of Modern Art Film Stills Archive)*

John and Francesca: the Hollywood years.

A Hollywood premiere in 1933 attracts Francesca and John, Fay Wray and husband John Monk Saunders.

Shirley Temple as *The Little Colonel* (1935) reigns over Evelyn Venable and John. *(Museum of Modern Art Film Stills Archive)*

Lunch with Clark Gable at the Paramount studio commissary in 1932, while Gable was filming *No Man of Her Own*.

Francesca in costume for her Hollywood Bowl ballet.

John's favorite film, *The Scarlet Empress* (1934), co-starring Marlene Dietrich.

John takes the punches in his only Western, *Under the Tonto Rim* (1933) with Verna Hillie. (*National Film Archive, London*)

Francesca and John's only on-screen collaboration, *Stasera alle Undici*, made in Rome in 1937.

John visits with family friend Edith Wharton in Paris in 1935.

John's last film, Max Ophuls' *De Mayerling a Sarajevo* (1940), a historical epic on Archduke Franz Ferdinand, with French actress Edwige Feuillère.

At Elstree studio John steps out of his sporty Lancia Landa. *(Associated British Pictures Corporation)*

Carol Reed's *Bank Holiday* (1938) co-starred John with young British actress Margaret Lockwood.

Broadway, 1941. John (standing right) played in long-running hit *Watch on the Rhine* with Paul Lukas, Ann Blyth, Lucille Watson, and George Coulouris.

John's first British film, *Ourselves Alone* (1936), with John Loder and Antoinette Cellier, made him an international star.

At the close of World War II, Lodge received the French Legion of Honor from Admiral Fenard. *(Official U.S. Navy Photo)*

John as U.S. Navy spokesman participated in numerous wartime defense plant ceremonies recognizing production goals.

Between summer stock rehearsals in 1940, the Lodges exercise on a Massachusetts beach.

Fairfield's first family (Lily, John, Francesca, Beatrice) in Washington, 1947.

On the campaign trail for Congress in 1946.

Villa Lodge, John and Francesca's home for more than forty years on Easton Road, Weston, Connecticut.

The Henry Luces and the Lodges, shortly after John replaced Clare Boothe Luce in the House of Representatives.

Francesca's sister and brothers and their spouses celebrate at the Governor's Residence. Seated, *L to R*: Francesca, Mario, Gloria Etting, Libby, Rama, Charo, John. Standing, *L to R*: Chadwick, Emlen Etting, Mary, Stiano. *(Look magazine)*

West Coast travels of Lodges in 1953 include return to Paramount lot and visit to set of *Casanova's Big Night*, with Basil Rathbone and Bob Hope.

1950 campaign postcard.

JOHN LODGE
for
GOVERNOR
A Man You Can Believe
PULL THE SECOND LEVER

Outgoing Governor Chester Bowles
with incumbent Lodge in 1951.

John and Cabot Lodge at Hartford inauguration in 1951.

Lodge welcomes President Harry Truman to Connecticut at the laying of the keel of submarine *USS Nautilus* at Groton in 1952.

John's Fair Play address at the 1952 Republican National Convention in Chicago helped to gain presidential nomination for Eisenhower.

John confers with Frank Lausche of Ohio and James F. Byrnes of South Carolina at 1954 National Governors' Conference.

At nine minutes to midnight, John takes oath as the first four-year term governor of Connecticut.

The Lodges greet incoming governor Abraham Ribicoff and Mrs. Ribicoff at January 1955 swearing-in. *(Hartford Collection, Hartford Public Library)*

John lost close-fought 1954 election while the rest of the ticket won office.

Chowder and Marching Club charter members Lodge and Richard Nixon.

Chief Justice Earl Warren, with Secretary of State John Foster Dulles, swears in John as Ambassador to Spain.

Spain's head of state Franco meets Ambassador Lodge after the presentation of his credentials in 1955.

At an Embassy party, Beatrice is co-host, welcoming Crown Prince Juan Carlos and future husband Antonio de Oyarzabal (right).

John encouraged American filmmakers to choose Spanish locations. On the set of *Solomon and Sheba*, he greets Gina Lollobrigida and Yul Brynner (left).

President Eisenhower shakes John's hand at historic meeting with Franco (right), as Spanish Minister of Foreign Affairs Fernando María Castiella and presidential aide Colonel Vernon Walters stand by.

Junior Achievement's new president John Lodge greets daughter Lily and son-in-law James Marcus in 1963.

At Washington swearing-in ceremony as Ambassador to Argentina, Francesca and John pause beside portrait of his great-grandfather, Frederick T. Frelinghuysen, Secretary of State in the 1880s. At left is cousin and New Jersey Congressman Peter Frelinghuysen.

Helen Hayes endorses candidacy of John for U.S. Senate in 1964 as Francesca and Westport artist Stevan Dohanos look on.

The palatial quarters in Buenos Aires reminded Lodge of Nixon's remark: "I'm sending you to the most beautiful U.S. embassy in the world!"

Visit of astronauts Michael Collins and Neil Armstrong (left) attracted thousands of Argentines to Lodge reception.

Chief Justice Warren Burger delivers oath of office to Reagan's Ambassador to Switzerland in April 1983.

President and Mrs. Reagan change partners with Lodges at White House gala in 1981. *(Ronald Reagan Library)*

Lodge and *Little Women* star Joan Bennett and director George Cukor share memories at 1981 RKO studio reunion in New York.

Former Governor Thomas Meskill (left), Francesca, and Governor William O'Neill dedicate the Connecticut Turnpike in 1986.

October 17, 1993 service of remembrance at Arlington National Cemetery.

State of Connecticut Governors' Gallery portrait, painted in 1954 by Deane Keller.
(*Photograph by Gus Johnson*)

CHAPTER 15

Strife and Fair Play
in the Political Arena

The Lodges' new home, the Governor's Residence, provided "luxurious shelter." The Georgian Colonial manse, with its nineteen rooms, was one of the most majestic governor's houses in the East, perhaps in the entire country, and somewhat out of character for an old entrenched New England capital. Although the chief executive's salary was only $12,000 a year, the job came with spacious living accommodations, an ample food allowance, and an efficient domestic staff, plus a limousine, an extra car, and an airplane flown by the National Guard.[1]

Hartford struck the Lodges as somewhat provincial and insular. Influenced chiefly by nineteenth-century Boston, the affluent city had later attracted factory workers and industrial managers. "But a few wealthy families still set the tone," recalled Florence Berkman, widow of *Hartford Times* political writer Moses Berkman and next-door neighbor to the Governor. "Hartford was reactionary and chauvinistic in the 1950s. John Lodge did not fathom its provincialism; his experience had mostly been within very urbane, artistic and intellectual circles. In turn, Hartford misjudged his shyness for arrogance."[2]

Regardless of the city's staidness, Francesca quickly made the Governor's house jump. She opened its doors for musical programs, dinner parties, and dances. The Lodges liked sharing its public rooms with their friends and backers, and there were Italian parties with tarantellas and Polish nights with polkas. They held the first public open house since the state acquired the dwelling in 1945. Some 3,500 people, from infants to nonagenarians, passed through the front door and met all four Lodges, ate cookies and candy, drank punch, and listened to a five-piece string ensemble.

Francesca straightway reached out into the community. She helped bring Broadway productions to Hartford theaters, often entertaining the visiting show people. At an Italian festival at the nearby Farmington Village Library and at the Oxford School, where Beatrice enrolled, she danced in native costume. Often she expressed bewilderment when the city's old guard frowned on her letting her hair down, especially after it had invited her to perform folk dances in full regalia.

John came in for his share of criticisms but in a more spirited and accommodating atmosphere. New York's Saints & Sinners Club chose him as their Circus "fall guy" for an afternoon of ribbing. For admission into the Waldorf Ballroom, the club set up its own Merritt Parkway tollgate, which yielded over $200 for charity. John was billed as the man who bowled over Bowles in a "thrilling drama" entitled "Hollywood to Hartford, or From B Pictures to Grade A Politician." Master of Ceremonies Walter Kiernan introduced humor-pegged highlights from Lodge's life and careers. The heaviest laughter came when a performer, outfitted as an old doctor, declared he had brought John into the world and that "he didn't cry until I took the silver spoon out of his mouth." John relished the lighthearted tribute, even appearing on stage as famed Connecticut circus-master P.T. Barnum, complete with frock coat, top hat, and cane.[3]

Back at the Capitol, it was a far cry from fun and games for Lodge. His work day frequently extended to sixteen hours, including Saturdays. New legislation and programs demanded long and arduous study and review. The preparation of speeches and messages necessitated much research and rewriting. "The Budget and appointments," wrote executive secretary Ray Watt to Cabot's counterpart Francis McCarthy, "are the demons which keep us awake."[4] The situation was also complicated by a split Legislature: a Republican House friendly to John and a hostile Democratic-controlled Senate.

While Bowles had purposely maintained an aggressive attitude on state issues, John moved in a cautious, non-hurried manner. He maneuvered carefully and hoped over the long four-year haul to "win on points" rather than a knockout punch. Several times the opposition came near to pinning him to the ropes on crucial issues. But he either avoided or parried blows aimed in his direction.

Rival factions battled intensely over the biennial budget and a growing deficit. Tied to the debates was a demand by 17,000 state employees for a ten percent pay increase. A thrifty New Englander at heart, Lodge believed that one cut his suit according to the cloth he could afford. Personally, he never owed a cent and even managed to avoid a mortgaged home. He viewed the state in those economic terms.

The state ended the first six months of Lodge's governorship with its debt slashed to a modest $25,000 or so. Unanticipated tax receipts, especially in sales and corporation taxes, moved the 1949-51 budget into balance. General prosperity from Korean war contracts (some $5 billion in total) buoyed the economy, albeit briefly. Lodge's chief legislative action was his espousal of the law banning legislators from accepting state and local political posts. His most damaging veto was of a bill permitting firemen's fairs and similar carnivals to employ gambling devices to raise money for public purposes.

For fiscal 1951-53, Lodge submitted a biennial budget of $241 million. It embraced new corporate and sales taxes. The Democrats counteracted with a smaller budget and no additional taxes. John Bailey convinced a few key Republicans to follow his reduced spending plan or face a special legislative session. Bailey figured that by 1953 Lodge would have to ask for tax increases to make ends meet, and the onus would fall on his party just before the next gubernatorial election. Bailey's budget strategy did work, and later Lodge clearly had to boost taxes and cut his budget.[5] Sometimes it seemed as if Bailey was calling the shots and writing the script for both parties, especially when Lodge declined to take a firm stand or make a hard-hitting rejoinder. John often refused to commit himself on certain state matters. Bailey quickly tagged Lodge "Silent John" and it stuck. John was unruffled by the epithet. He replied that the right of freedom of speech carried with it the right to be silent.

When it came to speechmaking and letter writing, John, however, was far from quiet or inactive. He delivered two 1951 Lincoln Day dinner talks. John often told his favorite after-dinner yarn of the "literal" tax assessor. That year Connecticut tax authorities had made a survey of real estate for state taxation. The report from one assessor in a small, isolated village had officials perplexed, if not buffaloed, John related. This assessor had listed "seven goats" as real estate. The puzzled officials asked for an explanation. The fellow cited an old law to include the goats. Real estate, he answered, took in anything "bounding and abutting on the highway."[6]

In a more serious vein, John gave the commencement address at Trinity College in Hartford that spring. President G. Keith Funston awarded him an honorary degree, his first, along with similar accolades to six business executives and two clergymen. Honored also by the Israel Histadrut (General Federation of Labor) in New York, he responded by calling for support of the new state of Israel, "a strong example of democracy and economic progress."

Lodge devoted an inordinate part of his day to correspondence beyond those letters of an official nature. He gave painstaking attention to his social and personal mail; it often concerned requests and favors.[7] During his tenure, for example, he provided information to a wartime friend in Toulon, France on the new drug cortisone and its availability; he arranged for the promised gift of a hat to South Carolina Governor James F. Byrnes from a Connecticut factory; he asked help from U.S. High Commissioner in Germany John J. McCloy for concert appearances for brother-in-law Mario Braggiotti; he wrote letters of introduction to U.S. ambassadors in Europe; he pursued employment opportunities for friends at the UN through Cabot; he expedited requests for personalized auto license plates; he inquired of MGM on their interest in a new book written by French novelist (and author of *Koenigsmark*) Pierre Benoit; he attempted to grant foreign diplomats hunting privileges in the state; he looked into a diplomatic post in Switzerland for a Harvard classmate; and he conveyed birthday greetings to friends near and afar. And there were Christmas cards—over 3,500 were mailed each December.

At the close of the long 1951 legislative session, Lodge anticipated a change of pace and a summer close to his family. Lily, a Wellesley College senior, graduated that June. A talented, attractive young lady, she had developed an interest in the theater and appeared in a number of school plays, notably *As You Like It*, *Macbeth*, *Julius Caesar*, and other Shakespearean dramas, and had leads with a stock company organized by Wellesley students and alumnae. Lily also had been chosen from hundreds of college women for a major role in a broadcast of the popular radio thriller *The Shadow*. She decided on an acting career. "You have chosen the hardest work anyone could possibly enter," her mother pointed out. "All we expect is that you study with humility and seriousness; that you be devoted to your craft; and that integrity and high standards be the foundation on which you will work."[8] With her parents' support, Lily Lodge enrolled in the Royal Academy of Arts in London, where she lived with the family of British actor Henry Ainley. As a combination graduation and twenty-first birthday gift, John mapped out an extended family trip to Europe.

On July 12, the Lodges sailed on the liner *Vulcania* for Italy. The first stop, Florence, provided a chance for a reunion with Mario, Chad, and Gloria Braggiotti at the old family villa. A highlight of the trip, a twenty-minute private audience with Pope Pius XII, gave the Lodges an ecumenical insight into the lingering problems of unemployment and poverty in Italy. John also talked with U.S. officers with NATO, met with Premier De Gaspari, and visited philosopher and poet George Santayana. John had hoped for many years to meet Santayana, the highly regarded teacher of his father and of Joe Stickney at Harvard. "I do appreciate your granting me the privilege of seeing you," he wrote the aged writer. "Your works have been a source of great stimulus to me."[9]

John flew home on September 3. Francesca, Lily, and Beatrice continued on to England, where Lily began her acting studies. The absence of fifty-three days, the first of lengthy departures from the state during his term, caused much criticism, particularly from caustic John Bailey and the Democrats. Two months in Europe after only six months on the job was too much, they protested. So they called John "the puppet governor." Nevertheless, the overseas holiday provided Lieutenant Governor Ned Allen with an unusual chance to gain on-the-job training. "No lieutenant governor, in my memory," Allen wrote, "had had such an opportunity and I hope that through this experience I may be able to assist you more intelligently in the tremendous job that lies ahead of you."[10]

Lodge returned to find an office beset with mounting problems, especially state employee pay-hour demands and other fiscal matters. There was no money on hand to finance a ten percent pay increase, Lodge reasoned. Moreover, there was a potential deficit of about $10 million because the split Legislature had failed to appropriate funds. The touchy political relationship with a number of the GOP professionals demanded attention too. While the Democrats had stopped their infighting, the Republicans now engaged in constant backbiting. It still rankled some regulars that John had bypassed the usual path up the political ladder, beginning for most at precinct, ward, or district level.

"The GOP is developing a rift between Governor Lodge and his personal group, and the regular party organization," observed reporter Jack Zaiman. "Governor Lodge has found himself in open conflict with big business leaders in the state who aided him considerably in getting elected." Zaiman claimed Lodge had almost completely ignored the GOP State Central Committee and the patronage factor of his administration. "It seems that a vital and basic political rule has been forgotten by the Governor's office. It is the traditional rule that is recognized in politics everywhere: 'Take care of your friends, especially people who put you in office.' "[11]

The governor's inner office group, his so-called "kitchen cabinet," composed of executive aide Raymond Watt, speech writer Albert Coote, and legislative consultant Charles S. House, seemed determined to build up John as a totally independent and unbiased governor. With it came growing isolation and much bad advice. Reporters complained that his office produced little solid news. But the picture changed considerably as the pivotal political year 1952 approached, bringing new controversies and momentous events. In particular, Connecticut citizens wondered where the Republican leaders stood on the race for the GOP presidential nomination and who would be the Party's nominee for the Senate race. While in Congress, Lodge leaned towards Senator Bob Taft as the party nominee in 1952. But the Republicans desperately needed a charismatic campaigner and vote-getter to end nearly two decades of Democratic occupancy of the

White House. Governor Tom Dewey had run twice in the 1940s; now it seemed Taft's turn. John had welcomed Taft to Connecticut on several occasions and personally admired the integrity and ability of the conservative leader. Before John came too close to backing the Ohio Senator, Cabot told him to hold off.[12] He was maneuvering to persuade wartime leader General Dwight D. Eisenhower, now Supreme Allied Commander in Europe, to enter the race on the Republican ticket. In his memoirs, Ike himself talks of a stream of visitors, both Democratic and Republican, with politics almost the single subject on their minds.

Cabot Lodge came to Ike's headquarters in September 1951. "He was different," wrote Eisenhower, "in that he was reflecting the known views of a number of large groups, many of whom now wanted to start organizing a nationwide movement to present my name before the 1952 Republican convention. Cabot, an associate and friend of mine from wartime days, presented his plea with the ardor of a crusader."[13] He argued for the two-party system and the need to bring the Republicans out of defeat. He agreed to let the Senator test his name in the primaries, and the wartime hero was soon publicly known as a Republican when Cabot entered his name in the New Hampshire primary that winter. Eisenhower had made it clear to Robert Burroughs, a GOP leader from New Hampshire, that he would not campaign actively for the nomination in that or any other state.

By the end of 1951, John Lodge had joined the Eisenhower camp. On February 5, in a state-wide broadcast, John formally announced his support of Ike. "With Dwight Eisenhower as the leader of this nation, the American people can express at last the bursting vigor, the sureness of aim and the breadth of compassionate spirit which are inherent in the very word American. If these famous American virtues are trained and centered upon our domestic and international problems, those problems will at long last move toward solution."[14] Rejecting the contention that Eisenhower's views were not sufficiently known, Lodge said that "on the great public questions of the day he has expressed himself repeatedly and convincingly." Ike, he added, exemplified the citizen-soldier at his best, and "his views on international affairs are those of a man who assuredly does not want the United States to become a nation in which the recruiting sergeant and the draft board are to be the perpetual arbiters of the future of American youth."[15]

Three days after his radio talk, John helped to organize a large-scale and widely supported "Bandwagon for Eisenhower" at New York's Madison Square Garden. The late-night rally was televised, and a kinescope was then quickly processed and flown by aviatrix Jacqueline Cochran to Paris for Eisenhower to see. An enthusiastic and determined turnout of some 15,000 "I like Ike" fans, including Clark Gable and Irving Berlin, gave visual proof to the General of his undeniably strong following.

But not all the mainstays in Connecticut preferred Ike. Brennan, Bradley, and State Controller Fred Zeller stood firm for Taft. John, as head of the party in Connecticut, believed he must deliver a united front for Ike. Happily, members of his state delegation increasingly leaned to Eisenhower after the New Hampshire primary. Both John and Cabot campaigned there for the General, and his remarkable victory *in absentia* and Taft's severe political rout jolted the Republican outlook. Similarly, President Truman met a resounding defeat in the Democratic primary against Senator Estes Kefauver. "The lesson [of New Hampshire] seems to be that the voters are tired to death of the old, over-familiar political faces," wrote columnists Stewart and Joseph Alsop. "They want something new to be added, whether an Eisenhower or a Kefauver. And judging by the remarkable size of the New Hampshire turnout, the voters are determined to get what they want."[16]

Lodge lost little time jumping on the Ike bandwagon with both feet, in spite of the General's statement that under no circumstances would he ask to be relieved of his European post before June. John and Francesca, at the request of the Republican National Committee, traveled south to speak at party rallies and before clubs in Florida and Mississippi. If he had been asked by the Committee to refrain from reminding audiences of his endorsement of Ike over Taft, he soon bypassed the advice. At a banquet of the Women's Republican Club of St. Petersburg, he clearly backed Ike, only tempering it by adding that he would support whoever the party's nominee happened to be.[17]

In April John again took to the road. As a member of the executive committee of the National Governors' Conference, he attended its meeting in Chicago. At a gathering of Midwest business leaders there, John sensed that they were nearly all for Taft, but he spoke up for Eisenhower. "I really don't know what General Eisenhower thinks, but he's a soldier, a graduate of West Point, and the chances are he has rather conservative views toward the maintenance of fiscal stability and limitation of budgetary deficits."[18]

From Chicago, Lodge made a whistle-stop tour of down-state Illinois. John told audiences that no man knew more about war and peace than Eisenhower. At the University of Illinois in Urbana, with a bow to his erudite listeners, he tossed in a quotation from Walt Whitman: "Out of the cradle endlessly rocking . . . come new leaders." His old Middlesex classmate John W. Wood heard John in Champaign. Highly impressed, he dashed off a letter: "I was bowled over by your growth in stature, self-control and assurance . . . the conviction with which you spoke, the light touch and good humor with which you handled difficult questions."[19] John's efforts in Illinois, however, made little headway against the Taft forces, which picked up forty-eight out of fifty delegates in the primary.

In Connecticut Senator Benton mapped out his race for a full six-year term. Banker Prescott Bush of Greenwich again maneuvered to oppose him, and Clare Boothe Luce characteristically took steps to get into the race without actually appearing that she was seeking the nomination. And John, too, was on the sidelines if not in the actual running.

Republicans met in late May to select the candidate. Out of a welter of confusion, Lodge clearly stated he would stick to his promise to serve the full four-year term. To his very closest friends, he spoke of his mother's antipathy to having two sons in the Senate at the same time.[20] Speaker of the House (and briefly State Chairman for Ike) Mansfield Sprague entered the race with a push from Bill Brennan. Businessman William A. Purtell, a former president of the Connecticut Manufacturers Association, soon moved into a leading position, but John publicly declared that he would not back any candidate. Bush, a proven vote-getter in 1950, still had a good chance. One evening, a group of upstate party leaders persuaded Lodge to favor Purtell. "It looked as if Dad was through as far as the Senate was concerned," recalls Prescott Bush, Jr., "and he withdrew." The party closed ranks behind Purtell.[21]

Bill Purtell stood out in contrast to Benton. An Irish Catholic laborer who rose to factory executive, he appeared too liberal for many Connecticut Republicans. But the party was hungry for victory. It believed it could only draw off Democratic votes by offering someone who, for all intents and purposes, might have been in Bailey's camp.

A festering animosity between Lodge and Bill Brennan surfaced during the two-day convention. Basically a personality clash between the national committeeman and the governor, it was compounded by the burly Irishman's closeness to Taft and his efforts to build up convention delegates in his camp. Antagonistic and stubborn, Brennan continually opposed Lodge and his backing of Ike. John had wanted Bill for the national post, thinking it would gain his cooperation in party councils. It proved a mistake, Lodge explained decades later. Brennan continued to be abrasive in his manner and hostile in his actions. John felt the post of committeeman should go to someone who would cooperate in the election of Eisenhower. Political reporter Jack Zaiman devoted column after column on the Republican Party turmoil and schism. Zaiman's headlines—"Lodge and His Advisers Rip GOP Party Wide Open," "Several Reasons Submitted for Lodge-Brennan Break," "What Happens to State GOP if Taft Wins Nomination?"—added fuel to the fire. A crafty manipulator, Bailey relished the strife, knowing the battles would weaken the Republicans. Newspaper editorials throughout the state picked up the theme of GOP self-destruction. The purge of Brennan as national committeeman and his replacement by ex-governor Shannon left scars that never healed.

There were always ceremonial activities to offer a refreshing interlude from John's political angst. He spoke at commencement exercises at Bay Path Junior College and at Worcester Polytechnic Institute, both in Massachusetts. Worcester made him an honorary doctor of science; he reminded graduates that education implies the capacity for consecutive thought: "It is vastly different from training. You can train a seal, but you can't educate him."

Earlier that day, Lodge welcomed President Truman on his first visit to Connecticut in four years. They shared the platform in the laying of the keel of the nation's first atomic-powered submarine, the USS *Nautilus*, at Groton. On June 28, John boarded a train for the annual Governors' Conference in Houston. Following the four-day meeting, he quickly returned to Hartford to join Connecticut's 144 delegates, alternates, and spouses preparing to attend the 1952 National Convention in Chicago. Firmly committed to Ike, John would gain national recognition in Chicago and more exposure than all his Hollywood films combined.

When John arrived at the Stock Yard Inn, his political future was at stake.[22] As head of the state delegation in what was then a state without a primary, he had cajoled and coerced most members to vote for Ike. A Taft nomination, he realized, would accelerate a slow but steady decline in his leadership and trim his grass-roots popularity. Besides, he really liked Ike. John had first met Eisenhower in Europe during the war, and they ran into each other the first day in Chicago's Conrad Hilton Hotel. "You brought the heavy artillery, John," the General quipped, referring to the recent conference of governors where Lodge had "crusaded" for Ike.[23] John was on his way to a meeting that Cabot, who had become Ike's campaign manager, had called. Cabot wanted a report on the Houston meeting and more details on the question concerning the seating of certain contested state delegations.

Ike's campaign for delegates was seriously threatened by Taft's high standing among party leaders, especially in the South. In Texas Taft supporters had arbitrarily ignored substantial Eisenhower support at local precinct gatherings in choosing the state's thirty-eight-man delegation. According to Texas law, delegates to the state convention were elected by the people at the precinct level. At its convention, the state organization barred Ike's elected delegates and sent a nearly solid Taft slate to Chicago. So Ike's people elected an opposing group. The pro-Taft National Committee, however, seated the Senator's delegates on the temporary roll, and these delegates were positioned to vote on their right to their own seats and against any group of challengers. (A number apparently had been moved into place by Democrats encouraged to enroll in the Republican Party and vote in the Texas primary.)

In Houston John had proposed to GOP governors a manifesto: delegates whose places were in dispute could not vote on the seating of any other delegates whose places were in dispute. Otherwise, contested delegations would become the "accused, judge, and jury." Virtually each of the twenty-five Republican governors okayed it. At Chicago, with the cry of "Thou Shall Not Steal," Cabot and Governors Tom Dewey of New York, Douglas McKay of Oregon, Al Driscoll of New Jersey, Dan Thornton of Colorado, and John turned the matter into a moral issue whereby thousands of citizens were being cheated out of their votes. It looked as though the convention was going to be a replay of 1912, when ex-president Teddy Roosevelt emerged as the overwhelming favorite, but President William H. Taft, Senator Taft's father, gained renomination from the powerful old guard. Forty years later, Cabot refused to compromise on the issue. He was determined to put the whole matter to the test of a vote by the entire convention at the very first session. When a last-minute deal to split the Texas delegation votes was proposed by Taft's people, Cabot made the memorable retort, "I will not consult with evil."[24]

Deft, experienced politician Herbert Brownell of New York, who was assigned by Cabot to get delegate votes for Ike, has described the issue as crucial: "It was set forth as a matter of 'fair play,'" he emphasized. Earlier, at the Governors' Conference, Brownell and Boston lawyer Ralph Boyd had actually drafted and tested the manifesto. "It was both a maneuver to advance Ike as well as a vote for fairness," Brownell pointed out.[25]

In Chicago John was assigned the duty to speak in favor of this Fair Play amendment to the convention's temporary rules. To prepare, he conferred with his legal adviser Charles House and close friend Meade Alcorn. Lodge knew political history and the ins and outs of the parallel situation at the 1912 Convention. The three men hammered out the speech for John, a "good part" in the unfolding drama to be aired nation-wide before the largest television audience in history. John already had played his role so well that he was emerging as a political leader in his own right. From the very opening of the convention, John and his fellow delegates were seen frequently by tens of millions on television sets, chiefly because they were seated less than twenty feet from the rostrum and right in the center of the amphitheater floor.[26]

John came to the podium wearing a white linen suit which stood out well on black and white TV screens. He first reminded his audience that the Republican governors at Houston had approved the Fair Play proposal.

At that moment, Taft people jumped up to hype their candidate. Waving placards and soaring balloons interrupted John's speech. He stood there while they shouted and paraded through the aisles. He smiled and laughed at the outburst, and waited for the demonstration to subside. Some twenty minutes later, the outburst ended and he continued with his talk.

"There is one ideal which has pervaded all our American theories of justice, and this is the ideal of fair play," John stated. "Whether in the field of sport, in the market place, in the court or in the political arena, we Americans want no loaded dice, no shoddy goods, no tampered juries and no packed ballot box. This amendment calls only for fair play at this convention. How can we attack, as we must, the appalling corruption of the present administration, if we do not go to the people not only with clean hands, but with hands that the American people know are clean? We must not only be honest—we must convince the people that we are honest. Fair play demands that the accused not sit on the jury which tries his case."[27]

John tore into the opposition and in a matter of minutes had many delegates cheering him on. Turning to the past, John explained that "every convention is at liberty to adopt its own rules. Each convention is a law unto itself. We are not bound by the 1912 rules any more than we are bound by 1912 policies; and future conventions need not be bounded by the rules of 1952." Then, he characteristically looked to Lincoln for inspiration: "In Lincoln's words 'As our case is new, so must we think anew and act anew. We must be imaginative. We must be resourceful. . . . There is no contract that men can devise which takes the place of good faith among men. If we are gathered to draft rules to guide men of no faith, then it were better had we not gathered at all. It would be better to disband and admit that we cannot, in the words of our founder 'rise with the occasion.' We can hardly achieve victory from such a confession of moral defeat. Let us reaffirm our faith in our party, our faith in our free system, our faith in our fellow man, our faith in America," John forcefully concluded, "by passing this amendment which is essentially a symbol of faith."[28]

At the end of the dramatically delivered talk, Lodge received a thunderous standing ovation from many of the 12,000 delegates and spectators. Recalls Connecticut delegate John Alsop: "He persuaded major opinion makers with that speech. The roll call favored Eisenhower's position. With open hearings before the Credentials Committee, we succeeded in seating many delegates pledged to Ike, as opposed to those committed to Taft. And when that started to happen, it was a psychological lift to Ike's candidacy. His supporters knew they were on the way to a nomination."[29]

John always described the speech as the best he ever gave (and one of his shortest). Delegates and home viewers alike rushed to praise his enlightening and persuasive argument. John's well-orchestrated call for fairness helped gain Ike the votes necessary for a first-ballot victory. John emerged as a farsighted statesman and a courageous politician (who, in addition, delivered all but one of Connecticut's twenty-two votes to Ike). And by the next day, he was being touted in some quarters as potential vice presidential timber.[30]

Although John's name never came into serious discussion, he comprised part of the group that picked the vice presidential candidate. Early on the afternoon of July 11, party leaders gathered on the 11th floor of the Conrad Hilton Hotel. Cabot called the meeting; he had rounded up twenty-five key GOP floor leaders, governors, senators, and congressmen. The windows in the hot, crowded suite were wide open, but there was no breeze from Lake Michigan to relieve the discomfort.

Cabot ruled that anyone who suggested a particular candidate would leave the room to permit frank and free discussion. Three names were raised and considered: Senator Everett Dirksen, Senator Taft, and Governor Driscoll. Then, William Knowland of California offered fellow Senator Richard Nixon. Several others spoke up on Nixon's behalf, including John, who had served closely with him in the 80th and 81st Congress. John pointed out that the Senator was young and would appeal to new voters. Nixon had served in the Navy during the war and came from a geographically strategic state. "Besides, Dick has become an experienced politician and proven campaigner," he expounded. After a half hour of discussion, thirty-nine-year-old Nixon emerged as the unanimous choice.[31]

Brownell picked up the phone to tell Ike the group's recommendation. The General, who had asked for "a young man," readily approved of Nixon. The young senator had worked for Ike in California and convinced the state delegation to cast its large unit vote for the Fair Play resolution. During the meeting, neither Cabot nor Brownell ever mentioned or produced a list apparently made by Ike of seven possible running mates.[32] "Ike preferred not to dictate the choice of a running mate," Brownell later emphasized. "He was, of course, entitled to decide but said to me that he'd like group recommendations."[33]

That fall Nixon was attacked over an $18,000 private fund contributed by friends in California to help with congressional expenses. There were some who wanted to drop him from the ticket. Because the story mushroomed into a national controversy, Ike's campaign was in jeopardy. Dewey suggested a way out of the troublesome and politically dangerous impasse. Nixon would go on television and state his case.

It was the speech of Nixon's life. In his so-called "Checkers" talk, Nixon told viewers that his spot on the ticket would be decided by the Republican National Committee. That implied his future was more in the hands of the professionals than of Ike himself. Favorable telegrams and letters poured into GOP headquarters.

In the meantime, Tom Dewey phoned John: "General Lucius Clay is on the Eisenhower campaign train, and he thinks that Nixon ought to be dumped from the ticket. But he wanted to find out what you and I and Governor Driscoll think." John responded: "Well, Tom, I'll tell you what I think. I don't believe Nixon's done anything wrong. There's no reason why a young man with no personal funds of his own shouldn't accept some financial help between campaigns, for doing things to help his image, so to speak, to publicize it, to give him a larger staff—things which he'd be perfectly entitled to do if he had the money to do it himself. A candidate can accept contributions to campaigns; why can't he accept contributions between campaigns? "I think that if Nixon were dropped it would be wrong. It would be immoral. And it would be admitting guilt for something that isn't wrong. I think we'd deserve to lose. And I think we probably would." Dewey agreed: "John, I feel just the same way. You'll be interested to know that so does Al Driscoll."[34] A short time later, Nixon flew to Wheeling, West Virginia, where Ike received him warmly, saying "you're my boy." The momentous campaign of 1952 continued in high gear.

John now was a highly popular figure both within his state and beyond. He returned to full command of his party, his prestige heightened by his success in helping to nominate Ike. Those who challenged Lodge were silenced, at least for the moment. And countless Americans were finally aware that Henry Cabot Lodge, Jr., had a brother.

After many weeks of political business, John left for a two-week vacation in the Virgin Islands. Just days after the Lodges' arrival in St. Thomas, word reached them that Senator Brien McMahon, ill for six weeks, had died of cancer. The forty-nine-year-old Democrat and chairman of the Joint Committee on Atomic Energy had served nineteen months of his second term. John interrupted the Caribbean holiday to attend McMahon's funeral, then returned to St. Thomas to mull over his next move.

An interim appointee for McMahon's seat was on everyone's lips. John thought about his own hoped-for wish to serve in the Senate. As Governor, he wondered if he should resign and have his successor, Ned Allen, name him. Then in November, he'd run for the job if he got the nomination. But he remembered his promise: to complete his term as the first four-year governor. Moreover, the concern of his mother over sibling discord in the Senate stuck in his mind. He decided to keep an open mind on the idea, and announced the second state convention that year to select a candidate.

A movement to draft Lodge went into motion, not particularly by his friends but by those elements who wanted him out of Hartford. Those who objected to Lodge's dual-job ban for legislators and his veto of the gambling bill joined to get him support for the nomination. Whereas a segment of his old Congressional district wanted him out of Washington for paying too much attention to foreign affairs, another state-wide clique sought his removal from Hartford and a ticket back to the U.S. Capitol.[35] At that point, John briefly wished he could push politics aside and assume an ambassadorship. His and Francesca's beloved Italy would be ideal for the Lodges, he thought. His support of Eisenhower and a Republican victory in November might fulfill his dream of taking that exciting post.

Cross-currents of his character, a bi-polar split, manifested itself as he dallied over decisions. Despite a self-assured imperious air, Lodge often evidenced a lack of self-confidence backstage. He seemed unsure of himself, bedeviled by a suspicion of inadequacy. He was given to asking of persons, "You think I'm a good Governor, don't you?" And on occasion he shocked some others by a plaintive question: "You think I'm a failure, don't you, because I've never made a lot of money?" His insecurity led him to parry questions, to decline answers on all sorts of pretexts. It accounted for his failure to give leadership when it was needed during legislative sessions. His gubernatorial speeches about "bold leadership" expressed a yearning to keep up with Cabot and the illustrious Lodges on his family tree, aspirations fulfilled only infrequently.[36] The whole tenor of John's persistent attempt to create a better standard for state business vexed many ward heelers, and so they organized a "draft." John remained on the sidelines. The nomination had to come without his seeking it. John was reminded of the wave of unpopularity that fell on Hiram Bingham in the 1920s, when he resigned as Governor of Connecticut to become Senator. Countless Republicans resented Bingham's maneuver, and many never forgave him.

John's advisors came forward with viable candidates for the open Senate seat. Some favored Purtell because he had been duly nominated at the May convention to run against Benton. Charles House suggested Prescott Bush as the logical person, "a strong candidate at the special convention." Clare Boothe Luce speedily launched her own campaign. Lodge was besieged with pro-Luce phone calls, letters, and telegrams from influential Republicans, not only in Connecticut but in other parts of the country. Eisenhower was said to have been one of those pushing her appointment.

"We were really for her," Francesca revealed many years later. "Besides, with Clare on the ticket, we expected Henry Luce to contribute plenty of money and media resources to the Connecticut campaigns." But Francesca was let down by a remark of Clare's: "Cesca, you know how wonderful it is to have a grand title, especially when you travel to Europe. I'd like to add that prefix of 'Senator' to my name." Francesca said years later: "I viewed her remark as unpatriotic."

Lodge refused to name Luce. He did not believe she could win the upcoming election. In turn, she charged him with a failure to show leadership. Bush had worked hard for the nod and now felt he was merely a backup candidate. "The public avowal of neutrality by Governor Lodge and State Chairman Clarence F. Baldwin," Luce declared, "is a smoke screen to hide the fact from our delegates that certain party bosses are preparing undercover to give our party the twice-beaten Prescott Bush." Luce claimed that she was 'the only available proven vote-getter." Lodge, she added in a press statement, "flatly and finally told me he would not extend me any support in seeking the nomination. So I must believe that he is also supporting Prescott Bush under the guise of neutrality."[37]

A week before the convention, John made one of the toughest political decisions of his career. He announced the appointment of William Purtell to fill out the remaining four months of McMahon's term in the 82nd Congress. With those words echoing in her ears, Mrs. Luce rolled out the heavy artillery. She announced plans to get the full-term nomination by carrying her fight to the convention floor. On a New Haven public-service TV program, a panel of five newsmen fired a bevy of questions. Had there been a political break between her and Lodge, one reporter asked. "There never was a political tie," she snapped. "There has always been a friendship."[38]

Luce, who that summer had been in Hollywood writing a movie script, scurried to line up delegates. "The free and open" convention soon attracted two more Senate aspirants: Ken Bradley and State Senator (and avid pro-Taftite) Tage Pearson. With more and more party stalwarts jumping on other bandwagons, Luce scouted for someone to nominate her. Many refused until Congressman James Patterson agreed to take the job. Meade Alcorn and Cappy Baldwin felt Luce had no place in Connecticut politics and couldn't possibly win. They went to Bush, a strong candidate, to build up his strength. "It was an incredible sequence of events," says Prescott, Jr. "Dad said that he would not seek the nomination. 'You deliver it,' he told Alcorn and Baldwin."[39]

Soon after the convention opened, Henry Luce wrote John a cryptic note on their "friendship":

At 3 A.M. this morning, Lt. Gov. Allen told Clare that you had been friendly to her and that she had not understood this fact. I want *you* to understand that I have studied the situation carefully from day to day and that I have found no evidence whatsoever that you have been in any way friendly to Clare or to me in this contest. Let there be, as of this morning, no misunderstanding as to my estimate of your position.

Very sincerely yours,
Harry[40]

John drafted a friendly reply, a clarification that probably was never sent.

Dear Harry,

I was very much taken aback by your note which reached me Friday morning.

We have been friends with Clare and you for so long that it would be impossible for 'Cesca or me to think, or to wish to act, toward you in any but a most friendly way.

Having made it emphatic that I would take no sides in the convention I held strictly to that decision.

You will recall that I took no sides either in the earlier Purtell-Bush contest. Neither man called my stand unfriendly, although one of them, like Clare and you, has had a claim on my friendship for a good many years.

My impartiality was based, not on indifference, but on the conviction that this was the right and only course for me to follow. Were I the sort of person to avow one thing and then covertly to do the opposite, I would have no right to your friendship or to any man's.

Your note was a kind of thunderclap to 'Cesca too. We can only hope (and we can all too well understand) that it might have been written out of your natural concern rather than in earnest.

We both think Clare's little talk after the convention was typically excellent. Some of the thoughts and phrases were so startlingly acute that I wonder if the convention fully savored them at the time.

'Cesca joins me in sending you both our friendliest and constant good wishes.[41]

Clare's persistent and almost desperate efforts to win her party's nod ended with a laugh. Her nominating speaker, after praising her integrity, dignity, vision and courage, concluded his remarks by saying, "and now I give you Mrs. Clare Moose Lou." The roll call of delegates netted her fifty votes.[42] Prescott Bush won the nomination on the first ballot with over 400 votes. The delegates seemed to welcome the chance to make him the nominee; after all, he had narrowly lost at the earlier convention. His opponent was Congressman Abe Ribicoff, a new Democratic hopeful.

Henry Luce seemingly retaliated against John through Cabot, himself a candidate for re-election in Massachusetts. Facing a formidable opponent in a tough match, Cabot conceded that young Congressman John Fitzgerald Kennedy had tremendous appeal in a state that had become increasingly industrialized, Catholic, and non-Yankee. Thus, he felt very put out when Luce's Republican-leaning *Life* Magazine published, in Cabot's eyes, "a most impressive and effective" editorial endorsement of Kennedy for the Senate. (Actually, the issue of September 29 referred to Kennedy as "a good man," "first class political talent," and "wasted in a battle of personal charm," but never backed him. The editorial reads more like an obtuse endorsement of Cabot.)[43]

Cabot made known his displeasure to Luce, his one-time employer at *Time* magazine's Washington bureau in the early 1930s: "You realize, of course, that this is a close fight and that this editorial could make the whole difference. You realize also that the question of whether or not we shall have a Truman type control of the Senate is also very close and could very well hinge on whether or not a Republican Senator is elected from Massachusetts. You may very well therefore have decided the control of the Senate in the next Congress by this editorial. . . . I have often had my opponent helped and myself hurt by editorials but never by an editor whom I thought a friend. . . . What has caused you to change I cannot imagine but I know you to be very intelligent and that you always know what you are doing. I write you so frankly because of our long friendship and because of my respect for your ability."[44]

The Lodge brothers gave little time to Senate races in their respective states. John attended numerous Ike rallies and GOP campaign dinners in New Jersey, New York, and Massachusetts. "Just as Abraham Lincoln was right for his time, so Dwight D. Eisenhower is right for our time," Lodge proclaimed. And in California, where he was Mary Pickford's guest of honor at a political gathering at her Pickfair estate, he campaigned for his Chowder and Marching buddy Don Jackson as well as for Ike.

Eisenhower entered Connecticut on a special campaign train, and John spent the entire railroad swing with him. Ike made speeches from the back of the observation car and on station platforms. Charles House remembers an Ike look-alike who stood in for him and waved to crowds as the train sped through small Connecticut towns.[45] Nixon, too, journeyed to the state to convince voters that the Stevenson-Sparkman ticket would only continue the policies of the Truman era.

The Ike-Nixon team lost ground by October, although it still led in the polls. Its weakness stemmed from lackluster campaigning, and anti-Catholic and anti-Semitic charges against Eisenhower.[46] Nonetheless, on Election Day, Ike rode to victory in 39 states. He carried Connecticut by 200,000 votes, a feat nobody had ever achieved up to that point. Both Purtell and Bush beat their Democratic opponents by substantial margins. In Hartford, both houses gained a Republican majority. Congressman Thomas Dodd of Hartford won as the only Democrat. The new Republicans in Washington included John's young cousin Peter H. B. Frelinghuysen, Jr., whom both Lodge brothers had encouraged to run for Congress, where he would remain for eleven terms. Above all, the 1952 elections were a triumph for Ike. Lodge shared in the victory. Eisenhower wrote a personal note to John for his "great contribution" to the campaign not only in Connecticut but elsewhere: "In the trying weeks ahead it will be comforting to know that we will have the support of strong state governments headed by such outstanding leaders as yourself. Such backstopping in our states is necessary if our crusade is to continue successfully."[47]

The Republicans emerged as the majority party in Congress, but Cabot Lodge would not be among them. His extensive campaign work for Ike overshadowed his own efforts to stay in office. A coalition of anti-Lodge people, including the wealthy Kennedy clan, irreconcilable Taft supporters, and diehard isolationists, steamrolled Cabot, a moderate conservative, into the ground. Before it all ended, there were even scurrilous rumors that Cabot had talked to Boston's Bishop Cushing about becoming a Catholic.[48]

Eisenhower aide Robert Cutler congratulated John on the victory in Connecticut and hinted that Cabot would probably go on to a high post in the new administration. The Boston banker wrote: "The last thing Ike said to me, as he and Mamie and I were walking down the corridor in the Commodore at 3:30 A.M. on November 5, when it looked as if Cabot might not come through, was this: 'Tell Cabot if Massachusetts doesn't want him I certainly do.' . . . He bore his defeat with remarkable courage and magnanimity."[49]

President-elect Eisenhower rewarded John with a special assignment. He represented Ike at the inauguration of Governor Luis Muñoz Marín of Puerto Rico. In San Juan, John made his first public remarks in Spanish. "I didn't know Spanish, but Francesca and Muñoz-Marín wrote out some words for me, and I said them," John later explained. The brief message in good Spanish surprised the crowd.[50] John stole the show, too, with music and dance. He serenaded guests with the French song "La Vie en Rose" and then persuaded Muñoz Marín to sing an American song with him. John and Francesca capped the evening by a brief exhibition of the tango.[51]

For Ike's inaugural, John and Francesca led a large contingent of Connecticut citizens to Washington. In the traditional parade, they rode together in an open car, followed by the brightly uniformed Foot Guard and 500 fast-stepping cadets from the U.S. Coast Guard Academy. Outfitted in a stylish black coat and homburg, John smiled and waved to the throngs lining Pennsylvania Avenue. When asked about John's headgear, Francesca pointed out, "He's brought both a top hat and a homburg. You can be sure John's head will be covered. He comes from the Hat State!"

John had earned his right to wear and wave his hat. Out of a year steeped in political struggles and surprises, momentous meetings and conventions, Lodge had stepped forward in high favor on both state and national levels. A friend and backer of Dwight D. Eisenhower, he now held center stage as a widely recognized team player, a trusted strategist, an unequivocal leader. Surely his hat would be in the ring again.

CHAPTER 16

A Lincoln Republican

In his two years in office, John Lodge proved Connecticut had
something more than a political neophyte for a governor. His
administration had been a refreshing manifestation of state government in
action, and one with a new standard of dignity and helmsmanship. *Town
and Country* devoted most of its March 1953 issue to Connecticut *haut
monde*. But in its section on Lodge, the magazine made inroads in casting
off his aristocratic glamour-boy image. Voters and politicians, it stressed,
now realized Lodge was not to be written off or underestimated. "Politics
he accepted as an instrument of government," the article noted, "but he
has balked all attempts of politicians to subordinate the interests of the
state to the interests of the party."[1]

Yet in the wings, amid the euphoria of Republican victories, party
wreckers conspired, wanting to divide and conquer. Several issues came to
the forefront to provide fuel for the nearly total self-destruction of the
party from its earlier high-water mark.

The controversial pro-gambling bill again fell in John's lap. His staff
suggested that he let it become law without his signature. But he regarded
that as a shirking of responsibility. "Don't be a boy scout," his aides
declared. Lodge was not against gambling on moral or puritanical grounds.
He had another basis. Law enforcement officers in the state told him that
games of chance would inevitably attract hoodlums and criminal elements,
and make the protection of law-abiding citizens difficult. Thereby, it was
a question of law enforcement, not an ethical issue. In spite of the bill's
approval by the Assembly and by many groups, he saw little good from
opening the doors to gambling on even a small scale.

One day, a displeased, carping Bill Brennan came to Lodge's office.
"Legalization of gambling is what the people want," he shouted. "You
better give it to them." John refused. The tall, heavy-set Brennan suddenly

became nasty and rough, practically strong-arming Lodge. John rose to his feet and ordered the Fairfield ward heeler out the door. To Capitol insiders, it spelled trouble ahead—this clash of wills between the powerful county boss, who thought government was the arm of politics, and the idealistic state leader, who believed politics was the arm of government.[2]

Meanwhile Connecticut's need for a cross-state superhighway and John's advocacy of it mustered together a vociferous cabal of anti-Lodge elements, augmented by some of John's former supporters and closest friends. A commercial route along the coastline from the New York line to the Rhode Island border had been discussed in the early 1940s. At that time, a bill was passed to give the highway commissioner full authority to build a road (I-95, the Connecticut Turnpike) to relieve the dangerous and irritating traffic congestion caused by private autos and trucks on Route 1, which meandered through scores of towns and villages on or near the Long Island Sound. Initially, most residents favored the construction of an all-purpose Greenwich to New Haven expressway, but opposition grew in the wake of the severe postwar housing shortage and rise in existing real estate values. Few landowners wanted the much-needed route in their backyard.

"Our highways are vital to our economic growth," reminded Lodge. "Every mile of improved highway benefits our whole state." The new six-lane modern highway would speed the transportation of manufactured goods and agricultural products, and open up great areas of Connecticut to increased development, both industrial and commercial. Its construction, Lodge emphasized, would be financed from a bond issue based upon projected toll revenues.

Republican leader and State legislator John W. Boyd recalls the bumper to bumper traffic on the Post Road. "On days of football games at Yale, it would take several hours to drive from Westport to New Haven, a distance of some 25 miles."[3] But just as many people opposed the route as favored it, particularly in Fairfield County. Only in the eastern part of the state were there few protests; in fact, they wanted the highway extended through their area on to Rhode Island. State Representative Lawrence Gilman of sleepy Bozrah insisted his area needed the highway in order to bring in new business and relieve unemployment. He introduced a measure to continue the route from New Haven to New London, then northward to Killingly. As House Chairman of the Roads, Bridges, and Rivers Committee, Gilman and Highway Commissioner Albert Hill were at the center of the heated controversy.[4]

Gilman's so-called "Nutmeg Turnpike" bill generated public hearings that pitted Republicans against Democrats, eastern residents against western folk, anti-Lodge segments against the Governor's boosters, homeowners against businessmen, and so on. At one of the largest public hearings ever held in Hartford, over 500 people crowded into the House chamber. Gilman opened the meeting but was immediately challenged by Democratic minority leaders as being too partisan. The Democrats even introduced a resolution calling for his removal as chairman for his alleged "discourtesy" during the hearing.[5]

Lodge's hometown supporter Herman Steinkraus, president of Bridgeport Brass corporation and a property owner near the proposed route through residential Westport, marshaled substantial opposition. (Even Harvard crony Bud Eames, a recent home buyer in Westport, voiced firm displeasure.) Steinkraus organized the Citizens' Association, an amalgamation of civic groups against the turnpike. He met with John at the Capitol and implored: "John, Westport is your hometown, and you're doing a great disservice to the community by approving a superhighway through some of the best sections of the town. Wouldn't you back down and come out for an alternative route through another area?" John characteristically took the broad view: "All the road building experts tell us that the proposed route is the most efficient and economical. Remember, I'm not Governor of Westport or Fairfield. I am Governor of Connecticut. Our state needs this road. I have no intention of playing favorites for any single community."[6]

For the final hearing on the road bill, the resolute industrialist sent up a motorcade of people with anti-turnpike banners and signs. During the seven-hour session, Steinkraus frequently injected his opinions. At one point, he eloquently described an old Catholic church that stood in the path of the highway and its pending destruction. When he finished, a priest raised his hand to speak: "I'm the rector of the church that would be leveled. "I say 'Thank you, State of Connecticut, for taking the building.' We're going to have a much more beautiful church in a better location as a result of the highway."[7]

Lodge's press secretary Richard Ficks clearly remembered the hostility toward the turnpike and Lodge's anger over being deceived after confirming an appointment for one "friendly" representative, but receiving a caravan of outraged Westporters. One such anti-turnpike arrival, a smartly dressed Greens Farms matron, shook a well-manicured finger under John's nose: "I voted for you but we won't vote for you again if this turnpike goes through." "Madame," Lodge replied sternly, with a faint smile, "if I allowed myself to be influenced by such intimidation I would be undeserving of your vote!" "Her jaw locked—open," Ficks recalled "Lodge turned, walked to his office, and the 'party' was over."[8]

In the spring of 1953, the State Assembly voted final approval, and on May 23, Lodge signed the controversial bill with its allocation of some

$350 million for construction. (The actual cost reached $465 million by the time of completion in early 1958.) "It was the best investment the state ever made," concluded Lawrence Gilman. "With some 100 exits and entrances, it allowed users, especially local commuters, to travel short distances without paying tolls. And it was the only turnpike at that time with 75 miles of lighting."[9]

Construction of the 129-mile state-wide highway began immediately on both ends of the route. Lodge admitted it went through a lot of private property. Some 3,000 houses were taken by eminent domain; many were moved to other sites. John visited many people affected by the project. "I was very sympathetic with their reluctance to part with their own dwellings," he later noted. "It wasn't all bad, however. These people were paid in almost every instance a good deal more than their land and house were worth."[10] Inevitably, the thruway dispossessed many people who didn't forgive their governor. It made enemies for Lodge in many quarters.

John added ammunition to the anti-Lodge camp with another politically touchy decision. When Chief Justice Allyn Brown stepped down at the State Supreme Court retirement age of seventy, Lodge broke tradition. He turned not to its senior member, Raymond Baldwin, to fill the highest judicial post. Instead he chose sixty-five-year-old Ernest Inglis. The selection of the experienced and able Inglis had its roots in the 1949 "sell out" to Bowles by Baldwin, at one time the best vote getter for the party.[11]

Lodge's appointments generally met with approval. The naming to the Supreme Court of his brilliant legal counsel, Charles House of Hartford, was applauded, as were such choices as G. Harold Welch to the Banking Commission and Ray Watt to commandant of the Rocky Hill Veterans' Home. Few appointees were from his old Congressional district, only 18 out of a total of 125. And approximately a quarter of his selections were women, a high average for the time. His Secretary of State Alice K. Leopold was the state's highest elected woman.

Lodge took a special interest in higher education and visited campuses of state colleges to get first-hand information on major issues. He urged the state to supplement private colleges with more public universities. By the end of the 1950s, the number of college students was predicted to exceed 19,000, an increase of over 35 percent. Many would seek public institutions, he pointed out. He also looked into primary and secondary education, viewing with suspicion an unprecedented movement to organize teachers and authorize strikes in public schools.

Lawyer Richard Joyce Smith, a fairly active Democrat and one-time advisor to Governor Wilbur Cross, served as a Lodge appointee on the State Board of Education. "It was a period of radical activities within the teaching system," he later recalled. "As a result, Lodge became suspicious of educational bureaucracy and believed that parents should have more voice in the educational setup. "I remember John wanted school districts to provide transportation to students going to parochial schools in order to ensure their safe travel. That caused a lot of controversy, as did his statistical survey of the number of pupils in parochial schools. It had never been done before. He became a marked man among those who rigidly believed in the complete separation of church and state. Many didn't know what it was leading to. The outcome was a series of bitter hearings. Lodge had courage. He fought the party bosses and faced the liberals with teeth. He was a governor absolutely in his own right."[12]

Conservative in some areas, forward-moving in others, Lodge looked at the potential for the economy of Connecticut and New England from the development of atomic-generating power. As Chairman of the New England Governors' Conference, he formed, with the help of Massachusetts Governor Christian Herter, a ten-man committee on atomic energy, the first in the country to survey and report upon its prospects for peaceful purposes. He believed that atomic-generating power eventually would be practical. However, the commission subsequently found out that atomic energy was not economical in the 1950s.[13]

While Lodge the actor had faced his share of scathing reviews, he readily signed a bill that prohibited theaters from barring a drama critic from its audience. The measure was introduced after a Hartford theater protested a "savage" review by a veteran critic and thereafter denied him access to the theater. With Lodge's backing, the legislation made Connecticut the third state, after New York and California, to pass such a law.

The ceremonial side of his governorship continued to fascinate Lodge, and he carried it out with great ease and presence. With theatrical flair, he cut the ribbon that opened southwestern Connecticut's first TV station, WICC, in Bridgeport. John soon inaugurated a weekly series of fifteen-minute TV programs on state departments and agencies. With various officials, he reviewed the scope of services from such units as the new Department of Mental Health, the busy Motor Vehicles Department, and the fast-growing Public Works Department. One of the first governors of any state to utilize television on a regular and informative public-service basis, he also created a Commission of Education Television. From time to time, he even "competed" with his former "self" when one of his old movies surfaced on the TV screen.

In 1953 John once again spent two weeks as a Naval Reservist on active duty. Promoted to full commander, he joined the *Roanoke* on Atlantic waters between New York and Norfolk. When his military tour ended, he hurried home to pack. He and his family then headed west to the National Governors' Conference. At the meeting in Seattle, John was named to the group's executive committee and introduced resolutions to simplify the federal estate tax, to study certain inequities concerning corporate taxes, and to ask state and inter-state groups to participate in planning and executing programs for the utilization of natural resources in their areas. All three were adopted at the Conference.

From Seattle the Lodges flew to Hawaii for a ten-day vacation. As a family, they always liked to travel to new and different places and try to understand the local customs, Lily explained to a reporter. She, along with her mother and sister, took hula lessons, and John learned Hawaiian songs to sing as they danced.

Back to the mainland via the SS *Lurline*, they debarked at Los Angeles for a visit with society columnist Cobrina Wright, Sr. They were again entertained by Mary Pickford and Buddy Rogers at Pickfair, their Beverly Hills estate, where two hundred film, business and community leaders surrounded them. On another day, actor Basil Rathbone accompanied the Lodges to the Paramount studios set of his film *Casanova's Big Night*, starring Bob Hope and Joan Fontaine. John's old pal John Carradine rushed over to see him, as did a dozen studio workers from his days on the lot.

Away from Hartford almost two months, Lodge once more came under attack by political opponents and columnists because of his long absence.[14] Many outside meetings did enhance the prestige of his state. But he stayed close to the capital that fall, and his in-state engagements in October numbered thirty-five speaking dates. They ranged from the dedication of a firehouse to participation in the installation of a new archbishop for the Hartford archdiocese.[15]

John soon initiated a popular in-state agenda of personal visits to various areas on a weekly basis. Known as "Touring Tuesdays," he stopped by schools, businesses, and community organizations. Overall, he worked diligently to find solutions to one of Connecticut's persistent problems: loss of industries and jobs to other regions. The situation had grown more serious after the Korean conflict ended in mid-1953. Along those lines, he helped form a New England Textile Commission to retain regional manufacturing in that sector. He supported the efforts of the Aeronautics Commission to enhance the air service and facilities at Bradley Field, an airport situated to serve both Hartford and Springfield, Massachusetts.

Close observers described Lodge as the most overworked "state employee" in Connecticut. His work day of fifteen or so hours, six days a week, earned him less money than a laborer in the Highway Department working the same number of hours, even taking into account his recent salary boost to $15,000 from $12,000.[16] "It is a tough, exacting schedule which only a man of very strong physical health and very high standards of public service could carry out at all," Republican National Committeeman Meade Alcorn observed.

In a rallying address called "Let Us Keep Pace with His Greatness," Alcorn noted that "the effort is all the harder in the case of Lodge, who abhors the second rate or the mediocre." Alcorn described Lodge as a hardworking, conscientious, intelligent chief executive: "He looks like a Governor, acts like a Governor, speaks like a Governor. . . . Leadership with Lodge does not consist of threats or of loud criticism and browbeating of the other branches of government. . . . Rather, he conceives leadership to be a task which can best be carried out by quiet persuasion, by consistent good example, and where necessary, by bold and resourceful compromise."[17]

Mix in stately bearing and superb eloquence and he stood out as a person in command. Eisenhower recognized this. In November the President asked him to lead, with the rank of Special Ambassador, two official delegations at ceremonies in Latin America. The first marked the fiftieth anniversary of the independence of the Republic of Panama; the second celebrated the inauguration of José Figueres Ferrer as President of Costa Rica. "Both of these ceremonies are events requiring special recognition by this Government," wrote Secretary of State John Foster Dulles to John, "and both the President and I are very anxious to have a public figure of outstanding qualifications as head of our delegations." Dulles concluded: "May I add that we realize this is a very difficult time for you to take on extra duties of this sort and that we would not ask you to make the sacrifice if we did not feel that this was a matter very much in the national interest."[18]

The Lodges left Washington for Panama on November 1. Jack Neal, then deputy director of the Office of Middle American Affairs, arranged the trip for the delegation of State Department officials, legislators and military attachés. "John," said Neal," refused to travel on a commercial flight; he insisted on a special military craft, although it was too big to land directly in Costa Rica. He also wanted to stay at hotels, not embassies or government houses. Throughout the two-week trip, John remained his usual magnanimous and gregarious self—singing, dancing and being the life of the party."[19]

Yet there were serious problems to wrestle with, especially in Panama. It was the fiftieth anniversary of the Panama Canal, and John and U.S. Ambassador John Wylie met with a group of Panamanians to hear their complaints on the control of that strategic link in the security of the hemisphere. Lodge stressed the vital common interests which bound the two countries together.

In Costa Rica, the newly named U.S. Ambassador Robert Hill of New Hampshire greeted John. It began a close friendship between the two New England Republicans. José Figueres Ferrer, who had helped install a measure of democracy in the small Central American republic, delivered an inaugural address with words unfriendly to the United States. He attacked his North American ally on its patronizing programs of technical assistance in agriculture, health, and other areas. Later Lodge told Figueres that he clearly took offense at his speech. His response was: "Oh, Ambassador Lodge, you know, of course, I had to say all that for public consumption."[20] Apart from this sour note, the Lodges relished the warm hospitality and responded in phrases of newly learned Spanish. At the official ball, they danced to the beat of every Latin tune the orchestra played. Francesca caught the eye of every diplomat and partnered many. She even exhibited an intricate and lengthy dance called the tamburito with Nicaraguan President Anastasio Somoza.

Back in Hartford, John reported in a nation-wide radio talk that both Costa Rica and Panama had been subjected to the "siren song of Communism" but had refused to be influenced by it: "The Communists knew, what we seemed to have forgotten, that if they could destroy or perceptibly weaken the unity of the Western Hemisphere, they would not only effectively compromise the security of the United States, but would also strengthen their propaganda in free nations in other areas of the world."[21]

The year brought a reconciliation between the Lodges and the Luces. Upon Eisenhower's election, Clare was offered the Cabinet post of Secretary of Labor. She refused but indicated interest in a diplomatic job. John, too, warmed to the idea of an important ambassadorial post, now that Republicans controlled the White House for the first time in twenty years. But he would leave Connecticut only if the President specifically requested his services as an envoy. Rome held a particular allure. But the fact that his wife had been born in Italy, although an American citizen from birth, worked against him. The State Department frowned on sending a high-level representative to a country where he or his spouse had ethnic ties. So when John heard that Clare Luce was being considered for Rome, he urged Washington to appoint her.

"He had felt badly about Clare not getting the Senate appointment or nomination," Francesca recalled. "He backed her completely for the job as Ambassador to Italy—by far the most important diplomatic responsibility entrusted to a woman up to that time. John's support brought us back together with the Luces. I even taught Clare some Italian words for her to speak on her arrival in Rome."

By early spring, her nomination was confirmed, and John and Francesca eagerly organized a large farewell dinner in Bridgeport. John spoke of Luce's ability to implement "the sound and mature foreign policy that the Eisenhower administration stood for." President Eisenhower's choice of Luce, he concluded, reflected the growing importance of women in public life. "The people of Connecticut take affectionate and deep pride in the knowledge that Mrs. Luce will represent us with grace and energy and distinction and will bring the friendly solicitude of the people of Connecticut and the whole United States to the people of Italy."[22] The Lodges presented Clare with miniature U.S. and Connecticut flags attached to small silver stands for her desk in Rome. And from Rome, Clare commenced writing affectionate and chatty letters to both John and Francesca. "The boring moments are so intermixed with the variety and spice of life that they pass unnoticed," she penned in typical Luce angst. "Political conversation flows around every dinner table with intensity, voices are raised in excitement, hands begin to fly, and an ordinary party takes on the aspect of a heated debate in Madame de Stael's salon."[23]

Luce didn't have to face an election for her new assignment. But the thought of another campaign in league with the "party wreckers" unsettled John. His smoking accelerated to the point of going through two or three packs of cigarettes a day. The opportunity for a weekend break in Westport didn't exist; Villa Lodge had been rented. John relaxed by horseback riding at nearby Avon Mountain. One January day while astride "Baron," his mount went down in a patch of snow. Unable to disengage his foot from the stirrup quickly enough, John injured his knee. No bones were broken, but he walked with a stiff leg for days.

Not long after, another family member fell. Bessie Lodge broke her hip at her apartment. John immediately made a trip to Washington to see her. The brief visit generated talk that John was being considered for a Cabinet post, namely as a replacement for Secretary of the Navy Robert B. Anderson, who was moving on to Deputy Secretary of Defense. Washington informants, noted the Associated Press, said the possible appointment stemmed from a recent private poll by the Republican National Committee. The survey showed that Lodge would lose re-election by 30,000 votes, findings of little comfort to John.

Facing the uncertainty of a second term, John hastened the completion of his official portrait as Governor. Deane Keller of Yale's School of Fine Arts had been selected for the task (at an appropriation of $1,500, including frame). John scheduled several sessions in his studio, but it was necessary for Keller to catch John for brief sittings on the run. "I am not a believer in psychic phenomena," the artist wrote Lodge's secretary Regina Tomlin at the completion of the commission, "But I do know that if I admire a sitter, this usually appears in the painted product, and if I don't, sometimes the dislike appears too. It is not all a matter of colors and a brush and a canvas. A couple of times when Mr. Lodge was sitting in my studio at the end of the day, pretty tired I'd judge, I believe I saw way into his thinking. What he had to say on these occasions was bedrock, sound and high-minded as he talked of the problems of the state and of people in general."[24]

What emerged on canvas remains a dramatic pose. Lodge stands at night on the steps of the State Library. He holds a homburg in one hand and his other rests on a briefcase. Over one arm is a Navy raincoat. He is dressed in a dark suit and a rep tie; a rosette appears on his lapel. In the background, the lighted State Capitol and a glimpse of downtown Hartford appear under a somewhat ominous dark sky mixed with both clouds and stars. The striking painting joined the more conventional portraits of other Connecticut governors in the Library gallery that year.[25]

As the political winds blew stronger, John eagerly anticipated his invigorating reserve training on the aircraft carrier USS *Coral Sea*, cruising in the Mediterranean. Once again his absence provided a chance for many to voice outrage over a governor, not merely out of the state, but out of the country.

And it couldn't be denied that John moved very slowly with policy-making decisions. He admitted that executive duties were laborious because he didn't have much confidence in his own judgment and needed to hold long meetings with department heads to come up with a course of action. And more and more matters fell under the control of an inner group surrounding John, a staff isolating him from different and diverse points of view. Republican control of both houses of the Legislature naively lulled the Governor's office into thinking that perhaps there would be little or no party opposition to his programs.

His closest day-to-day advisor, Al Coote, was no more than a political novice. First hired as a publicity aide and speech writer, he advanced into an all-round assistant. A well-educated fellow, an avid reader, and an able editorial craftsman, Coote prided himself on being on the same intellectual wave length as Lodge. He'd often finish a famous quotation John started, supply the last line of a poem, or identify a literary source. He was a perfect alter ego, but lacked know-how on politics and government. A handicap to John, he refused to bring in experienced and savvy political experts. Coote's style prompted the oft-repeated complaint that Lodge was aloof and unapproachable.[26]

Coote seemingly placed John on a throne, sequestered and hidden from the everyday ebb and flow of state business. Very possessive of John and jealous of anyone maneuvering too close, he rationed his "man-on-the-street" junkets. "Al Coote thought John was some sort of deity," Francesca once ruefully admitted. "He didn't like me. To him, I was *de trop*. All my ideas were unacceptable. He was an Ivy Leaguer and writer. I was an unlearned interloper who couldn't speak his language. I tried to bring in other and less lofty points of view. But he cut me off, and in doing so, increasingly isolated John within a circle of idolaters. He was the man who ruined John's governorship."

John's ego was being fed at the expense of his common sense. A bit myopic, he had difficulty playing with the Lilliputians of the Connecticut political scene. Now he was being enveloped by a palace guard and picked to pieces by his own party pros, not to mention Democratic forces. Francesca urged John to break out of the protective shell. She reminded him he always emerged as pretty much of a regular guy when he came out of the executive inner sanctum. She pleaded with John to meet informally with Bill Brennan and his pro-Taft crony Fred Zeller, and Jack Zaiman, who always seemed to put down Lodge in his columns. "Get to know them better on a one-to-one basis," she advised. "Have it out with these people, then work out a compromise with the opposition within your own party. Once they see you and get to know you better, things could change in your favor." "They're against me," John replied. "They dislike me, and I don't want to see Zaiman, Brennan or any of that gang. Besides, Coote says 'no.' He tells me to stay away from any arguments with them." Had Lodge drifted away from acting on his own firm belief that "politics is the art of inclusion?" And was Lodge, to borrow the words of Oscar Wilde, not being "too careful in the choice of his enemies?"

Lt. Governor Ned Allen tried to restore Republican harmony so the party could go on and win again in 1954. Republican leaders met at Allen's cottage in Enfield on the banks of the Connecticut River. They adjourned in apparent amity. But for reasons unknown, "the treaty of Enfield" lasted only a few days. Coote may have broken the peace by pointing out that Brennan's ongoing patronage deals in Hartford benefitted his insurance business. These contracts struck some as a probable conflict of interest. These back-room arrangements, Coote concluded, could backfire at Lodge and smear his unquestioned honesty and scandal-free administration. The collapse of the Enfield accord, says Zaiman, signaled the beginning of the end of the Lodge regime. "Brennan wanted his own way. He needed to cut John down to size in the election of 1954 if he was going to retain any influence and position. And I think Brennan played with the Democrats, and they eventually rewarded him with some insurance work and appointments for his guys. "My newspaper was liberal Republican and supported Lodge. But in the 45 years I wrote for the *Hartford Courant* no one told me what to say. John complained about my columns to the publisher, who told him that I was on my own on reporting state politics. And I believe I called it right."[27]

At heart, Lodge did not have an overriding drive to run for governor again. He wanted to return to Washington. On a visit there, Eisenhower's Chief of Staff Sherman Adams remarked to John, "You know the President is never going to ask you to run again in Connecticut, but if you don't run, who is there?"[28] It was one way of saying that the White House preferred John to stand for re-election. He dragged his feet on making a clear-cut decision. In retrospect, John realized that he made a mistake by not coming to grips faster with his future plans. "I kept postponing it. It was a basic error."[29]

Not until late spring did John announce his candidacy. In July he won renomination by unanimous acclamation at the state convention. The Republican team included Charles Jewett for Lieutenant Governor; Fred Zeller, Comptroller; John Ottaviano, Treasurer; John Bracken, Attorney General; and Mildred Allen, Secretary of State. Cappy Baldwin remained as chairman of the State Central Committee.

Among the Democrats, John Bailey pleaded for harmony in order to overcome the GOP sweep of 1952. Abe Ribicoff, with his formidable backing, moved into the front ranks as a gubernatorial candidate. The first Jew to run for governor of any New England state, he had made a spectacular run for the Senate against Bush. Ribicoff, who had served with John on the House Foreign Affairs Committee, was nominated without opposition, along with running mate John Dempsey, Mayor of Putnam. Bailey's formula for political success that year was simple: good candidates, good issues, and good organization. Besides, he had a candidate born and educated in Connecticut, while Lodge remained for some a foreigner.

John stepped up his official activities, making political hay from his "Touring Tuesdays" and ceremonial duties. He attended an anniversary of a synagogue, met with Cub Scouts, participated in firefighter tributes, celebrated with Italian-Americans, and accepted honorary membership in veterans' groups. One day he even played softball. His legal aide Edmund O'Brien remembered the athletic club game well: "John wasn't good at baseball, and I thought his participation on the field would be a disaster. But he had a very lucky day! The Governor hit a triple and a single in three trips to the plate and played errorless ball at first base. He also scored a run. His team, the Executives, downed the Old Timers 7-2 in three innings. And a photo of Lodge at bat ran on the front page of the *Hartford Courant* the next day!"[30]

John's unexpected success at sports may have won a few votes. But a number of his own party remained in the dugout. Columnist George E. Sokolsky noted a Republican split and lukewarm enthusiasm for Lodge in some quarters. "While whenever I have met Republican politicians in Connecticut," he wrote, "they speak well of John Lodge personally, they seem to go out of their way to praise the Democratic candidate, Abraham Ribicoff. It is an unusual demonstration of lack of partisanship in a campaign year. Its significance cannot be missed."[31]

Francesca realized that her husband was making little headway in the campaign. It was again time to gear up and take to the campaign trail. She mapped out a broad agenda. She appeared in country Grange halls, joined drum-beating workers on campaign trucks and trailers, urged an isolated community of French-born nuns to vote, reminded hospital patients to cast absentee ballots, distributed "We Want Lodge" T-shirts on street corners, and broadcast Lodge ads in Italian. Her unique charm, tested know-how, and hard work gained support for John among the rank and file. And sharp-eyed feminine critics agreed that her beauty was authentic, not synthetic. There was no end to her energy: even in the midst of all this politicking, she turned to a non-political project close to the hearts of the Lodges and many actors and theatergoers and helped to break ground for the American Shakespeare Festival Theater at Stratford.

John entered the campaign with solid accomplishments, but hardly the substance for front-page news. He reorganized the welfare department at an estimated annual savings of $5 million and eliminated overlapping and duplicating services which helped save money, consolidated municipal courts in adjoining communities, and took steps to repair damage to shorelines and to study beach erosion control.

State employees benefitted from the establishment of a forty-hour week, again bringing savings of some $3½ million. Underpaid by comparable standards, state employee salaries were upped an average 27½ percent. There were fewer employees, but they were better paid. Connecticut had the lowest unemployment rate among all the industrial states and was the first and only state in the nation with a seventy-five-cent minimum wage law. And he picked heads of departments on the basis of merit, honesty, and ability. Moreover, Lodge strengthened anti-discrimination laws.

Within the areas of health and education, the Governor directed legislation at the needs and wants of individual citizens, without concern over potential votes. He set up a Mental Health Commission, an agency that made tremendous strides and was recognized as one of the most advanced in the country. He backed a commission to study the problems of the aging. Its recommendations included expansion of placement services for older workers and development of pre-retirement preparation courses, enlightened legislation for the time. State hospitals expanded as did campus facilities, particularly at the University of Connecticut. Grants to towns in aid of expanding school systems were stepped up. And nearly 10,000 homes under public housing programs helped to meet the crucial housing shortage. Most of these measures required an increase to tax rates, amounting to 3.2 percent, never a popular move by an administration yet at a rate lower than many states. Meade Alcorn concluded: "The general issue of taxation was probably the most troublesome for Lodge."[32]

Throughout his political career, John believed that with freedom came responsibility. He defined freedom *as* responsibility: "If people are going to transfer their responsibilities beyond a certain point to the State, they are certainly not going to retain their freedom." He called himself "just enough of an old-fashioned puritan to think that it's good for the character and good for the soul, too, for the individual to assume the responsibilities of freedom."[33] And he called himself a Lincoln Republican as well, based on the premise of a government of, by, and for the people—a government that did only what individuals could not do for themselves. The state, he believed, should be run in the best interests of all its citizens and on the basis of fiscal probity.

Lodge and Ribicoff, in essence, had a good deal in common and were friends. Each had a basic independence stemming from a belief that good government is more important than political loyalties. Not even John's bitterest enemies could breathe the slightest hint that he was, in any way, motivated by the thought of personal or monetary gain. Personal integrity stamped his administration. No scandal touched his team. The state maintained a sound, efficient, forward-looking administration. The tax burden on a per capita basis was still one of the lowest in the nation. Gambling cabals, liquor lobbyists and state employee groups often pressured him for special consideration. Large property owners inconvenienced by the highway threatened reprisal. Through it all, Lodge refused to put any individual interest above the well-being of the entire state. And he managed to achieve most of his program in less than four years.

In the midst of the campaign, he wrote a challenging article that aroused national attention. Called "Politics is Everybody's Business" and published in the *New York Times Magazine*, it summoned all Americans to take part in public affairs: "Political activity is the prerogative of no special group. As Americans, one of our main efforts should be to encourage every citizen to make the business of government his own business. As more and more citizens become politicians in that sense the full range of meaning in 'politics' will be more generally understood and the duties and enormous satisfaction of public service will attract more and more of our capable and high-minded men and women."[34] This philosophical clarion call may not have registered with the average voter in his state, but it expressed a statesman-like analysis of Lodge's American Dream. Later, it would be read by countless students as an example of superior prose in the textbook *Improving College English Skills*.

As the campaign moved into the final stages, few major differences came to the forefront. The Democrats failed to raise a major issue, beyond the increase in the state sales tax. Their plank stressed sweeping constitutional reforms in legislative representation and abolition of county government. Lodge seemed to have the edge because of his modern-minded labor legislation, increased state services, and surplus-building budgetary operations. Most newspapers favored his re-election, based on his record as "The Man Who Gets Things Done." As a campaigner, he understated, rather than overstated, believing that the exaggeration which fails to convince is better left unsaid.

Behind the scenes, Bailey was worried. To keep his leadership position, he had to win the state race. A defeat would mean another four years of Republican rule and the end of his chairmanship. Moreover, he had not had a winner in any Senate races since 1950, and his part in those victories was comparatively slight. His party would have to come out of the five largest cities (Hartford, New Haven, Bridgeport, Waterbury, and New Britain) with a large plurality. Bailey had to inject some issue, some twist, some angle, into the final weeks of the contest. He had emphasized the absentee governor theme to the extreme, shouting that Lodge's "frequent junkets" were often at the expense of taxpayers. "He should remove himself from the state payroll," the Bailey camp proclaimed. "And where was the Governor on election day in 1953? Attending a bullfight in Latin America!"[35]

The only pronounced issue in the campaign, according to Ribicoff, emerged in the last weeks. It stemmed from a member of his own party. Former Congressman John McGuire of New Haven, who had served with him for two terms, had been denied a renomination. McGuire and several brash cohorts visited Abe to plead for help to get him back on the ticket. Abe resisted. In desperation, McGuire said, "Get me the nomination or I'll destroy you." His form of revenge was a whispering campaign over Ribicoff's religion. "He was the one," Ribicoff pointed out, "who started to float anti-Semitism. And a lot of it. It was very ugly and nasty." McGuire, meanwhile, backed Lodge.[36]

Ribicoff felt he had to respond to the rumbling maelstrom. On October 24, at a dinner of the Italian-American Democrats of Connecticut, Ribicoff asked to be judged only by his ability and integrity. His election, he stated, would show "that any boy regardless of race, creed or color has the right to aspire to public office. Where else but in the Democratic Party could you find a boy named Abe Ribicoff becoming a candidate for Governor?" Bailey, too, spelled it out to the gathering: "If we elect Ribicoff on November 2nd, we may have a governor of Italian-American extraction in the next decade."[37] Many quickly voiced outrage over the statement. Ribicoff's hometown paper termed it an insult to thousands of voters, Democrats, Republicans, and Independents, "who Mr. Bailey apparently believes will vote for a man solely because of his race, creed or color rather than because of his ability, record and accomplishments. . . . Mr. Bailey must be worried over the outcome of the election to resort to such reprehensible tactics."[38]

Far from disassociating himself from Bailey's tactics, Ribicoff added innuendoes. His answer to the charge that an appeal had been made to voters to cast their ballots for him because he was a Jew (or in spite of the fact that he was a Jew) stemmed from a lot of "ugly rumors" and behind-the-scenes bigotry, by word of mouth as well as by mail. He indirectly suggested that the Republican Party was never "liberal" enough, or courageous enough, to nominate a Jew or a Catholic for high office. Blatantly ignoring facts and the posts held by former Governor James Shannon and Senator John Danaher, Ribicoff and Bailey twisted their appeal for tolerance into an appeal for votes based solely on religion and the promise of future racial and ethnic standard bearers. A number of life-long Democrats protested the fact and repudiated the "vicious and un-American way of courting political favor."[39] The Republicans failed to counterattack. John was told that any hard attack on Ribicoff would be considered anti-Semitic. Besides, there was little time to overcome the slur against the party and aspersions against John personally (as, for example, "the Brahmin from Boston who doesn't know what it's like to be homeless").

Lodge kept his campaign on the high road. He hoped the visit of Eisenhower to Hartford would build support, particularly from independent voters. The President first spoke in a non-political vein at Trinity College when he received an honorary degree. After the talk, Ike went to Bushnell Park at the foot of Capitol Hill for a gigantic birthday party for John. An estimated 50,000 cheering people turned out to see Eisenhower cut a 400-pound cake to celebrate the governor's fifty-first birthday. He referred to John as "the first citizen of your state, who does a worthy job in your service." The President might have given John a stronger personal endorsement, aides concluded.[40] The Democrats observed that Ike or anyone who could stimulate a get-out-the-vote appeal would only benefit them because Hartford was a Democratic stronghold.

In the final week, John campaigned fifteen hours at a stretch, criss-crossing the state to speak at clubhouses, restaurants, factories, and street corners. Radiating optimism, he shook thousands of hands as he walked through three plants in New Haven on a single day. But at a New Britain factory gate, homeward-bound workers avoided him, tossing campaign flyers and buttons onto the street. A campaign aide observed to a disconsolate

Lodge that "even Babe Ruth didn't hit home runs every time he came to bat." John turned to party worker John Ericson and said, "I didn't expect to hit a home run, but I thought I could at least lay down a bunt."[41]

Francesca covered nearly as much ground. Neither spared themselves as the election developed into a neck and neck race. Three or four hours of sleep each night was a luxury as they combed the depth and breadth of the state. Tired and weary, John remained confident of victory. Like the MP he played in *The Tenth Man*, he'd come through with a slim majority of votes at the last minute. "But he had lost his sense of humor and knack of laughing at himself, of enjoying the repartee and hurly-burly," Francesca remembered. "Fatigue drowned his natural flair. 'I'm no political operator,' he'd say. 'Others have the politicians but I have the people.' He felt the vox populi would recognize his good points and honesty, and want him to continue for another term."

Ribicoff and Lodge ended their contest in front of a television camera in New Haven on the Friday evening before election. The challenger spoke first. He again cited the ugly anti-Semitic rumors and whispers that "would cut you to the quick." He wondered if the American Dream was still alive—that anybody regardless of race, creed, or color had the right to aspire to public office. "The important thing," he declared in a low-key, one-to-one earnestness, "is that I should have the *opportunity* to be elected." In this highly emotional talk, he proclaimed that the American Dream "is still alive and no matter what happens on November 2, Abe Ribicoff still believes in it."[42] John followed with a dry speech, full of statistics and budgetary and other accomplishments. He lacked spontaneity. Years later, Ribicoff recalled: "He should have said 'I have no prejudices. I have always been against anti-Semitism.' Without my American Dream speech, I would have never won."[43] The home-stretch address made a tremendous impact on voters and apparently swung to his side many who were still uncommitted.

The polls on Election Day opened to heavy voting. Crowds continued to line up to cast ballots all day, in spite of heavy rain. By early evening, 157 of the state's 169 towns reported in, and Lodge was ahead. Yet, in town after town, he failed to keep pace with his earlier 1950 totals. Radio commentators began to hedge on Lodge's chances. John, his family, and a crowd of friends waited the final results in the library at the Governor's Residence. John sat impassively with Francesca at his side and Cabot in a chair behind him. There were rumors that TV reports were far more encouraging than local radio newscasts. "It's hard," Francesca whispered to a bystander, "to watch someone else's trouble. I feel so helpless. I can do nothing to help him."[44]

He lost ground, but there were occasional bright spots—in New Haven and in some Fairfield towns. Reports of a *Hartford Times* poll seeped into conversations. It showed the Governor gaining, coming abreast of Ribicoff, and finally passing him. Suddenly, at 9:45 P.M., John's press secretary Jack Tierney (who replaced Ficks in May 1954) put down a telephone to announce that Lodge had won by 5,000 votes in the *Times*'s unofficial poll. "Cut it out, Jack," John snapped. "I'm losing town after town. Don't try to fool me."[45]

But his reluctance to accept the newspaper's count was battered down by the mob sweeping into the library to congratulate him. A radio station had announced his victory. The well-wishers broke into loud cheers. A special edition of the *Times* with headlines of Lodge's re-election already was on press in downtown Hartford, someone proclaimed. John, still dubious, smiled, and reminded all within earshot that it was still all very unofficial. Amid talk of a victory parade to Republican headquarters, a glum Lodge remained apart from it all. The phone rang. It was New York Governor Tom Dewey. "Congratulations, John," he exclaimed. "Well, it's uncertain yet, Governor. Thank you very much, but it's hard to tell now."[46]

John resisted the efforts of reporters to have him issue a victory statement. Francesca, dressed in a blue silk dress bedecked with campaign buttons and a paper GOP elephant, was not overjoyed at the election news: "Five thousand votes? Where is the vote of confidence? At this point our armor is dragging."

Meanwhile, Ribicoff at his home in Hartford heard the news of the *Times* count. He began to prepare to concede. But just before 11 P.M., radio reporter Rudy Frank of WELI-New Haven ran into the living room from the press room in Abe's basement. "Don't concede! We show you winning." The *Times* had left out the complete Bridgeport vote. Ribicoff had carried that city by 8,000. By 11:30 it was clear. Abraham Ribicoff had won the governorship. It turned out John was right all along. The "victory" was erroneous; the Lodge election, unfounded. The celebration ended abruptly. John moved to a corner of an enclosed sun porch and asked for a drink. "It is too bad," Francesca repeated, "but it is life. It is all right." At 11:45 P.M., John conceded in a brief statement over radio. Francesca stood at his side, as she had often during the grueling campaign.

John lost his bid for re-election by merely 3,115 votes. His defeat was traced primarily to a poor showing in Fairfield County, a traditional Republican stronghold. Actually, Lodge received 24,000 more votes than he had in 1950, picking up a total of 460,735 votes to Ribicoff's 463,530. Perennial Socialist Party candidate Mayor Jasper McLevy of Bridgeport in his thirteenth run for governor polled about 11,000 votes, and write-in contender Vivien Kellems picked up some 1,500 votes. Political analysts concluded that Republicans in party strongholds either abstained from voting or perhaps even voted for Ribicoff. Bill Brennan had apparently instructed his "machine" in Fairfield to sit it out. Perhaps he did not want Lodge to lose. But he certainly wanted to punish him for his political sins. A win by the narrowest of votes, he concluded, would clip his wings. Brennan and other dissidents publicly advanced the theory that he lost because he didn't submit to their guidance. "John kicked some old politicians in the ass," concluded John Alsop. "An incumbent governor with a good record should win."[47]

Construction of the controversial Turnpike hurt John, too. Irritating differences among highway commissioner, local officials, and homeowners in the path of the route were factors in losing votes. Ribicoff later concluded: "I think the building of the turnpike hurt John Lodge in the election. Not because it was a toll road. . . . It hurt because of constant turmoil in condemnation proceedings as they cut a swath through the State."[48]

Campaign donations for Lodge had lagged too. Fund-raisers found it difficult to generate money for the governor. Over $5,500 of the $11,455 raised for John came from his relatives; more than half of that amount was a gift of his well-do-do Lodge cousin and legislative aide William Minot of Greenwich.[49] In comparison, the Ribicoff for Governor Committee received $67,000 in contributions and used a large chunk of its treasury on effective roadside billboards.

The election left Francesca more a public woman than before. Some complained she butted in too much, and they blamed her for John's fall. But most people said that she wanted to help her husband in every way possible and that her active role was admirable and commendable. And she appeared at so many events because she was invited and begged to attend. Reporter Tere Pascone, who had followed both Clare Luce and the Lodges from the time they entered politics, claimed Francesca broke all precedent in the state and compared her to Eleanor Roosevelt, who similarly traveled far and wide to sing the praises of her husband: "She will probably go down in history as the most active First Lady Connecticut ever had."[50]

The defeat of the Governor signaled the end of Republican dominance in the state. The party's hold in the Capitol slipped measurably because of those 3,000 votes in Ribicoff's favor. Jack Zaiman terms it "the turning point in the history of Connecticut politics and government." He suggests that those votes "killed careers and built careers. It's not the greatness of the winner; it's the stupidity of the loser that often shapes events."[51]

From a more discerning perspective, *Hartford Times* political analyst Moses Berkman summed up John's defeat: "He could not form a partnership with the professionals whose primary interest was patronage and personal security, without sacrificing principle and independence. He chose the latter."[52] For John personally, the cruelest blow on election night was the discovery that every Republican on the ballot save one had been triumphant. (Incumbent Congressman Thomas Dodd handily beat his Republican opponent in the First District.) Even his Lieutenant Governor had ridden to victory with some seven thousand more votes than he himself had attracted. Lodge had run behind his entire ticket, in several places by as many as 14,000 votes.

Dejected and downcast, John had lost his first political race, and with it a job he had come to like and thrive in.

CHAPTER 17

New Constituents

The sudden twist from joyous near-victory to painful rejection left John bewildered and numb. Minutes after he conceded defeat, Cabot bid good-bye to his exhausted brother.

"Cabot," pleaded Francesca, "I wish you wouldn't go now. It's going to hit John very hard."

"It's too late to tarry. I'll talk to him on the phone tomorrow."

The house emptied quickly. In the stillness, John vanished into the darkness of the night. A half hour later, at one P.M., Francesca became worried. When he failed to return, she called their next-door neighbors, Florence and Moses Berkman. Had they seen John in the neighborhood? Yes, they had spotted him earlier walking on the road in the rain. Francesca waited, and soon heard the sound of the opening of the front door. John was back to the once-jubilant Governor's house.

Cabot did call the next day. To comfort John, he told a story about Winston Churchill's defeat in 1945. The Prime Minister, it seems, had retired thinking he had won re-election. He woke up the next morning to find that he and his party had been swept out of office. His wife Clemmie was waiting for him at the foot of the stairs. She had been wondering what to say to him in order to soothe the sting of defeat. When he descended the stairs, she took his arm and led him into the dining room. "Oh, my dear Winnie. You know, I do think this must be a blessing in disguise." To this Churchill tartly replied: "May I say, my dear, that the blessing is most effectively disguised."[1]

The tale gave the disconsolate brother little solace. "Cabot and his damn story," thought John. Yet with mixed feelings, he would remember the anecdote and tell it to others many times in the future.

Sifting through the post-election political ashes, he grieved over his loss and struggled to explain it. Defeat suddenly made John very vulnerable. "I never trusted some of those guys," he muttered over and over. "A mere 3,000 votes. All I needed was half that to win. I should have blasted the Democrats over the ethnic matter. Cesca worked so hard. I should have listened more to her advice. And couldn't have Ike praised my administration more? And it inherited nearly $7½ million deficit and left over $17 million surplus! What will I do next?"[2]

Those closest to John soon realized he was having some sort of a nervous breakdown. He had difficulty sleeping. At times, he stood and stared quietly out the window. An immediate period of rest was prescribed. The Lodges prepared for a vacation in Bermuda. But before they left, Eisenhower wired a message. It expressed disappointment over the defeat, yet noted that his services would be utilized elsewhere in government. Cabot, too, quickly reassured John. "You have many attractive prospects before you," Cabot wrote two days after the election, "and you can look back on everything that you have done with real satisfaction." He also commented on John's magnificent self-control and general deportment on election night, and that "to me means far more than a political victory."[3]

John's stay in Bermuda did help to bring him back to his old self. But doctors and psychiatrists urged still more rest and a change of scenery. He canceled a number of end-of-the-year engagements. Francesca asked Tom Dewart and his wife and the recently widowed Dick Aldrich to go with them to Hot Springs, Virginia. Long walks through the bucolic countryside and hours of jokes and storytelling with his old cronies from college and the war did boost his spirits.[4] Yet his physicians continued to recommend rest, and even electric shock treatment, a not-uncommon method of psychiatric therapy in the 1950s. "Do what the doctors tell you," his mother, and just about everybody in the family, begged.

In the meantime, there were rumors that John or Cabot would replace Sherman Adams as White House assistant. Eisenhower, however, offered John a diplomatic post, in Spain as his Ambassador. The President needed a proven "troubleshooter" to bring that country closer to America, especially as a partner in the defense of Western Europe. John spent hours pacing the floor, saying to Francesca: "I just don't know how I can do it. I don't know Spain. I don't know the language. To me, it's like going to Japan. Cabot feels I can't do it." A nervous tic around his mouth, a facial twitching stemming from his school days, accelerated. Indeed, Cabot, witnessing his brother's continued vulnerability in the wake of defeat, ruled out such an assignment, according to Francesca. "John should never run again for public office," Cabot stated at a family gathering to consider the "fate" of John. "And he can't handle any foreign job in government, at least for the time being."[5]

A week or so later, John went to the Wardman Park Hotel to see his mother. Trying to console him, she urged retirement. John felt he needed to talk with someone besides his mother and brother. He phoned his brother-in-law Chad Braggiotti at UN headquarters in New York, where he was an advisor on the staff of Cabot. A Foreign Service career man since the war years, with postings in Colombia, Argentina, Belgium, and Poland, he had reluctantly joined Cabot and the U.S. delegation, not wanting to be with his brother-in-law's brother and encountering innuendoes of nepotism. But Cabot insisted, and Chad had little choice in the matter.

"Chad, I want you to come to Washington this evening on an urgent matter," John explained. Chad had agreed to fill in for Cabot at a UN-related dinner, but he said he'd make up an excuse to get out of it. He always had to be very careful about any meetings with John because Cabot often became quite nosy and jealous. Chad told Cabot that it was essential that he go to Washington that evening for an early morning meeting at the State Department. "Why didn't they call me first and ask my permission?" Cabot replied. "After all, I'm not a nobody. I was General Eisenhower's campaign manager. And I have Cabinet rank!"[6]

Chad arrived at Mrs. Lodge's apartment to find John nervously debating with himself over his future: "President Eisenhower has been pushing me to accept the post as Ambassador to Spain. But I don't think I can handle it. Perhaps I could if I were his man in Paris. I don't know anything about Spain and really don't speak the language. I have to give an answer tomorrow morning at the White House to Sherman Adams. Please help me. I value your judgment."

John and Chad talked all night and into the morning. "John, I think you'll make a great ambassador. You've a unique aptitude for languages. You'll learn Spanish. You picked up enough Italian to make pictures in Italy. You're fluent in French. I don't think you'll have any trouble."

"I'll accept the job. But you must come and be my deputy."

"I can't. I'm working for Cabot. The State Department won't agree anyway. But I'll give you all my support, all my ideas."[7]

Francesca remembered that period. " 'He must get to Spain,' I told his mother. She said I was absolutely crazy and that he couldn't handle it. I explained John needed something to completely occupy his mind, a challenge of a different nature, a job that would restore his sense of worth and rekindle his talents." John resisted Francesca's reasoning and efforts. There were other less taxing tasks at hand to fill the vacant space in his life. He gave a well-received talk on Mark Twain at a library in Hartford at the close of the year, and other similar requests came to him. A casting director for TV's *Masquerade Party*, *The Name's the Same*, *I've Got a Secret*, and other game and panel shows offered him guest shots at the top fee of $500 a broadcast.

His appointment to Spain was still unofficial as the year drew to an end. Then, on December 28, President Eisenhower from Augusta, Georgia announced the selection of Lodge to succeed Ambassador James C. Dunn. John received official word in Hartford. On Connecticut's inaugural day, the Lodges were hosts at a luncheon for incoming and outgoing state officials. The next day they flew to Washington, where they took an apartment for the winter while John received briefings on his new career in diplomacy.[8]

Nevertheless, John worried over being in one of the few major European countries with which he had no familiarity. He didn't even consider Spain truly a part of Europe. To him it seemed more oriental than Mediterranean. Cabot reminded him that it was a wonderful break and he was lucky to get the post. The ambassadorship, a Class I post, carried a top diplomatic salary of $25,000. In addition to the regular embassy complement, the job entailed supervision of all U.S. economic, military, and Information Service operations.[9] Besides, a new seven-story modern embassy, in the final phases of construction, would bring the various staff members and employees under one roof. The building included a 210-seat theater for American films and lecture programs.[10]

A month before departure, Chad asked about their travel plans. John explained that they would sail on the American Export Line and disembark at Gibraltar, then motor to Madrid.

"That's English territory. It's a sensitive place for the Spaniards, almost a slap in the face. Why not fly?"

"We can't do that. We've tons of luggage, plus two dogs."

"Call the Line and ask them to land you in Algeciras."

"What? That's right on the Bay of Gibraltar."

"Yes, but it's Spanish soil. This way you don't start out on the wrong foot as Ambassador. Tell the State Department you can't possibly land on British turf."[11]

Washington resisted the move. John finally called the steamship company directly. As a favor, the *Constitution* would stop at Algeciras and allow the Lodges to go ashore from a launch. Going directly from American to Spanish ground, and not the usual route through British territory, made an instant hit with the Spaniards. A thousand or more people waving American and Spanish flags lined the waterfront to welcome the new envoy. Cheers and shouts in English of "hello, hello" greeted them. This was no ordinary diplomatic couple, they thought.

"We were met by the Deputy Chief of Mission Homer Byington, Jr., and went by car to Madrid, slowing down at little villages to wave and say 'hola' which is 'hello' in Spanish," related Francesca. "Our 40 trunks, as well as our dogs, were quite a curiosity. There was great commotion when someone mislaid the keys of the luggage and Beatrice and Lily had to search in all the bags. Beatrice, tall and blond, and Lily, shorter and dark, were greeted by the natives who sang out the popular song 'La Rubia y la Morena,' a romantic melody meaning blonde and brunette."

Once John had boarded the *Constitution* in New York, he soon became his old self—alert, convivial, outgoing.[12] Conquering Spanish became a priority on the voyage. They discovered a cabin steward who knew English and Spanish well. He was engaged to converse with them in Spanish three or four hours each day. John absorbed the language quickly and easily, and by the time the steamship reached the Mediterranean, he had prepared a short greeting in Spanish with the help of the steward and a fellow passenger. John was thrilled about learning more about Spain and its people. "John clicked right back and was himself again," Francesca explained. "Soon the newspapers were saying that the new American Ambassador had stepped onto Spanish soil and into their hearts."

Within days the formally attired Lodge entered a horse-drawn eighteenth-century carriage for an Arabian Nights-like trip through the streets of Madrid to the Oriente Palace to present his credentials. The coach, escorted by 100 picturesque Moorish guards in native costume and carrying burnished lances, attracted thousands of onlookers. At the palace gates, aides unrolled a long red carpet to the portico. Inside, John presented members of his Embassy staff to General Francisco Franco, head of the Spanish State. John was then invited by the General into a side room for a private conversation. Franco spoke warmly of John's attempts in Congress in 1947 to include Spain within postwar aid programs. The long meeting was considered a good omen, and the talk, according to John, was extremely cordial.

That week John gave his first official public talk—in Spanish: "It is my belief that the common bonds which now join us will grow even stronger as our two countries stand together against the menace of Communist aggression and for the maintenance of peace in the world." Apologizing for his Spanish, he commented: "Such a beautiful language should never be spoken so badly. But I promise you that in a few months, I'll do better than today."[13]

Spanish-American relations were moving into a comparatively amiable period by the mid-1950s after having fallen to a low ebb in the previous decade. Earlier opinion abroad had been split violently between those who saw in Franco a peremptory savior of his country from the economic and social disasters of the 1930s and those who saw him as a Fascist dictatorial poser in the mold of Hitler and Mussolini. When war broke out in

Europe, Spain had leaned toward the Nazi-Axis alliance and apparently even promoted subversion and sabotage against the United States in Latin American countries. By the end of World War II, nearly every major country had criticized, if not denounced, Franco's links to the Axis powers or Spain's non-belligerent neutrality. Few had normal diplomatic ties by the mid-1940s, and as a result, Spain grew isolated and insolvent.

It was another sad chapter in Spanish-American diplomacy, contentious relations that went back to the late eighteenth century, revolving around control of the Mississippi and later Florida and Cuba, and coming to a peak of intensity with war in 1898. Although Spain had not sent troops to help George Washington's army, she did lend the cause nearly a million dollars in 1779 and engaged the British in fighting at Gibraltar. Diplomatic relations were established six years later. Among the early American Ministers were statesman-jurist John Jay and authors Washington Irving and James Russell Lowell. More recent ambassadors included Claude Bowers, Norman Armour, and Stanton Griffis and Lincoln MacVeagh, the latter two of Connecticut and appointees under Truman.

Before the latter two representatives arrived, there was a move among U.S. military circles that the areas of defense against the Soviets should be drawn to include Spain. The idea was bitterly attacked by labor unions, anti-Catholics, and liberal journals, and especially by those who had fought against Franco with the anti-Fascist International Brigade during the Spanish Civil War. It became readily apparent that from the American viewpoint, the two great areas of disagreement concerned labor policies and religious freedom. Nonetheless, Congress in late 1950 voted a loan of $62 million, although the purposes and distribution were not fully determined nor in place for over a year. There also existed the matter of the desire to arm Spain against the common enemy Russia, which soon took the form of the establishment of bases as part of the defense of Western Europe.

In September 1953, after lengthy negotiations between Franco and U.S. Chief of Naval Operations Admiral Forrest P. Sherman, Spain and the United States agreed to the building of strategic air bases on Spanish soil at Torrejón, Zaragoza, and Morón, and a naval base at Rota on the Bay of Cádiz. The treaty allowed a 485-mile jet fuel pipeline running from Rota to link the three air bases. In exchange for the right to have these military installations on Spanish territory, Washington agreed to provide $350 million in arms plus economic assistance to its 28 million people, a population that was growing at about 3,000 a week. The United States justified its dollar input to the Franco regime on the grounds that in the long run the survival of a free Spain depended on a sound economy.

The base-building program had an immediate effect on Spain's well-being. "Although at least 70 percent of all materials required for the bases were imported from the United States," writes Benjamin Welles in his book *Spain: The Gentle Anarchy*, "the acquisition of the remaining 30 percent spurred Spanish producers and imparted valuable techniques. At the height of the program, in 1957-58, the U.S. contractors had 5,000 Spaniards employed directly, and another 15,000 indirectly, through Spanish subcontractors. When the bases were complete, Spain acquired $30 million worth of American construction equipment free."[14]

Major General August Kissner, head of the military mission, made frequent reports to Lodge and accompanied him when occasions arose to turn over U.S. aircraft, tanks, and even a refitted destroyer to Spanish forces. (A well-kept secret was the apparent nuclear weapon capability of U.S. B-52s.) Apart from Kissner's strategic defense duties, he tactfully maintained a tight rein on the thousand or more American servicemen. He ruled uniforms out of order off the bases, prescribed Spanish lessons for everyone, and brooked no trouble-makers. The combination of U.S. discipline and Spanish friendliness began to work, notes Welles, who served as *New York Times* correspondent in Madrid. "U.S. service families found themselves as happy in Spain as at any post in Europe."[15]

General Stanley J. Donovan, as chief of the Joint U.S. Military Group, carried on the smoothly laid operations of Kissner, and Lodge became very supportive of the ongoing programs. They were augmented by technical and military exchange programs whereby Spanish engineers and specialists traveled to America to study modern construction techniques and Spanish jet fliers went to American air bases in Germany for special training.

The Lodges settled, not into the new modern living quarters adjacent to the multi-story embassy building, but in a nearby house at 75 Avenida Lagasca rented from Prince Pio of Savoia. This smaller yet exquisitely furnished dwelling seemed to Lodge to be a more conducive setting for entertaining officials, especially Spanish acquaintances of every rank and occupation. Rarely seen paintings by Goya and Velázquez decorated the walls of the reception areas.

Lily Lodge soon returned to New York to pursue her stage career. She became a protégé and companion of Helen Hayes, learning a great deal about the theater. John was pleased that his younger daughter wanted to remain in Spain. Beatrice, who at first missed her Hartford classmates and Jonathan Dugan, the boy next door, readily became a part of the official entourage in Madrid and sort of a junior ambassadress. She broke away only briefly to complete her senior year at Marymount International School in Barcelona. Unusually tall and attractive, she received many a "piropo" or compliment from Spaniards. One day on a street in Madrid, a group of young men who were a foot or so shorter than her height looked up and remarked, "It must be cold up there." On other occasions, groups of singing students called "tunas" serenaded her under her window. Often they were invited into the residence for refreshments.

John went to great lengths to bring over his closest political aides and friends, even relatives, to form part of his embassy staff of 112 Americans. He tried to nail down an assignment for Al Coote with the USIS or ICA, but a job didn't pan out. He urged his cousin Bill Minot to leave his Canada Dry Bottling operations in Connecticut and take an overseas government post. Bill was assigned not to Spain but France, where his father Grafton Minot had served with the American Embassy before the war.

Before John had left for Madrid, he said to Dick Aldrich, "I would like nothing better than to have you with me there." Actively producing plays and managing theaters, Aldrich thought no more about it. After John reached Spain, he brought over Dick as part of the United States Economic Mission to Spain.

John again sought to include Chad Braggiotti in his circle of advisers. Shortly after John arrived in Spain, his young brother-in-law left the UN for an assignment as Deputy Chief of Mission in El Salvador under Ambassador Bob Hill. A year later he was in Washington as Congressional Liaison Officer at the State Department. John still felt frustrated by the fact that Chad had not been assigned to Spain. A certain amount of criticism circulated in Washington that Chad was using political influence to secure a job on Lodge's staff. It was unfounded. Apparently, John's mother spoke out in Chad's behalf. She was very distressed that he was living with his wife and children in a small rented house, struggling to make ends meet in a period of fast-rising living costs. Chad had long been close to Mrs. Lodge, ever since he regularly dined at her home while studying for the Foreign Service examinations just before the war. She followed his career as vice consul and consul in South America and Europe, and rejoiced over his marriage to the daughter of the former Foreign Minister of Ecuador. At his mother's urging, John spoke to Loy Henderson at State to consider Chad's qualifications for an assignment in Spain. In early 1957, Chad received word that he would be the new Consul General in Seville, not exactly a part of John's official team but certainly close by.

And not long afterwards, a distant Cabot cousin and career officer joined John's staff. One day in Washington, while walking down the corridor in the State Department to check in at the Spanish Desk, Cabot Sedgwick had met Lodge coming out. John said that he looked forward to seeing Sedgwick in Madrid one day, which proved to be prophetic: Sedgwick became an officer in the Political Section under him in 1958. "In my 30-some years in the Foreign Service I had many posts but Spain was probably my favorite," Sedgwick recalled.[18]

With the Lodges established in Madrid, they lost little time in traveling about Spain. John became the first American ambassador to pay an official visit to the Canary Islands, Spain's outpost in the Atlantic. He presented a comprehensive technical library on the peaceful uses of atomic energy to the Junta de Energía Nuclear on behalf of the U.S. Atomic Energy Commission and its chairman Lewis Strauss. He opened a new USIS Center ("Casa Americana") at Cádiz. At La Rábida near the Gulf of Cádiz, he attended the annual Mass given in the Chapel of the thirteenth-century monastery where Columbus had visited prior to setting sail in 1492. John presented a box of earth from Mount Vernon and an American flag, and made a few remarks in Spanish. To Al Coote he explained, "I think you would have appreciated the historical interest and the wonderful romanticism underlying the whole affair. . . . I am very active and life is full of interest."[17]

To those closest to John, it seemed that he had found himself and was born again. His letters to his mother were cheery and loving, if not boastful. He reminded her of his growing facility with Spanish, described by the most critical Spaniards as "splendid and sonorous," with a praiseworthy Castillian accent. Mrs. Lodge responded in kind: "Francesca says that you spoke a half hour in Spanish. Bright boy Johnny. How can you do it?"[18]

Each summer the Spanish government, particularly the Foreign Office, carried on business in the northern coastal city of San Sebastián. Most foreign diplomats joined the exodus, after celebrating the most important Spanish national holiday, July 18, the day the Civil War started in 1936. The Lodges moved to the summer capital, taking a house across from the beach. In 1955 their stay at San Sebastián was interrupted by a serious illness of Beatrice. "Pa gave me so much courage," she recalls. "He held my hand even as I was wheeled into the operating room for the removal of my appendix."[19]

John made his first trip back to the States at the end of 1955. On his arrival in New York, he conferred at the United Nations with Cabot on strategy to bring about the admission of Spain to the UN. Cabot had asked him to talk privately on the most important questions in Spanish-American relations to the U.S. delegation, Foreign Service officers, and other career people from the State Department, some fifty in all. Lodge described Spain as "a strategic fortress and a dependable ally." In response to questions about the fact that Spain was not a democratic country, he observed: "I think it is a mistake for us to try to reform the world in our own image, and not to recognize that there are diverse backgrounds that influence people. Spain was never exposed to the forces of the French Revolution or to eighteenth-century French rationalism, and had been exposed to the Industrial Revolution in only a limited way."[20]

Spain came into the United Nations that December as part of a package plan that allowed five Communist countries to join in exchange for membership for Spain and a dozen other non-communist nations. An offshoot of the admission into the UN was the first visit of a Spanish Foreign Minister to the United States. In April 1956, Alberto Martín Artajo paid a visit to the White House, the Capitol, and Georgetown University, where he received an honorary degree.

Lodge found the job as ambassador more pleasant and interesting than the rigorous back-stabbing political years in Hartford. His enormous energy burst out in all directions. He enjoyed meeting people, and everybody seemed to know who the tall, dignified yet accessible American was. Strangers would wave to him on the street, smile, and call out "Mr. Lodge" or "Mr. Ambassador." Madrid taxi drivers would shout "Hola, Juanito" when they spotted him. Spaniards in restaurants would point him out and sometimes gather around his table. In country villages, he attracted clusters of townsfolk. There was no mistaking him, for he looked like an ambassador and stood out among other diplomats like an oak tree among shrubs.

Outgoing and friendly, he commanded attention among Spaniards from every walk of life. Playwright Joaquín Calvo-Sotelo commented on Lodge's widespread cordiality with a phrase which became popular: "Spain has a new boy friend and his name is John Lodge." And the affair would last for six years.[21]

His facility with Spanish amazed many and endeared him to countless others. His continuous travels along the length and breadth of its historic peninsula in so many places gave rise to an affectionate jest: "Is His American Excellency running for Senator from Castille?"[22] His growing affinity for Spain warmed the hearts of Spaniards. He was Eisenhower's personal representative, a non-bureaucratic political appointee and friend. "Without such ties and backing, an ambassador is nothing but a clerk in the eyes of many," observed Albert Gelardin, an American businessman who lived in Madrid for decades. "He was the most celebrated man in Spain after Franco. The people did not know what Americans were like. He popularized the United States in Spain. The Lodges made America popular while making themselves popular. They were the right people at the right time in the right country."[23]

Yet, at the same time, in America there were numerous high-level people who looked with disfavor on Franco and his militaristic, and often uniformed, retinue.[24] Oregon's crusading Congressman Charles Porter, for one, spoke out against all forms and degrees of totalitarian governments. An Air Force Reserve officer, he planned to stop in Madrid during a fact-finding tour with a planeload of generals and colonels. Porter wanted to lambaste Lodge face to face for his close dealings with the Spanish Foreign Minister and gain a measure of approval from other Washington legislators and many average citizens who still shook their heads over the Spanish regime. The feisty Porter intended to tell John that he ought to quit pampering Franco and resign. Just before heading for Spain, Porter was shown a letter from the U.S. Air Attaché in Madrid, explaining there was no reason to stop there, since the country had only twenty-five U.S. reserve air force officers. The visit was crossed off the group's itinerary.[25]

The *New York Times* tended to slight Spain. Correspondent Ben Welles regularly filed stories but knew few would be printed by his anti-Franco editors. Time after time, John reminded Welles that in all fairness the *Times* shouldn't ignore the country. More and more Americans, he emphasized, were encountering the "ineffable magic of this enchanted land," and it deserved as much newspaper space as any other major European nation. Spain had an authoritarian form of government, but not a totalitarian regime, and the country was coming into the mainstream among Western nations. That fact had to be acknowledged, John stressed. He followed the foreign policy of Eisenhower, who believed that the United States should not try to reform the world in its own image but try to understand rather than judge other countries.[26] "Lodge did very well on this score," points out Antonio Carriques, a leading lawyer and diplomat who was married to an American. "He had a good understanding of the political area. I faced some of the same complex problems and negative resistance as his counterpart, Ambassador from Spain to the United States, later during the Kennedy years."[27]

An increasing number of American tourists began discovering both the great cities and friendly villages of Spain during the ambassadorship of Lodge. He raved about Iberia, its matchless art treasures, ancient monuments, majestic landscapes, and noble people to his friends back home, and they and their friends came in droves. Many received the VIP treatment by the Lodges—a reception or dinner invitation, occasionally a room at the residence. Quite a number were government or administration officials. One of the first visitors was Secretary of the Interior Douglas McKay. Soon Cabot and Emily came to see John, as Cabot told him, "in all your glory." Cabot added: "I want nothing done for me officially at all—unless it helps you in your job." At the end of the visit, Cabot wrote: "No matter what else you may do in life you will never do anything which will be more important or which will give you more satisfaction."[28]

Then came Attorney General Herb Brownell on his first vacation since Ike's election. No sooner had he unpacked his bags and jumped into a bathing suit for a swim in the Mediterranean when an urgent call reached him. Eisenhower had suffered a severe heart attack in Denver. John quickly arranged for a small plane to pick up Brownell and take him to Madrid for a commercial flight to Washington.[29]

Dulles, taking advantage of a day's respite from a conference in Geneva, paid a flying visit to confer with Franco. He was the first Secretary of State to visit Spain. Vice President Nixon stopped briefly to meet with John, as did Supreme Court Justice Tom Clark and Senator Alexander Wiley. Many visitors of lesser rank greeted John informally in his Embassy office. The Navy influence predominated. In every direction were photos of aircraft carriers, fighting ships, naval officers, and military groups. The display reminded callers that John was a part of the military service as well as the diplomatic corps.

Reserve duty for Lodge every year was a well-heralded event in the press. Most Spaniards admired his commitment to military service. With the Sixth Fleet in the Mediterranean, he one time was hoisted into the sky by helicopter from a submarine. His training that summer encompassed this unforgettable lift into the air, as well as a dive below the sea waves.

John's two weeks with the Navy often revealed his life-long incapability of dealing with domestic chores. His family all agreed if he ever lived alone, he'd just starve to death. Captain Jack Noel of the Sixth Fleet recalled his complete lack of know-how with ordinary everyday tasks: "One time John tossed his expensive tennis shirt into the ship's laundry. It came back a foot long. No one had ever told him that woolens didn't go into the regular wash."[30]

John's ongoing Reserve obligation and fascination with the military establishment both in the United States and Spain gave rise to the feeling that he was overly pro-Pentagon. If he appeared closer to defense and security matters than to other aspects of his job, he was just carrying out his duties. If the State Department felt overshadowed by Lodge, a political appointee, he was, in a sense, also a professional diplomat. Ben Welles noted that Lodge's concept of his role was uncomplicated:

He played it like a successful American politician, keeping the constituents happy. Franco and the regime were his "constituents," and unless they were happy, American policy in Spain would fail. Spain, in Lodge's view, was a nation emerging from civil war and from twenty years' isolation and Franco was a phenomenon cast up by Spain's own historic evolution. Franco was not perfect, but he was necessary until Spain could stand on its own feet. U.S. aid admittedly helped keep the Franco regime in power, but what was the alternative? To cut off aid? Would cutting off aid hurt the dictator, backed by the army, police, church, and business interests, or would it hurt the masses recovering from years of poverty and international ill will, he would ask. The "tough" techniques, Lodge noted, had already been tried in 1946, and Franco had emerged stronger than before.[31]

Lodge once remarked to young Kit Pinto-Cuello, daughter of Naval attaché Captain Henry Jarrell, that he felt more of a politician than a diplomat in Spain. "I think he meant he couldn't leave a room without feeling that he had gotten his particular message across to each and everyone there," Kit explains. "He didn't want to be merely 'decorative.' "[32]

The growing importance of Spain as a partner in the security of Western Europe gained further recognition when U.S. intelligence officer Archibald Roosevelt was named special assistant to the ambassador, or more accurately, station chief. Roosevelt became part of Lodge's official circle, if not family. Indeed, his grandfather Teddy Roosevelt had been John's godfather, and few Washington families had been closer in the early decades of the century. Theodore Roosevelt's first wife, Alice Lee (1861-84), was the daughter of George Cabot Lee of Massachusetts and a distant cousin of Lodge. With these ancestral connections, Archie on his arrival received the "big hello" from John and soon was best friend with all the Lodges. At staff meetings, John often embarrassed him by saying, "Archie here really knows what's going on. Just ask him."[33]

The Embassy's DCM, Roosevelt recalled, was of no help to him. Park Armstrong, Jr., had replaced the very capable Homer Byington, Jr. Armstrong had long been ensconced in Washington until an order went out that all State career personnel had to have overseas experience. He requested Madrid, when that post opened up. During Lodge's absences from Madrid, Armstrong—no admirer of John—apparently capitalized on this opportunity to upset a good deal of the ambassador's *modus operandi*. The fact that Roosevelt's duties focused on the top secret interrogation of Spanish expatriates from the Soviet Union (as apparently did some of Dick Aldrich's CIA work) made the DCM feel left out of some of the most vital activities at the Embassy.[34]

John, nonetheless, was astute enough to realize the importance and necessity of having all his staff work as a team, yet allowed his section and agency heads considerable latitude in planning and carrying out their responsibilities. "He enjoyed the give and take of staff meetings, which were usually protracted sessions," remembered Second Secretary of Embassy William B. Sowash. "As is the fate of many ambassadors, his staffs included many yes-men, but he recognized and valued differing opinions and advice when solidly based and those few who ventured them had his respect and friendship."[35]

As a political appointee, John had his foes back at the State Department. They apparently took a cue from political kingpin John Bailey, who in the euphoria of the hard-fought and successful gubernatorial contest had been chosen Democratic Party National Chairman. They compiled statistics showing long absences from his Madrid post. A half-dozen other political appointees and non-career men were singled out, too, for taking so-called excessive holidays and junkets. State Department data revealed that these envoys were absent from duty more than twice as often as career ambassadors during 1955-56. For Lodge, they counted up 143 days off the job. John endured the slur in silence. Only months later was the record corrected. Senator Mike Mansfield, who twenty years later would become a political appointee to Japan, apologized to Lodge in a Senate speech and noted his "distinguished service" in Spain.[36]

Mansfield revealed that Lodge's absences totaled only 127 days, distributed this way: vacation, 16 days in 1955 and 8 days in 1956; 29 days on active naval duty (during which he wrote himself off the ambassadorial payroll); 58 days for official consultation in Washington and elsewhere (including a summons to the capital by Dulles and a meeting of European ambassadors in Paris); and 16 days off on weekends not counted as vacation. "As an example of official stupidity, involving the improper use of statistics to injure a representative of the country," the *Hartford Courant* editorialized, "this report is in a class by itself. . . . Why wasn't the record based on the accomplishments of the Ambassador in helping to win the Spanish people over to our side? Why was the report issued in the first place, and why did it take so long to correct?"[37]

After nearly two years in Madrid, the Lodges returned for their second home leave. Student organizations at the University of Bridgeport had asked him to speak on Spain and his role as ambassador. John explained: "Spain is insufficiently known in the United States. For our own benefit we should make every effort to familiarize ourselves with her history and her lasting contribution to the culture of the West. Spain is important not only in a military sense, but in what she has to contribute to the great occidental tradition of individual dignity which is, of course, the very opposite to the test-tube, soulless man with whom the Red czars hope to build a communist empire."[38]

He explained that the organization of the U.S. embassy in Spain was quite complicated, but things worked reasonably smoothly. He cited two factors that made this possible: "One is that the Ambassador at any given post is the final authority among the several agencies and departments represented abroad, whether it be consular, public relations, military, political or in other fields. A necessary adjunct to this fundamental concept is what we call in the field 'The Country Team Meeting,' at which department heads meet weekly to thresh out conflicts, mutual problems, manners of approach, courses of policy."[39]

Lodge asserted that the United States must have leaders who could recognize the very core of world problems and devise successful solutions for them: "Only the finest and most rigorous education can equip our leaders to do this. In my opinion the heart of this indispensable training must be the liberal arts, living acquaintance with the best minds of the past leading to informed speculation on the problems of the present."[40]

In January John left the philosophical for the practical. He had been instructed by Dulles, as had all the diplomatic corps, not to attend the 1956 Republican National Convention in San Francisco the previous summer and not to campaign for the renominated team of Eisenhower-Nixon. But he made sure he'd not be absent from the Inaugural. Vice President Nixon secured VIP tickets for the Lodges. John's presence at his party's second victory celebration in two electoral turns at bat would serve to remind the home team that he was still a viable player in the big leagues.

CHAPTER 18

Life in Spain

I f Hollywood had cast the Lodges in roles as America's diplomatic team in Spain, it could not have found more accomplished players. John and Francesca were ideal co-stars in a production that became a hit overnight. They were a tremendously successful partnership, a triumph that John never expected and could not have visualized in his wildest daydreams.

It was an exceptional moment in Spanish history, and the Lodges fit perfectly into its latest and most pivotal chapter of the mid-twentieth century. They arrived at a time when Franco was at his peak of power and acclaim, with the bad years largely behind him. John and his family personified America to a country that had had remarkably little contact with the land their Iberian forefathers had helped to discover and settle. Together with the military installations and personnel, Lodge's dynamic presence facilitated the opening of more doors to the once-cloistered regime. And back home, the Lodges conveyed the importance of being a friend of Franco and his government at a point when a new way of dealing with changing global needs came into focus. And what was gained was never lost. Some observers called John the most prominent foreigner in Spain.

The indefatigable Lodges were ever on the job. They entertained extensively at the Embassy Residence and opened its doors to all kinds of people. They invited Spanish people who would not ordinarily have been asked to ambassadorial functions, and they would greet them as warmly as a cabinet minister. The Spanish Foreign Minister Artajo once remarked to the American-born Aline, Countess of Romanones: "I'd wish you'd tell your friends, the Lodges, that at their luncheons, it's a little embarrassing to be with people from such different walks of life." At one such gathering, the Lodges' guests, it seems, included a former political prisoner of the Franco government![1]

The Lodges felt that they must be open and fair to all sides, and put their best foot forward to everyone who came through the front door. Their party and dinner invitations were much sought after, once people learned how full of fun and dazzle they were. And they hardly were inconspicuous at the parties of others. Guests at a Ministry of Foreign Affairs formal dinner one time were taken back, then totally amused and charmed by Francesca's entrance. With a fan and castanets, she clapped and danced her way into the reception hall.

To brighten up many assemblages, John might tell a joke in colloquial Spanish (or French, if the guest list called for it). Usually he broke into a song at some point, raising his solid baritone voice with a chorus of the familiar *schotis* of Mexican composer Agustín Lara, "Madrid, Madrid," or the ballad "A mí me gusta Madrid" with words by the influential Spanish grandee, the Count of Romanones—sung, of course, in Spanish. If a group of musicians were nearby, John and Francesca often started the dancing with a sprightly pasodoble or lively fandango. And so among the diplomatic corps and far beyond, the Lodges emerged as the most talked-about and most-photographed couple in Spain. "Nobody came near to being as good as John and Francesca as ambassadors or as well loved by all levels of Spanish people," concludes Aline, who has written of her life in Spain since the 1940s in *The Spy Wore Red* and other autobiographical stories.[2]

The movie industry, in particular, discovered Spain during the Lodge years. The government, through John's urging, made space and facilities available to international film producers, offering them a country of such varied landscapes as to afford scenic background for almost any type of film. Besides, extras by the thousands were on call for a handful of pesetas a day. John happily put out the welcome mat for American filmmakers. Oscar-winning producer Robert Rossen brought Richard Burton and Frederic March there to shoot *Alexander the Great*, and producer-director Stanley Kramer filmed the $5-million historical epic *The Pride and the Passion* with a trio of big Hollywood stars: Cary Grant, Sophia Loren, and Frank Sinatra. The cast and crew of *John Paul Jones* (including Robert Stack in the lead role) were enthusiastically greeted by Lodge, who loaned press aide Joseph McAvoy and others at the embassy to portray eighteenth-century historical figures in several brief scenes. MGM brought the all-American duo Debbie Reynolds and Glenn Ford to Madrid to film *It Started with a Kiss*, a comedy about U.S. airmen in Spain. Producer Ted Richmond filmed the Biblical Western *Solomon and Sheba*, with Gina Lollobrigida and Tyrone Power (who died of a heart attack during shooting and was replaced by Yul Brynner). Richmond encouraged other producers to go to Spain, feeling it could become the film center of Europe once a new studio with modern facilities was built.

One day John visited the set of *Solomon and Sheba* and as he watched, a costumer from Hollywood asked him whether he felt like the proverbial firehorse smelling smoke. Lodge mentioned that upon his arrival in Madrid, he had been asked to play the ambassador in Norman Krasna's light-hearted comedy *The Ambassador's Daughter*, opposite his Hollywood Bowl co-star Olivia de Havilland. But he wasn't interested in moviemaking; he didn't miss it. Moreover, he did not think the real and celluloid roles would mix.

He was happier playing host to film people, such as Myrna Loy after she completed her part in the Krasna picture. She stayed at the Madrid Ritz, which was very unusual. Actors were not welcome there because they attracted the press and photographers, but Myrna was considered "government" because her husband Howland Sargeant had been Deputy Assistant Secretary of State.

Reports of the genial hospitality of John and Francesca, and indeed of the Spanish people, spread. Before long, a steady stream of prominent performers and celebrities passed through Madrid, including Red Skelton, Maureen O'Sullivan, Danny Kaye, Agnes de Mille, Grace Kelly, and the Duke and Duchess of Windsor. Party-giver and gossip columnist Elsa Maxwell brought the young soprano Maria Callas to the embassy while on a trip through Europe to introduce her to the world of high society and diplomacy.

Bob Hope landed with his troupe to entertain servicemen at the air bases. At Torrejón he filmed a segment for his NBC television show with Gina Lollobrigida. He ran into Ambassador Lodge during his travels. "Bob, if you ever get tired of show business, we can use you," said John. "You'd make a great ambassador." "Me, an ambassador?" he quipped. "What country are we mad at?"[3] In Hope's book of travel stories, *I Owe Russia $1200*, he noted that underneath it all, it gave him a warm feeling to have a man like Lodge think so highly of him: "It wasn't till much later that the thought occurred to me that John Lodge, too, is a man highly trained in diplomacy."[4]

From Connecticut, Helen Keller and her secretary Polly Thompson came to visit the Lodges. Keller, both deaf and blind, met a group of blind Spanish girls, a day none of them ever forgot. Keller had been the beneficiary of work for the blind carried on by John's own family. His mother had learned how to transcribe books into Braille. When she read of the sad loss in a fire of the personal library of Helen Keller, she secretly worked on a classic admired by both women, *Walden* by Thoreau, and sent it to her. Mrs. Lodge asked what other books she wished hand-copied into Braille, and during the 1950s she regularly toiled half the night to send packages to Keller. One of them was the monumental five-volume set of *Familiar Animals of America*.

John also welcomed a special group of performers to Madrid, the Theatre Guild American Repertory Company. The troupe launched a 15-week State Department international cultural exchange in Spain. The audience at the gala premiere enjoyed an outstanding performance in English of the classic American play *The Skin of Our Teeth*, with an all-star cast, including Helen Hayes, Leif Erickson, June Havoc, and Helen Menken. "It was our good fortune that John Lodge was then American Ambassador," recalled the play's director Marcella Cisney. "He met our plane . . . and gave a splendid dinner party for the stellar cast. We opened with 'The Skin of Our Teeth' and received a standing ovation and a brilliant press to begin our long trek to all the leading theatres of Europe, the Near East and Latin America." (The other plays for the tour were *The Glass Menagerie* and *The Miracle Worker*.)[5]

After the final ovation from an audience that included Prince Juan Carlos, Lodge accompanied Foreign Minister Fernando María Castiella back stage. There, Castiella honored Helen Hayes with the coveted Order of Isabel la Católica. John actually had arranged the presentation to the acknowledged First Lady of the American Theatre and Lodge family friend. "Helen Hayes' reply was talked about and remembered," Francesca recalled. "She said, 'after all, Isabel la Católica was really the mother of all Americans.' "

Lily Lodge continued to work with Hayes back home and toured with her in summer stock. Beatrice radiated a star quality of her own in Spain. She quickly made many friends and attended countless parties and receptions. When asked what she liked best in Spain, she quickly answered "Los Españoles" and won the hearts of all. The list of fiestas and balls she graced grew long. She reigned as queen of the picturesque Fiesta de la Vendimia in Requene, sweetheart of the annual Valentine Ball in Madrid, and Princess of the famous fair in Seville. She graduated from Marymount in June 1956 and then made her début in Madrid before an array of Spanish nobility, diplomats and government officials, and a sprinkling of Americans.

"In Spain the coming out party," noted Francesca, "is called Puesta de Largo, meaning putting on a long dress. It is often treated more importantly than a wedding." Francesca had been at a loss to pick out a debutante dress from the many designers who sought her favor. So she asked them to submit sketches of a gown, and then she'd select one. She decided to accept the design of a young unknown artist. It revealed an exceptional talent and gave Oscar de la Renta his first opportunity as high fashion dress designer. The boost from Francesca launched him as an international couturier.

In Spain, Francesca found a new interest, activity, or hobby everywhere she turned. Animals, however, took precedence. Rarely without a dog or two at her side, she discovered a tremendous need for seeing eye dogs in Spain. She encouraged their use, brought in trainers from the United States, and eventually helped to establish a school for guide dogs for the blind. "Americans at first protested," she remembered. "They said 'We are not going to send our pure-bred, expensive and well-trained dogs to Spain where they'll be eaten by the natives.' A talented young man, Ramón Arenas from Bilbao, whom I sent on a scholarship for the blind in Morristown, New Jersey—a leading center for dog training—became a chief instructor in Spain."

Every animal in Spain was her friend. The sight of a Spaniard beating or mistreating a dog, horse, or donkey so upset her that she'd go to the aid of the poor animal right then and there. And she refused to attend bullfights, events that were *de rigueur* in diplomatic circles. She even spoke up against them among Spaniards: "I actually got Mrs. Franco's permission not to go to bullfights. She told me, 'I only go once a year for charity.'"

The Lodges regularly traversed the Spanish countryside on horseback, breathing in the soothing scent of jara and tomillo in the air. John usually wore a Connecticut Horse Guard jacket and an old Navy officer's hat. Many Sundays they rode with the city's cavalry commandant Jesús Lugue Recio to rustic towns surrounding Madrid. At midday they'd spread out a picnic lunch under a large shady tree. Colorfully dressed townspeople frequently came to talk and to play music and to dance for "el Ambajador de los Estados Unidos de América." In response John let go with a song or two.

Their mounted excursions took them to a sheepherders' village near Madrid called Villanueva del Pardillo. They gradually "adopted" the town and at Christmas gave all the children of the area dolls or footballs. One year the village was the recipient of a community television set bought with dancing class fees collected by Francesca in Madrid. When the Lodges left Spain, the town named its main street "Calle Mr. Lodge" and commemorated the tribute with a bronze tablet.

A Spaniard later remarked of Francesca's generosity: "If she had stayed longer in Spain and had had more time and money, there would be a statue of her in Madrid today."[6] Nonetheless, she received a high honor—the Order of Isabel la Católica—for her work among children and animals. No single undertaking of Francesca remains more vividly etched in her memories of Spain than her 500-mile cross-country horseback ride from Portugal to Madrid. Organized by Spanish and Portuguese cavalry and legionnaires, the race, called a "raid," rarely if ever included women. But she was an exceptional rider, determined to participate with her friends in the cavalry. She especially was intrigued with the idea of testing

the group's horses for distance and endurance. Besides, the mayor of
Madrid had given her a superb Spanish-Arab mount called Quitín, and she
was eager to put him to the test.

Francesca explained: "The greatest joy was that John was in favor of
my acceptance to join the 60 ranchers, horse breeders and cavalrymen in
the marathon that began at the Portuguese town of Elvas, just on the
Spanish border." Tina Hawkins, wife of the Chief of the Political Section
of the Embassy, and a shy and quiet but highly competent horsewoman,
joined Francesca, as did one other woman.

The first day, Francesca rode an easy eleven miles from Elvas to
Badajoz; most days were much more strenuous with a daily course that
covered over sixty miles. The cavalcade stopped at shrines along the way
and often camped gypsy-style at night in the hills. In many villages,
townspeople waved flags and pressed bouquets of flowers into their hands,
and mayors greeted them. Frequently, there were banquets and toasts that
lasted well into the night.

Tina Hawkins, who had never made such a long distance on
horseback, complained that the late-night festivities were too tiring after
a rigorous day in the saddle. "Let's figure out a way to get off the hook
and get some sleep," she said. Francesca thought a while. Then an idea
came to her. Secretary of State Dulles had just died. "There's our out.
We'll tell the local dignitaries that we are in mourning. We'll say that it
is impossible for us to attend any public celebrations or banquets."

At the end of the eleven-day trek over rugged mountains and
sweltering plains, the group had dwindled to fewer than thirty riders.
"Francesca's participation," Tina Hawkins remembered, "engendered much
enthusiasm. An Ambassadress, so game and sportive, captured the
imagination of the pueblos. We were there for all to see and criticize. At
the end of many hours in the saddle, we managed to smile in answer to
the greetings of local people, so interested in such an undertaking by
women."[7]

Perhaps the most enduring legacy of the Lodges in Spanish-American
relations is not in Spain but in New York. It is the cultural link between
the two countries called The Spanish Institute. Modeled after The French
Institute and founded shortly before they left for Madrid, it promotes
friendship and understanding between the people of Spain and the United
States. Banker George S. Moore recognized the need to bring together
those interested in bettering cultural and educational ties. The early
partners in the venture included Angier Biddle Duke, Lucrezia Bori,
Theodore Rousseau, Edward Tinker, and Melvina Hoffman. The group
viewed that the best prospects for such an organization lay with a broad
intellectual base that would reach out and bring in both the people who

were on Franco's side and the émigré and avant garde community for whom the Spanish Republic was still a worthy cause.[8]

Ambassador Lodge rallied to the side of the Institute, recognizing the validity of its mission to provide a forum for in-depth discussion of history and culture, art gallery programs, language courses, roundtable luncheons and lectures, and a research collection of books—all in the name of friendship, goodwill, and knowledge. From Madrid he facilitated the appearances in New York of Spanish artists, musicians, and lecturers. By 1960 the Institute had grown to 500 individual members and twenty-five corporate subscribers. It soon acquired its own building, a Park Avenue mansion donated by the granddaughter of John D. Rockefeller, the Marquesa de Cuevas. In the 1960s, after his return from Spain, Lodge became chairman. In the words of George Moore: "He assumed a strong role, which kept the Spanish Institute independent, influential, and helped gradually to build the support it now enjoys. . . . As one of our greatest public leaders and our best ever Ambassador to Spain, John Lodge was and will always be one of the pillars of the Institute."[9]

In 1982 John received the Institute's coveted Gold Medal in recognition of his significant contribution to the betterment of relations between the two countries and joined the company of such past honorees as Andrés Segovia, Alicia de Larrocha, Henry Ford, James Michener, and Plácido Domingo. Earlier, the government of Spain awarded him that country's highest civilian decoration, the Grand Cross of Carlos III, along with the Gold Medal of the City of Madrid, which made him an honorary citizen of the Spanish capital.

Many of the Spanish-American cultural, social, and economic missions and peripheral endeavors of the Lodges, oddly enough, might not have come to fruition, nor succeeded or been fully developed, if John and Francesca had left Madrid after the usual three or four years in one post. Midway in his assignment there, John faced a potential career crisis, a possible recall that perplexed and annoyed him. The matter eventually resolved itself, and he forged stronger links to the land that was becoming his second home. But it took most of the year 1958 to unravel the governmental knots and repair the political snags of a situation that in the end clearly reaffirmed John's commitment to public service in an international milieu.

CHAPTER 19

A Spanish Abrazo

At the end of a State Department conference on Spain in February 1958, Christian Herter buttonholed John. Herter, who had served two terms as Massachusetts Governor before becoming Under Secretary of State, apparently mentioned a four-year limitation on ambassadorial assignments. In his chat with John, Herter pointed out that the only current exception to the so-called four-year limit was a non-career fellow named Thomas E. Whalen from North Dakota. Whalen was being kept on as Ambassador to Nicaragua after seven years in order to placate Senator William Langer, who threatened to vote against all ambassadorial candidates unless Whalen or some other North Dakotan served in an overseas post. (Langer was the only Senator to vote against Lodge's confirmation in 1955.) Herter concluded his brief talk by asking John what he intended to do at the end of his time in Madrid early the following year. John expressed a wish to be ambassador to Paris or Rome. Herter made no comment.

John gave much thought to the conversation as he traveled to Atlanta, where he delivered a speech entitled "Economic Aid and Foreign Trade: How They Help to Protect Our Freedom" at the Southern Regional Meeting of the American Bar Association. On his return to Washington, John secured an appointment with Herter to discuss the matter of his "retirement." Lodge voiced his confusion as to the full import of what he had been told earlier. John brought up the names of a number of career and political appointees who had recently served in various diplomatic capacities beyond four years. Herter said that he could not really explain those extensions; he was, as a matter of friendship between two former New England governors, simply telling him about a policy which came from the White House.

John had been hearing rumors about this so-called strategy. It was being pushed by Democrats in order to replace non-career appointments, especially Republicans, with professional envoys. The last five ambassadorial appointments, indeed, had been career men. John concluded that Chris Herter had not been fully informed for the unpleasant job of telling him that after four years as Ambassador to Spain, his overseas services would no longer be required.

That spring John wrote Cabot a confidential letter and sent it, not to his UN office, but in care of their mother. "I am hoping that perhaps you can explain both the policy and the exceptions to it," John asked his brother. John discussed the administration's stated need for experienced, qualified individuals. Yet in practice they were often ignored. Instead, businessmen with lots of money and little diplomatic know-how were appointed. An important member of the Eisenhower team, he wished to stay in government service at a job as good as, or better than, the post in Spain. John added that the White House had indicated that he was doing a good job.

Presidential assistant Sherman Adams had told him, John explained to Cabot, that both his personal and political qualifications were above par. Adams mentioned the possibility that Lodge might replace former Arizona Governor Howard Pyle as deputy assistant to the President with responsibility for governors' conferences. John ruled out all interest in that position. Through the capital grapevine, John also learned that Arthur Hill, chairman of the Greyhound Corporation and a big Republican Party contributor, was angling for his post in Madrid.

John made it clear to Cabot that he did not want to go into a job in the business world. Unless he were offered another governmental appointment on a suitable level, he hoped to stay in Spain, where all the Lodges had been very happy, "especially Beatrice who has truly blossomed." He concluded that if the administration had no interest in retaining his services, he wanted to be told in no uncertain terms. "I should, of course, welcome advice on what, in that eventuality, I should say both to the press and to my many friends on both sides of the aisle in both houses of Congress so that I can protect the administration."[1]

Cabot replied by offering his help in the situation. But he could not give an authoritative explanation of the "policy and the exceptions." There was a big "grab-bag" element in the whole business, he pointed out, and said that time and chance, hit or miss, play a great part. Cabot believed that John had earned the right to think about private employment after twelve years in public office: "It is important to get one's new career 'in orbit' while one is still vigorous physically." Cabot took note of the high regard for his brother throughout the administration, and asked for a government job list from John—one strictly confidential for his own guidance in Washington. He made it clear that Paris and Rome were not in the cards.[2]

Several weeks later, John responded. He reiterated his desire not to retire from public life; he had counted on public service at least as long as the country had a Republican administration. Turning to a specific list of jobs, John believed a meeting of Cabot with Dulles and Herter could be very helpful as to his future role in government. Turning to posts in Paris or Rome, John clearly stated: "I assure you that I have the financial means to swing either of these posts. I have been fortunate with certain investments and I am after all the best judge of what I can afford."[3] He wanted to stay in Europe, perhaps at NATO or the European Economic Community. But Madrid, he made clear, had lost none of its appeal after more than three years.

Cabot apparently talked with Herter. Again he wrote John on the impending recall: "It appears that no exceptions are being made on the four-year rule for political appointees to major diplomatic posts. There also is great pressure from well-qualified people with political stature, but everyone is being turned down as far as major posts go. For the future, therefore, you should start *making plans* to return to private life," Cabot concluded. "You need not *execute* them now but the planning and the hard thinking should begin now. A strong position in private life is not only good from the standpoint of making money, but it also provides a base from which to jump again into public life if you want to do it for elective or appointive office in 1961 if you are still interested. "I am sorry to give such a discouraging report but these are the facts as I got them from Chris and they are confirmed by my own observations. If you think of anyone else I can talk to or anything I can do, please tell me."[4]

John reacted to what he called a "pretty brutal" conclusion. He again wrote Cabot: "The fact is, as you well know, that I have ruled out no jobs. I have merely made some suggestions which, as I stated, are not intended as a comprehensive list. I simply gave you a short tentative order of preference as far as foreign posts are concerned. Actually I have been offered no federal position of any kind since the question of my transfer came up. . . . Why then is this administration which I have served faithfully, and I truly believe successfully, anxious to be rid of my services? Under FDR and Truman such men as Harriman, Bullitt, Lew Douglas, Bob Lovett, and many others were continuously used in posts of importance, both at home and abroad over a period of many years. Under this administration such men as Bob Hill, Douglas Dillon, Randy Burgess and others have had steadily developing careers both in Washington and on foreign posts."[5]

John reaffirmed that he had no intention of returning to private life.

Sick at heart, John felt the rug had been pulled out from under him: "This is becoming a far worse experience than political defeat . . . Where have I failed? In what way are my personal and political qualifications deficient? . . . When career people, business men and certain Democrats are treated more fairly and generously than people who have gained valuable experience in public life, one is, I think, at least entitled to an explanation."[6]

The correspondence between the brothers concluded with a legal brief-like rundown by John, seemingly obtuse to the ways of Washington under either political party. He analyzed the entire matter and again raised a half-dozen unanswered questions. He also brought in the longevity of Cabot. Why didn't the four-year rule apply to Ambassador Henry Cabot Lodge, now in his sixth year at the UN? He also noted that son George Lodge was about to become assistant secretary of labor for international affairs: "I do hope that this will come to pass and that it is as much a recognition of ability as is the fact that you and Foster Dulles and many others in and out of the Cabinet are kept in your posts beyond four years."

Cabot apparently had spoken to Dulles about John's desire to stay in public service. Dulles called him "a very valuable man." John ended the unresolved imbroglio by stating that he wished to serve in Madrid at least for an additional year, into the spring of 1960, at which time he would resign to work in the Presidential election. "I think that I could be helpful to our party," he suggested.[7]

Lodge's pride, as well as his sensitivity and vulnerability, which Cabot often piqued, had been stepped upon by the administration. The White House, it seems, had only casually considered a four-year rule. Apparently no such policy on ambassadorships really existed. More likely, it was a matter raised at some point by career diplomats, particularly Democrats in the State Department who wanted the likes of Lodge moved out to make room for long-term professionals. The ongoing need for John's unequivocally solid experience, background, and commitment at a period of military and defense exigencies and economic and monetary readjustments ultimately ruled out a recall from Spain.[8]

But at the time, the uncertainty and confusion led John to consider running for political office in Connecticut. A movement spearheaded by Republican town leader Robert Bliss of New Canaan sought to bring Lodge back to vie against Governor Ribicoff, who had compiled an imposing record in four years and would not be easy to beat. Although the Republicans had done well in the 1956 elections with Eisenhower leading the national ticket, John sensed that the State contests in 1958 would favor the Democrats. And indeed they did. Bill Brennan successfully gained for his favored candidate, State Controller Fred Zeller, the gubernatorial nomination. Purtell gained renomination for the Senate race. But both went down in defeat that fall. Ribicoff won by a record landslide of more than 245,000 votes over Zeller. Congressman Tom Dodd downed Senator Purtell by a similar margin. And Ribicoff's popularity was so overwhelming that he carried the entire Democratic ticket, including all six House seats. Lodge concluded that the so-called "professional" politicians had had their time at bat and struck out. It proved, he felt, that they needed the Ivy League players in the game after all.

Francesca urged him to maintain an ongoing visibility in Connecticut affairs. She decided to engage a public relations counsel to develop a statewide public image for John. In retrospect, there probably was little need to publicize and promote Lodge. Events in Spain brought that country into the European mainstream, and through it, Lodge benefitted, albeit never becoming an international luminary or a household name in the mode of Cabot Lodge, Dulles, or Mrs. Luce.[9]

By 1959, all major facilities of the U.S.-Spanish base program were nearly complete and virtually a hundred percent operational. Although the signing of these agreements seemed, on the surface, an obvious act of self-interest on the part of both countries, the achievement was a question of much greater complexity and more lasting significance than any simple physical arrangement. The U.S. military aid of $400 million affected Spanish economic development to a high degree. Inflationary pressures, caused in part by wage increases plus shortages in exports and increases in imports, precipitated a marked deterioration in the Spanish economy. Therefore, a much-needed stabilization plan was formulated in mid-1959.

"It was a top secret project of high priority," says Milton Barall, then deputy director of the economic mission at the Embassy, "and the most important job in my entire government career. It encompassed vigorous and fundamental measures to end inflation, to overcome the balance of payments drain, and to stabilize the Spanish peseta at a new and realistic rate, according to conditions laid down by the International Monetary Fund. John, by the way, gave me free reign to negotiate. He was the best kind of guy you could have in Spain at that time."[10]

The deficit and decline in foreign reserves were stopped, and substantial increases in foreign exchange holdings were realized by the end of that year. Prices in Spain were held in line and inflation was arrested. The adoption of the stabilization program was an expression of mutual confidence between Spain and the leading Western powers. A bold new departure, in which Lodge's country team played a significant part in planning and execution, it led to greater economic cooperation and trade expansion in the Western mold.[11]

Lodge hoped the plan would take Spain on the road to full and equal partnership in the European community of nations. He favored Spanish entry into NATO. Norway, however, felt that Franco still bore the stigma of a pro-Nazi affinity. Lodge responded by pointing out that Franco actually had blocked Hitler's request that German Panzer divisions be allowed to go through Spain and occupy British-held Gibraltar. Franco's firm stand and Spanish neutrality indirectly helped the Allies, Lodge explained. But Norway thought differently. It would resign from NATO if Spain became a member. Lodge felt it was in the best interests of NATO to invite Spain to join, believing that as both an Atlantic and Mediterranean nation, it was *de facto* a part of the defense of Europe. But not until 1983 did Spain come into the organization.

John's duties centered not just on high-level economic and political concerns and diplomatic turns. Behind the governmental agendas, he, as chief representative of his country overseas, was called upon to expedite personal matters on a one-to-one basis. And with the influx of summer tourists, Ambassador Lodge encountered his share of back-street incidents.

The week-long festivities tied to the annual running of the bulls through the streets of Pamplona always attracted many American students. At the Fiesta one July, he learned of an American recently thrown into a cell for disturbing the peace. The young man turned out to be the son of Mathias Plum, a former classmate at Harvard Law. Lodge arranged for his release and insisted that he write home and explain the incident before his father heard of it from another source.[12]

At the same Pamplona fête a year earlier, John came to the rescue of two students on a wild school holiday. During the running of the bulls, law school classmates Ted Kennedy and Varick (John) Tunney, apparently while drinking, tossed cushions and pillows at the bulls and townspeople from a balcony. Such an act was a serious breach of the law. Kennedy and Tunney, both future U.S. Senators, were arrested and thrown into jail. John was called to be their friend "at court." John realized the whole affair had the makings of a tantalizing story for every paper in the United States. He readily acknowledged that it would cause distress among both families, one of whom defeated Cabot in the 1952 Senate race. John vowed to keep the entire incident off the record. He secured their release after a fine was paid. Varick Tunney's father, Gene Tunney, was profoundly grateful to John, especially for keeping the episode involving his son and his fellow jailbird from the press.[13]

An event that Lodge was eager to see in every newspaper soon came about. For several years, the Spanish government had waged an ostensible campaign to get President Eisenhower to visit Madrid, even for a single day. It envisioned a stop at Torrejón air base, where Ike and Franco would meet and dedicate the defense facility. But the hope didn't materialize; even Eisenhower's participation in the 1957 NATO meeting in Europe brought forth no interest to see any part of Spain.[14] Then, two years later, Foreign Minister Castiella and Ambassador to the United States Motrico flew to London, where Ike, on a brief trip to England, agreed to see them. Castiella and Motrico learned that Ike had planned a world tour that fall. They invited him to Madrid as a guest of Franco. Surely he could fit in Spain, they assumed, and inspect an American base. Eisenhower remained noncommittal, still concerned over probable anti-Spain protests at home from such a stopover.

Lodge stood completely behind Castiella's idea. No American president had ever set foot in Spain, John reminded Washington. Behind the scenes, he argued the case for a meeting between the two heads of state. Eisenhower's itinerary listed a flight from Paris to Casablanca, directly over Spain. There was no way he could diplomatically avoid paying a call on the post-war ally. Just a month before Ike's departure on the twenty-day, eleven-nation world tour, the President added a landing in Spain.

The visit hit the embassy at a time when personnel was in short supply. A number were on home leave; others had just been rotated. John's capable public affairs counselor, Frank Oram, acted as the chief buffer between the White House advance team and its Spanish equivalent. Both countries stood anxious to have maximum television coverage of Ike's arrival. The large motorcade with many dignitaries and mounted cavalry necessitated detailed planning. Eisenhower and Franco would ride together in an open car in the procession, slated to get underway shortly before dusk. According to Spanish protocol, the most important individuals always appear last.

"I argued that this procedure would eliminate TV pickup because of darkness," Oram remembered. "There were numerous meetings between the two groups. The Spaniards kept reminding us that their protocol was older than ours. We told them that by the time the two heads of state came into view in the heart of Madrid it would be much too dark for a clear telecast. Finally, we compromised. Ike and Franco's car would be moved up closer to the front of the procession, and thus come into view on TV screens sooner."[15]

On the afternoon of December 21, 1959, Ike landed at Torrejón, 13 miles outside of Madrid. He was accompanied by his son John, his daughter-in-law Barbara, and Under Secretary of State Robert Murphy. "The main thing I remember about our arrival was not so much Franco but Mrs. Lodge," Barbara Eisenhower says. "Mrs. Lodge was wearing all of her 'I Like Ike' buttons. They were pinned to her coat and hat, and even on her stockings."[16]

Franco in full dress uniform greeted the Eisenhowers. The General had never set foot on the U.S. base, but now with Ike could inspect the

American installation. *New York Times* correspondent Ben Welles described
Ike's first encounter with Franco as somewhat stiff and coldly correct.
After a review of troops, the party left for the twenty-minute drive to
Madrid. On the outskirts of the city, they changed into an open car for
the parade to Moncloa Palace, Ike's residence for the overnight visit.[17]

The cavalcade moved along the streets of the capital. As it approached
the center of the city, thousands of onlookers lined the route. Once they
recognized the face of the President from magazines and newsreels, they
burst into shouts of "Ee-kay, Ee-kay," their translation of the name Ike.
The President stood next to Franco, taking everything in, responding to
the huge crowds, waving his hat over his head. The voices of welcome
grew louder as the procession moved along the tree-lined Castellana. An
estimated three million people greeted Ike. "Even Franco could not have
ordered such a large turnout," Eisenhower's interpreter Vernon Walters
noted. "The opposition had said that if one was against the Franco regime,
'Don't go on the street.' But they disregarded the directive. The
spontaneous outpouring of the wildly cheering crowd was the largest
reception for Ike on that trip outside of New Delhi."[18]

That evening Franco was the host at a formal state banquet at the
royal palace. Dinner commenced at 9:30, an unusually early hour for
Spaniards, but travel-weary Ike requested a dinner that would end by 11.
In the absence of Mrs. Eisenhower, Franco escorted Francesca, resplendent
in a stunning gray net Fontana gown massed with white and silver
beading. Ike accompanied Señora Franco. "I sat on Franco's left," Barbara
Eisenhower remembered 30 years later. "All I can recall of our
conversation was talk of my children (and his) and also Ava Gardner! This
was about the time she was prancing around Spain with her bullfighter.
Franco got a twinkle in his eye when he told me some of her escapades.
We had a simultaneous translator so it was fun to talk to him."[19]

During the banquet, he toasted the First Lady back in Washington,
and thanked the United States for "the peace we enjoy and the
preservation of Western Europe against falling under the Communist
yoke."[20] "There were tears in his eyes," Francesca recalled, "as he put down
the text to his prepared speech and ad libbed an emotional ending of
blessings and thanks." He noted that the day, December 21, was the third
birthday of Eisenhower granddaughter Mary Jean. This especially pleased
Ike and his family." Franco, the President wrote in his memoirs, was
personable and agreeable, "a small man of regular features and modest
manner." Ike wondered if Franco could win in a free election. He certainly
didn't seem like a dictator.[21]

The following morning, Eisenhower and his party met for an early
breakfast and conference with Franco at the Pardo Palace. Franco

endeavored to eat a Texas-style menu of thick steak, toast, and coffee. A heavy silence hung over the small gathering of Spanish and American guests who were not used to such an early hour after a State dinner (and a nightclub excursion with the Lodges to observe a show of fiery flamenco dancing). Bob Murphy broke the ice with a joke, and Lodge followed up with a humorous story. Soon the anecdotes came from all directions, including Franco's. In the wake of the laughter, Eisenhower plunged into a review of his global trip and the status of world affairs. He managed to inject a request from Protestant churchmen in the United States that Spain allow Protestant church activities.[22]

Shortly before ten o'clock, the meeting ended. U.S. Air Force helicopters stood on the lawn near the palace. The party piled into the craft for the short hop to Torrejón. For Franco, it was his first flight in a helicopter. As Ike prepared to board his plane, he complimented John and military chief Stanley Donovan for a job well done. A round of handshakes between all the dignitaries preceded a last good-bye between the two heads of state. Grinning broadly, Ike threw his arms about Franco in a traditional Spanish *abrazo*. The army of photographers jumped forward to record it. Most historians agreed that these photographs are among the most human ever taken of Eisenhower or Franco. The latter's expression is filled with real emotion and genuine appreciation.[23] "Merry Christmas and a Happy New Year," Ike called out from the top of the aircraft's steps.

The brief visit was tangible proof of an expression of friendship toward a nation much isolated by the rest of the world. Lodge and his team had organized a very successful meeting at a time when such rapport was highly important to national security. A Spanish joke circulated after Eisenhower's departure: Ike was like a lover: he came at night and left in the early morning. The warm memory of this Western leader remained. "And Franco," Ben Welles writes, "the onetime outcast, had been elevated from a stiff handshake to a demonstrative embrace from the President of the United States."[24]

An official visit to Washington by Foreign Minister Castiella contributed to the growing affection between the two nations. Just three months after Ike's meeting with Franco, Chris Herter, now Secretary of State, was host to Castiella, and the Lodges accompanied him. They were on home leave or in Washington for consultations for much of early 1960. The days there provided time to see Bessie Lodge, who had suffered several mild heart attacks. She spent most days in her bedroom, which her sons insisted be air-conditioned for the steamy Washington summers. Her nemesis, Mrs. Woodrow Wilson, lived nearby, still treating her as the widow of arch-enemy Henry Cabot Lodge, not the unpolitical widow of his long gone poet-son. The grudge that Edith Wilson carried was so intense that she had refused to greet Bessie after Sunday church services at St. John's on Lafayette Square. And one morning when Bessie fell leaving church, Mrs. Wilson, who was close by with her car, would not offer assistance or a ride. Mrs. Lodge stoically accepted the incivility as part of the legacy of a political rivalry.

That summer Vice Admiral William "Smeddy" Smedberg suggested to John, now a captain, that he serve with his old prep school classmate in the Pacific for his two weeks on active duty. He agreed and stopped in Washington en route to join the Seventh Fleet. He spent several days with his mother. On June 29, he flew off to Japan to rendezvous with his ship. En route he received a message that his mother had died. He returned immediately to Washington, flying for three days and a distance of nearly 14,000 miles.

No one in the family was exactly sure of her birth date—she never celebrated birthdays. They calculated her age to be eighty-three years. Bessie Lodge was buried, not in Cambridge, but in the Davis family plot at Washington's Rock Creek Cemetery.

If Bessie Lodge had lived another month, she would have seen Cabot gain the nomination for vice president at the Republican National Convention. As chief delegate to the UN and a member of the Cabinet and National Security Council, he had become one of Eisenhower's senior policy advisers. He was even permitted to speak for Washington in UN debates without prior clearance from the White House, an unusual privilege. Watching him in action for seven years on television screens, U.S. viewers were unmistakably reassured that the country had in that world body a sturdy champion who presented the U.S. case with force and eloquence and answered every Russian thrust with a hard-hitting counter-thrust. Cabot made a point of replying to Russian attacks promptly so as to get his country's answer into the same wire service story that carried the Russian charge around the world. His frequent exposure on television and on the front pages brought celebrity status as well as political clout.

Cabot represented the United States in important debates during the Suez crisis and Hungarian revolt of 1956, and explained American action in sending troops to Lebanon two years later. In 1959 he accompanied Soviet Premier Nikita Khrushchev on an unprecedented twelve-day tour through the United States. From San Sebastián, John penned a brotherly note to Cabot on this unusual assignment: "If he [Khrushchev] makes things unpleasant for you, I think you can be relied on to make things appropriately unpleasant for him."[25] At the conclusion of the Soviet visit, he praised Cabot's role: "I like very much the way you straightened out Mr. Khrushchev on September 18 on economic humanism and the role of capitalism in American life. Congratulations."²⁶ In spite of his growing acclaim, Cabot had shown no interest in running again for the Senate from Massachusetts in 1958. The formidable Senator Kennedy waged a tremendously successful re-election campaign, and Lodge probably would have been on the losing side for the second time.

In early 1960, the idea of the highly visible and exceptionally able Cabot Lodge as a vice presidential running mate with Nixon gained some momentum. John, too, had his boosters. Republican National Chairman Thruston B. Morton publicly said that he felt John Lodge was one of the eminently qualified candidates for the nomination. He noted that Cabot also had been mentioned by some party leaders for the second spot. "I don't want to get in the middle of a family situation," Morton explained. "Both men are able, dynamic and articulate."²⁷

Early on, John realized that he had very little chance of being asked to join the ticket. He was genuinely more interested in campaigning vigorously for all Republicans throughout the country as well as in his home state. Nixon had a clear-cut edge on the presidential nod, and in April John offered his services. Unlike the 1956 convention, he gained a green light from the Secretary of State to attend the Republican gathering as a Connecticut delegate. At the convention, a group of New Jersey delegates pulled him aside, asking if he would object to running for vice president. He ruled it out because of his brother's position as a highly possible candidate.²⁸ Nixon actually had approached Cabot several months before the convention. As Nixon's choice, he was readily accepted by the party and soon resigned his UN post to vie against his formidable past opponent on the Democratic ticket, Jack Kennedy.

The day after the convention, Nixon and Thruston Morton urged John to enter the campaign, suggesting that he quickly resign as ambassador. John hesitated, although a number of anxious Republicans in Connecticut, also, wanted him back to help the state ticket. He wrote for brotherly advice, truly believing Cabot would summon him back to the campaign trail. On August 30, Cabot cagily replied:

> As you know, I am very mindful of your future in Government. Clearly this future would not be served by defeat—or by our winning in spite of a "brother act" which had misfired. The more the campaign develops, the clearer it becomes that the unrehearsed newspaper and television quiz on delicate topics—rather than the usual political speech—will be the big feature. This unrehearsed quiz is a really new campaign development—one which makes the old style "straight" speech very secondary.
>
> It would obviously be impossible for you and me to make the

same answers to the same questions and when each of us answered differently, it would provide a new "focus of interest" which would make us both look ridiculous. I have thought about this a great deal and do not see how such a ridiculous situation could be avoided.[29]

John then asked his brother how he should reply to inquiries on his role in the campaign. Was he about to leave his post and enter the campaign, everyone asked? Francesca too started to receive urgent requests for her presence back home. A Connecticut candidate for Congress wrote saying her appearance would make the difference between victory and defeat. Many people were going to be "disappointed and surprised by my failure to return home to campaign," John added.[30] Cabot abruptly wired back: "Believe it extremely inadvisable for you or Francesca to campaign. That is my frank opinion. . . . Am sorry because I would love to have you here to enjoy your company."[31]

John, stymied and annoyed, pointed to Lily Lodge, who had begun to campaign for the Nixon-Lodge ticket. Why couldn't the rest of the Lodges do so as well? Again, he set forth his case, concluding with a paragraph on the matter of the "pleasure of his company" on the campaign trail: "Certainly, I fully reciprocate that sentiment. We have seen little enough of each other over the years. Yet a campaign in which you are running, and in which, if I were involved, I would not be on your campaign train but would be making speeches, seems hardly a good opportunity to enjoy each other's company. I hope that we can do that when the campaign is over."[32]

To the very end, John believed his participation in the campaign would be helpful, and Francesca's too. She could boost local candidates—chiefly among the Italian-, French-, and Spanish-speaking populations. As it turns out, she would have avoided a serious accident by returning to Connecticut. In October, on a ride with Beatrice in the hills near Madrid, her horse tried to jump across a deep ravine but went down into the hollow. Francesca held on, landing with her right shoulder against a large rock. The spill broke her upper arm: "I stayed on my horse through it all. If I got off, the horse would have tried to rear and try desperately to get out of the hole. My chief concern was to control the animal and bring it up safely. It took a handful of cavalry to do it. I was in agony from my injury until they came two hours later." At a hospital, her arm was put in a cast. She left just in time to welcome guests at an Embassy party.

When it came to sensitive issues during the 1960 campaign, Cabot failed to take the advice he gave John. Speaking in upstate New York, he announced that a Black would be in the Cabinet if Nixon was elected. The statement took Nixon by surprise. The Vice President pointed out that "with respect to appointments to the Cabinet, I will attempt to appoint the best possible without regard to race, creed or color."[33] Apparently, there was a growing misunderstanding between the two running mates. Nixon increasingly felt that Cabot was upstaging him into second billing on the ticket. John knew the feeling. Besides, Cabot approached campaigning somewhat cavalierly. He tended to cancel daytime appearances at rallies and whistle stops, not infrequently in favor of an afternoon nap, and to antagonize newsmen by prefacing replies to their questions with the words, "my good man." By election day, the race was too close to call. The outcome did not become clear until early the next morning, when Kennedy topped Nixon by fewer than 120,000 votes. In any event, with defeat Cabot didn't have to concern himself with a post for John in a new Republican administration.

John realized his days in Madrid were coming to an end unless the Democrats re-appointed him. By 1961 no other high-level political appointee of Eisenhower had served longer overseas in one single post. In mid-November, he wrote Nixon a letter expressing his regrets on the Republican defeat. "You can be proud of the fact that over 33 million, or nearly half the voters, voted for you and Cabot," John pointed out. "This is a great achievement and augurs well for your future. You have rendered enormous service to our Country since we entered the Eightieth Congress together in January 1947. You are at the top of your strength and I do not doubt that you will render distinguished service in the years to come. You have many loyal friends, not only in the United States but abroad and in particular Spain."[34]

John wrote again to Nixon, this time to explain that Loy Henderson at the State Department requested that he not resign on the prescribed January 19 or 20 because the simultaneous departure of so many ambassadors created a problem. "Since I am in no hurry to leave," he recorded, "I am quite willing to oblige, and I assume that there is no objection to my remaining until the next administration decides what it wants to do with respect to the ambassadorship to Spain." John noted a number of moves by both Spaniards and Americans to persuade the Democratic administration to retain him. John asked for the outgoing Vice President's thoughts.[35]

Nixon advised John to stay on if asked, or to take any overseas post it offered. "There is a need for some continuity in the conduct of foreign affairs and for demonstrations of bi-partisanship to the extent it does not inhibit the right and the responsibility of the minority party to provide constructive opposition to the policies of the party in power. You have done a superb job in Spain and I am sure that no one Kennedy could appoint could do better."[36]

John made cautious overtures to Kennedy, who, like Nixon and Lodge, had entered the Congress in 1947. Kennedy and his Secretary of State-designate Dean Rusk remained completely noncommittal on all ambassadorships. John heard that there was a fair chance he could stay on because no Democrat wanted to get close to the still-controversial Franco regime in the way John and the Republicans had. John submitted his resignation, hoping it would be "for consideration only" and not a "request to leave."[37] But Kennedy soon made his selection: a two-fisted "Brahmin from Philadelphia," Anthony J. Drexel Biddle, the aging scion of a wealthy and accomplished clan with significant political and diplomatic achievements. Biddle replaced Lodge in the spring of 1961.

One of the reasons John was anxious to remain in Madrid was the forthcoming marriage of Beatrice to a young Spanish diplomat-to-be. She had met the earnest and engaging student, Antonio de Oyarzabal y Marchesi, not long after they arrived in Spain, and he was a frequent guest at embassy parties. During her only year away from home, Beatrice kept in touch with Antonio. At age 17, she decided to convert to Catholicism. John thought she was too young to make that decision, yet he did not think he could withhold his consent. He told Foreign Minister Alberto Martín Artojo about it during one of their friendly get-togethers. Artojo had been upset when one of his eight children had married a Protestant: "Mr. Ambassador, all I can say is, you're more broad-minded than I am about these things."[38]

After living in the country and studying its language, history, literature, philosophy, and art, and having little contact with her homeland after 1955, Beatrice thought of herself as Spanish: "My father never liked me to say that. But I loved the Latin pace and temperament, and European way of living. I enjoyed being with my parents in Madrid and traveling through Spain with them for six years."[39] The relationship with Antonio became serious during the final year of his studies at Spain's diplomatic school. His father had served in the diplomatic corps, and Antonio prepared for a similar vocation. An orphan since his early youth—his parents during World War II were killed when the train compartment in which they were passengers en route from Berlin to Madrid was wrecked by a bomb—Antonio was well-educated and well-traveled. After attending the prestigious Le Rosey School in Switzerland, he enrolled at the University of Madrid and also studied briefly in France and England. Antonio and Beatrice decided to wed soon after his graduation in June 1961.

The regal couple were married, not in Madrid, but in New Jersey on July 6, the 32nd wedding anniversary of John and Francesca. Cousin Matilda Frelinghuysen gave the wedding reception at her country estate

"Whippany Farm" in Morristown. Among the 200 guests were Lillian and Dorothy Gish, Fannie Hurst, Helen Hayes, Anita Loos, and Mary Roebling. Many still remember the magnificent reception, and not surprising, the rendition by the father of the bride of the Lodge perennial, "La Vie en Rose." After a wedding trip to Bermuda and Italy, the Oyarzabals settled in Madrid, where Antonio began his career as third secretary at the Spanish Foreign Office. Francesca's and John's wedding gift was an eye-catching Mercedes convertible.

The Lodges' last Christmas in Spain became the most festive since their arrival. Francesca, ever the energetic Santa Claus, gave presents to everyone, in addition to sending over 8000 holiday cards and helping Spanish charities. She also concluded the sale of the old Braggiotti villa, a property that required much maintenance and yielded little rental profit.

In a farewell letter to John, travel writer Temple Fielding described the Lodges as "the most beloved, most successful, the most delicately sympathetic and aware U.S. Ambassadorial family since the days of Washington Irving."[40] The Spanish newspaper *Arriba* editorialized on the departure. "Gentlemanly, frank and generous," the article said of Lodge, "he has penetrated the mysterious stronghold into which not all are able to enter: the soul of the Spanish people. He was our friend back in 1948 when it was neither easy, popular nor, indeed, wise for a man in American politics to be one. Lodge, the diplomat, may be leaving, but Lodge, the man, can never leave us."[41]

A flurry of laudatory press comment poured down like rose petals. The Madrid newspaper *El Pueblo* observed that John Lodge had not lived among the Spaniards as an island apart but rather in the Spanish way:

> He has seen us from the inside, not over the fence of the amused, casual observer. Studying Spain's present problems or the meaning of its history; living side by side with the high level of society or in contact with the ordinary people; enraptured in a library or admiring the dome of a cathedral, the Ambassador has always tried to reach the bottom of a matter which is difficult for ourselves as well: our own self-understanding. Even when he paraded on horseback as the principal figure of the San Antón festival, down Hortaleza street, among gentlemen, farmers and soldiers; or when he prepared codfish, from the vicinity of Boston, "pil-pil" style, in a gastronomic society in the old section of San Sebastián, John Davis Lodge was carrying out his determination to understand Spaniards as they really are. And, since those who seek do find, he found that understanding which has served him so well for the success of his mission.[42]

The simplicity, dignity, and passion of the Spanish temperament awoke responsive echoes in Lodge. It was, in the very words of John, "this beautiful friendship of ours." More than friendship, it became love on both sides.[43]

On April 13, 1961, the Lodges packed their carrying luggage, and gathered their dogs for the last leg of their Spanish adventure. They flew to Barcelona to embark on the SS *Constitution* for New York. At the pier, to their surprise, was the Spanish Foreign Minister to personally say good-bye, a gesture few, if any, diplomats ever received. "Good-bye, Mr. Lodge," was the page-one headlines in dozens of journals that day and in the weeks that followed.

As the giant steamship left the port of Palma Mallorca, Francesca dashed off one of her characteristic notes to her husband. She reminded him that his success in Spain made history. Now, they must utilize the interlude between careers or jobs to refuel their energies: "We must rest & get refreshed & do some clear thinking. We start tonight on this project in preparation for our next adventure. Count on me to be strict, helpful, understanding & willing, not to mention so many other aspects of my love & devotion & ambition for your health, happiness & success."[44]

The Lodges had much to attend to upon setting foot on American soil, including the obvious question of John's future employment.

CHAPTER 20

Casting About

A week before the Lodges returned to Connecticut, a fire broke out in the children's playhouse on their Westport property. Before firemen arrived, the four-room live-in dwelling was gutted by the blaze. Also destroyed were Francesca's pony cart and riding equipment. The main house, rented for the past ten years, escaped damage from the fire which was attributed to sparks from a backyard incinerator that ignited a woodpile. No thought was given to replacing the structure where Lily and Beatrice had spent countless hours as youngsters amusing themselves with their friends and where an occasional overflow of house guests slept. Both daughters had long outgrown this pastime, and besides, they now were infrequent visitors to Villa Lodge. John was interested in only one kind of rebuilding in the early 1960s, that of mending his political fences.

Many of Lodge's friends, both in politics and not, wondered about his future. A number believed he had gained in stature since he was beaten by Governor Ribicoff. Others noted a serenity about both Lodges which was not apparent when they first entered the political arena.

The returning Ambassador's first obligation took him directly from the SS *Constitution* to Washington for debriefings at the State Department and a meeting with his successor in Madrid, Anthony Drexel Biddle. From there he traveled to Hartford for his first public address as a private citizen in nearly fifteen years. A talk before a Trinity College alumni group, it covered the status of Spain as a partner in the defense of Western Europe and stressed the feeling that the country should not be left out of NATO. He spent the night in Hartford at the house of his Lt. Gov. Ned Allen, and the conversation there covered a range of state and local matters. Allen urged him to meet with Republican leaders. John returned to Hartford a week or so later to take political soundings, with a view to determine his standing in the party after a six-year absence. He also had a reunion with members of his old gubernatorial staff. He began to accept political speaking engagements around the state. Soon hardly a week passed without several dates as guest speaker at a GOP committee gathering or testimonial dinner.

In the wake of the heavy drubbing in the 1958 elections, the party struggled to regain a footing as a viable alternative to Democratic candidates. John spoke out to remind his audiences of the need for a functioning two-party system, "the heart of representative government as we enjoy it in the United States." He described the independent voter as one who depends on the survival of the two-party system. "In nations which have more than two effective parties," Lodge noted, "the independent voter has little influence. Such nations tend toward minority rule. The proliferation of political parties is apt to produce weakness and chaos. George Washington said, 'Government is not mere advice; it is authority with the power to enforce its laws.' A country which had less than two parties, or in other words, a one-party system, is a country on the road to dictatorship."[1]

Turning to local issues, Lodge viewed the Republicans as having a matchless opportunity to unite and to present to the people of the state a program which would counteract the large increase in state debt, government expenditures and taxes, and the loss of important industrial concerns: "A determined effort must be made to retain and to attract business and industry, to diminish unemployment, and to increase take-home pay by tax adjustments and by tax reductions. Nationally the Republican Party, I believe, contains elements well-suited to lead America and the non-Communist world in this time of difficulty and danger. We can produce the leadership which we must have in order to cope successfully with the Communist onslaught abroad while maintaining a strong currency at home."[2] More and more, John was sounding and maneuvering like a candidate for office in his old home territory.

His political forays were interrupted by a statesman-like commencement address on the country's educational system at Vermont's Middlebury College. There, he received an honorary degree, as did early screen star Mary Pickford. "Our society is based not on equality of accomplishment but on equal opportunity to excel," he pronounced. "The pursuit of excellence at Middlebury College constitutes a bright beacon light of hope in a darkening world in which standardization tends to suffocate individualism, and, indeed, to crush freedom itself. For our vaunted freedoms under law will avail us little if the feat of excellence gives rise to the cult of mediocrity. The mass man is out of place in a free society."[3]

A flood of speaking invitations at varied events poured in at Lodge's doorstep. In Connecticut he spoke in Weston at the forty-fifth anniversary of the Theatre Guild at founder Lawrence Langner's open house, before the Bristol Women's College Club, at the Canterbury School, and to the Garibaldi Mutual Aid Society of Middletown. Out of state, he addressed the War College at Maxwell Air Force Base in Alabama, the Zach Chandler Republican Club banquet in Lansing, Michigan, and the New England Daily Newspaper Association in Boston. His increasingly full schedule was interrupted only by his long-standing annual two-week Naval Reserve training cruise. When his 1961 tour of duty with the Sixth Fleet in the Mediterranean ended, Captain John Lodge joined Francesca for an August vacation in Spain.

By fall John still evidenced little interest in assuming full-time employment. Financially, he had no overriding need to take on a regular job. He shared in the nearly one million-dollar estate his mother had left, and this inheritance augmented his growing portfolio of investments and a decade of rental payments from Villa Lodge.

More and more, Lodge looked to the state-wide elections of 1962. He decided not to take on any business ties that would interfere with his hoped-for return to public office. The last Republican to have been governor, he was entitled to be called the titular head of the party. But being a titular head of the party was a long way from controlling the machinery of the party, he discovered. Many of the Republicans in high office when Lodge was governor now were no longer there. Lodge admitted that he did not control the party machinery and had to set about meeting the new people in command.

By the beginning of 1962, fifty-eight-year-old John had done a good job of reminding people that he was still around, stirring with strength and vigor, brimming with opinions and ideas, bursting with zeal and eagerness. Yet, instead of avidly and actively pursuing the gubernatorial slot on his party's ticket, he decided to position himself on the sidelines as a readily available compromise candidate for the office he once held. His stance reflected the feeling that a proven vote-getter named Lodge need not do any asking about for support. And John seemingly failed to realize that the field of other would-be runners had grown to six men, all younger, and included two serious contenders, his long-time confrère John Alsop and former Congressman and GOP State Chairman Edwin H. May.

His friends opened the Westporters for Lodge headquarters and the Republican Town Committee supported him for governor. But a local primary contest developed. John was challenged by ultra-conservative State Senator John M. Lupton of neighboring Weston. The day before the primary, this forty-five-year-old opponent with considerable financial backing had a red rose delivered to the home of each of the 3,200 Republican voters in Westport. Each rose was accompanied by a letter urging party members to vote and listing Lupton's view on state issues.

Lodge took virtually no active part in the contest and consequently polled thirty-one fewer votes in his hometown. Undaunted by this loss, his backers continued their plans for a statewide Lodge-for-Governor drive.[4]

Ned Allen came forward to head the committee. Nonetheless, he leveled with John, comparing the present party circumstances with the strategy in the 1954 campaign. Allen stated that the Republican organization was not begging him to run for office in 1962, and some leaders were not excited over the idea of "getting off their coats and working like hell for Lodge, even though they truly want to see a Republican victory." Allen expressed his conviction that John could not win the nomination without the help of a united party—one that included the political bosses, even to some degree the retired Bill Brennan. He also advised John to take heed of Francesca's intuition and presentiment.

With less than a month before the Republican state convention, Lodge still had not announced his candidacy. But on May 10, he all but tossed his homburg in the ring at a party gathering in Stamford.

Then a bombshell hit GOP circles on May 16. Senator Prescott Bush decided not to seek re-election to a third term. This totally unexpected announcement caused shock waves throughout the state. Bush for all intents and purposes had acted as if he wanted to keep his seat in Congress. The hardworking, well-respected legislator had compiled a fine record in Washington, sponsoring the interstate highway bill that created the country's road system and playing an influential role with armed forces and urban renewal matters. Described years later by his son and namesake as "fiscally conservative and humanely liberal," he had had the good fortune to run for office twice during an Eisenhower landslide.[5] But by 1962, he was not overwhelmingly popular throughout Connecticut, and party members thought his chances of re-election a bit doubtful. In any event, at the advice of his physicians, sixty-seven-year-old Bush, because of ill health, planned to retire from the Senate at the end of the year.

Within hours after the Bush bombshell, Lodge switched political goals. He and his Lodge-for-Governor backers launched the Lodge-for-Senator Committee, and the following afternoon he announced a new campaign for this long-desired post. That evening Lodge spoke at a dinner of the Stamford branch of the NAACP. Town Republican Chairman John DeForest recalls the program in his daily journal: "I thought he was quite good, but some people didn't like the frequent reference to Abraham Lincoln. It was something of a political speech although he didn't refer to his earlier statement of this afternoon when he came out seeking the GOP nomination for the Senate. . . . After the dinner I was one of the five delegates from Stamford that agreed to count ourselves the first bona-fide delegation to the June Convention which offered its support to Lodge."[6]

John faced competition for the Senate nomination. Congressman Horace Seeley-Brown had made known his candidacy less than an hour after Bush's surprise move. Former Congressman Antoni Sadlak jumped into the race, too. Both were so-called upstate contenders.

Lodge felt more comfortable facing national and international issues. He handily zeroed in on the world situation: the menace of Communist aggression, America's allegedly declining prestige abroad, shaky relationships with key allies. At a Republican gathering in New Haven, he spoke forcefully and intelligently on how the party could win:

> *We can win* if we plan to stop wasting time arguing about which Republican is a "real" Republican and decide, instead, that there is room in the Republican Party for all Republicans and a good many others. We *must* achieve a unified front for our Fall campaign. Narrow factionalism, petty jealousies, and individual ambitions must be subordinated to the well-being and strength of the Party. Let us remember that politics is the art of *inclusion*, not of *exclusion*. Let us not allow ourselves to be divided by an exercise in semantics. Conservatism, liberalism, me-too-ism, and indeed "realism" have been bandied about so much lately that they have lost their meaning.[7]

Less than three weeks remained before the gathering of 660 delegates at the nominating convention. John felt that he was the party's best known, strongest, and most-likely-to-succeed Senate candidate. And he seemed eager to run against the expected Democratic entrant, his onetime opponent Abe Ribicoff, who had resigned as governor in 1961 to join President Kennedy's cabinet as Secretary of Health, Education, and Welfare. One of the first nationally prominent backers of Kennedy for President in the 1950s, along with John Bailey (who in January 1961 had gained the party's coveted National Committee chairmanship), Ribicoff felt his position was being undercut by the White House. A few insiders claim his feeling of overblown self-importance in Washington led to the suggestion that he go home to Connecticut. Bailey greeted such an idea with much enthusiasm. Just when circumstances seemed to be forcing Bailey to run his weakest ticket since 1946, his leading vote-getter was heading for Hartford.

Campaign manager Ned Allen urged John to get out into the field and hustle for delegate votes. Francesca, as venturesome and energetic a partner as in past races, echoed Allen's wise advice. But John pointed to a party poll wherein he emerged with a recognition quotient of 96.6 percent. In this survey, made when Lodge was still in the gubernatorial lineup with six others, he out-polled all of them put together on the question, "Which of these men do you believe would have the best chance of winning against Democratic Gov. John Dempsey?"[8] Meanwhile, Seeley-Brown, an amiable apple farmer, rushed about to cover every nook and cranny he could find in the state to ask for the votes of delegates and leaders. John never came near to most delegates to ask their support on a one-to-one basis.

The GOP convention opened on June 4. Delegate Jack DeForest recorded his impressions:

> We all filed up to Bushnell Hall where we gathered in our respective county sections, ours being way up front on the left. . . . The keynote speaker was U.S. Senator John Sherman Cooper from Kentucky who was very colorless and a poor speaker, although what he had to say read well in the paper. . . . It was agreed that Don Zezima and I were to make seconding speeches for Alsop and Lodge, respectively. But Lodge's manager decided that they wanted an Italian-American to speak for the former Governor so it had to be Don Zezima or no one.[9] So Don agreed to second Lodge's nomination, and we then went to Alsop, after we'd caucused and decided to back him for governor, and asked if he'd accept someone other than Don for a seconder. He said he'd be happy to have anyone we wanted so I was selected. He was very happy to have Stamford support him."[10]

The convention developed into a heated and divisive battle. Among the six gubernatorial candidates, including Speaker of the House Anthony E. Wallace, no Republican built up an unqualified lead. The frenzied struggle continued past the first day and into the next. After an unprecedented sixteen-hour session with eight tense and drawn-out roll calls, John Alsop squeezed into first place by twenty votes over closest rival Ed May. More work still remained to complete the delegates' task. They adjourned for a few hours sleep before returning on the third day to pick a nominee for the Senate.

DeForest recalls the final session:

> Finally, on the vote for Lodge for Senator, he lost by a tremendous vote to Rep. Horace Seeley-Brown of Pomfret, whom no one down this way in Fairfield ever heard of. Lodge supporters call him the "Hyphen" or the "corruptible Boy Scout." Seeley-Brown is famous for campaigning on a door-to-door basis, and is said to be a real worker. Around convention hall he was really

working while Lodge sat back and did nothing. This morning some oversized campaign buttons appeared with the names of Lodge and Alsop on them in large black letters, Lodge's name appearing on the top. This apparently bothered many people who felt Lodge was taking too much for granted. So with a combination of things causing it, Lodge was defeated.[11]

A plain-talking little-known congressman and pre-convention underdog, Seeley-Brown had led a grass-roots rebellion against the wishes of party leaders. The uprising of delegates was aided and abetted by party wheeler-dealers. Among them were those who had broken with John when he was governor. The shadow of Bill Brennan, it seems, fell over the Lodge forces. Seeley-Brown had swamped John on the first ballot, 476 to 149.

Political observer Jack Zaiman, not unexpectedly, had the last word. "Lodge's mind," declared Zaiman, "revolves around issues, around government, around a liberal or a reactionary Republican Party, around international affairs. He thinks on a grand scale."[12] Lily Lodge once analyzed her father's mind in a letter to him. "You're someone who is cursed with a sensitive awareness of the overall view of things, and this is what makes you great. It's also what makes you complicated."[13]

The longest and most exhausting state convention in years ended just two days before the Lodge family gathered in Westport for the marriage of Lily. John had urged her to set the wedding date in a week that would be apart from the convention. But after a long courtship and a very short engagement, she wanted a ceremony in early June at the local Episcopal church and a reception at Villa Lodge.

Lily had met her future husband, James L. Marcus, at a summer theatre colony in 1960. An attractive, witty, and charming young man of thirty-one, he nonetheless struck John and Francesca as a somewhat mysterious, insecure opportunist. A daydreamer, he projected a Walter Mitty-quality of empty fancy. And at his first introduction to the Lodges, Marcus made an unpardonable mistake. He lied, telling his future father-in-law that among other things, he had completed college, played semi-pro baseball, and performed professionally as a trumpet player. Jim, it seems, had to enlarge the fabric of his life through a rich imagination.

John's disenchantment came quickly. When he realized the extent of Marcus' fables, he secretly investigated him and his family through a lawyer and Lodge's New York political connections. John discovered that Jim's father, a none-too-successful Schenectady lawyer, had pleaded guilty in 1960 to income tax evasion and was fined $10,000 and suspended from practicing law for six months. A check of Jim's background revealed that he seldom completed anything he started. His business dealings were shadowy and inconclusive. He claimed to be a partner in a small New York chemical company, a concern about which no records were ever found. Overall he seemed imbued with the idea that success could be measured only in terms of money, social status, and a position of public celebrity.[14]

The fact that he came from a Jewish background seemed a much less insurmountable obstacle. It was his little boy-like and almost desperate eagerness to impress the Lodges and ride on the coattails of an influential and affluent dynasty that disturbed John and Francesca. But their thirty-two-year-old daughter made up her mind to marry her soft-spoken, pensive suitor. After a decade working in and about the theatre, she now wanted to settle down as a housewife and raise a family, as had Beatrice a year earlier. Indeed, her younger sister had just given birth to the Lodge's first grandchild, Matilda, named for spinster cousin Matilda Frelinghuysen.

John finally acquiesced to Lily's wish to be a June bride. The wedding, not quite as grandiose as Bea's, nevertheless captured the attention of society reporters. Uncle Cabot made one of his very few visits to Westport for the nuptials. After his vice presidential defeat, he had become director general of the Atlantic Institute, a research and conference organization to further a united Europe and link it with the United States and Canada.

The morning after the wedding, John left for Geneva, New York, to deliver the commencement address at Hobart and William Smith Colleges. President Louis Hirshson conferred an honorary Doctor of Laws degree on its weary recipient. The president's words, however, uplifted John's spirits after the unexpected convention defeat: "The poet's line 'and to the things his fathers learned to do' wasted itself upon the trivial. You sir, have restored dignity to that fine phrase for in you are your fathers' worthy and several capacities revived. Your career has certified that 'public office is a public trust.' . . . You have served with integrity, vision and honor."[15]

By early July, Lodge eagerly anticipated his tour of duty with the Navy. He joined his ship at San Francisco for a cruise with the Seventh Fleet in the Pacific. When he finished his military stint at Tokyo, he undertook a reporting assignment for the Hearst newspaper chain. He wrote a half-dozen geopolitical articles based on his Asian travels to Formosa, Laos, and other locales. The articles did not get the play the Hearst Headline Service expected, chiefly because the news focus that fall was temporarily on the Cuban crisis and places far distant from Asia. The byline features did kindle an interest on the part of lecture bureaus for his services at fees up to $1,000 a speech. In the fall, he began the first of a long series of speaking tours crisscrossing the country, travels that continued throughout much of the 1960s.

Between his lecture dates, he campaigned for Republican candidates, pleading the party cause energetically and eloquently in his home state as well as in New Jersey, Washington, Oregon, California, Missouri, and Ohio. During an extensive swing through five towns in Ohio for Congressman Charles Mosher (who won by a margin of 11,600 as compared with some 4,000 two years earlier), John, according to Mosher, delivered one of the best speeches the people of Norwalk, Ohio, had ever heard in the long series of addresses which had characterized the McKinley Day banquets there.[16] But the results of the elections elsewhere were deeply disappointing to John.

In Connecticut the Democrats scored well in both the cities and the suburbs. Gov. Dempsey came into his own, beating Alsop by 66,000 votes. Ribicoff topped Seeley-Brown by 26,000 votes in the Senate contest. Future governor Ella Grasso emerged as the most formidable vote-getter, winning the post of Secretary of State by 83,000. Four of the five congressional seats were nabbed by Bailey's boys, who also took the State Senate by a sizable margin. At a victory dinner, Ribicoff commented that he had won on Dempsey's "coattails." Dempsey promptly replied that Ribicoff had provided him with the "coat" by resigning as governor in 1961 and permitting his lieutenant governor to advance to the governorship.

Many of those who lost that November were close to John. His old political ally Richard Nixon fared badly in the race for governor of California against the victorious Pat Brown. And nephew George Lodge, with Washington experience as an assistant secretary of labor, bowed to the dynastically powerful Ted Kennedy in the contest for senator from Massachusetts. George had decided to run a year before the election, not knowing who his opponent would be. When it turned out to be a Kennedy (and a brother of the President, who had reappointed George to the Labor Department post), he knew the situation was practically hopeless. For the third time, the Lodges fell victim to the Kennedy mystique and clout. (John offered to campaign for George but was turned down.)

Shortly after Election Day, John was about to take his first full-time non-governmental job since he had gotten out of uniform in 1946. During his mid-summer reserve duty, Francesca had been contacted by S. Bayard Colgate, board chairman of his family's soap company and resident of nearby Darien. He spoke about a unique opportunity for John to sell the free enterprise story to large segments of the public while simultaneously gaining an excellent opportunity to remain in the public eye and to maintain widespread contacts for possible future political endeavors. Besides, the activity paid well—a salary of $50,000, significantly more than John had ever made from any job or post. Francesca encouraged Colgate to spell it all out in a letter to John.

The proposal entailed not a position in the corporate world *per se*, but rather an offer to assume the national presidency of a non-profit organization of volunteer businessmen-advisers and business-oriented young people. The group was Junior Achievement, which had now grown to the point where it needed a permanent salaried leader at its headquarters in New York. Junior Achievement's retiring president Edwin H. Mosler, Jr., wrote John a detailed letter inviting him to do for the organization what General Alfred Gruenther had done for the Red Cross. Mosler, whose family had founded the bank safe company, believed the prestige of Lodge would open doors for him at business conventions and meetings of the NAM, AMA, Chambers of Commerce, and Rotary Clubs, where he would be given an opportunity to present the Junior Achievement story and solicit the support of business leaders. "Almost every prominent business in the United States currently supports Junior Achievement in some form or another," Mosler explained. "Our needs basically are to increase this support in funds for a growing program to new areas, in securing sponsors and advisors for Junior Achievement companies and in securing good talent for our national executive committee and regional boards of directors."[17]

John was quite intrigued with the public-speaking aspect of the post. It would give him the freedom to speak to the public on the free enterprise system and better economic education for teenagers on a non-political basis virtually anywhere in the country yet under an umbrella of a public service youth activity. He accepted the job but made it clear that he would continue an active interest in politics, which "after all is the life blood of representative government as we know it in the United States."[18]

John started work on January 15 and almost immediately was off to build up enthusiasm for the JA programs in Providence, Minneapolis, Detroit, Cleveland, Chicago, Philadelphia, and Des Moines. In Portland, Oregon he was met at the airport by a local "fun group," the Rain Makers, who presented him with sundry gifts, including bottles of the rain water for which the northwestern city was famous. During the Oregon trip to four cities, a business reporter interviewed John at the airport as he waited for a midnight flight back to New York. Even for an audience of one after a grueling drum-beating schedule, Lodge regaled *The Oregonian*'s Gerry Pratt with a lot of political wisdom. John recalled the old Congressional period story of the Connecticut voter who told him that he probably didn't know that the majority of his constituents were against the Taft-Hartley Bill and if Lodge had known that, he undoubtedly would not have voted for it. "Your representative owes you not only his industry, but his judgment," John said to Pratt of that long-ago encounter. "He betrays both you and his judgment when he sacrifices it to your opinions." Lodge grinned recalling the incident. "It was a declaration of Sir Edmund Burke's. He was a tall man who could stand in a strong wind and not bend."

Lodge continued: "The legitimate object of government is to do for a community of people whatever they need to have done, but cannot do at all or cannot do so well for themselves in their separate and individual capacities. In all that people can individually do for themselves, government ought not to interfere." It was a recital that brought a broad smile to his face—warm enough, noted Pratt, to chase the stuffiness of his cultured accent: "As an American, I hope to God that deadly effect of non-productive enterprise, which is what government is, will not dilute that magnificent sense of enterprise and self reliance."

Lodge swung into full campaign voice with that, and airline ticket personnel across the room were picking up their ears: "Freedoms and responsibilities are inseparable. And as you delegate your responsibilities to government, you give up freedoms to government. I am more afraid of the deadening hand of government than I am of nuclear fission in the hands of the enemy. The danger is much more that we won't live up to the best that is in us."

It was an eloquent speech for a tired campaigner. As John pushed his black felt hat on his head and began to wiggle into an old Navy greatcoat, he turned to reporter Pratt with a last ominous warning: "As our people become less creative, less aggressive, our survival is much more in jeopardy." His flight was called. Pratt watched him walk through the brisk gorge winds toward a ten-hour, all-night flight and still another speaking date back East. He too was a tall man, thought Pratt, who could stand in a strong wind and not bend.[19]

During 1963 John traveled far and wide, reaching large and small cities in twenty-seven states and Canada. In one single month, he made thirty-two speeches. The turnout for his appearances was usually large; the events, well publicized; and the results, productive in fulfilling JA goals. He was instrumental in starting new programs and miniature corporations among high school students in previously untapped communities. For the first time, over 100,000 students participated in a single year.

Junior Achievement Executive Vice President Joseph Francomano remembered the beginnings of JA in Puerto Rico: "While we were flying down to San Juan, John asked if anyone had contacted the Governor of the island about his visit. No one had, so he suggested the Governor be alerted and plans be made to see him. It was rather an unusual request to JA aides. I called the Governor's office and explained the purpose of our trip. The Governor immediately expressed the wish to see Lodge the next day. In John, we realized we had a man very well-known and highly respected with prestigious acquaintances in every direction."[20]

But often it was the man on the street that couldn't identify or place John Lodge. JA's offices were across the street from the famous Toots Shor restaurant, and one day Francomano and Lodge walked over for lunch. A long line waited for seats in the crowded dining room. John told Francomano to inform the maître d' that Ambassador Lodge was here and would like a table. "Bring the Ambassador up front and I'll seat you immediately," the waiter accommodatingly replied. As John came forward, the maître d' looked at him rather quizzically and continued to stare as he seated him. Finally, he asked, "You did say you were Ambassador Henry Cabot Lodge, didn't you?" John, in an icy Brahmin tone, responded: "There are, my good man, two Ambassador Lodges!"[21]

In his travels, John gave out awards to deserving JA youngsters and, in turn, picked up numerous community, school, and club awards himself. But the almost constant running to airports and boarding planes to attend banquets and luncheons and meetings paled by the end of a year. Francesca accompanied John to few such activities. She much preferred politically geared trips and gatherings. John soon began to dislike the traveling part of his job and to a lesser degree the ever-present pressure to increase company sponsorships. His time with Junior Achievement, albeit highly successful for the expanding organization, was later looked upon by both Lodges as a sort of bridge between campaigns.

CHAPTER 21

Political Tightropes

Frequent challenges and confrontations at home and abroad tested the Administration of John F. Kennedy. At the start, the anti-Castro counterrevolutionaries' landing at the Bay of Pigs in 1961 failed to overthrow the Cuban communist government, even with the orchestrated backing of Kennedy. Yet the Cuban missile crisis a year later demonstrated Washington's new and intense awareness of the threat to American security close to its shores. Khrushchev retreated and met Kennedy's demands to remove all Soviet offensive arms from the Castro stronghold. The President brought the world back from the brink of possible nuclear disaster. Election results a week later solidified the 1960 gains of the Democrats.

Freedom-loving Europeans were uplifted, too, by Kennedy's appearance at the Berlin Wall. He spoke before a tumultuous crowd of West Germans who cheered the American Commander-in-Chief's words: "Ich bin ein Berliner" (I am a Berliner), expressing his solidarity with the isolated people of the city, surrounded by the totalitarian Communist bloc.

By 1963 Kennedy was devoting more of his time to the military problems and political reforms of a small Asian country called Vietnam. It was the only place in the world where American military "advisers" were shooting and being shot at, and it was generally viewed as a keystone in the defense of southern Asia. If Vietnam fell, it was thought, then the tide of Communist domination might engulf many surrounding countries. The President sought the advice of a number of military leaders and statesmen. One in particular impressed him. Former UN Ambassador and Army reserve officer Henry Cabot Lodge struck Kennedy as the self-confident liberal internationalist he needed in Vietnam. He asked this recent Republican adversary—an experienced and French-speaking negotiator—to take the ambassadorial post in Saigon. Many Republican confidants clearly advised Cabot to stay clear of the burdensome and undoubtedly dangerous chore. John stood among them. But Cabot Lodge replied that he, indeed, would go to Vietnam, explaining he always had a sense of patriotic duty to answer his country's call without regard to party politics: "I'll give it everything I've got," he said. Cabot too was anxious for hands-on involvement in government in a career that to some had "lacked clear direction."[1] He realized without any misgivings that Kennedy preferred to give a Republican the job that might backfire politically.

Cabot's confirmation before the Senate Foreign Relations Committee, on which he had served for six years, was unanimous. In late August 1963, he landed in Saigon and into a cauldron of seething repression and persecution by the increasingly unpopular Ngo Dinh Diem government. Its Catholic leaders vigorously oppressed the Buddhist population while engaging in anti-Communist forays. Over 12,000 American troops were already deployed in the midst of the inexorable attack, infiltration, and terrorism by the Communist forces of North Vietnam.

"In those crisis-ridden days," writes Lodge's biographer William J. Miller, "Lodge's lean, energetic figure and his rugged, determined face became again as familiar to millions of Americans as they had been in his years tilting with the Communists at the UN."[2] On October 31, Cabot was due to fly to Washington for consultations, but at the last minute he postponed the trip because of an imminent coup by mutinous generals, an uprising which he had anticipated, if not encouraged, months before the plot coalesced.[3] These insurgents captured and assassinated Diem and his brother and chief political adviser Ngo Dinh Nhu. Cabot expected a shorter U.S. involvement because of the coup. Just before rescheduling his trip home, word suddenly came of Kennedy's death by an assassin's bullet in Dallas. Cabot immediately made his Washington journey, joining the scores of diplomats who paid tribute to the slain President. On November 24, 1963, he met with the new president, Lyndon Johnson, whom he had known in the Senate. Johnson asked him to stay on in Saigon to retain, as Kennedy wanted, a bipartisan, national-unity cast over U.S. military efforts there.

Just days after Cabot returned to South Vietnam, Eisenhower urged his old campaign manager to come back home and make himself available for the 1964 Republican presidential nomination. It paralleled Cabot's push in 1952 to bring Ike back from his post as Commander of Supreme Headquarters Allied Powers, Europe (SHAPE). This public statement of the former president carried weight and lit fires in various political camps, not the least of which was brother John's. He had been slowly mustering support for a run at the Senate nomination. Now the mushrooming interest for a Lodge presidential candidate both bolstered and complicated John's grassroots efforts in Connecticut.

Cabot's unofficial organizers in Massachusetts, including son George Lodge and political amateurs Arthur Goldsmith and Paul Grindle, moved to the forefront. John too wanted to be more than a "listening post" for Cabot, many thousands of miles away on the strategic Asian line of defense: "What I have in mind is to point out that while I as your brother cannot very well be a front man at this time, there is nothing to prevent your supporters from organizing. Nobody remembers better than you that it was not only the response to your visit to Paris but to the clamor which arose in the United States that Eisenhower resigned his post as head of SHAPE and returned to the United States. Arthur Goldsmith has called me and wants to lunch with me to discuss the situation. . . . I shall of course handle all these matters exactly as you desire and, as I have already said, I fully recognize that you can have nothing to do with it."[4]

Cabot responded by again pointing out that he was not running for anything and considered his greatest usefulness "the work at hand in Saigon." And by law, as an ambassador, he could not participate in political activities, either firsthand or from afar. To John, on December 16, 1963, he concluded:

> I am not at all afraid of the "brother act" but I really and honestly have no political ambition whatever. I admit that I used to have when I was younger. Also I cannot possibly leave here at any *proximate* future without neglect of my duty here and this I will not do. I will, of course, always try to do my duty as regards our two party system.[5]

John, meanwhile, was accepting nearly every invitation to GOP gatherings, party dinners, and politically-oriented cocktail parties, regardless of the size and makeup. He had learned a bitter lesson from the 1962 foray, when his aloofness and overbearingness lost him much support. Well-wishers reminded him and Francesca that, although they were a striking and charming and loquacious couple, they sometimes created the impression that they were above the average citizen. "John could be very stiff and unbending with people he didn't know," recalled Alice Harlow, wife of his Harvard classmate Brooks Harlow. "At Republican gatherings, John would come over to talk with me when he should have been circulating and seeing key politicians. Francesca was much better with all kinds of people."[6] Graceful, gentle, and generous, she struck her godchild Marge Chain Ellinger as "a democratic Republican."[7] More than in any previous campaign, Francesca took charge of lining up backers for John in Connecticut. With his obligations on the road for Junior Achievement, he had to rely on her political antenna and assiduity.

The Lodges soon courted the party stalwarts. From Stamford they invited five key Republicans to dinner at Villa Lodge. John DeForest, a Party leader in that city, was included. In his anecdotal journal, he described the evening as one of the most interesting in a long time. The Westport house struck him as almost a museum with so many fascinating mementos, photos, and curios in nearly every room. "On our arrival," he recorded, "we were escorted to a family living room downstairs where there were a bar, fireplace and comfortable chairs, the room having something of a Spanish influence mostly because of the pictures and objets d'art. The huge coffee table had a copper top made up of varied sizes of copper riveted together. This, along with a floor lamp, had been given to the Lodges by the Spanish Chamber of Commerce."[8]

"On finishing dinner," DeForest continued, "we retired to a solarium where Francesca proudly showed her plants. Here we enjoyed coffee from large painted cups given to John by the Fiat Company, and on which were depicted ancient models of this automobile. Besides two dogs, one a Scotch collie and the other a Spanish dog used to herd sheep, John also has a mynah bird which speaks Spanish . . . sneezes and coughs."

The group finally got on the subject of politics when it returned to the downstairs sitting room. The guests began to bring up the matter of where Lodge fit into the political landscape of 1964. John stated that he thought Stamford GOP leaders ought to be active in the struggle over the control of the state chairmanship, but he himself expressed the importance of staying aloof. He struck DeForest as still sensitive over the fact he was defeated for re-election ten years back.

John soon started to regale his guests with entertaining stories and anecdotes. He told about the distinguished lawyer Joseph Choate and an episode as U.S. Ambassador to the Court of St. James at the turn of the century. As American envoys wear no uniforms, Choate was mistaken for a butler when a young British lord asked, "Call me a cab." "You are a cab!" replied Choate. The same request brought a sarcastic retort. The lord was livid and went to tell his host of the insult received from his servant. When the fellow realized he'd made a terrible blunder, he tried to apologize. Choate brushed it off by saying, "Young man, if you were better looking, I'd have called you a hansom cab."

John then related a yarn about Daniel Webster, who was in a hotel once, and on paying his bill, the clerk remarked that there was a question as to what he should charge. "If that was your wife that spent the night with you, the charge is $5; if not, it is $10." Webster handed over a $10 bill and replied, "Here is $10. If this is a hotel, you may return five."

The conversation later turned to Cabot and his chances for the GOP nomination. "John naturally favors his brother," noted DeForest. "He is afraid his brother may be killed if he remains in the Far East. He often makes reference to 'my brother' or 'my brother Cabot.' Well, it was all so entertaining that we never got away from Westport until after 11:30. The new Lodge grandchild is still awaited. The final bit of décor to which we were exposed was John's bathroom, the walls of which were papered with covers of a well-known Spanish magazine (*ABC*) over which lacquer had been coated. It was quite interesting."[9]

The March primary in New Hampshire gave non-candidate Cabot Lodge an unprecedented write-in sweep. A stunning landslide, the upset brought him 33,000 votes, compared to nearest contenders Barry Goldwater and Nelson Rockefeller with 20,000 and 19,000, respectively. Nixon followed with some 15,000, or 17 percent of the Republican ballots. The early state contest propelled Cabot into the front rank of prospects for the GOP ticket. John hailed the victory. A New England "favorite son," Cabot, of course, never spoke a word in New Hampshire. But the voters favored his liberal international orientation, although he could not speak regarding his policies. The Lodge write-in had a profound effect on the candidacies of Goldwater and Rockefeller, since the aloof, uncommitted Cabot, thousands of miles away, won without campaigning and against two men who campaigned vigorously for weeks and spent enormous sums of money.

On March 12 John appeared on Johnny Carson's *Tonight Show* in connection with his Junior Achievement work. But the talk turned to New Hampshire. Lodge told viewers that he thought Cabot's stunning sweep stemmed from a deep preoccupation with foreign affairs by voters, and his brother had proven experience and mature judgment in that area. A week later while in Cleveland, John received on behalf of Cabot a petition signed by 25,000 people, asking him to return from Vietnam to campaign for the nomination. Many party leaders told him to come back to Massachusetts and start to build on his initial success. Cabot refused to move or encourage his backers.

John increasingly felt frustrated and bewildered over Cabot's insistence that he serve the Johnson administration and the Democrats, rather than his own party and campaign workers. As always, Cabot was receiving from John attention bordering on reverence. He had long viewed Cabot as a much better politician than he was. Helena, John's sister, tried to console John: "Cabot doesn't know when he offends people and is often hurt himself as he tries so hard to be good and considerate and wonders what the trouble is."[10]

John and Francesca, nevertheless, pushed the presidential bandwagon in Connecticut. A Fairfield County Lodge-for-President Committee came into being with Stamford ally Jack DeForest as chairman (who also became a director of the state-wide Draft Lodge Committee). Other state primaries were on the campaign trail that spring. In Illinois Cabot did well as a write-in candidate, although the down-the-line conservatism of Goldwater won 63 percent of the vote. The next important test, the Oregon primary in May, gave Cabot more solid backing, albeit not as impressive as New Hampshire's. Had he been there, he probably would defeated Rockefeller, who expended enormous effort and money. In the pivotal California primary, a narrow majority of registered party voters leaned toward Goldwater. The *vox populi* groundswell for Cabot seemingly faded as it moved west into Goldwater country.

In June Cabot and Emily decided to leave Saigon; he advised Johnson that he would like to come home as soon as the President could find a suitable replacement. His wife's health played a major part in the decision to leave the unrelieved heat and humidity of that Asian outpost, in addition to the ever-present dangers to the civilian population and foreign community. Cabot was too late to help himself in the quest for the presidential nod. So he jumped in to boost the slow-moving campaign of Governor William Scranton of Pennsylvania. But time was running out for both men to put the brakes on the two front-runners.

With Francesca's unstinting and generally behind-the-scenes buildup and promotion, John's own move to nail down the Senate nomination accelerated. Only briefly was it sidetracked when John waffled a bit over switching races with incumbent Congressman Abner Sibal, thus letting the ambitious Fourth District representative run for the Senate while permitting Lodge a try to regain his old Congressional seat. The possibility of an ambassadorial post was also bandied about, but Johnson, the president whom John seemingly knew the least, was about to run for the White House on his own. He was hardly one to tap another Lodge for an overseas assignment.

Francesca kept an almost running account of her non-stop efforts to bring her husband to the attention of party leaders as well as to the rank and file: "When the party wants you and you refuse, you're a dead duck. If there is a Johnson landslide and the Republican, *et al.*, loses, yours is not considered a loss just as to some it was never considered victorious. You must go around & be your own candidate. No one else is as good. There's no disgrace in fighting for something & losing but not fighting & losing is bad. I am out for an unanimous nomination—nothing less. Most feel the party will unite behind you and you'll be the focus point. You must get around & talk to the delegates. Meade Alcorn thought my idea of setting up meetings in various parts of each county excellent & I have the plan & the staff all set to go." And in 1964, John had an added advantage because the name Lodge evoked much favorable comment within the presidential race.

In early June, John, not willing to sit back as an elder statesman or king-maker, announced his candidacy for the Senate. He lined up Prescott Bush as honorary chairman of the Lodge for Senator Committee, and secured state legislators Peter Mariani and Louis Padula as co-chairmen, and Fairfield fund-raiser Gordon Lamont as treasurer. Lodge agreed to conduct the same kind of fighting campaign to unseat Democratic Senator Thomas J. Dodd as he had to defeat Governor Bowles.

Bush nominated Lodge, the obvious convention favorite as measured by a twenty-minute demonstration by delegates who surged into the aisles parading and chanting. A half-dozen seconding speeches boosted John's image as the front-runner. When the roll call came, he led by a wide margin. His sole opponent was Eugene Scalise, a retired Air Force officer and college teacher who sought to remake the party into a more progressive outfit. Scalise had planned to run for the post of Congressman-at-Large, but the seat was abolished by the General Assembly in April 1964. An Italian-Catholic, he felt the party's movers and shakers had not given minority groups their due. After being heard, Scalise withdrew his name, making Lodge the unanimous choice.[11]

In his acceptance speech, John described himself as a Lincoln Republican who would unite all elements of the party and "welcome with open arms all who wish to join us in advancing the cause of responsible government and renewing the forward march of our people." He described the times as one of "lost allies, lost friends, lost wars, lost face." He saw a sense of frustration and futility on the part of Americans both in the country's world position as well as with its major domestic problem: "They are distressed at the realization of the long-standing wrong under which our Negro citizens have lived. And they are frightened at the violence and hatred that have been unleashed in the process of the correction of those wrongs." He pointed to the Civil Rights Bill, which he supported:

> But let us be frank. The law is necessary—but we cannot expect it to solve the problem. No law can impose tolerance and love. Neither can a law set right, as if by magic, the effect of decades of discrimination in education, in employment, in economic opportunity. The best a law can do is to insure rights that never should have been denied, open doors that never should have been closed, extend horizons that never should have been shortened. If a law, or implementation of that law, tried to do more—tried to operate retroactively—it can quite easily begin to infringe upon the equally endowed rights of other citizens. You cannot base civil rights on civil wrongs, civil disobedience cannot generate equal protection under our laws.[12]

The times called for a firm, forthright position on a burning issue, and Lodge spoke out with an incisive and enlightening Lincolnesque exhortation.

No other state convention ran so smoothly in John's favor. Following his acceptance address, Governor William Scranton delivered the keynote speech. In turn, he garnered twelve national delegates to the GOP convention in San Francisco. The four remaining Connecticut delegates pledged their votes to Goldwater.

A few days after the Hartford meeting, Lodge, after eighteen months on the job, resigned as national president of Junior Achievement and turned all his energies to his campaign. The Republican National Convention in July did little to boost John's chances for a victory at home. He still hoped Cabot would somehow win the nomination, but realized only a deadlock would favor his brother. John pushed for party unity at every opportunity, taking no sides in the Goldwater-Rockefeller-Scranton tussle. He'd support whomever the delegates chose.

Goldwater forces and their cry "we'll offer a choice, not an echo" dominated the gathering. Scranton, out-gunned at every turn, tried to rally his backers for a last ditch effort. Rockefeller fell by the wayside because of the clamor over his recent divorce and remarriage. The Arizona Senator won the nomination on the first ballot with more than 200 votes to spare. Connecticut was the seventh state to jump on the Goldwater bandwagon after the completion of the roll call. John addressed the convention as the spokesman for Republican candidates for the Senate, praising the platform and party unity. The final session confirmed Goldwater's choice for second place on the ticket, former National Committee Chairman and Congressman William F. Miller from upstate New York.[13]

Goldwater's acceptance speech was anything but conciliatory toward those who had opposed him for the nomination. His bold statements— "Any who join us in all sincerity, we welcome. Those who do not care for our cause we do not expect to enter our ranks in any case" and "Extremism in the defense of liberty is no vice. Moderation in the pursuit of justice is no virtue"—produced some fairly violent reactions among many delegates.[14] John believed the conservative Senator's address had many good things in it, but it augured little good for many of the party regulars.

"Those of us who were trying to hold the Party together," John wrote to Senator Thruston Morton two days after the convention ended, "had our hands full on the Connecticut chartered plane, on our return trip from San Francisco. The principal problem seemed to be the interpretation of Barry Goldwater's remarks on extremism as an endorsement of the Ku Klux Klan and the John Birch society. I don't believe this was an endorsement, but his comment did cause a reaction among many. I had considerable difficulty with my own staff. If he had only issued a clarifying statement of the kind that I understand he made to General Eisenhower, it would be very helpful here in slowing the disturbingly numerous defections from our ranks."[15]

John waged an uphill battle in Connecticut. Moreover, he actually liked his opponent, Senator Dodd, whom he considered a friend and had once entertained in Spain. He said any "hatchet" job on Dodd must be done by others. President Johnson, who handily gained his party's nomination, had briefly considered Dodd as his running mate but soon turned to Hubert Humphrey when he realized that the Connecticut Senator's attitude toward the cold war was much more in harmony with Goldwater's stridently anti-Communist rhetoric.

John remained the underdog in the campaign and had no delusions of an easy climb. When asked by voters how he felt being on the same ticket as Goldwater, he admitted he differed with the GOP leader on some issues. Then he quickly aimed at the Democrats and said he thought Humphrey should feel uncomfortable with Johnson, whose civil rights record before 1960 was one a Mississippi governor would envy. The Goldwater question continued to pop up. One day in Bridgeport, he encountered a large sign in big red letters: "Republicans for Johnson." John looked at it, then remarked. "Well, they might vote for me." Later in a shopping center, a woman told him, "I'm giving you my vote but not Goldwater." Two men told him the same thing within fifteen minutes. That night an aide told John forty-two of sixty-five homes canvassed that day in New Britain were for him and twenty for Dodd. None was for Goldwater.

John walked a political tightrope. It was necessary to endorse Goldwater for the sake of party unity, but this alienated many. All-out warfare against Johnson and for Goldwater would cause numerous votes to shift to Dodd among pro-Johnson Republican and independent voters. Lodge, therefore, had to minimize references to Goldwater and minimize negative remarks about Johnson. Anti-Lodge sentiment seemed greatest, percentage-wise, among Republicans.

John's own political following never really grew in numbers, strength, or commitment. His philosophy and ideas didn't seem wrong or misplaced; they just failed to catch fire in a region that had become markedly liberal since the end of the war. For some, the substance and content of his addresses proved unacceptable. And for others, his highly sermonized and imperative style of delivery registered poorly.

The campaign trail held moments of both hard-earned satisfaction and inescapable frustration. It was a schedule so busy, so changeable, and so wide-ranging that it was difficult to measure success and failure. A proposed "John Lodge Day" in Stamford was planned, then dropped when the date set could not be confirmed by state campaign headquarters. The switch annoyed local organizers as well as Francesca. Upset over the cancellation, she proceeded to get on the phone and complain to John's public relations coordinator, campaign manager, and several others until she finally got assurance that John would be in Stamford as agreed upon earlier.

"It was quite a show we witnessed but she got results," wrote Jack DeForest of Francesca's machinations. "She was critical not only of the fact that Stamford was not getting an opportunity to expose John, but there were also other things that bothered her. Apparently there is no organization to the whole thing. It's ridiculous that our city of 100,000 with the largest GOP registration in the state has so little exposure for John." Following Lodge's "day," DeForest recorded that Lodge had given one of his best speeches: "The reaction was excellent. In fact, I had many fine compliments that the entire day was a real success."[16]

Francesca's unflagging persistence, contagious vitality, and exceptional creativity helped the campaign immeasurably. At a "Ladies Like Lodge for United States Senator" luncheon, she persuaded Helen Hayes to speak for John. The first lady of the American theater recalled first meeting Lodge in 1932 in California, where "Hollywood grabbed him after one look, as nothing looked as aristocratic, American and honest as John Lodge."[17] Hayes continued her praise: "I think he's sustained every role in everything that he's ever undertaken. John in my mind is not a flashing star or a twinkling star. He is a steady star—a star that glows steadily. I think we have a lot of bright stars, maybe shooting stars, in our political arena. But don't we need a good steady one. . . . Let's follow John Lodge."[18]

Along with Helen Hayes's glowing endorsement came Eisenhower's backing and campaign visits by Nixon, Scranton, and Miller. (Goldwater virtually conceded Connecticut to the Democrats and never came into the state.) John anxiously anticipated some help from Cabot. Closely identified with the drive to nominate Scranton for President, Cabot was not willing to approve his party's ultimate choice. He did send his brother a campaign contribution of $300 and promised to swing into Connecticut for a day of speechmaking in late October. One of his most ardent Connecticut supporters, Royal Cowles took charge of the logistics. Cabot chose United Nations Day for the visit, giving him a suitable peg to focus his remarks on world peace and the role of the UN. At a later rally in Waterbury, he said the United States should "use and thus build up" the organization. He praised John's record in public service: "When you consider John's record, you will see that it fits him to pass on the great foreign policy issues of our day."[19]

But was it the enthusiastic and stirring endorsement John anticipated? Cabot's concluding message echoed the similarly tepid approval voiced in the gubernatorial race of the 1950s: "It is not for me to come to

Connecticut and tell anyone how to vote and I am not going to do so. I will simply close these remarks by saying that my brother, John, from long experience, does understand the dangerous and disorderly world in which we live, and could therefore be counted on to make a constructive and useful contribution as your United States Senator from Connecticut."[20] The much-desired endorsement by Cabot of Goldwater never came about. As the envoy from Democratic administrations in Vietnam, Cabot distanced himself from the Republican platform on the conduct of the war. As the brother of a bipartisan representative in southeast Asia, John felt constrained from attacking Washington's stance. He would never publicly air family differences, politically or otherwise. Besides, John generally favored a military victory short of all-out war. Very clear and articulate on voicing America's interests as a nation, he recognized U.S. responsibilities and limits. And to him party politics ended at the water's edge. The importance of this Lodge precept hit home when in the middle of the campaign Cabot undertook, at the request of President Johnson, a tour through Europe to explain U.S. foreign policy.

John was gratified, albeit quite surprised, when the never-too-friendly *New York Times* came out in favor of his election. The paper voiced the hope that Connecticut voters would show greater awareness of individual merit than they had in the recent past. The *Times* editorial pointed out that Lodge would constitute "a valuable addition to the bloc of moderate Republicans in Congress who must strive to regain control of their party from the extremists now holding its reins." The endorsement added that his views on foreign policy were "more akin to those of the Administration than are those of Senator Thomas J. Dodd, whose belligerent line toward the Communist bloc is reminiscent of Mr. Goldwater."[21] The support from the *Times* may have ultimately confused some voters who looked upon Lodge as a conservative and not a moderate, in contrast to Dodd.

Almost every daily newspaper in Connecticut supported Lodge, as did New York's two preeminent morning journals, the *Times* and *Herald Tribune*. Yet John still felt that it was a lonely time for a Republican. For one thing most contributions to Goldwater from Connecticut residents went not to the state committee but directly to Washington. This struck him as an indication that there would be lots of crossing over between party levers. He looked more and more to the tremendously large block of some 400,000 independent voters.

The contest proved to be a gallant, last hurrah for Lodge. It was a Democratic year, and undoubtedly no Republican in Connecticut could have won against the insuperable odds. Dodd received over 779,000 votes, topping Lodge's 425,000 by a wide margin. Goldwater was clobbered by

Johnson two to one, hardly a surprise to most. All in all, John ran some 80,000 votes ahead of Goldwater in the Democratic landslide. In a note to Richard Nixon, penned November 7, Lodge wrote that he was "swamped by the anti-Goldwater feeling in Connecticut. Ironically enough, I think I conducted the best campaign of my life."[22]

Elsewhere, his old Chowder & Marching Club ally, New York Senator Kenneth Keating, took a drubbing from Robert Kennedy. But in the Senatorial race in California, John found a measure of satisfaction. Former Kennedy press secretary Pierre Salinger failed to win over a political novice. The Republicans had nominated a candidate close to John's heart, a former Hollywood actor. After over forty films and several terms as president of the Screen Actors Guild, George Murphy took up politics as an avocation. Urged both by Eisenhower, for whom in the 1950s he organized large-scale campaign rallies, and Walt Disney, who wisely told him that he'd get elected if he could just talk to enough people, the sixty-two-year-old ex-actor and dancer, became—after Lodge—the second Hollywood performer to gain high political office.

Lodge made it clear that he would continue to work for a vital two-party system. He would persevere in the struggle against a policy of appeasement of communist enemies, believing that it merely multiplied the hazards of war. And he noted that he would persist in the battle to make government "more responsive to the individual responsibilities which are inseparable from freedom." In a reply to a post-election letter from Barry Goldwater, in which he stated that he did not think any Republican could have beaten President Johnson, John reminded the defeated candidate that the Democrats seemed to understand better than the Republicans that "politics is the art of inclusion."[23]

At the close of 1964, John provided a personal insight into his campaign. He wrote to William J. Miller, Cabot's biographer: "Regarding the election, I knew pretty well what I was getting into. It seemed to my friends most unwise for me to give up a good job to engage in what looked like a losing battle from the beginning. Call it a sort of puritanical quixoticism which impelled me to become involved in a campaign which was possibly the most difficult within living memory. . . . I do truly believe that there are times when it is better to fight the good fight than shrewdly to sit on the sidelines. Time will tell."[24]

But at age sixty-one, time seemingly had run out for John Lodge, the political office-seeker.

CHAPTER 22

Relations, Foreign and Domestic

After the Republican debacle at the polls, Lodge took steps to become an active lieutenant at the side of the country's next GOP leader. But he also turned to pursuits which he had generally avoided in the past: academia and high finance. These endeavors remained secondary, yet figured significantly in a life unusually full and diverse.

Before running for the Senate, Lodge had accepted the invitation of the University of Pennsylvania to become chairman of the committee for its Foreign Policy Research Institute. This group in a short period had achieved a nationwide reputation for effective and constructive research and writing against communism and for the alliance known as the Atlantic Community. Many studies were undertaken at the request of the U.S. Senate Foreign Relations Committee. Directed by Professor Robert Strausz-Hupé, a leading political scientist and author, the Institute saw in Lodge an apt ally with a penetrating understanding of global problems and dangers as well as opportunities.

The Foreign Policy Research Institute's quarterly journal of world affairs, *Orbis*, invited academic and political figures to contribute articles. John's writings were well received. His "Can NATO Be Restored?" explained the importance of keeping that Western Alliance "modern" and adaptable to the needs of the times. He urged the United States to grant its European allies, including West Germany, a greater voice in the determination of NATO strategy and especially in planning the use of nuclear weapons in the defense of Western Europe: "I conceive of a 'modern' alliance, integrated militarily, united politically, and not dominated by the United States."[1]

In the mid-1960s, John gained belated recognition for his legislative role in foreign relations. The Polish government-in-exile awarded him the Order of Polonia Restituta, a high civilian decoration. It acknowledged his efforts to assist the people of Poland and particularly some 18,000 Polish refugees and their families who immigrated to the United States as a result of his legislative efforts while a Congressman.

In 1963 Lodge had also begun an affiliation with a small coed liberal arts college in Illinois. Founded in 1847, Rockford College placed strong emphasis on individual self-reliance for its 400 students. John came to the attention of the school through his Junior Achievement activities and their compatibility with the private enterprise philosophy of Rockford. In an introductory letter to Lodge, its president, John A. Howard, pointed out that the school was "unafraid to take an unequivocal institutional stand against communism, or against Federal aid to education." Howard also suggested that John from time to time make appointments for Howard to solicit gifts from people of similar convictions who might be interested in helping the college.[2]

John joined its Board of Trustees, emerging as a valued adviser and skillful public relations practitioner for Rockford. On several occasions he acted as master of ceremonies at the presentation of the college's Jane Addams Medal. "Lodge," observed Rockford President John Howard, "was gifted with poise and graciousness and wit which made any occasion over which he presided a memorable one."[3]

The school's Chicago public relations firm sized up Lodge as a resourceful ally and actually placed him on a retainer to promote enrollment at Rockford. His most widely heralded move tapped the stock in trade of the Lodge family itself. It seems that in the 1950s a student doing research at the Illinois Historical Society unearthed the only known photograph of Abraham Lincoln made after his death. The rare picture showed the slain President lying in state at New York's City Hall. At the side of the open coffin stood Rear Admiral Charles H. Davis, great-grandfather of Lodge. The young researcher brought the picture to the attention of Dorothy Meserve Kunhardt, daughter of Lincoln collector Frederick Hill Merserve. Her daughter, Nancy, was married to John's nephew, George Lodge, and because his ancestor was in the photo, he presented a print to the Lodges. John offered an enlargement of the photograph to Rockford College. A symbolic gift (the original photo remained at the Illinois Historical Society, which had often made copies available to scholars and historians), the presentation gained considerable press coverage, due in large part to a well-publicized ceremony on the very eve of Lincoln's Birthday in 1967.[4]

Lodge's ties with academia grew. In 1965 he addressed an audience of 300 people at a summer session of the Monterey Institute of Foreign Studies. Gaspard Weiss, its president and his classmate from the École Droit in Paris, had named him to its Board of Trustees. The California-based school chiefly prepared students for careers in the foreign service, and Lodge was particularly impressed with the institute's expertise in the teaching of languages. "Americans don't learn enough languages, and we must," he told its student body.[5]

Nearer to home, a search committee sounded out Lodge on the feasibility of assuming the presidency of Bennington College in Vermont. Its forty-eight-year-old president Dr. William Feis had died, and the college, one of the least orthodox women's institutions in the nation, sought a replacement. John's lawyer, Colin Ives, investigated the academic pros and cons at the rather anti-traditional and liberal Bennington and advised his client not to take the post.

Lodge often visited campuses for commencement exercises and conferences. He delivered the graduation address at Wilbraham Academy in Massachusetts and at Vernon Court Junior College in Rhode Island, where Francesca's niece Landa Braggiotti received a degree in 1966. In Connecticut at Wesleyan University, Lodge participated in a Spanish Civil War symposium, and at Fairfield University he joined a Spring Cultural Festival salute to Spain and was awarded his fifth honorary degree.[6]

John's widespread Junior Achievement acquaintances occasionally asked him to join corporate and financial organizations. Few interested him, even on a part-time basis. He turned down the position as vice chairman of Thomas J. Deegan Company, a New York public relations firm that offered a salary of $10,000 a year for two days a week on its Coca-Cola account. But he did go on the advisory board of the Newport National Bank in California at the urging of its president George L. Woodford, a national director of Junior Achievement. As a member of the New York Bar, John also attracted offers from law firms. He was tempted to become a partner and share in the large fees of the 1960s, a far cry from the $40 a week he labored for as a young clerk.

Holtzmann & Holtzmann, counsel to theatrical and film producers as well as governments and corporations, made a tempting proposition. Partner Fanny Holtzmann, seemingly awed by John's glamour-filled life and worldly charm, prodded him to write his memoirs for which she would act as his agent and lawyer. When that failed to interest John, Fanny offered him a partnership. Francesca strongly advised against it. "It will *never* be good," she clearly warned in no uncertain terms. "Let's be poor instead, PLEASE. She could easily do you harm." Francesca never argued at length with John on such matters. "With his judicial mind, John debated with himself and sort of 'blew it out.' "[7]

A persistent Holtzmann gained the services of John indirectly. A client in the development of oil and gas properties and the production of crude oils in Canada elected him to its board. This firm, National Petroleum

Corporation, also contracted with him to negotiate with overseas oil operators. John fell into a web of risky deals and circuitous concessions among foreign wildcatters. Then came a threatened stockholders' suit. In less than six months, he severed his ties to the company. Francesca's guiding intuition had been right again.

John's success as a leader or catalyst for charitable fundraising was unquestioned. He served as chairman of the Leukemia Society Drive in Connecticut and on similar campaigns. Francesca worked beside him. But her strongest commitment revolved around the performing arts. With her proven knack for bringing diverse groups of people together, she coordinated the efforts of local committees in Connecticut in raising over $100,000 for the construction of Lincoln Center. Part of the money went for the placement of an entrance column at the new Philharmonic Hall, designated the Connecticut pillar.

Lodge rarely passed up an invitation to help a fellow Republican, in or out of Connecticut. At a dinner in New Jersey, he spoke against Gov. Richard J. Hughes in his re-election bid against Republican State Senator Wayne Dumont. A burning issue in that 1965 race was Hughes's support of Dr. Eugene Genovese of the State University at Rutgers, who said he would welcome a communist victory in Vietnam. "I have a question for Gov. Hughes," Lodge said at the GOP banquet. "If he had been governor at the height of World War II and a Rutgers professor had said he hoped Hitler would win, would he have said that the professor was merely exercising his right of free speech?"

Members of the Chowder & Marching Club too could always count on John. "He did indeed enjoy being around those of us who were still running for re-election every two or six years," reflected former Congressman Robert Michel of Illinois. "He loved to swap stories and he did enjoy hobnobbing with politicians, probably more so than with the diplomatic set where protocol and a more reserved demeanor were the order of the day."[8]

His love of public speaking brought him to the attention of the World Wide Lecture Bureau for the Metropolitan Dinner Club series throughout the country. Armed with a copy of one of his forceful clarion calls—"The Challenge of the Hour: No Place To Hide" or "How Real is the Threat of War?"—Lodge played his part well in an evening of "good food, good company, good minds."

Francesca recalled his appearance at the Hispanic Society dinner-dance in Chicago. She forgot to pack a pair of evening socks for John to wear: "It was only my second packing error in nearly forty years of marriage. I had to hurry out of the hotel to buy another pair." The first packing *faux pas* occurred, she noted, when her husband was a young law clerk.

One of the firm's partners invited the newlyweds for a weekend in the country, including a command-performance black-tie dinner: "And I forgot to pack John's tuxedo! We managed to borrow one from old *Vanity Fair* editor Frank Crowninshield, who was about half John's size. The jacket was so tight and small that the sleeve came up to John's elbow."[9]

A popular ladies' luncheon speaker, John was regularly booked by the Federation of Republican Women's Clubs. These engagements renewed earlier acquaintances and made new friends. One particular lecture tour through southern California was as much a homecoming as a money-making venture. In Los Angeles, the Lodges visited columnist Cobina Wright, Sr., and Paramount studio chum Jack Oakie. In Palm Springs, they stopped by the house of Ike and Mamie Eisenhower, and had a reunion with old screen stars Janet Gaynor and Charles Farrell. Many Californians urged John and Francesca, now in their 60s, to retire and settle in the West. But they had no desire to leave Connecticut, where John still had a role to play.

In July 1965, he returned to Hartford. A delegate from the Fourth District to the Constitutional Convention ordered by the U.S. Supreme Court on the question of reapportionment, John was one of eighty-four members to face the one-man, one-vote matter. The special session was convened to formulate provisions for districting the Senate, apportioning the House, equalizing representation in both bodies no less than every ten years, and developing new procedures for amending the state Constitution. One of fourteen convention members from his old congressional district, Lodge was named to the Committee on Constitutional Resolutions, co-chaired by John Alsop and Chase Woodhouse. John relished being with a cross section of leaders in both parties: Raymond Baldwin, Thomas Meskill, Ella Grasso, Horace Seeley-Brown, Meade Alcorn, Wilbert Snow, J. Tyler Patterson, and Malcolm Baldridge.

The Convention met in twenty-five sessions over four months to update the Constitution of 1818. At its conclusion, Lodge urged all voters to okay the new Constitution. He did report, however, that he would have found it difficult to support the reapportionment provision "had it not contained an escape hatch to allow for Constitution amendment . . . which leaves the decision as to the composition of state legislature to the electorate which may wish to have at least one house chosen on a basis other than population." On December 14, 1965, only a paltry 20 percent of the state's voters turned out to vote. Those who went to the polls favored the new Constitution by a better than two-to-one margin.[10]

Connecticut's Constitution preserved the best of the old and added the most fitting of the new. Lodge had a similar outlook for Spain in the 1960s. He followed its progress into the economic mainstream of the free world and its role in the Western military alliance. He frequently preached on good relations with the United States, citing common interest and common cause. In a letter published in the *New York Times*, Lodge stressed this view: "We should not reject the friendship of nations simply because they do not enjoy representative government as we understand it." He praised Secretary of State Dean Rusk for recognizing Spain's contribution to "our common cause." Lodge concluded that Rusk "should be applauded, not censured, for attempting to continue the fruitful policy of friendly collaboration which characterized our relations with Spain during the Eisenhower Administration."[11]

As a place to be, Spain stood on a par with Westport. The Lodges had frequently spent holidays in Madrid with Beatrice and her growing family and vacations on the Costa del Sol in picturesque fishing villages along the Mediterranean. Not unlike the coast of southern California with its semi-tropical climate and mountain and sea vistas, the region had only recently become a resort attraction. European aristocracy had discovered it in the 1950s. Prince Alfonsos von Hohenlohe, for one, was charmed by a particular pine forest near the beach at Marbella, an hour's drive from the port city of Málaga. He built the first hotel there, the Marbella Club. His friends Count Rudolf von Schonburg and his wife managed the club and welcomed a procession of dukes and duchesses, diplomats, industrialists, and movie stars. A number rented or bought summer bungalows built by land developer Pomposa Ecanolon near the club.

The Lodges easily fit in among the affluent and celebrated visitors. Moreover, before John had left his post in Madrid, he had purchased a tract of land close to the Marbella Club. It overlooked the expansive waters of the Mediterranean; on clear days, one could see the distant yet imposing Rock of Gibraltar. "It would have been very convenient to build a house on this property while John was ambassador," Francesca pointed out. "But we waited because we didn't want any criticism of using his rank for personal comforts."

Francesca made frequent trips to Spain, often staying weeks with Beatrice, who by 1967 had three children: Matilda, Marta, and Juan. Antonio's career in government had prospered. He had served as governor of the Canary Islands and was destined for posts in London, Ecuador, Tokyo, Denmark, and Washington as well as an appointment as governor of the northern province of Guipuzcoa. To be with the Oyarzabals, the Lodges insisted that every August be set aside for a holiday in Spain.

Nearly ten years passed before the Lodges constructed a house on the site in Marbella, the first and only dwelling they ever planned and built. For its architect, they came upon an expatriate American who had lived in Spain since the mid-1950s. A student and disciple of Frank Lloyd

Wright, Robert Mosher moved to Madrid when the United States began building bases, having been called in by the State Department to help design them. The enterprising Mosher, whom Francesca would soon tag "Bumblebee" because of his perpetual bustle and verbal dash, remained in the country and established a business in Marbella.

"The Lodge property," Mosher remembered, "was no more than a plowed field of about two acres. At first we planned a villa right on the edge of the sea. But we learned that the dwelling would block the view of the adjacent house, a pseudo-Moroccan beach bungalow owned by the Duchess of Alba. So I pushed the house back and placed a lawn, garden and pool in front. The change proved auspicious. The move farther back provided an uninterrupted expanse of more than a hundred meters just above the sand."[12] A protective sea wall of large native stones separated the property from the sand and surf which occasionally wreaked havoc on less fortified beach houses. Mosher also had perceived some of the negative aspects of living at the water's edge. When the beach was filled with sun worshippers, the Lodges' view still remained private and unobstructed.

Construction of their villa, named Santa Matilda for the family's beloved octogenarian Matilda Frelinghuysen, proved to be a major undertaking. The transport of tons of river bed sand for use in cement required enormous efforts. Mosher had ruled out the more accessible beach sand because it was saline and prone to structural faults.

Within the house, Francesca added a special touch, an upraised area at one end of the large living-dining room complex for flamenco dancing. Appropriate wood had to be secured, cut, and set down to give the right sound from the tap-tap of dancers. Before the final stone was in place, the Andalusian-style villa and its servants' cottage cost five times the original estimate, boosting the outlays to more than six-and-one-half million pesetas, or some $100,000 in 1968 currency.

John referred to Santa Matilda as the house that IBM built. His stock holdings of that lucrative investment provided the wherewithal for this sumptuous and airy Spanish Shangri-la, a striking contrast to his comfortable yet low-key New England Villa Lodge. The Lodge coffers could now maintain two large homes. By 1967 John was receiving, in addition to a growing income from investments, fees from lectures and honoraria from writings, a large pension as a former Connecticut governor, and a monthly check as a retired naval officer. Later he would become eligible for a sizable stipend from his time as congressman and ambassador. On top of that, in 1969 he received $300,000 from the principal of grandfather Lodge's estate trust. All in all, John and Francesca could glide from Westport to Marbella with first-class ease and gusto.

Spanish conviviality figured more and more in their lives, but U.S.

politics remained close to John's heart too. In early 1968, the Westport *Town Crier* published an article on Lodge called "Connecticut's Prophet Without Honor Seems to be Riding a 'Winner' Again." The paper saw John, the state's last Republican governor, helping to elect Richard Nixon as president, in spite of Connecticut's determination to "sweep their most articulate spokesman and literally most distinguished example of Republicanism under the rug." The *Town Crier* noted that the Republican Party in the state went to extreme lengths to "snatch defeat from the jaws of victory." Their treatment of Lodge, "the most distinguished individual member on the record of victories and accomplishments," was a perfect example. But, it proclaimed, "he's out to put the State's Republicans in the lead again, whether they like it or not."[13]

John Lodge looked to a strong national leader to unite the party in Connecticut as well as all Republicans countrywide. Lodge thought Nixon was in the best position to pull together the party. He said so in 7,000 letters addressed to GOP county leaders, state chairmen, national committeemen, and others throughout the United States. As he had with Eisenhower, and would with Reagan, John fortuitously cast his lot on the side of the ultimate winner in a presidential race. Young Richard Nixon had entered the halls of the House of Representatives with Lodge, and they had developed an amiable working rapport as members of the 80th Congress. Both lawyers and navy veterans, they were enthusiastically committed to strengthening their party. As founding members of the Chowder & Marching Club, they were active in its midweek meetings on Capitol Hill and its weekend get-togethers in clubs and homes.

John admired Nixon for his involvement in drafting and debating the important Taft-Hartley legislation. Nixon's election to the Senate in 1950 brought him into the higher echelons of the party and into the field of potential presidential running mates. During the 1952 campaign, John welcomed the future vice president into his home state. Francesca even took Nixon under her wing to win over large blocks of predominately Democratic Italian voters. At a 1952 rally in East Boston, she wore a red, white, and blue dress bedecked with campaign ribbons and the inscription "I like Ike" on her shapely ankles. But she made certain the crowd knew the California Senator was the man of the hour. She introduced Nixon in Italian and then virtually crowned him the favored candidate of Italian-Americans by removing her blue cloak, her old "lucky" Italian regimental cape, and placing it on the shoulder of a smiling Nixon. She took him into the crowds and offered a few pointers on the game of boccie, a favorite Italian pastime. He joined in with much alacrity. At the close of the successful outing, Nixon described Francesca as "the best politician of the Lodge family."[14]

Both the Connecticut and the Massachusetts Lodges figured measurably in the rise of Richard Nixon. In his Cabinet-level UN post, Cabot participated in White House meetings with Vice President Nixon. In his run for the Presidency, the Republican bellwether chose Cabot as his running mate. But in the mid-1960s, private citizen Nixon appeared a loner. If, from time to time, Nixon seemed standoffish and noncommittal, Lodge would overlook it. Nixon, he firmly believed, would rise from the ashes of defeat and lead the country in the post-Kennedy-Johnson era.

In New York, John visited Nixon intermittently at his Broad Street law office and Fifth Avenue apartment, and spoke up for him as the man to restore the image of the party to popular acceptance. While many Americans viewed the former Vice President as marching into a field of battle with a hundred defeats, both at the polls and off-stage, John described him as "a loser who could win." "The 'can't win' theory now being used against former Vice President Richard M. Nixon is based on the fact that he lost the election of 1960 against John Kennedy," Lodge pointed out in an editorial in July 1967. "Yet, out of 69 million votes, a shift of 11,778 votes in four states would, under our electoral college system, have put Nixon in the White House." He went on to describe those "come-back presidents"—Jefferson, Jackson, Cleveland, and William Henry Harrison—who lost a race for the presidency and later ran again and won. "If election defeat were to rule out a person's chance for the presidency," Lodge argued, "then today Democrats would not be having Jefferson-Jackson Day dinners, and Republicans would not be having Lincoln's Birthday celebrations."

His intelligent analysis cited many examples of politicians who came back. "At this time of difficulty and danger of war abroad and lawlessness at home," he concluded, "we Americans should elect the most qualified person available to the Presidency of the United States which is, after all, the most important office in the entire world."[15] He left no doubt that only Nixon could fill those shoes. As early as 1965, he had spoken up for Nixon in Connecticut and begun lining up delegates to the national convention.

John soon joined the Republican National Committee's Task Force on the Conduct of Foreign Relations, chaired by former ambassador Bob Hill. Various tours were assigned to its members, who included conservative-minded past and present congressmen and governors, political science professors, ex-diplomats, and retired generals. John prepared a paper on the Middle East and served with those completing an analysis on U.S.-Eastern Europe relations.

Cabot played no role in such Republican foreign policy study groups. President Johnson had reappointed him Ambassador to South Vietnam, where U.S. troops strength in 1965 stood at 200,000 and American planes stood poised for bombing raids against North Vietnam. Cabot eased more and more into the Democratic camp as the President's representative; in any event, he was barred from taking any political, or even semi-political, positions. When he left Vietnam in May 1967, the veteran diplomat next agreed to become an ambassador-at-large and move to another key post, West Germany.

John assumed leadership within a group organized to oppose foreign trade with Russia. The Committee to End Aid to the Soviet Enemy (CEASE) lined up many Washington sponsors, including 36 senators and representatives. Nixon was not among its directors, but CEASE had his support in the fight against aid to and trade with the Communists. With headquarters in Washington, CEASE stood firm against making war weaponry available to the Communists, particularly in North Vietnam. "It is monstrous to attempt to build bridges with the Soviet Union," sounded Lodge in an address to the Sons of the American Revolution in New York, "while we are engaged in a brutal war in which Russia is supplying to our enemies in North Vietnam 80 percent of their arms and equipment—that is, all the petroleum, all the MIGs, all the SAM missiles, all the anti-aircraft weapons, and all the sophisticated weapons systems."[16] CEASE played its hand well. It forced the State Department to tell Congress that it would not seek legislation to expand U.S.-Soviet trade. The group influenced the Senate decision not to make four billion dollars of Export-Import Bank money available for trade with the Soviet bloc.

Nixon was pleased with Lodge's work and contacts. "Because of your stature," the presidential hopeful wrote, "you, of course, can talk to people around the country whom very few individuals in our organization could contact. This kind of approach is invaluable." Pro-Nixon Republicans would meet in Washington in June 1967, and Nixon expressed pleasure in knowing that his old friend could lend his "prestige and eloquence to the occasion."[17] John added a strain of genuine Ivy League distinction and refinement to Nixon's strategy. The would-be candidate encouraged Lodge to make as many television and other personal appearances on his behalf "as you can work into your schedule." John's efforts on platforms promoting Nixon encouraged him. After one particular program, Nixon wrote: "There will be other programs of this type where you will be able to hold up my end against the opposition."[18]

As 1967 drew to a close and the winter primaries approached, John became more and more part of the Nixon team. Then, without warning, a family crisis occurred, news so startling that it frightened and numbed both Lodges. He later described the ensuing dilemma as "by far, the greatest trial of my entire life."[19]

Fifteen months earlier, in September 1966, son-in-law Jim Marcus had been appointed to the coveted post as New York City Commissioner of Water Supply, Gas, and Electricity by Mayor John Lindsay. Jim had left his oft-changing venture capital jobs not long after the Lodges introduced him to the young Republican Congressman and mayoralty candidate. The affable Marcus volunteered to work in the Lindsay campaign. After the 1965 election, he was named an unpaid assistant and troubleshooter to the new mayor. He quietly climbed toward the top rung of the Lindsay administration, gaining the $30,000 a year commissioner's job, and in July 1967 the additional responsibility as administrator of EPA and the proposed Department of Air Pollution and Sanitation. Few officials were closer to John Lindsay, who, earlier that year, became godfather to George Griswold Frelinghuysen Marcus, the younger child of Jim and Lily.

To all observers, Jim's star finally was on the rise. He had a well-paying municipal post, complete with such perquisites as a chauffeured limousine with a still-uncommon mobile telephone that he enjoyed using to surprise friends. John believed his thirty-seven-year-old politically minded son-in-law had found at last a worthy vocation. Lily, too, seemed content and able to manage roles as a mother and an actress. Then, several weeks before Christmas 1967, the Marcuses rushed to John with an incredible and frightening story. Unless Jim delivered some $50,000 in cash to loan sharks, his career was in jeopardy, perhaps his life. He had borrowed heavily at astronomical interest rates after losing money in various business dealings and unsuccessful market transactions.[20]

John at first refused to give any money to Jim to clear his nightmarish debts, thinking there was more to the sordid tale than what he was told. Matilda Frelinghuysen, however, decided to loan the cash. A few days later, city newspapers carried front-page stories on Marcus' resignation as water commissioner and District Attorney Frank Hogan's investigation into his business affairs. Jim was quoted as saying personal problems and the recent death of his father were to blame. The press soon provided greater detail on the developing scandal. Marcus was being held with Mafia leader "Tony Ducks" Corallo on charges of a $40,000 kickback on a $835,000 city contract to refurbish the Jerome Park Reservoir in the Bronx. In the words of a *New York Times* editorial on corruption, the facts of the indictment left "no doubt that organized and experienced criminals and labor racketeers moved in, found a mark, and tried to make a score."[21]

Further investigation by the DA's office and the FBI soon uncovered another kickback plot, a scheme by Marcus and labor lawyer (and undercover FBI informer) Herbert Itkin to obtain monies on all municipal repair contracts issued to a private water system company. At a trial in Federal Court in June 1968, Marcus testified that his life had been threatened four times and his debts totaled more than $100,000. He admitted taking about $16,000 in payoffs from a contractor on the Bronx reservoir job. In September Marcus began a fifteen-month sentence at a Federal prison. He also pleaded guilty to charges of conspiracy to commit perjury, taking unlawful fees, and receiving a bribe when he was water commissioner. Ultimately, Marcus served about eleven months.[22]

Jim's in-laws received prominent mention in nearly every newspaper and magazine article on the affair. It was a bitter and embarrassing situation for the honest and upright Lodge. He apologized for his son-in-law's actions in a note to Lindsay. The Mayor replied in kind: "I'm sure it was a difficult one for you to write, but the wrench that you must have suffered in doing it is made up for by the comfort that it gave me. This has been indeed a hard one and I've suffered muchly, but no more so than yourself and Francesca. I think of Lily and pray for her because she is a lovely person."[23]

Lily stood by Jim, appearing in court during the grievous trial and sentencing. When he went off to prison, she visited almost every week, month after month. "Lily's loyalty to him," her father wrote to a friend in London, "has been total. It is all terribly tragic and quite unbelievable."[24] The tragedy seemed like an incredible nightmare to the Lodges. In January 1968, after a month of dealing with the unfolding scandal, Francesca and John had to get away. They spent nine days at the isolated La Costa Spa near San Diego. One day while relaxing at the resort's health center, they struck up a conversation with a gentleman nearby. He introduced himself as "Mr. Marcus." And a few minutes later, they turned around and spotted an old friend, John's college classmate Stanley Marcus. It seemed there was no escape from a Marcus. The Lodges later laughed about it, and the odd story brought a refreshing smile to their faces.

Upon their return to Westport, both Lodges immersed themselves in the Nixon campaign. Nixon asked John to stand in as his proxy in the presidential primary in New Hampshire. Polls showed that Nixon was ahead of his nearest rival, Gov. George Romney of Michigan, by as much as five to one. Extolling Nixon's experience and dedication, Lodge said that campaigns were a test of the electorate as well as of the candidates. He hoped the former would be influenced by basic realities, not concocted surface imagery.[25] Confident that his man practically had the nomination, John returned several times to New Hampshire to speak on Nixon's behalf. John added that he himself was not a conservative or a liberal but took a middle-of-the-road stand with Nixon—namely, a firm stand on Communism, crime, and the integrity of the dollar.

In the March 12 primary, Nixon gained 80 percent of the vote and immediately wrote the Lodges: "Your moral support would have done the job, but your active assistance is what really put the frosting on the cake—our New Hampshire victory would not have been possible without your help. Pat joins me in sending warmest regards and deep personal appreciation to you both."[26] On the Democratic side, President Johnson won the state primary, despite a strong showing by Senator Eugene McCarthy of Minnesota.

John eagerly moved forward to make Nixon the convention favorite. He served with the Nixon Network, a nation-wide group of community-level supporters positioned to spark a hard-hitting communications program. He played a major role in organizing "Ambassadors for Nixon," a group of seventeen inactive U.S. diplomats, mostly from the days of the Eisenhower administration. John became chairman of the organization, which included Spruille Braden, Bob Hill, Clare Boothe Luce, Henry J. Taylor, William Pawley, and Val Peterson.

Both John and Francesca took to the road for Nixon. In Palm Beach they circulated among the party's big contributors and picked up major donations. In Palm Springs they discussed Nixon strategy with publisher Walter Annenberg, who would in the next administration serve as ambassador to Great Britain. They called the Eisenhowers at nearby Indio. "When you come to see us tomorrow," Mamie Eisenhower insisted over the telephone, "please wear your 'battle clothes,' Francesca. It would delight Ike to see you in one of your red, white and blue campaign outfits."

As soon as he spotted Francesca in a navy jacket and red and white striped skirt, Ike greeted them with his arms up over his head in his famous victory pose and hugged the patriotically dressed old friend. At the reunion, she gave Mamie a large colorful umbrella bedecked with a big Nixon badge. In a thank-you letter, Ike told the Lodges that Mamie was going to a Republican Women's luncheon that week and would wear the Nixon badge: "Her attitude is 'Well, I am for Dick Nixon—why do I not have the right to publicize my support.' To such a statement I can see no possible objection because after all, as she says, she is over 21." It was the last time the Lodges saw Ike.[27]

As the May primary in Oregon approached, John predicted a Nixon win on the second convention ballot, despite Nelson Rockefeller's entry into the race. He also predicted that Nixon would face Vice President Hubert Humphrey in the election, rather than Robert Kennedy, who had less chance of uniting the Democratic party. (Johnson, encountering growing opposition to the Vietnam war, had withdrawn from the race in March.)[28]

In August Nixon gained the nomination on the first ballot, pledging in his acceptance speech to bring an honorable end to the war. A member of a special six-man Nixon advisory committee, Lodge had been asked to submit his views on the choice of a vice president. He first considered Senator Charles Percy ("He has come out for Governor Rockefeller," Lodge noted) and Senator Mark Hatfield ("He is a notorious 'Dove' on Vietnam," Lodge added). Turning to Ronald Reagan, who had been elected California's governor in 1966, he analyzed his strengths and weaknesses. "He is the accepted heir of Barry Goldwater and therefore would inherit much of the opposition to Goldwater," he wrote Nixon. John pointed to recent polls. Reagan was weak in his home state, John explained. He concluded that Reagan, a former movie star, "is an expert scene stealer" and it might be difficult for him as number two on the ticket "to take his signals from the nominee for President."[29] For vice president, John submitted Governor John Volpe of Massachusetts, "a liberal without being a spectacular, controversial liberal like Senators Percy and Hatfield." A Roman Catholic of Italian extraction, Volpe, said John, would have strength where Nixon needs it the most.[30] Nixon, to the surprise of virtually all his advisers, picked the little-known governor of Maryland, Spiro Agnew. In any event, John felt both Nixon and Agnew and their families made a tremendous hit at the close of the convention. "Your singing and piano playing," he told Nixon, "struck a new note of harmony."[31]

The Lodges hit the campaign in full force that fall. The "trail" aspect inspired Francesca to come up with the idea of a fully outfitted house trailer to travel New England to promote the ticket, especially among inner city ethnic groups. She called it The Nixon-Agnew Rolling Home. Agnew's daughters Susan and Pamela launched the brightly decorated vehicle, which served to dispense campaign literature and souvenirs, broadcast taped speeches by Nixon, and provide refreshments.

With the advancing women's liberation movement, women played a greater role in the 1968 campaign. Francesca, however, had long felt liberated in political campaigns and in her forty-year marriage. She stood firm with her increasingly out-of-fashion credo: "Man and woman are one—and the man's the one." For decades, she had believed that "the emancipation of women had tended to blunt their most attractive quality—flexibility" and that women in many ways were too free, "which I believe is why so many successful women are unhappy."[32]

Francesca joined her other half to help light up the skies above Times Square. John pressed a button that signaled the lights beaming on a 106-foot-wide billboard at Broadway and 48th Street with the single word "NIXON." Erected by master sign builder Douglas Leigh, whose company had designed the smoke-puffing Camel cigarette display and the Chevrolet and Canadian Club advertisements along the Great White Way, the campaign message hoped to "turn on" voters.[33]

With Nixon in lights on the skyline of Manhattan, John soon flew to Europe to persuade overseas Americans to vote Republican. In Spain Chad Braggiotti, now retired from the Foreign Service and chief of mission of the Intergovernmental Committee for European Migration, organized businessmen and citizens for Nixon. He set up a speaking schedule for his brother-in-law to reach the 50,000 Americans in Spain and an even greater number in Italy.

On Election Day, the Lodges voted in Westport and then drove into New York to wait out the returns at Republican headquarters. Not until the early hours of the next morning was it clear that the "new" Nixon, whom they had backed more than three years earlier in his political comeback, had edged out Hubert Humphrey. For John still another campaign was about to begin, one that tested his mettle and patience. He soon learned that even for those close to the victors the spoils did not come easily.

CHAPTER 23

The Road to Argentina

I n early spring of 1969, President and Mrs. Nixon were ingratiating hosts at a twentieth anniversary for members of the Chowder and Marching Club. The occasion brought together many GOP legislators who had served in the House in the 1940s and 1950s. Retired "old-timers" did not know some of the "newcomers," so much effort was spent seeing that everyone met everyone else. The three-hour White House party, a very nostalgic gathering, passed all too quickly, according to those guests who had known Nixon as a young Congressman.

A fair number of the forty or so Chowder and Marching members had moved up in the political world but no one, of course, quite as far as their host. The new President had already appointed some of the Club's early mainstays to important posts: Melvin Laird to Secretary of Defense and Hamer Budge as chairman of the Securities and Exchange Commission. Don Jackson's nomination as a member of the Interstate Commerce Commission had just been announced. Rogers Morton was about to take over the reins as chairman of the Republican National Committee, and Ken Keating, his new assignment as Ambassador to India. Virtually all of Nixon's original Capitol Hill friends and campaigners who wanted jobs seemed to have them in the new Administration.

Everyone but John Lodge. Where was his hoped-for assignment? When would a reward come for his long and arduous team-playing? These thoughts occupied him during much of the White House celebration.

Right after the elections, most political observers had predicted a key job for John: probably in the State Department, perhaps even Secretary of State. His experience both overseas and at home seemingly earned him the appointment. But former Attorney General William Rogers, close Nixon ally, gained the top Cabinet post. In December Richard Kleindienst had called to ask John what type of work the former ambassador had in mind.

He quickly responded, describing three offices that could utilize his qualifications.

As a retired Naval Reserve Captain, he first suggested Secretary of the Navy. But he moved on to stress his diplomatic skills. "It is in the field of foreign policy, however, that my qualifications are quite specific," Lodge reported. John mentioned ambassadorships to Paris and Rome. On an enclosed page, he listed additional information on his qualifications for France: early education in Paris, military liaison with French forces in the Mediterranean and southern France, linguistic ability, House Foreign Affairs committee membership. As qualifications for service in Italy, he described his speaking knowledge of Italian, World War II contacts with the Italian Navy and the landing at Salerno, friendship with de Gasperi and other leaders, Congressional activities to help rebuild the country, and a wife fluent in Italian.[1]

John mentioned the three other Class I posts in Europe. He dismissed London. Brother Cabot, he stated, was currently ambassador to another, Bonn. The third, Madrid, was very desirable. "It has been conveyed to me from high sources that I would receive a most friendly welcome were I to return to Madrid as Ambassador," he wrote Nixon. "My son-in-law Antonio de Oyarzabal, who was your aide when you last visited Madrid, is an aide to Foreign Minister Castiella, with whom I have maintained close and friendly relations during these intervening eight years. I have had several recent talks with the Spanish Ambassador to Washington and to the United Nations with respect to the Spanish bases. I am familiar with the subject [renewal of the agreement on maintaining military installations] and I am ready and willing to help Bill Rogers to arrive at a satisfactory settlement with our Spanish friends."[2]

On a brief trip to Madrid not long after the inauguration, Francesca wrote John with hopes of a possible homecoming: "Gosh! How everyone remembers you & asks after you with the greatest affection & treats me like a Queen!"[3] Her son-in-law recalled the situation: "Many people insisted he come back. What they really wanted was to bring *back* the days of Mr. Lodge—to recapture a period when America could do everything for Spain. But new forces within the Franco regime were changing the country and looking ahead and convincing Franco to adapt to the European countries surrounding Spain."[4]

Lodge might have returned to Madrid if he had not advanced himself so assertively as the best go-between on military base negotiations. According to a commentary written by Flora Lewis, he gave Nixon foreign affairs adviser Richard Allen a "compromise" proposal that he thought he could get the Spanish government to accept. The secret document was, in effect, the Spanish government's own plan. Moreover, John had advised the Spanish ambassador in Washington to wait out the last months of the Johnson administration and negotiate with Nixon's. At the State Department, it seemed like potential, if not actual, conflict of interest.[5]

Meanwhile, in the last weeks of 1968, as John stood in the dark as to his own assignment, he was being hounded by friends for jobs in the new administration. Then, unofficial word of the choice of Lodge as envoy to the Vatican spread. But the thought of some form of relationship with Vatican City, the first contact since World War II, stirred up a wave of protests. Opposition to American representation at the Holy See stemmed from within Congress. It led Nixon to back down on establishing ties with the Catholic hierarchy.[6] The diplomatic assignment was a post that both Lodges would have liked and undoubtedly would have handled well.

To add a measure of insult to injury, Nixon enthusiastically announced the appointment of Lodge's fellow Connecticut campaigner worker, J. William Middendorf, as Ambassador to the Netherlands. As treasurer, he had raised millions for the Republican National Committee and virtually produced a surplus for the party. And another nearby Connecticut acquaintance, Frank Shakespeare, an executive at CBS, took the job as chief of the U.S. Information Service.

By the night of the Chowder and Marching Club White House dinner on March 19, Lodge was annoyed, perplexed, even testy. That evening Nixon pulled him aside and urged him to confer the next day at State with Bill Rogers and to accept whatever position the new Secretary might offer. The next day, Rogers discussed the position of permanent representative to the Organization of American States and sent John to confer with the incumbent delegate Sol Linowitz.

That evening, at a gathering at the Washington Marriott, Nixon again buttonholed Lodge. In the presence of other people, including newsmen, he repeated his advice to accept whatever job Rogers put on the table. John took it to heart, and a few days later, on March 24, wrote the President a letter accepting the ambassadorship to the OAS, an organization formed in 1948 to foster cooperation among the countries of the Western Hemisphere. A week later, he wrote still another letter to Nixon, expressing his high regard for the "profoundly moving and beautifully delivered" eulogy by the President on Eisenhower, who had died that week. Lodge also hoped to confer with him on "certain aspects" of the OAS post before a public announcement was made.[7] Yet within a few days and before Lodge had a meeting with Nixon, newspapers carried stories of the "expected" announcement by the White House.

From Spain Francesca had been urging her husband to see Nixon directly and "appeal to him that you are being 'knifed all around.' " She felt he was being "both used and sacrificed." Nixon, she thought, had many crises on his hands. "But he had left you far too long and now is the time to push, kick & scream. BUT—not obviously." At the same time, there was talk among White House aides of the ambassadorship to Argentina for John. "Perhaps if this OAS is so in the air . . . Argentina would be best," Francesca concluded. "If, when you see Nixon, you can manage it, it *may* be possible to make another stab for Rome. . . . There is something about being the Ambassador which is particularly interesting & rewarding—*no te parece*? Argentina is important & if Nixon plans a South American tour it will be especially so, more so than Brazil or any other (Gosh! I wouldn't like to cope with Portuguese—*et tu*?)."[8]

However, with the belief that he would soon be located in Washington, John made a few missteps. He practically insisted on government housing, a limousine, and similar perquisites as the U.S. delegate to OAS. John then flew off to Spain for a brief Easter holiday. No sooner had he landed when word reached the Lodges of the death of aged cousin Matilda Freling-huysen. He immediately returned to the States and while there, faced several front-page *New York Times* articles on his "fate." He was soon contacted by White House job scout Peter Flanigan, who urged John to forego the OAS "non-offer" and head elsewhere, perhaps South America. Apparently, the State Department career establishment took issue with Lodge's effusive and outspoken nature, in contrast to the more reserved style of Secretary Roger's chief subordinates, and wanted him out of Washington.[9]

The White House had never actually announced the OAS appointment, therefore avoiding an embarrassing impasse. Lodge felt humiliated. William Rogers blamed John for the news leak to the *Times* of the OAS job. John denied it, replying that "as these matters drag on, rumors tend to circulate." Moreover, the stinging and inexplicable words of Rogers— "We can't use you"—reached John and remained foremost in his thoughts.[10]

In mid-April Flanigan, after repeated telephone calls to a puzzled Lodge, convinced him to go to Buenos Aires. On April 20, John again wrote Nixon, this time to accept the post. Hadn't the President back in March off-handedly remarked to him, "John, I am sending you to the most beautiful embassy we have." But that was all he said about it until Flanigan made it official. "I have been greatly distressed by the unfortunate intrusion of the media in what must be regarded as a confidential matter," John wrote Nixon. "Ever since I became President Eisenhower's Ambassador to Spain, the *New York Times* has been, by and large, rather unfriendly to me. You, sir, are in a unique position to understand this. It can hardly be said they have always been friendly or fair to you."[11]

Ten days later, the White House announced the appointment to Argentina. Flanigan apparently had been so frayed by the Lodge-Nixon experience that he even forgot to inform John of the upcoming official pronouncement. John first learned of it from the radio and from newsmen's queries.

If there existed a cabal, diplomatic or political, working against the interests of John Lodge, it could have readily gathered ammunition on several fronts. In the 1968 elections, the Republican Party leadership in Connecticut had once more demonstrated their expertise in defeat. Nixon lost the popular vote in the state. Lodge had made some 400 speeches for the President, but in the way of fundraising, he brought little into the party coffers from his own resources or collegially. On the other hand, Middendorf and his Connecticut-based team raised millions for the campaign.

Meanwhile, Cabot grew into a saint-like figure among the State Department professionals. He followed the establishment line as Ambassador to South Vietnam, then moved under Johnson to Bonn. After the elections, Nixon asked Cabot to become the chief U.S. negotiator at the Vietnam peace talks in Paris. Surreptitiously, Cabot communicated the feeling that there was room for "only one Lodge" in Europe.[12]

And in all the off-again, on-again confusion, sixty-five-year-old John Lodge wondered whether those past the traditional retirement age were being cast aside. But he was more concerned about Nixon's personal thoughts over the Marcus scandal and a family member serving a prison sentence. Perhaps all these factors, singularly and collectively, gave Nixon cause to drag his feet from November to April, until finally he gave the official word that Lodge would have an ambassadorship.

In late May, the nominated Lodge appeared before the Senate Foreign Relations Committee. Senators Dodd, Mansfield, Aiken, and Mundt warmly greeted their "old friend and colleague." Senator Clifford Case, who also served in the House with John, suggested that the group might adjourn to another room and watch some of his old movies. Chairman William Fulbright questioned John on his financial holdings, then tried to pin him down as to the character of the government of the country for which he was headed. John suggested it was a democratic regime. It was far from the truth. Argentine President Gen. Juan Carlos Ongania gained power as the result of a *coup d'état* that overthrew his civilian predecessor in 1966.[13]

On June 6, 1969, Lodge was sworn in as Nixon's Ambassador to Argentina. Under Secretary of State Elliot Richardson delivered the oath before a sizable gathering of Congressmen and Senators, White House staffers, political supporters, foreign service aides, Connecticut friends, and family members—and in front of a portrait of John's great-grandfather Frederick T. Frelinghuysen, Secretary of State during President Chester Arthur's term. A flurry of farewell parties and receptions filled the calendar for June. Among them was an informal supper at the Spanish Embassy in Washington that followed "A Nostalgic Night at the Movies" presenting *The Scarlet Empress*. GOP Chairman Rogers Morton took one look at the on-screen Lodge's shoulder length hair and beard and exclaimed: "Good Lord! Look at the hippie haircut."[14]

On the last Friday in June, some fifty friends and relatives and a handful of dignitaries, headed for the Moore-McCormack steamship line pier on the Hudson River. At long last, after eight months of uncertainty, confusion, and harassment, John was about to sail aboard the SS *Brazil* to a new and challenging post. Aboard the South American cruise ship, on one of its last voyages, was John's old aide in Madrid and new DCM in Buenos Aires, Milton Barall, and the recently named Ambassador to Brazil C. Burke Elbrick. On July 6, as the ship crossed the Equator on her 18-day sail, the Elbricks gave a party to celebrate Francesca and John's 40th wedding anniversary and their journey "to greater renown."[15]

As Nixon had offhandedly remarked to the Lodges that he was sending them to the most beautiful U.S. embassy in the world, the ambassador's house in Buenos Aires proved to be the grandest of residences. A small-scale Versailles palace with almost a city block of gardens, a swimming pool, and a tennis court, it had been built in 1914 as a private house. This marble and granite structure on the Avenue del Libertador impressed every visitor with its regal entrance hall and spectacular curving staircase leading up to spacious reception rooms. Not long after Lodge presented his credentials to President Juan Carlos Ongania, the dwelling opened its doors to one of the largest receptions ever held there by an ambassador.

Two of the three members of the Apollo 11 lunar landing team, Neil Armstrong and Michael Collins, greeted enthusiastic guests at the top of the circular staircase. The first men to land on the moon, they visited Buenos Aires as part of a twenty-two-nation, round-the-world goodwill tour. The line of over 2,500 well-wishers stretched from the front entrance down the outside terrace steps and into the garden. Many also waited for hours on the street for a glimpse of the astronauts and a chance to cheer the lunar explorers. The celebration set the pace for future galas of the Lodges in Buenos Aires during the months and years ahead.

John had never been to South America (although in his 1938 film, *Just Like a Woman*, he played a jeweler's agent on an assignment in Buenos Aires). But in Argentina he felt very comfortable. The country was greatly influenced by Italy and France as well as by Spain, and its ties to Europe were considered very significant. Buenos Aires, a city of eight million people, very much resembled Paris with its broad avenues, many parks, and splendid monuments. Yet, being so isolated from Europe and North America, it created its own cultural institutions and developed a sort of aloof elegance.

Frank Oram, who had served John in Madrid and now joined his staff as public affairs officer, describes the typical cosmopolitan Argentine: "He speaks Spanish, lives in a French house, dresses like an Italian, but thinks he's British. Argentina has never had a social revolution, fought a war, or faced famine. In 1969 and 1970," he adds, "the country was in a holding pattern politically with no forward motion."[16]

Italian and Spanish immigrants established the strong European flavor of this, the world's eighth largest country in area. A million square miles of mountains, grasslands, deserts, and tropical forest, the land stretched from swampy Gran Chaco of the north to the windswept desert of the south—all backed by the Andes, with many peaks towering over 20,000 feet. The Lodges could hardly wait to see the diverse regions of the farthest-south country in all of South America. As in Spain, John sought to venture beyond the capital at every opportunity. His first trip, to a co-operative housing project in La Plata, had him talking in Spanish to the community and stretching out his hand in greeting to everyone along his route. Soon he traveled to Patagonia, visiting farms, sheep ranches, and oil well riggings.

An invitation to participate in the opening of a national highway in the Pampas, named for John F. Kennedy, gave John an opportunity to see the provinces of Corrientes and Misiones. A reporter from *La Mañana* in Corrientes noted his remarkable quality of winning everybody's goodwill, "of putting them in his pocket" with his genuine friendliness and engaging smile: "He showed with remarkable eloquence that he was not only helping economically to complete a much-needed and wished-for public work but that he understood the people, that he identified with their customs and way of life."[17]

Lodge's executive assistant Donald Stewart recalled these frequent trips, often by plane and arranged by a defense attaché in the course of his duties: "The travels to distant areas and provinces were viewed as a sincere gesture of goodwill and made John extremely popular. Francesca accompanied him on many. Their pattern of seeing the country was precisely like the one pursued in Spain."[18]

Lodge arrived in Buenos Aires at about the same time as the new British Ambassador Michael Hadow. Within diplomatic circles, the two major power envoys were quickly compared. Each had a different and contrasting approach. Hadow believed in quiet diplomacy, the traditional mode of being seen but not heard publicly. He demonstrated an ability in person-to-person contacts, especially in carrying out one of his principal objectives, to secure a greater Argentine interest in British imports.

John immediately radiated personal charm. With a flair for promotion, he took the plunge of making a national broadcast on the Apollo 11 moon walk before the presentation of his credentials. That, and his talks with newsmen, normally would have proved a handicap for a mission in a country noted for rigid adherence to convention. But for Lodge, the occasion of the space odyssey warranted the unusual step. The message, delivered in perfect Spanish, won him popular as well as official applause.

Thus, his flamboyant, highly theatrical style quickly gained favor among the Argentines. "They loved it," recalled international banker Peter B. Smith, who grew up in Connecticut in the 1940s and 1950s:

> His egocentric nature appealed to the masses. But it turned off a number of career diplomats and made him rather controversial, especially within the U.S. State Department. To some, he came across as a buffoon, who, no matter how serious the social occasion, always at some point broke into a song. One time, when he invited me to an embassy reception, he announced that in honor of his Connecticut friend Peter Smith he would sing the Yale "Whiffenpoof Song." Some people abused his confidence when he let his hair down. His off-the-record liveliness often backfired.[19]

The American community tended to criticize Lodge for developing stronger ties with the Argentines rather than his own countrymen in Argentina. Businessmen complained that he was attuned to cultural affairs but not to trade and economics, particularly in contrast to his predecessor Carter Burgess, a corporate executive and former president of American Machine and Foundry.

Lodge applied the collaborative team-player approach that had worked so well in Madrid. In spite of a frequent turnover in personnel, it proved successful. "He didn't become directly involved in the team's duties and responsibilities on a daily basis," Donald Stewart pointed out:

> Yet, if a person came to him and presented reasons why something should or should not be done, he'd listen and respond. You could persuade him to take a certain course of action. However, he would not yield easily. Everyone had his day in court.
>
> He was astute, generous, and well meaning. But he could be demanding and exasperating. He wanted things done well. He

often remarked that he saw himself as a professional career ambassador, not a mere political or presidential appointee handed a job because of his name and pedigree and party support. One time we were together in his office. He was complaining about his secretarial staff using staples to hold documents together instead of paper clips. As he tried to remove a staple, he pricked his finger. "There," he exclaimed, "I'm bleeding. All right, you're my witness: See it's not blue!"[20]

At times Lodge tended to bully associates, not unlike the adolescent verbal jabbing he periodically received from brother Cabot. "John could be derisive and run people down," observed Milton Barall. "When that occurred, you had to piss back."[21]

In the 1960s, United States zeal and sense of mission toward Latin America tended to increase dependence on North America for ideas, for direction, and for money. When Nixon came into office, he made several deliberate decisions regarding the country's posture toward Latin America, and Lodge applauded them. First, he resolved to avoid taking these Latin neighbors for granted, assuming that they were irrevocably linked to the United States by commerce and friendship. Nixon looked toward a new relationship in which Latin America would assume increasing responsibility for ideas, initiatives, and for action. Rising nationalism and internal weaknesses called for greater understanding and patience on the part of diplomats to counter xenophobic and anti-American attitudes.[22] Economic changes also increased the country's volatility. In Argentina the high living standards that had long distinguished the nation from the rest of Latin America had largely eroded by the year of Lodge's arrival. Chronic inflation and recurrent cycles of recession and recovery stymied the country's growth. Historian David Rock writes that Argentina had become a second-rank nation "unable to find a stable international position and was largely isolated in the world community."[23]

Lodge had hoped that Nixon would re-enforce his policies by undertaking a major tour of South American countries during his first term. The president's travels, however, focused chiefly on Europe and Asia. John encouraged not only Washington officials and legislators to include Buenos Aires on their agenda but friends and political allies. He had more visitors than most diplomats and businessmen. "Few travelers or tourists from the United States actually made the long journey or passed through Buenos Aires," pointed out Peter Smith, who represented Morgan Bank interests in the capital from 1968 to 1972. "It was isolated, with communications with the rest of the world still rather difficult."[24]

The State Department apparently kept close watch on Argentina and the Embassy. Charles Meyer, Assistant Secretary of State for Latin American Affairs, came to Argentina to meet President Ongania and Foreign Minister Juan Martín during John's first year there. Meyer publicly commented that the United States would be more neutral in its dealings with Latin American governments.[25]

Less than a month after these meetings, Ongania was ousted as president when the chiefs of the country's three military branches made a sudden and successful grab for power. With the full support of the armed forces, Army General Alejandro Lanusse, Fleet Admiral Pedro Gnavi, and Air Force General Juan Carlos Ray advised the Argentinean Supreme Court that they had taken over. The coup on June 8, 1970 was announced by radio to the country's twenty-three million people and the foreign community. The triumvirate chose to remain in the background and allow the presidency to pass to General Roberto Levingston, who attempted to restore a price stabilization program of a pre-Ongania administration. The takeover by the generals, however, signaled a rise of terrorism and counter-terrorism, including kidnappings and bombings.[26]

The diplomatic community was a prime target. Additional armed security guards now protected Lodge in his daily travels. A follow-up car with two officers trailed his vehicle, and often an advance vehicle was used; at least one bodyguard was always at his side. John often said that if anyone tried to kidnap him he'd flop down as a deadweight and would not move. It would force any kidnappers to carry, he joked, some 200 pounds of "largesse." Somewhat fatalistic, he refused to be hampered by extremists or hemmed in by terrorists. Abductions, which by 1971 occurred on the average of two a month, often ended in murderous attacks. And the following year, in the wake of the kidnapping and murder of the Fiat auto head in Buenos Aires, Francesca's name was found on a list compiled by terrorists.

One day a rock tossed at John's bullet-proof automobile sent another chill through his staff. The stone hitting the roof of the car sounded like a bomb about to explode. Undaunted, John wanted to stop the vehicle and find out where the stone came from. And at the back end of the residence, a large high-rise apartment overlooking the property caused a problem. One afternoon in the garden, the butler looked up while bringing a snack to Lodge: "Mister Ambassador, someone has a gun on you. Get out of the way quickly!" John stood up and shouted, "Where is the jerk?" The butler pointed up to a person on an upper apartment balcony. The figure had a gun aimed in their direction. They suddenly realized the would-be assailant was a child with a toy pistol. But the times spent relaxing outdoors or playing tennis now demanded precaution and protection. Even Francesca had to be careful while walking her dogs in the backyard.

Agitators seemed on the verge of engineering popular insurrection.

The furor brought another change of government. General Levingston handed over the reins of office to General Lanusse who, in turn, promised elections to restore civilian government. The residence itself became the target of terrorists, and one day a policeman on outside duty was attacked and relieved of his pistol and machine gun. On another occasion, Francesca received a call from the wife of the French Ambassador. She urged both Lodges to come for dinner that evening. Francesca checked with John, and he agreed. Usually they dined together in the dining room if alone. While they were guests at the French embassy, a stolen lorry sped by the residence. Three bombs were thrown at the dwelling; one went through a dining room window and exploded. Apparently, the French embassy knew something nasty was afoot and managed to spare the Lodges from serious injury or death.[27]

Francesca was as brave and undaunted as her husband. Bomb scares and shootings failed to detract her from her role as the U.S. ambassadress. She emerged as one of the most admired and scintillating diplomatic wives in Buenos Aires, just as she had been in Madrid. Once again there were dance and exercise classes. This time she stressed the tango and the hula for distaff members of the foreign community and Argentine friends. Before too long, there were fashion shows, tango contests, and dance exhibitions to benefit local charities. Professional tango experts Juan Carlos Copes and María Nieves often helped with instruction. Another highlight was an evening outdoors of ballet and modern dance, including a performance of a number reminiscent of *A Midsummer Night's Dream*. And Francesca, who celebrated her seventieth birthday during rehearsals, led the troupe in several leading roles to the "bravos" of John and the enraptured audience.

"She had a terrific sense of 'people' and political judiciousness," Donald Stewart recalled.[28] Others on the staff remember that she was the first wife of an American ambassador to actually go up to the servants quarters on the top floor of the residence. She wanted to see how they lived, and to her dismay discovered that in the midst of a house of much luxury, their areas had no heat. She set about making their rooms more livable and pleasant.

On a late December day in 1970, John brought Francesca news that stunned and saddened them both. Their youngest daughter, twenty-eight-year-old Edith Lodge, had died suddenly of heart disease in Connecticut. Since the 1940s, this retarded youngster had lived under the care of a surrogate mother in Fairfield, but supported with a generous monthly stipend from Francesca. She occasionally visited the child, now called Diane. Her real name was never divulged, according to the dictates of the Lodges. A death certificate, however, was filed under her given name, listed her parents, and recorded a burial on Christmas Eve in a nearby cemetery.

Then, in early January, something happened that focused world attention on the virtually unknown child of the Lodges. A reporter from the *Bridgeport Post*, while going over records in relation to some other matter in the town clerk's office, unexpectedly discovered a recent death certificate on file. The name "Lodge" caught his eye, and the document became the nucleus of a story. Shortly thereafter, the newspaper wired John for family clarification. Several follow-ups by phone still failed to receive a response. After four days, the *Post* on January 16, 1971 ran the disclosure of the "Lodge Kin Death." The article was seen and picked up immediately by the Associated Press. Within days stories appeared in papers throughout the country. The existence of Edith Lodge, unknown except by a few family intimates, was now common knowledge. Kept out of the public eye, the tragedy of a daughter with Down's Syndrome had always been a very private matter. The grief borne by John and Francesca forever remained sequestered.

Raising money for charities became Francesca's favorite avocation in the midst of any personal anguish or setbacks. Thousands of victims of floods in the southern province of Neuquen were aided by her efforts, as were those injured in the General Pacheco train wreck. She organized many fundraising programs for worthy organizations, such as a children's hospital, a home for blind women (where a dormitory was later named in her honor), a trade institute, and a school-home for the retarded. One year she arranged for 8,000 poor and physically disabled children to attend the world-famous "Holiday on Ice" skating show. By the end of four years, she had personally aided over forty deserving projects and helped in some way a hundred or so more. To show their appreciation, the Argentine Public Opinion Institute named her woman of the year in 1972, the first non-Argentine to be so honored. Earlier, she received a high accolade when the wife of Argentine President Lanusse presented her the "Golden Venus" Award from the Buenos Aires Women's Club for translating diplomacy into friendship.[29]

Virtually every visitor to the embassy residence was struck by the display of flags of the fifty U.S. states adorning the balustrade that crowned the grand double staircase. They were put there by Francesca and John to provide a warm yet dazzling introduction to the palatial dwelling. And a diverse and notable array of individuals came through the front door, including Ford Foundation president McGeorge Bundy, bandleader Duke Ellington, Federal Reserve board chairman Arthur Burns, Marine Corps commandant Leonard F. Chapman, historian Samuel Eliot Morison, Governor Jimmy Carter, violinist Isaac Stern, Secretary of Commerce Maurice Stans, singer Sarah Vaughan, and chess champion Bobby Fischer. For the Tenth International Film Festival at Mar del Plata in 1970, the

Lodges organized a gala reception for the local film community and Hollywood guests. Jack Valenti, president of the Motion Picture Association of America, arrived with producer Mark Robson, director Alan Pakula, actress Julie Newmar, and actor John Gavin (who in the Reagan Administration would himself serve as ambassador to a Latin country, Mexico). Valenti brought a special gift for John: a mint copy of his 1934 lavish spectacle *The Scarlet Empress*.

Connecticut politician Jack DeForest journeyed to Buenos Aires soon after Lodge presented his credentials. Two days after his arrival, he found himself the guest of honor at a small but formal luncheon at the residence. He was ushered into a drawing room by Francesca's secretary. As he waited, Jack heard Francesca calling his name: "Jack, Jack, where are you in this big house?" She entered the room with a small dachshund in tow and a camera in her hand. When he kissed her on one cheek, she remarked, "We kiss both cheeks here." They sat and sipped drinks until the other guests arrived and lunch was announced. "Mamie Eisenhower's autographed photo smiled across at me from a corner of the room," recorded Jack in his journal. "Lunch was served formally in the State dining room in a very grand manner with the appropriate china and silverware."

Returning to the drawing room, the group enjoyed coffee, brandy, and cigars. "John Lodge was in his glory," DeForest reflected, "and the old 'ham' in him shone through lucidly as he poured forth his pure Castillian Spanish. . . . He is great on telling stories which were translated for my benefit." Jack wished he could stay longer in Buenos Aires; everyone was so cordial and accommodating to make his visit pleasant.[30] A day or so later, Francesca telephoned Jack's hotel with an invitation to play tennis. He was out, and when he finally reached her, it was too late:

> In fact, I had to call her a second time as she was out with her dogs. . . . She said the U.S. Ambassador to Peru is there today and she is giving him my name and the name of my hotel in Lima in case I wish to pay my respects; he'll know who I am. She was very concerned that I had enjoyed myself in Buenos Aires and I assured her that I had. It is obvious that John is enjoying himself greatly in his role as Ambassador.[31]

Yet John's triumphant personal acclaim south of the border carried little weight among his superiors back in Washington.

CHAPTER 24

Showing the Flag

Americans in Argentina describe the early 1970s as the beginning of a time when people disappeared. The conflict-ridden country witnessed an alarming number of abductions and kidnappings, extortions and murders, amid escalating urban terrorism and counterterrorism. The brutality was directed against American and other foreign businessmen as well as ordinary Argentine citizens. Guerrillas gunned down a Ford Motor Company executive. And Exxon once paid over eleven million dollars to ransom one of its kidnapped employees. The U.S. Information Service was a frequent target of firebombs.

The U.S. embassy felt that Washington should receive frequent and detailed reports of Argentine political and social turmoil. And throughout this chaos and tumult, Lodge subscribed to an energetic American presence of "showing the flag," and was viewed as being extraordinarily successful in this regard because of his high public profile and degree of participation in cultural events.

In the spring of 1971, John journeyed for a week's consultations in Washington. Appointments with Secretary William Rogers and other State Department officials were followed by meetings with CIA Director Richard Helms, FBI chief J. Edgar Hoover, Commerce Secretary Maurice Stans, Attorney General John Mitchell, and various Administration aides. John also requested a meeting with President Nixon. He felt the need to talk with him about his mission and the internal changes, not only in Argentina and in South America, but also shifting U.S. policy toward that part of the world.

On an earlier visit to the capital in December 1969, he likewise had been anxious to see Nixon. Lodge felt that an ambassador must absorb information one on one, not just from letter, cable, or phone. He was told to proceed through White House aide Dwight Chapin, who quickly passed word to the State Department that since John was to attend a dinner at the White House in honor of Republican nabob Elmer Bobst, that was an adequate opportunity to converse with Nixon. It came as a surprise in light of John's long-standing friendship with the President. Inexplicably, Nixon never again invited John to the Oval Office.

By 1971 John felt even more out of touch with the White House machinery, and it, in turn, kept him at arm's length from the President. He had never had any trouble getting to see Eisenhower. John once again wondered if the unseen hand of Cabot was attempting to freeze him out of the highest councils in Washington. By June 1970, his brother had himself returned to an overseas assignment after a six-month rest following the unproductive and frustrating year as chief U.S. negotiator at the Vietnam peace conference in Paris. Nixon now named Cabot Lodge his envoy to the Vatican. The move was a compromise between the President's desire to improve contact with the Pope and his reluctance to establish full diplomatic relations. The appointment required no Senate confirmation and carried no diplomatic rank nor salary. But it rankled John to see his brother fall into a job that he had particularly wanted and nearly secured a year earlier. One thing he was now certain of: the coveted Ambassadorship to Rome would never be his as long as Cabot remained in Europe.

Their relationship continued as it had for over 40 years—cordial, perfunctory, and without much intimacy. John's loyalty to Cabot, however, remained constant and total. John again mulled over Cabot's opposition to his marriage, acting career, and public service. He concluded that Cabot would have been happier if he had had another sister rather than a younger brother. Overall, the words of uncle John Lodge came to mind: "Cabot is vainglorious!"[1]

Geographically, and perhaps politically, removed from the mainstream of the Administration, John and Francesca, nonetheless, fared exceedingly well and put their special stamp as envoys from a country whose people had not always been greeted too warmly. For one thing, John claimed that he was a descendant of the Italian explorer Sebastian Cabot, who in the 1520s was the second European to reach the coast of Argentina.[2] Often, when he met an Argentine with an Italian name, John would point out this fanciful bond. "Maybe we're related," he'd remark. "Old Sebastian, you know, sailed to Argentina. Perhaps he left a bit of himself in the Chaco."

Apart from would-be kinsmen, Lodge memorialized a visit to the Embassy residence by President Eisenhower in 1960. John installed a plaque given by recipients of Eisenhower Fellowships in Argentina. It was the second plaque honoring a U.S. President: Franklin Roosevelt had spent two nights in the residence during a pre-World War II goodwill tour.

Francesca unveiled a plaque of another sort. She commemorated the world-renowned Argentine tango with an inscription on a bronze plaque placed on a building on Buenos Aires' famous Corrientes Street. The event was celebrated with a fiesta in the roped-off street, and Francesca danced the tango's long gliding steps and intricate movements and posed for several hours, captivating bystanders.

When Argentine literati and bibliophiles learned that the ambassador was the son of a poet, they asked about Bay Lodge. To fill their requests, John gave sets of his father's poems and plays, plus the Henry Adams biography, to the esteemed Lincoln Library in Buenos Aires. At the presentation, he read several of Bay's passages in Spanish and noted Bay was part of that legion of early twentieth-century creative Americans, not unlike "the legion of writers and poets in which Argentinians abound."[3]

John showed unusual mettle in his travels. He'd journey a thousand miles by plane just to attend a luncheon in a distant province and return home that night. It was said that he knew the country better than most Argentines. And as a former Naval officer, he readily accepted an unusual invitation. The Argentine Navy asked him to sail on a supply ship to their isolated bases on the icy terrain of Antarctica, and he eagerly prepared for the long journey in February 1971. No ambassador from the United States or any foreign country had ever expressed genuine interest in venturing to that polar continent. Accompanied by his thirty-two-year-old executive assistant John Kriendler, Lodge flew to Argentina's southernmost port for the three-day crossing aboard the Bahia Aguirre. "The cruise clearly contributed to his understanding better the activities not only at the Argentine bases at Esperanza and Petrel but of the U.S. station on that continent," recalled ex-Naval officer Kriendler.[4]

In his travel notes of February 14, 1971, John spoke poetically of the wonders of an unfamiliar clime and terrain. He described the vast battlements of ice as "serene and stark . . . these guardians of the silence float in the Antarctic night." Of a careening albatross: "he points his beak up at the sky, then swoops upon the frigid water." Of waddling penguins: "dressed in their gay attire, they romp and dive in ice cold seas—for them it is a life of ease." Reaching the rocky shore of the polar shelf, he then flew inland by helicopter. One particular thrill was an invigorating ride in a sleigh pulled by nine barking huskies.

At the Soviet base, the officer in charge welcomed John with a plate of sardines and a bottle of vodka. "He began to feel quite high," John related, and "wanted to wrestle me in Judo, saying he was a brown belt. He lifted me in the air and I thought for a moment that he was going to break my back. He wanted us to go in the launch to visit the Russian scientific ship lying a mile off the beach. She is large (6000 tons) and carries scientists and equipment. We declined and returned to the good ship *Bahia Aguirre*, our cozy warm home in the ice."[5] The voyage back to Argentina tested the equilibrium of crew and passengers alike. "We encountered very rough seas with 70-knot winds," Kriendler remembered. "The ship keeled over to such a degree that most of us were quite uncomfortable. But Lodge wasn't fazed a bit."[6]

At the beginning of John's fourth year in Buenos Aires, the 1972 U.S. Presidential campaign was well underway. Lodge was not asked to resign in order to play a part in the re-election of Nixon. Nonetheless, he visited Washington in August for a brief round of meetings, but many of those he had hoped to see were preoccupied with the Republican Convention in Miami. The State Department's Charles Meyer reminded him that his speeches had better stay clear of partisan overtones. John acquiesced. Meyer consented to John's forthcoming participation as grand marshal in the New York City United Hispanic-American Day parade in October, but pointed out the undesirability of his being away from his post for too long at "this key period in Argentina development."[7]

The Watergate break-in was increasingly a subject of conversation overseas. John knew justice must be done, and explained this to Argentine friends. They found it difficult to understand why Americans insisted upon making such fuss over an incident which had frequent parallels in many other countries where comparable incidents had been nine-day, or even one-day, wonders and then had been replaced in the public attention by other, more urgent, matters. "These abuses," Lodge explained, "have no place in American politics, and the President has publicly deplored them and has been emphatic that his Administration will be more vigilant to make sure they do not take place." He acknowledged that the mistake was harming the country. "It has induced some to lose confidence in our system of government. It has become a significant element in the political worldwide conflict in which we are engaged. It is adversely affecting American national interests." He concluded that Watergate should be appropriately dealt with, "But let's not throw the baby out with the bath."[8]

At the time of the initial clamor over Watergate, the Lodges welcomed their friend and *Washington Star-News* writer Betty Beale and her husband George Graeber to Buenos Aires. Betty had long covered the capital social scene, and her feature stories were popular and widely syndicated. A house guest at the residence, she wasted no time in reporting on John and Francesca in glowing terms, describing their highly visible diplomatic approach and vibrant style. Beale viewed it as U.S. diplomacy at its best. "If the United States could be represented around the world the way it is represented in Argentina, it would be loved by the peoples of all nations," she exclaimed.[9] Her two-part series on Argentina received banner headlines in the politically conservative *Star* and in many papers throughout the United States. "I wrote what I saw," Beale later said. "It was true. The Lodges in their comings and goings and travels were very popular. Faces of total strangers would light up in recognition and broad smiles."[10]

Anxious to put the *Star* out of business and perhaps tarnish a staunch Nixon ally in the wake of Watergate and the overwhelming victory of the President in the November 1972 elections, the rival *Washington Post* sharpened its ax for what, on publication, would be perceived by some as a hatchet job on the Lodges. Editor Ben Bradlee assigned his South American correspondent to Buenos Aires to counteract the laudatory coverage of the Nixon political appointee. *Post* reporter Lewis Diuguid arrived there to pick up and extract every bit of negative comment and feeling from dissatisfied embassy staff, bemused newspapermen, envious foreign envoys, and unimpressed Argentine officials. In February 1973, Diuguid wired his feature to Washington.

Lodge, he proclaimed, was best known by diplomats in Buenos Aires "for his boisterous after-dinner songfests and an apparent lack of interest in political discussion." The *Post* story of February 18, 1973 quoted an Argentine foreign ministry official who pointed out that for anything not strictly social "we should go to the deputy chief of the embassy." Diuguid added the comment of a Latin American ambassador: "I've never been able to carry out a serious conversation with him."[11]

Diuguid also wrote that one of the principal concerns of the U.S. Information Service under "former actor" Lodge was turning out publicity on him and "one-time actress" wife, Francesca. He indicated that four Americans worked full time on press releases and photography of the Lodges, and two photographers during a recent twelve-month period produced 5,000 prints of the couple:

> Newspaper editors often joke about the latest Lodge photo to cross their desks—always marked *urgent*—showing him foremost, smiling broadly and shaking hands, usually with some visiting American of no news interest. Lodge is particularly sensitive to the absence of these photos in the English language *Herald*. The higher-ranking USIS officers periodically are sent forth to ask why a particular shot was unworthy of publication. Another function of the USIS men is to maintain liaison with local reporters, convincing them that they should not print remarks that Lodge occasionally makes in public places.[12]

Diuguid explained that he tried for a month to obtain an interview with Lodge and was finally told that it would not be possible. "I have met him only once, four years ago at the Argentine Embassy in Washington, when he spoke at length on the thesis that acting was the best preparation for a career in diplomacy. He inquired of all attending whether they had seen his film the previous night on the late, late show, an early Shirley Temple movie in which he shared billing."

The *Post* correspondent cited the 1972 visit of Secretary of the Treasury John Connally: "Most of the visit was spent on a cattle ranch, with pictures of Lodge and Connally, arm-in-arm, urgently posted to the newspapers. Connally's one chance to meet important Argentines in business and politics came at a formal dinner at that ambassador's residence. The Argentines were anxious to exchange views with Connally but they described later their dismay when Lodge kept the conversation on trivialities through drinks and supper. President Lanusse later spoke of his disappointment in the brief and superficial visit just before Connally was whisked off to the airport."[13] Years later, Francesca emphatically noted that Connally himself canceled or modified the carefully prepared formal agenda. He explained that his visit was not an official trip: "He did not want any tralala—only to see cattle ranches and the like, and we had to cancel people, food."

An annoyed Lodge termed the *Washington Post* article "a tissue of fabrications, half-truths, distortions, and just plain mistakes of fact." In a detailed memorandum to the State Department, he pointed out the misstatements and errors. USIS operations, he noted, had not been expanded for his or anyone's self-promotion, but actually reduced in personnel and funds. He defended his conduct of diplomacy in an atmosphere of gaiety and good fellowship, "an approach which has proven to be far more effective, especially in Latin countries, than the routine bureaucratic approach." At a Class I embassy, he further explained, it was natural and customary for the ambassador to delegate matters of substance to his DCM and to other senior staff members.[14]

Turning to the wide photo coverage of his activities, Lodge admitted that many photographs were taken, "a practice common to the condition of any prominent American family serving officially either in the United States or overseas." He noted the 200 daily newspapers and over 400 magazines in Argentina: "The potential press outlets that exist in Argentina are enormous and their appetite for information is voracious." And "urgente" on press packages was a commonly used flag on envelopes and releases for all types of media material.

Lodge also stated that Lewis Diuguid had been invited to the embassy on various occasions. (To his aides, he later expressed genuine regret over not giving him an interview.) As ambassador, he had held meetings with President Lanusse and his foreign minister. "In any case," he concluded, "an informed reporter would know that in any country an Ambassador's principal contacts are not with the Chief of State, but with the Foreign Minister."[15]

Meanwhile, Francesca wondered what harm could stem from extensive on-the-job publicity: "Is there any better public relations than a lot of good comments and pictures of the U.S. representatives in both the host country and in our own? Don't we in the U.S.A. want to know how our ambassadors are doing? And how we are being represented? It seems elementary that this is a good thing."

The English language Buenos Aires *Herald* reprinted the *Post* feature, adding fuel to the widely discussed stir over the Lodges. In a follow-up editorial, the *Herald* pulled John's leg. As an example of his "weakness" for publicity, it reminded everyone of the Lodges' 1971 Christmas card that carried no less than six photographs of the couple: "Christmas 1972 was a bit of a disappointment. Although printed in full colour, it bore only four photographs of the Lodges."[16] The *Herald* called the *Post* article "a fair piece." In general, the embassy staff thought otherwise. DCM Max Krebs, who replaced Barall in 1971, issued a statement that the aspersions cast on relations between Ambassador Lodge and his staff were wholly without foundation, "as anyone familiar with the embassy is fully aware."[17]

Back in Washington, certain liberal cabals in the State Department and White House capitalized on the derogatory write-up. It probably squelched the potential assignment there for Lodge to succeed Meyer as Assistant Secretary of State for Latin America. No doubt it bolstered the reputed efforts of a Foreign Service officer named John Crimmins to pull John out of Argentina. And it fueled hearsay of John's dalliance with one or more local ladies, thus titillating some circles in Washington while undoubtedly exciting the "macho" Latins in Argentina.[18]

The coverage of the Lodges was indeed extensive. By 1973 it filled a dozen large press scrapbooks, and that didn't reflect his radio and television exposure. "Sometimes you'd switch on the TV," John Kriendler recollected, "and Lodge would be there as much as local politicians. To some it was a positive impression; to others, even within the staff, it was a turnoff."[19]

The die was cast. No amount of praise from past visitors, official or social, could remove the stigma in Washington. It seemed only a matter of time before the White House brought him home.

Then, in mid-April, the *New York Daily News* picked up on the theme and ran an article on Lodge's precarious position, under a characteristically tittle-tattle headline, "Envoy to Argentina to Get Sack." John looked upon the press speculation as "an unhappy concatenation of circumstance." To his politically savvy friend William F. Buckley, he wrote: "Obviously, if, within a decent period of time, I were transferred as Ambassador to another appropriate post, much of the poison would be removed."[20]

Within Argentina itself, a new government was moving into power. In 1972 President Lanusse lifted the eighteen-year ban on Perónism and the exile of its once-powerful leader. Lanusse sought to undercut the country's drift toward revolt by bringing the larger-than-life hero Juan Perón home for a brief visit. He returned from a long exile in Spain to the acclaim of his supporters and amidst a growing wave of a widespread populism. Anticipation of Perón's arrival in Buenos Aires brought a turnout of several million people at the city's air terminal. It also caused the ranks of the opposition to chant disparaging insults and slogans. Before he actually landed, the welcome exploded into bursts of gunfire between the two rival segments. Perón's aides diverted his plane to a military airport where he was transferred to a helicopter for the final lap.

Later, in the elections of March 1973, the Perónist alliance emerged victorious with Perón's personal choice, Héctor Cámpora, as the new president. In June Perón returned to Buenos Aires for the second time in less than eight months. An estimated half-million people filled Ezeiza airport to greet him. As they waited, pitched battles erupted between leftist and rightist followers, killing twenty and wounding several hundred. Francesca remembered watching Perón's arrival on television:

> It became a battleground as shooting broke out. In the middle of scenes of turmoil and frenzy, the station suddenly cut off its coverage of the arrival. Then, an extraordinary thing happened. The TV channel switched to a movie. Lo and behold, there was John on the screen, tramping through a dark woods and holding a gun in pursuit of some villain. The scene was the dramatic climax to "The Little Colonel." I don't believe it was a deliberate move. The station just turned back to the regular film series that had been interrupted. It soon switched back to Perón and the special pickup of his dramatic landing.

Secretary of State William Rogers journeyed to Argentina to represent Nixon at the inaugural of Cámpora and to tell the Perónist government that the United States would start relations afresh with the new president. That confirmed the rumors that Lodge was headed home. Relations between Rogers and Lodge went from cool to somewhat frigid during the Secretary's visit. After an official meeting with the new government, the American group emerged from a building. Rogers and his party entered the embassy limo, then quickly drove off. The move left John standing alone on the sidewalk. Stunned and solemn, he walked briskly on his own to a nearby taxi stand, jumped into a cab, and went to his next appointment. For the breach of etiquette, the Rogers entourage was solidly reprimanded by bystanders and reporters.

John interpreted the personal snubs, deliberate or otherwise, as a sign from Washington that his usefulness was nearing an end, and he regarded the journalistic slurs as chiefly attacks on the beleaguered Nixon. He wrote a number of letters to Gerald Ford, House Leader and longtime Chowder and Marching companion, to solicit his support in remaining in Buenos Aires or receiving another post. On April 25, he explained the circumstances to Ford, who that summer would become Vice President upon the sudden resignation of Agnew:

> I have received praise for keeping the United States, for the first time in many years, uninvolved in the recent election campaign.[21] The slogan "Yankee Imperialism" has been muted by this method. Mine is an exuberant type of diplomacy which would probably not find favor with joyless carping, left wing critics. It might find favor with certain professionals of the diplomatic career. Quite frankly, however, it does appeal to our Latin friends, as the results in Spain and Argentina conclusively demonstrate. It would be rather unfortunate if the impression were left that we react obligingly by an early removal of the ambassador to such unsupported and unwarranted attacks from an unfriendly source. It would also be unfortunate if the idea were to get around that there are people in the Embassy who are disloyal. This could result in much injustice. It would be disadvantageous to U.S. interests if the Argentines, among whom Francesca and I have many friends, should get the impression that I am leaving because I was stabbed in the back by individuals on the Embassy staff. Indeed, this might be a problem for my successor.[22]

John's departure became official by late June. Nixon wrote him a personal note saying that the administration wished to change its representation in Argentina and requesting his resignation. The President concluded that Lodge would now wish to devote himself to personal affairs after many years of public service. He then added the hope that he and the Secretary of State might call on him "from time to time to undertake special missions and other special duties related to our foreign affairs."[23] The message was the first communication from Nixon during a period of rather frequent and unanswered letters by Lodge to the President. John had felt shut out by the White House, which he had always looked to first, rather than the State Department. More and more, he felt disinclined to put up a struggle to remain in Buenos Aires.[24] Nonetheless, the Lodges made no secret of their desire to continue. "Given the tragedies soon to occur in Argentina," later remembered political affairs counselor William Sowash, "the Lodges might have been thankful for the relief. But I am sure that had they stayed, they would have regarded those events simply as challenges to be met and overcome."[25]

In August the Lodges broke away from the unsettling turn of events with their annual holiday leave in Spain. During their absence, DCM Max Krebs, who was Chargé d'Affaires, was unanimously voted *persona non grata* by the Argentine Chamber of Deputies. Krebs, it seems, wrote several memorandums to the Finance Ministry on how best to proceed with several draft laws on foreign investment and re-nationalization of banks. This intrusion in domestic matters backfired. Krebs was nearly expelled from the country and seen as a vulnerable target to embarrass the United States and damage relations with Argentina. To shore up the U.S. position there, John suggested that the length of the gap between his departure and the arrival of his successor be minimized.[26]

Meanwhile, in August 1973, President Cámpora and his government resigned. He had been unable to abate the conflict among opposing extremist forces within the Perón movement. Many concluded that only Perón himself could stem the confusion and achieve stability. The presidency passed to Raúl Lastiri, a former president of the Chamber of Deputies, pending new elections. That fall, Perón received 60 percent of the votes, and on October 12, with his wife Isabel as Vice President, was inaugurated for what could be considered his third term since his initial victory in 1945. Perón was the sixth president to take office during the four years that John had been in Argentina.

The Lodges had planned to leave for home by ship on October 3. But a high level U.S. representative was required at the inaugural. The Argentine government frowned upon the appearance of Krebs on this state occasion. At the last minute, Lodge was asked to delay his departure and attend the ceremonies. Back in Washington, the appointment of Henry Kissinger as Secretary of State generated a measure of hope that he would continue John as ambassador. Senator Carl Curtis, who traveled with Herbert Brownell to Argentina for the Perón inaugural, urged the new Secretary to retain Lodge. "I gave it the strongest pitch that I could," Curtis relayed. "I mentioned the good job that you had done, that the Peróns had a great respect for you and Francesca, and that you had a distinct advantage from the standpoint of language. I also mentioned the problems that would occur if you should depart."[27]

Again the Lodges rescheduled their departure. A round of farewell parties and tributes, highlighted by the celebration of John's seventieth birthday on October 20, filled the final weeks. Buenos Aires' largest television channel even invited them to bid all their Argentine friends a good-bye from the studio. The program became a lively, good-humored adieu covering a wide range of subjects, including Francesca's many charitable endeavors. At a lunch in Lodge's honor, he was praised by Foreign Minister Alberto Vignes for his mastery of the Spanish language and his openness of communication with others: "These have brought him close to all levels of Argentine society. They have enriched his life here, I am sure, and have permitted us in Buenos Aires diplomatic circles, to include an eminent personality among our number. His is a home with open doors."[28]

Indeed, in four years at the embassy residence, they had held some 100 formal dinners, 25 formal receptions, and welcomed an average of 7,000 people a year. Francesca alone organized nineteen benefits, including art, musical, and fashion shows. Moreover, they visited seventeen of the nation's twenty-two provinces. John served longer as U.S. ambassador there than any of his predecessors since World War II and was one of the very last of Nixon's original ambassadorial appointees to depart his post.

Lodge, too, was commended for keeping a low political profile in the turbulent South American country. "A main objective was not to get involved in internal affairs," he later noted. "To me the essence of diplomacy is that relations between countries are somewhat like the relationship between a man and a woman. A man spends years trying to understand a woman and doesn't succeed and finally gives her love and affection. I think that's what we have to do with other countries; judge them less and love them more."[29]

With a total of more than ten years in diplomatic posts, John had gathered wisdom and know-how for handling overseas assignments. He was eager to continue to put it to work and share it with others. His primary rule, he often explained, was to take seriously the business of representation: "Be an observer and a guest, but don't make public statements on political matters."[30] In a conversation with Joseph Verner Reed, upon his nomination as Ambassador to Morocco in 1981, John elaborated on his guidelines. "Don't just entertain for the sake of entertaining. Yet do it as much and as often as possible with the idea of creating goodwill toward the United States. And bring into the embassy every sector of the foreign country—businessmen, artists, military figures, union leaders, even dissidents of various sort."[31]

John also reminded Reed that an ambassador works *for* the President and *with* the Secretary of State: "A political appointee is a permanent outsider from the Foreign Service." In the eyes of forty-three-year-old Reed, he was journeying off to Morocco in the mold of a young John

Lodge. When Reed arrived at Rabat, he felt the U.S. flag at the embassy was not big enough, so he had the largest possible American flag made to replace it. The U.S. Marine detachment, too, didn't seem quite up to snuff in civilian clothes, so Reed put them back in uniform.[32]

During the last months in Buenos Aires, the mail brought a package from Cabot. It contained his just-published autobiography, *The Storm Has Many Eyes*. John anxiously welcomed the book, and acknowledged its receipt, yet expressed dismay over the scant reference to an extant younger brother who had served in various high governmental offices. "Needless to say," Cabot replied in his usual brotherly bruising bluntness, "I would have liked to have inserted much more about you than I did, but I know that had I done so it would have been attacked as nepotism and it would have been bad for both of us."[33]

John delivered a sharp rejoinder:

> Your attitude regarding nepotism has never been entirely clear to me, and yet you have expressed it frequently. Perhaps sometime you can explain it to me more fully, since apparently these inhibitions apply to your relationship with your brother but not to your sons. I find this rather puzzling, although certainly it is your privilege to make that distinction. I must say that I have never looked at things that way as far as my efforts across the years to help you are concerned. This particular restriction has certainly never affected anybody in the Kennedy family, whatever that means. In any event, I do think your book is very superior and well worth writing and reading.[34]

In late October, the Lodges left Argentina as passengers on a cargo freighter bound for Brooklyn. They selected such a ship so that their six dogs wouldn't be crated in an airplane or locked up in a steamship kennel. The leisurely sail provided solitude and quiet after months of turmoil and uncertainty. They both thought about the future. Even at age seventy, John said he wasn't ready for retirement.

During his debriefings in Washington in December, he made known the fact that he was available for public service and wasn't ready for a rocking chair. Once again, he had hoped to visit the White House, but the closest he got to Nixon that winter was the opportunity to hear his State of the Union message from the floor of the House. Before the new year, the White House announced John's successor in Argentina: Bob Hill, whose most recent overseas post had been Madrid. Meanwhile, Max Krebs gained the ambassadorship to Guyana, the small former British protectorate in South America.

Francesca was happy to be back in Connecticut, even after the exhilarating overseas experience: "I didn't realize how much I belonged to the past. What one had been one is always pleased to come back to." But life in Europe continued to draw them. Before the end of the 1970s, they welcomed three more Spanish grandchildren, Gloria and twins Borja and Iñigo, to Beatrice and Antonio's household. John mulled over the sale of Villa Lodge to save the expense of running two sizable dwellings. He suggested the purchase of a condominium in Connecticut or long visits to New York and rooms at the Women's National Republican Club. But without the Westport property, Francesca reminded him, they'd have to give up their pack of dogs and other house pets. So that settled the matter.

One of their new objectives, to acquaint their New England neighbors with Argentina, occupied their time. "It's a pity people know so little about that country," they pointed out. "It's a land of the future, very much European with a tremendous middle class."[35] The nearby University of Bridgeport feted the couple at an Argentina Fiesta, which they had encouraged and promoted. The Lodges soon played an active part in the university's efforts to raise funds for the Argentine Graduate Scholarship, spearheading dinners, balls, and even polo matches featuring Argentine cuisine, music, and costumes. For one such international scholarship benefit, the invitation read: "Black tie or native dress." Francesca took it literally, appearing outfitted as an American Indian with a colorful, twenty-foot long feathered headdress that extended from the top of her head down her back to the floor. She even let out a few war whoops during the gala.

She readily returned to other enduring interests. The American Shakespeare Theatre needed help, so she rushed to the forefront as chairman of fundraising projects. John, she pointed out, had signed the original charter as Governor and she had worked with founder Lawrence Langner for a site. The Women's National Republican Club, too, faced financial problems. Francesca went to its rescue. She brought in member-building programs and speakers. In 1975 she spearheaded a luncheon to honor First Lady Betty Ford.

Life at Villa Lodge was nearly as unstructured and hurly-burly as it had been in the days of the political campaigns. Francesca described one typical morning in a book of random notes, circa 1975: "Finally one hour outdoors to catch up on my important correspondence . . . then telephone friends to listen to a special program. Two male dogs start fighting over Mona—put her in the house. John comes out to ask about invitations. . . . The housekeeper wants to know what to cook for lunch. The wind blows my papers and scatters them across the yard . . . time out to catch them. Again, time to phone others about the TV show." She labeled her jottings, "Interruptions"—commonplace at home, whether in Westport or Marbella.

John kept busy with his correspondence and study of current events. Neither a gardener nor a handyman, he would never push a lawnmower or paint a fence. To visit neighbors, the Rogers Porters or Charles Speakses, he'd back out the car to drive there, not caring to walk or take a shortcut across his woods onto the back of his friends' property. Many local residents anticipated his annual appearance in Memorial Day ceremonies when he marched head and shoulders above most in his Navy dress whites complete with rows of bright military decorations. From time to time, he gave the principal address honoring the town's veterans and war dead. He admitted the old uniform got a bit tighter every year.

Their travels remained an important segment of their lives: not just to Philadelphia, Washington, or Palm Beach, but overseas for Mediterranean cruises with Spanish friends aboard full-rigged sailing ships, family holidays in Italy with Mario Braggiotti at his flourishing music school, and official assignments, such as observing elections in Rhodesia as a guest of the Rhodesian government. In 1977 he flew to Argentina and Uruguay after a three-year absence.[36] His visit led him to wonder why these countries "in the uttermost part of the earth understand the greatest challenge to freedom since Hitler better than the so-called sophisticated societies of Western Europe":

> Why should Marxism, whether Communist or Socialist, have any appeal? Marxism, while newer than Christianity and newer than the concept of individual freedom, still dates back to 1840. Hardly a fresh thought for a brave new world. Moreover, Marxism has failed dramatically wherever it has been tried. It is bankrupt as a viable philosophy of government. Is Western Europe tired, cynical, weary of war and disillusioned in the ideals which once formed the basis for passionate conviction?[37]

After Nixon resigned the Presidency, Lodge felt his successor should be reminded that his old friend from the 81st Congress was "available." In the spring of 1975, the Ford White House apparently gave a somewhat optimistic reply to John's eagerness to serve the administration. Again, he waited and waited in readiness for an assignment. By summer he realized that his particular situation had been handled "with unnecessary clumsiness" by presidential aides. In a letter to Republican Minority Whip Robert Michel, he stated: "I hope the President can be protected in the future against this manner of dealing with such problems. It is not necessary to be inconsistent, insincere and unkind."[38]

The official word expressed concern over John's age: "I am worried for fear that this particularly monstrous, bigoted and selective discrimination against older people may become known. Just think of the millions of people in the United States," he pointed out to Michel, "who are older than seventy, perhaps too old to fight in a war, but not too old to vote."[39]

Finally, in a message to Ford after the President had visited Connect-icut later that year, John put his cards on the table: "Mr. President, I am the only former Republican Governor of Connecticut who is active politically. I have no intention of retiring. I am fit and full of vim and I am confident that I can successfully handle any assignment given me. The political pot in Connecticut is simmering and I shall appreciate it if you will give me some kind of a signal in order that I may make plans.[40]

Lodge rarely declined an invitation to stand before an audience as a keynote speaker or master of ceremonies. At the convention of Foreign Language Teachers in Hartford, he spoke on the importance of foreign languages in diplomacy ("Common language is a bridge . . . creates an immediate rapprochement and entente . . . a knowledge of languages can be an enormous asset, sometimes even decisive—in dealing not only with our friends but also with our enemies").[41] At luncheons and testimonials of the USO (for which he served on its national board of governors), he frequently introduced special guests and honorees, and delivered apt commentary. During the American Bicentennial, John was in even greater demand on a podium. His talks covered an historical overview of 200 years, then zeroed in on the country's diminishing power in the face of Russia's increasing strength. "Our influence extends only as far as our power. Sometimes we do not grasp even what is within our reach."[42]

Before patriotic societies, medical associations, and academic groups, Lodge helped to celebrate the country's birthday with a clarion call to preserve and improve the free enterprise system against those who wanted to destroy it and those who had produced no constructive alternative. "That is the struggle. That is where the battle is joined."[43]

When the State Department discounted the large one-sided election vote for Chilean President Augusto Pinochet on the grounds that normal political activities were banned and human rights violated in that country, John entered the fray. He took over the leadership of the American-Chilean Council, a people-to-people group based in New York, and defended the anti-Communist leader: "How does it advance our national interest to preach sanctimoniously to the Chilean government in Santiago about human rights which don't exist in Peking?"[44]

Periodically Lodge drafted newspaper articles on subjects that particularly interested him—Spain, the semantics of politics, non-career diplomats, the Panama Canal treaties, defeatism in Western Europe. His writings to the Op-Ed section of the New York Times were often rejected. His account of the "miracle of Spain" under Franco was initially turned down because, as John correctly surmised, it might unearth the liberals' distaste for this regime. His old fellow classmate and Wall Street lawyer Paul Williams, who was a friend of publisher Arthur Sulzberger, stepped in when John complained about his failure to get a decent hearing. The *Times* ran the piece and received the expected angry letters complaining of distortions and errors of fact in John's commentary.[45]

In spite of detractors, both Lodges enjoyed a full measure of tributes and honors. Thomas P. Melady, President of Sacred Heart University in Fairfield, Connecticut, awarded Francesca an honorary degree of doctor of humane letters. The school cited her devotion to improving the quality of life for others—culturally, through the performing arts, and civically, through her humanitarian work. Upon acceptance of the University accolade, she felt overwhelmed, nearly speechless. "It is not to be believed—a doctorate for one who hardly finished the equivalent of high school in Italy. Accustomed to public appearances," she added, "I have done so mostly as a dancer. I spent a great deal of my youth training my feet to talk. I wonder if I should be standing on my head to make better sense."[46]

A year later, in 1979, the University of Bridgeport conferred not only an honorary degree on John but one on his "partner" as well, making them, according to school president Leland Miles, the first, and still the only, couple to receive double honorary degrees from that institution. Five years later, in 1984, John received the University of Bridgeport Law School's annual Raymond E. Baldwin Award for distinguished public service.

Lodge's only political efforts at this time focused on the 1976 Republican National Convention in Kansas City and his participation as a Connecticut delegate. Francesca got into the spirit of the gathering by wearing a red, white, and blue dress splashed with red elephants. "This is my campaign uniform," she told everyone. "And John can find me better in that crowd of 5,000 in Kemper Auditorium."[47] He backed Ford on the ticket as did all thirty-five state delegates. Meanwhile, Ronald Reagan entered the race from an opposing camp. But the former California governor did not count on President Ford's candidacy as being so viable. Nonetheless, Reagan gained national exposure for his conservative stance; it helped smooth the way for another try. That fall Ford lost the election to Jimmy Carter, thus dashing any hopes of Lodge for an appointment in a Republican administration. Nonetheless, he wrote President-elect Carter, congratulating him with a reminder of the Lodges' hospitality in Argentina: "I should very much like to pay my respects to you in person when you might find it convenient to receive me." John offered his services "particularly in the realm of foreign affairs," and closed emphasizing his availability "in rendering public service to our country."[48]

As the 1970s neared an end, John and Francesca marked a familial milestone: their fiftieth wedding anniversary. The occasion reminded them of the many old Bostonians who had given the marriage six months. They laughed about the Back Bay debutantes who had such mad crushes on John that they practically suffered nervous breakdowns at their engagement. Francesca still subscribed to the adage that it took two people to make one career. Nevertheless, they owed much to one another for their individual accomplishments as far back as the early days in New York and Hollywood.

That spark of young lovers still seemed evident to many observers. Yet they remained in numerous ways as different as fire and ice. John could be stubborn and temperamental, even boyishly rigid. Francesca unfailingly stepped into every situation as a strong calming influence with unswerving devotion. She rarely let anything get her down. She always remained pleased and proud of his success. Together they were an extraordinary pair, an unbelievable team, an unforgettable couple.

At their anniversary party, full of eloquent toasts and vintage songs by John and Cabot, Francesca uttered a few remarks. "John and I have lived as a team and luckily have the same tastes for so many vital aspects of life. The one we do not agree about," she injected, "is that he does not enjoy climbing over six dogs in our small bedroom. He puts up with it bravely and it has kept him agile. We are a team. He is the better half. I am the lucky half."

John grinned, then added this postscript: "The greatest asset in my life has been Francesca."

CHAPTER 25

Man of the Right

In the last weeks of his 1984 re-election campaign, President Ronald Reagan flew into southern Connecticut for a rally on the green at the Fairfield town hall: "I'm always glad to visit again with the good people who have given America some of its greatest Republicans—John Davis Lodge, Clare Boothe Luce, and, yes, a fella named George Bush, who's been a great friend and my strong right arm."[1] Reagan's remarks pleased John Lodge, who was thousands of miles away from Connecticut and serving the President in Europe. It was the sort of high-level public recognition that every public figure seeks, and John welcomed the words, albeit a brief salute in a political talk on John's own turf.

A half-dozen years earlier and some eighteen months before the 1980 Republican Convention, Lodge had come out strongly for Reagan. It surprised a number of state leaders who were leaning toward Bush, the son of John's old ally, Senator Prescott Bush. But young Bush's plans to run for President were still unsettled by the end of 1978. In fact, Bush announced his decision to seek the office some months later, well into the spring of 1979. By then, Lodge was fully committed to Reagan, whom he saw as the only GOP candidate thoroughly grounded in conservative principles. Bush, on the other hand, seemed tied to the moderate wing of the party.

In another sense, John felt on common ground with Reagan. Both were former movie actors. In the 1960s, he had supported the ex-movie star for the California governorship, declaring that an actor could surely aspire to high public office. Now he reaffirmed his belief that a film actor could have the makings of a good president: "He has been tested in the fires of high political office. He has a perceptive understanding of large affairs. We agree that a government which panders to immediate demands for superficial solutions can only continue to erode the public confidence on which it rests. We agree that we must, at long last," Lodge said of their mutual stance, "recognize the hostile intent of our enemies and take the necessary steps to shore up the crumbling ramparts of our national security."[2]

In early 1979, Lodge moved into the post as chairman of Connecticut's Reagan for President Committee. Before long, John introduced Reagan to the Chowder and Marching aggregation on Capitol Hill. Already some half-dozen Republican hopefuls, including John Connally, Lowell Weicker, and Howard Baker, were competing for the state's relatively modest thirty-five-member delegation to the national convention. Well in advance of that gathering, Lodge began extending his pro-Reagan message throughout New England.

When Reagan hit the campaign trail in the Northeast, Lodge often played a supporting role. While many voiced dismay over bringing "that California cowboy" into Connecticut, John helped set up a Reagan rally in New Haven in May 1979. He introduced the Republican forerunner as "a man for our time." John, a vigorous seventy-five, met the matter of Reagan's age head on. The Californian, an equally energetic sixty-eight, had been facing criticism because of his age. No president, they both were reminded, had been elected past the age of sixty-seven, and he (William Henry Harrison) had died a month after his inauguration. Lodge pointed to Winston Churchill, Konrad Adenauer, and Charles de Gaulle as leaders who served their governments when in their seventiess and eighties. General Douglas MacArthur at seventy, he noted, commanded the Inchon landing in Korea. "To discriminate against a person on the basis of age is self-defeating," he observed from his own experience. "Ronald Reagan is a man for all seasons. He is right for our time. He is the steady hand at the tiller, which our distraught and floundering nation needs at this trembling hour of decision and destiny."[3]

Lodge later added that the prejudice against Reagan because he was an actor had been hardly voiced. It was the age question that many held against him. John mustered the support of senior citizens for his candidate, reminding party rank and file that older Americans were a large and powerful voting force. John's declamations paid off. By the time of the convention, it was a dead issue.

In the March 1980 primary in New Hampshire, Reagan won a landslide victory over Bush and Baker. By July he was positioned for the nomination, pledging to cut taxes and bolster defense. After he won handily, many delegates to the convention in Detroit expected him to select Gerald Ford for second place on the ticket. But after various ideas and proposals as to executive responsibilities and cabinet appointments flew back and forth, the former president declined the post. To the surprise of most Republicans, Reagan picked his chief rival George Bush as his vice presidential running mate. Connecticut Republicans, who for the most part had been divided between the two contenders, one a lapsed favorite son, had cause for celebration.[4]

"The Vice Presidency was a strenuous question mark," Francesca wrote for the *Westport News* on her return from the convention, "and groups everywhere were in a football huddle discussing with great feeling."[5] She described the convention banners, the loud noises, and the colorful get-ups and hats. All the Nebraska delegation had red caps and red check shirts copying their football team. The Kansas delegation wore blue Stetson hats and large sunflower badges. The Connecticut delegation and guests all had blue sun visors with the map of the state on the front.

She told of greeting Nancy Reagan in the stadium, and of her desire to show her the dress Oscar de la Renta had designed with its splashes of red and blue stars and the lettering "Reagan '80": "I always feel more in the mood of the occasion if I dress in the spirit of the event." She saw little of Detroit, but thought it fascinating that the convention should have chosen the oldest city in the Midwest for the party's new beginning: "We returned home very happy and inspired with our ticket. One might say that we came to Detroit as fighting soldiers of our party and we went back home as heroes united for our country."[6]

Cabot Lodge stayed at home. He had happily retired from public service in 1976, shortly after attending the Republican National Convention as a Massachusetts delegate that year. Apart from occasional writing projects, he shared his on-hands experience in government with students at Gordon College in Massachusetts and periodically lectured on foreign affairs at North Shore Community College in Beverly. Cabot and Emily remained in their comfortable dwelling in that Boston suburb. Always more family-oriented than John—Cabot had helped raise his grandchildren when his daughter-in-law became ill—Cabot and his sons lived only several hundred feet in distance from each other. He relished the long daily walks and the summer picnics that gathered together ten or twenty members of his growing family. Both Cabot and John often retreated to a basement office with a desk and file cabinets. Here, amidst floor to ceiling bookshelves crammed full of family books and favorite authors, they read, researched, and wrote. Cabot turned to recording his role in world affairs; John concentrated on correspondence and by-line editorials as well as organizing Reagan's campaign.

In recognition of Lodge's leadership and perseverance, Reagan quickly appointed him and Malcolm Baldridge, a former chairman of the state's Resources Recovery Authority and a leading industrialist, co-chairmen of the Connecticut Reagan-Bush Committee. And when the Reagans returned to campaign in October, John stood beside them as an unrefuted friend and worker.

Election Day brought few surprises. Reagan swept the nation, picking up 489 electoral votes to President Carter's 49. Reagan had promised "to put America back to work again," while Carter struggled over the release of the Iran hostages. At a GOP celebration in Greenwich, John got up on a platform after Carter conceded defeat. "This is an historic night," Lodge proclaimed. "It's a victory for the United States. We were on a toboggan slide." Later he said that Reagan would make a great president: "He brings an ability to analyze the issues before us, analyze them correctly. There's a long list of things for him to do in January."[7] Lodge hoped he'd be on that list.

The actor-governor who helped make politics safe for fellow actor Ronald Reagan waited and waited for a call to return to government service. "I'm available," he said, "and will be as long as I stay stuck together."[8] He believed that he could fill the post as envoy to France best. Meanwhile, standing in the wings, he represented the President at a function in Hartford. He stood in for Reagan at the funeral of Governor Ella Grasso. The first woman elected governor of a state on her own, Grasso had succeeded Republican Tom Meskill in 1975. She had entered politics as a Republican in the 1940s, but soon encountered insuperable odds as both an Italian-American and a woman. John regretted her switch to the Democratic Party yet admired her rise to the Executive Mansion. In fact, the Lodges were among the few high-ranking Republicans to attend her inaugural festivities.

There were invitations to a State Dinner at the White House for German Chancellor Helmut Schmidt and to a special tribute on Capitol Hill for former Senator George Murphy's eightieth birthday. The administration was naming many Republican comrades-in-arms to high posts—Arthur Burns to Germany, Mac Baldrige as Secretary of Commerce, Strausz-Hupé to Austria, Frank Shakespeare to the Vatican. John expressed willingness to serve in Spain, Belgium, Brazil, Chile, NATO, or in some other post where his languages, experience, and loyalty would be useful in the implementation of foreign policy. Connecticut allies, especially members of the Sons of Italy, pushed the White House to name him envoy to Rome. But Max Rabb, a Reagan confidant and former aide to Cabot, got the post.

In a letter to Reagan, dated August 21, 1981, John, ever-sensitive to exclusion, wrote: "While some people received early appointments, I, a linguist, your campaign chairman in Connecticut, with my long history of involvement in foreign affairs and chairman of the Reagan-Bush Connecticut electors, have been completely ignored. I hope I have not disappointed you. Of course, I have enemies, your enemies. The left wing liberals don't like me, they don't like Reagan Republicans. I never thought, however, that they could reach into the Reagan Administration."[9]

Vice President Bush offered little encouragement and exercised no apparent clout: "The word from the Presidential Personnel office is discouraging on an embassy for you." The office, however, did have Lodge down for inclusion in an official delegation overseas.[10] A month later, Bush again emphasized John's dim prospects. "The competition for those few posts amongst longtime supporters of the President is intense," he wrote. "I was sorry to be the bearer of negative tidings."[11] Bush, no doubt, remembered the "negative tidings" from Lodge when Bush asked him for early support of his candidacy for the Republican nomination for President in 1979.

For any other septuagenarian, life would have been full and complete. There was more time to spend in leisurely collegial get-togethers. He did gather a bit more with his family, often drinking an extra round of Martinis and devouring a second helping of his favorite French cuisine. And when sweets were served, Francesca looked over his shoulder, aware of his tendency to over-indulge. His Braggiotti nieces remembered a dinner at Uncle Rama's when Francesca gave a firm "no" to a second slice of chocolate cake. Before too long, John disappeared from the table. A few minutes later, Aunt Libby turned a corner near a downstairs toilet. As she did, she spied John coming out of the bathroom carrying an empty dessert plate. Everyone kidded him about sneaking off to eat a second piece of cake in the "john."

Around his own and other dinner tables, Lodge more and more a man of the right, frequently debated world issues. On one occasion, he got into an intense discussion about the CIA with University of Bridgeport President Leland Miles. "We obviously disagreed on the issue," Miles recalled, "and finally after 15 minutes of mutual harangue, I said to John mildly, 'John, let's just say that we disagree on this matter.' Whereupon to my amazement, he leaped up from the table, grabbed me by both lapels, put his face about one inch from mine and shouted, 'We do not disagree on this matter.' Everybody burst out laughing and we got onto another world subject."[12]

Increasingly, John's cinematic past came to the forefront. With the introduction and popularity of the video cassette recorder, along with cable TV, films with John Lodge became accessible to home viewers. As a result, the mail brought a letter or two each week from some movie fan, seeking more information on his career or commenting on a particular performance. Many were from Europeans who were rediscovering the fourteen pictures made overseas. With a former movie star in the White House, he felt no qualms over the increasing attention on Lodge the actor.

He encouraged the showing of his print of *The Scarlet Empress* at his birthday parties and other celebrations. When the Alliance Française in New York presented *De Mayerling à Sarajevo*, he eagerly provided the introduction and did the same for a French cultural group in Philadelphia. And later that year, he mingled with a group of old RKO Pictures players— Erik Rhodes, Ann Miller, Arlene Dahl, Dickie Moore, Betty Furness, Van Johnson, Margaret Hamilton, Kim Hunter, and Farley Granger—and *Little Women* co-star Joan Bennett and director George Cukor at a reunion to kick off an RKO retrospective at the Carnegie Hall Cinema.

John also turned to establishing a "think tank" to deal with foreign policy issues from the conservative stance. His close admirers Roger Stone, Paul Dietrich, and Bill Buckley shared this hope for a conservative-based center for international conferences and studies in Washington. "We had conversations about what I call 'mediating structures,' " Dietrich recalled. "We agreed that these structures are the bridge between the individual and the states, and have more power collectively. John loved institutions, and thought they were useful. He had a very sophisticated view of the world and of institutions. He believed the more mediating structures you could have, the more stable government and society could be."[13]

Under the leadership of Dietrich and Stone, plans for a non-profit foundation progressed. Named by them the John Davis Lodge Center for International Studies, the organization soon announced its purpose: to produce studies, papers, and analyses on major foreign policy questions, sponsor lectures and forums, and provide scholarships to appropriately selected foreign service students. In January 1983, Jeane Kirkpatrick gave the first foreign policy lecture for the center.

As a sop to the delays on finding a post, which in the best of circumstances usually encompassed many months to orchestrate, Reagan added John and Francesca to the Special Presidential Delegation to China in September 1981. Led by Chief Justice Warren Burger and U.S. Information Agency head Charles Wick, the group sought to expand cultural ties between the two countries. The trip only whetted John's eagerness to serve his country. Not that there was any lack of activity in his life: there were Spanish Institute board meetings and balls, Sons of Italy after-dinner speeches, Argentine-U.S. polo match galas, Women's National Republican Club gatherings, USO benefits, prep school reunions, Harvard-Yale football games, St. Patrick's Day celebrations, Explorers Club dinners, Dutch Treat lunches, and trips to Hawaii, Hong Kong, Spain, Palm Beach, Ecuador, and the Galapagos. But John sorely wanted a full-time administration job worthy of his experience and expertise. Finally, after almost two years of anticipation and campaigning, Reagan delivered a post, albeit of short duration and limited responsibility.

On September 22, 1982, Lodge began serving as a delegate to the three-month session of the 37th General Assembly of the United Nations. The President also indicated that a decision would soon be made regarding his appointment to an ambassadorial station.[14] John served on the delegation led by U.S. Chief of Mission Jeane Kirkpatrick, who, in his words, became "the pacesetter, the guide, philosopher and friend."[15] Day after day, there were delegates' meetings at 9:30 A.M., followed by morning and afternoon sessions of the General Assembly. John tackled complex issues—the nuclear freeze, the Polish ban of Solidarity, the Russian occupation of Afghanistan. On the latter issue, John delivered a ringing and eloquent rebuke to the Foreign Minister of Afghanistan Shan Mohammed Dost on the occupation of over 100,000 Russian troops and the flight of two and one-half million Afghanistan refugees from repression. Lodge declared that Dost represented a regime which remained in power only by force of massive Russian weaponry:

This monstrous travesty, this caricature of democracy, this martyrdom of a noble people, this ruthless and brutal crushing of freedom continues despite three resolutions of the General Assembly—approved by overwhelming and growing majorities—which called for the withdrawal of foreign forces, restoration of Afghanistan's non-alignment, self-determination, and return with honor of the refugees.[16]

John's loyalty, energy, political wisdom, and sense of humor enlivened the delegation meetings and strengthened its performance. "It spurred me on," Kirkpatrick remembered. "I needed the encouragement."[17]

At the close of the three-month session, at times exhilarating but often frustrating, he concluded that the Soviet bloc was completely coordinated and virtually monolithic in its actions. "The member nations accord the Soviet Union knee-jerk confidence," he wrote to Reagan. "You are, I feel certain, entirely right in your determination not to allow the Soviet bloc to grow larger." But a more permanent post still required all the field ammunition Lodge could gather.[18]

In a letter, he turned to conservative ideologist and friend Bill Buckley to ask why:

Having been governor of our State, I am often called by the media. The other day I was asked how come that Mac Baldridge, Connecticut Chairman for Bush, was appointed to the Cabinet shortly after November 1980, whereas I, Chairman for Reagan, have not yet been appointed in spite of my many years experience as Ambassador and my linguistic qualifications. . . . Of course I am controversial—I'm a Reagan Republican as you are. It is also apparent to me from my journeys about the state that I still have a substantial following in Connecticut. What do you think I should say to defend and protect the President when the press and Reagan people ask me why I have not yet been appointed?[19]

John felt humiliated and frustrated by swaying gently in the wind. What is the explanation, he asked. He wanted to be judged not just on loyalty to the President but on the basis of qualifications. From time to time, John heard talk of Reagan's intention to reappoint him to Spain. (Reagan retained careerist Terence Todman; Lodge apparently was the runner-up.) Yet no official word, yea or nay, reached him. He blamed his lack of success on the State Department and its bureaucracy. His nominal monetary contributions to the Party worked against him more decidedly. He felt buying power was vulgar.[20]

A few close to Lodge urged him to back down and stop "begging at the door." At his age and station in life, they said, he should be aloof, perhaps play hard to get. Hadn't that approach worked well when the movies first took an interest in signing him to a lucrative contract? To some, his "campaign" not to be forgotten in his little corner of Connecticut bordered on megalomania.

Helene von Damm, Deputy Assistant to Reagan and solidly pro-conservative, perhaps did more than anyone to bring Lodge into the Administration. She recognized his keen desire to serve abroad and finally put the matter into focus. She discussed possible posts with him. The Class I embassies that John expressed interest in were occupied; the smaller posts, he felt, were not commensurate with his experience and knowledge. White House executive assistant Tad Tharp and Helene set up a meeting with the President. He reassured John that he did want him to serve and that it was only a question of time. Tharp and von Damm kept on top of the matter.

She was proud that the percentage of non-career ambassadors had reached a peak of almost 40 percent after six months of the Reagan Administration. Then, in the spring of 1982, she learned that the Senate was considering legislation which would limit non-career ambassadors to 15 percent of the total. "The bill never really went anywhere," she wrote in her memoirs *At Reagan's Side*, "but I was getting a strong message from the State Department." Yet she persisted in placing conservatives as ambassadors.[21] The next post that became available was Switzerland with an annual salary of $67,200. Reagan's first envoy there had been the devoted and outspoken Reaganite Faith Whittlesey. But she had been called back to Washington to take over the Office of Public Liaison in the White House when Elizabeth Dole moved over to become Secretary of Transportation.

Von Damm was behind John Lodge for Bern and knew there would be a fight. The State Department had indicated that at age seventy-nine he was too old to handle the responsibility. "I knew John," she recorded. "He was old, yes, but people age at different rates mentally. John was still very sharp and he seemed to have more energy than men half his age. Though I too would have liked him to be ten years younger, I pushed hard for Lodge, and even enlisted the President's help. State at last decided that Switzerland wasn't worth fighting the President for, and John Lodge went to Bern."[22]

John heard the news in Quito, Ecuador, where he and Francesca were on an end-of-the-year holiday to visit Beatrice and Antonio, who was serving as the Spanish ambassador there. But the press for the most part took a dim view of the nomination to the Class I post. The *Washington Times* dredged up John's idiosyncrasies in Argentina: showing his B films at the embassy, disregarding certain security measures, evidencing favoritism with junior diplomats who played tennis. "His custom of wearing an opera cape around town," the *Times* wrote, "also appealed to the Argentines, who like a certain amount of flair."[23] John took issue with the article. He termed it remarkable for its fabrications and pointed out that he never attempted to slip out of the residence without a bodyguard: "It happens that I do not own an opera cape, although I would very much like to."[24]

Closer to home, the Stamford *Advocate*, in its lead editorial of January 22, 1983, suggested that Reagan would do better to keep Lodge where he is than in Bern. "The embassy in Switzerland is a sensitive spot because of its proximity to West Germany and other European countries where political parties preaching anti-Americanism are reaching for power," the newspaper stated. "Those parties are a potential threat to the continuance of NATO. Mr. Lodge, who was a one-term governor, is known as an uncompromising opponent of the Soviet Union, somewhat like Mr. Reagan himself. He has not shown that he possesses the suppleness nor the sophistication to understand that this kind of steely position can further alienate those in Europe who should be our friends and the Soviet Union's enemies. We think that, if Mr. Reagan is determined to appoint a non-career ambassador to Switzerland," it concluded, "there are other deserving Republicans to whom he owes a political debt who can do the job better."[25]

By spring John received unanimous Senate approval. Earlier, when asked during his security clearance probe, "Have you ever been involved in controversy?" he replied with a grin. "I've hardly been involved in anything else. The only things worth getting into are controversial."[26]

On April 15, John was sworn in as ambassador to Bern by Chief Justice Warren Burger. Following a welcome by U.S. Chief of Protocol Selwa Roosevelt, John spoke in a loud, clear, and studied manner: "For Francesca and for me this is an exhilarating, a memorable moment, posed as we are on the threshold of a great experience." He viewed Switzerland as a "haven of tranquillity in a sea of discord; a friendly oasis of civilized living in a jungle of hatred and violence; an island of hope in an ocean of despair; a beacon light of beauty and peace in the Stygian darkness of the ignorance and ugliness spawned by convulsive currents of change." He concluded that Switzerland was a refuge for the homeless and forlorn, for expatriates and the dispossessed, a great tourist center of health and comfort, of security and peace. "Switzerland is indeed unique. What would we do without her?"[27]

The Lodges looked forward to this new adventure with optimism and high excitement. Again their friends back home joined together for a round of farewell parties and tributes for John's new "star role." The Swiss, however, were less enthusiastic over the latest American envoy. Many Swiss looked upon him as just another political appointee and a White House payoff. They were accustomed to welcoming American ambassadors of questionable stature and ability, even ethics. More and more, Bern seemed to be a dumping ground for little-known golf-playing partners of presidents or would-be diplomats with health problems and hopes of a cure in a Swiss sanitarium. The Swiss readily acknowledged that John Lodge was not a political greenhorn like some of his predecessors and would bring a high degree of experience to Bern. But the posting of a seventy-nine-year-old man was of much concern. To some it signaled the insignificant status their capital had in U.S. diplomatic circles. "The Americans always act as if Switzerland is of importance to them," commented an indignant Walter Renschler, President of the Foreign Political Commission of the Swiss National Council, "and then they send us an old man. The American Embassy in Bern seems to have become a government subsidized institution for aged people."[28] The Chief of Protocol in Geneva, Robert Vieux, was concerned too over the age factor, as were other prominent Swiss.

As the Lodges packed for their overseas assignment, Lily came upon a small framed portrait of an early U.S. Cabinet member who had been a friend of their New England forebears. Statesman Albert Gallatin, she remembered, had been born in Switzerland, then journeyed to Boston during the American Revolution. He won election as a Senator, served as Secretary of the Treasury, and became an envoy in Paris and London.

Henry Adams later edited his writings and wrote his biography. Lily pointed out the accomplishments of this Swiss-American of long ago. At once, her father stuffed Gallatin's picture into his briefcase. Upon his arrival, he would remind his host country of the remarkable contributions of Geneva-born Gallatin to the early course of American history.

Francesca too was eager to tell the Swiss of her ancestral ties to their country. Her grandmother, the Countess de Pourtales, had been a member of a distinguished and old aristocratic family in Neuchatel. She soon discovered dozens of cousins, several of whom still ran the Pourtales vineyards near the Swiss-French border. The head of the clan, Rudolf de Pourtales, welcomed Francesca at his Palais du Reyrou, and at a reunion introduced her to many members of her extended family. Once more, she found herself fascinated by a culture, its folklore, customs, costumes, and traditions.

The residence in Bern, in contrast to the palatial and vulnerable quarters in Buenos Aires, looked more like a bucolic Alpine retreat. A stone house in a picturesque setting of trees, flowers, gardens, and grassy knolls, yet not far from the center of one of Europe's best preserved cities, it was cozy and secure. An unusual touch in back of the house emphasized the countrified atmosphere. Two sheep, Heidi and Brigitte, grazed freely on the rolling knolls behind the dwelling where grass cutting was extremely difficult. Known as the "embassy lawnmowers," the sheep were a fascinating attraction and a frequent conversation piece among the eighty or so diplomats posted in the capital.

The Lodges were amply compensated by a tranquil and safe atmosphere. One sunny day while sitting on the terrace, John exclaimed: "Thank goodness we're in beautiful Switzerland. Remember Argentina, Cesca. Remember those problems. I know at my age I could not handle them."[29]

To the Swiss, John's age quickly became of no importance because of his outstanding intellectual and human qualities. Instant friendships sprung up with Swiss President Pierre Aubert and federal and regional authorities as well as with many colleagues in the diplomatic corps and with scores of private citizens. "The fact that he was a great patriot, and reliable, true, honest and direct in the defense of his country's interest," declared lawyer-journalist Hans Sellhofer, "made him even more popular with most of the Swiss (who like clear situations)."[30]

The Lodges' 4th of July party in the garden of the Residence made many friends too. They extended invitations to every member of the Swiss-American Society for the first time in many years. The celebration encompassed a flag-raising ceremony by the Marine guards and a brief speech by John. Henry Steiger and his American-born wife Virginia were highly impressed and very touched by his historical account of the meaning of the 4th. The subject matter was by no means new, but the delivery was stirring. They agreed that Lodge looked and moved like an elder statesman of the striped-pants school. But an appearance so distinctive and words so beautifully spoken pushed aside the years. No other ambassador had ever impressed them so favorably. To the Steigers, Lodge represented the best of America.[31]

Multilingual Switzerland provided a spirit-stirring opportunity for Lodge to utilize his language skills. Along with his ease in French and Italian, he mined his school-boy knowledge of German. And if he had stayed longer in Bern, he would have, no doubt, learned the basics of the fourth and least spoken language of the country, Romansh. Jack DeForest, a visitor from Connecticut, remembered a talk by John in French, and Francesca's subsequent reminder to John that the Washington-circulated press release should have stated that he had spoken in French. "Apparently this would have been good," DeForest wrote in his journal, "and he agreed with her, but it is too late now. Another example of how helpful she is for John. She has many talents that can help him."[32]

Along with his speeches, press interviews, and ceremonial visits, John conducted an intensive public diplomacy program on the U.S. policy priorities established by Reagan. Switzerland, he recognized, was a neutral country. Nevertheless, he believed history had demonstrated that America could "unfailingly rely on Switzerland's commitment to the survival of Western Civilization of which they are such a vital part."[33]

Earlier that year, he had participated in a weekend party at Baron Hans Heinrich von Thyssen-Bornemisza's Villa Favorita near Lugano. After viewing a display of the American art from the Baron's great collection, Lodge again commented on the survival of Western civilization: "It is good that while others are assaulting Western civilization, you should bring to the fore some of the most distinguished accomplishments of that civilization in order to preserve some of the treasures which others are attempting to destroy."[34]

Lodge toiled effectively over a number of U.S.-Swiss issues during his two years in Bern. The Marc Rich case involving tax fraud and evasion occupied many meetings. Rich had pulled his commodities futures trading operations out of New York to Switzerland to avoid a crackdown, and the matter of extraterritoriality led to prolonged and sensitive negotiations. Another issue focused on civil aviation and agreements on fares and the approval of U.S. carriers to increase their market share in Switzerland. Technology transfer became a matter of concern. Under Lodge's direction the Embassy developed a highly effective mission-wide strategy using all appropriate resources to counter the flow of U.S. technology through Switzerland to the Eastern communist countries. He also took the lead on narcotics control, resulting in increased cooperation between the two nations, and when the Swiss dragged their feet on setting up a mechanism to cut down the flow of drugs, Lodge managed to add a drug enforcement officer to the American staff.

"I think he always took the world view," summarized the Embassy economic counselor Richard Dugstad. "It was a question of geopolitical forces and the use of power, rather than just communism versus Western democracy—although sometimes it would come down to that. He was extremely vocal, for example, after Korean Airline Flight 007 was shot down in the fall of 1983. Time after time, with Swiss leaders or business people, he would buttress, he would explain, he would go into a Churchillian type of explanation of the historical perspective for Europe, and the Swiss appreciated that. This is where he was extremely articulate and competent."[35]

On a more parochial level, Lodge directed a program of increasing the physical security conditions at the Embassy on Jubilaumstrasse, along with more rational allocation of space among the Embassy sections. And after considering the problems of maintaining a lease on the Embassy property and the unavailability of appropriate land or buildings for a chancery, he decided on and arranged for its purchase. He also completed negotiations for the subsequent acquisition of the adjoining building, which was a small hotel. He thus provided expanded space for various agencies, gained tax savings, and improved the compound appearance.

Overall, Swiss-American relations were enhanced by the visit to Washington of Vice President Kurt Furgler. John arranged and participated in the five-day visit in February 1984, which included an appointment with President Reagan. John's meeting at the White House gave him a chance to give the President a large Swiss Army knife with a personal engraving that read: "To Ronald Reagan, with high esteem and fond greetings."

Lodge corresponded regularly with Reagan, who, in turn, kept in touch with his man in Bern. He sent a cable of good wishes for John's eightieth birthday. (The Lodges celebrated at Bad Ragaz, a spa in the Alpine Rhine valley). When the President ordered a rescue operation to rid the Caribbean island of Grenada of Cuban military personnel, John praised him in several letters. Reagan replied with gratitude for his words: "The people met our troops with open arms, flowers and fruit. We brought home a treasure trove of documents—Soviet, Cuban, Libyan and even North Korean plus enough Soviet and Cuban weapons to fill an airplane hangar at Andrews Air Force Base."[36]

When the Lodges happened to switch on an old Reagan film called *Louisa* on Swiss television, John dashed off a note to the White House. "You spoke perfect German and we watched it while there was a beautiful snowstorm. I thought you were really excellent."[37] Copies of John's speeches to such groups as the graduating class of the American School in Lugano ("Our Moment of Truth") and the Swiss-American Society of Basel ("American Foreign Policy in a Troubled World") were regularly sent to the Oval Office. Reagan rarely failed not to wire words of praise and encouragement. On July 17, 1984, the President wrote:

> The clear and unequivocal tone of the speech which you delivered to the Swiss Bar Association/International Bar Association is a refreshing refrain from the cold and uninspired speeches we hear too often. I appreciate your forceful presentation of the precepts which we are trying to defend in our sometimes unfriendly world. I encourage you to continue your efforts to explain our policies to the Swiss. My best wishes to you and Francesca.[38]

More and more, John assumed a tough conservative position whereby the world was either black or white. And he amplified Reagan's vivid description on the rampant "evil empire" of the Soviets. In the battlefield mode of a General Patton, he often used his stentorian voice to rally followers into his geopolitical camp.

When Reagan was reelected that year, the Lodges helped to organize a formal inaugural celebration in Geneva for 250 Americans from the Middle East and Africa as well as Europe. Their indefatigable hospitality to both the Swiss and overseas visitors in Bern filled their calendar with engagements as it had in Buenos Aires and Madrid. From the States came Bill Buckley, William Casey, Anna Chennault, George Bush, Vernon Walters, and Claire Boothe Luce, along with a steady stream of neighbors and relatives. Among the "new" European cousins was Enrico Braggiotti, president of the Banca Comerciale Italiana in Milan. The comings and goings of American delegates to international organizations and conferences in Geneva added to their diplomatic obligations. John greeted many. He was not, however, involved with the critical disarmament talks there.

Yet in the midst of this brilliant diplomatic setting, a puzzling and painful illness struck the hardworking and conscientious envoy who, in a very short time, had energized and enhanced Swiss-American relations.

CHAPTER 26

The Last Homecoming

A good mind is a terrible thing to waste, Lodge often remarked, and this thought was foremost as he began his second year in Bern. In carrying out his diplomatic duties, he was not about to sit back and not speak out, even at eighty. But John was anxious to take leave from the Embassy in the summer of 1984. He anticipated a change of pace and atmosphere awaiting at his villa in Marbella where, as he frequently explained, he could be "transported into another world free of the violence and vulgarity which afflicts ours." It turned out to be the last summer of total relaxation and good health for Lodge.

Soon after his return to Switzerland in September, John experienced discomfort and pain in his right shoulder. Annette Veler, U.S. Consul at Bern, remembered the expression of acute anguish on Lodge's face when the president of the Swiss-American Club lightly touched his shoulder as he led him into a room for a luncheon talk. A local Swiss doctor diagnosed the affliction as bursitis and prescribed shots of cortisone. Lodge was relieved that it had no connection with his cardiovascular system. He had had several minor heart seizures in the past; the first, shortly after his return from Argentina. In each instance, after a week's rest, he had recovered completely from these attacks. He refused to acknowledge them as anything serious. He generally brushed aside any medical advice. He kept on smoking, drank only a bit less alcohol, and expressed a dislike for any ongoing medication to control high blood pressure. His physician diagnosed a prostate problem, but John was relieved that no operation seemed necessary.

The persistent and bedeviling pain in his shoulder, however, stultified and, at times, incapacitated him. To cure the malady, he visited several Swiss clinics and spas. The discomfort only grew, and he took to putting his arm in a sling to ease the ache. The embassy chauffeur, Erik Kohn, even had to drive extra carefully to avoid unnecessary bumps in the road. Then one day after an appointment with a specialist in Bern who administered several shots of cortisone, his entire right shoulder became swollen and inflamed. He was rushed to a nearby hospital where on October 25 an operation was performed that night. The doctors discovered an iatrogenic infection in his shoulder joint, which apparently stemmed from a contaminated hypodermic needle. John was in such serious condition that Beatrice hurried from Madrid to Bern. His physicians advised her to stay until his recovery could be ascertained.

On one of her frequent visits to the hospital, Bea carried a wrapped box of her father's favorite home-made muffins. But when John opened the package, out fell a shoe brush. "Idiots!" he shouted. Beatrice had picked up the wrong package in the residence kitchen. John's normal outburst indicated that he was feeling better. But the use of his shoulder and arm remained limited, and he had to give up a trip home to vote in the November Presidential elections. The exact cause of his affliction baffled the doctors. The whole affair made John ruefully observe, in the words of Noel Coward, "I have come to the point where I am grateful to my friends if they live until lunch time."

Aside from his physical torment, John faced the unraveling of Lily and Jim Marcus' marriage. They had stayed together through his incarceration and readjustment. But Jim drifted from job to job, usually in sales, and often faced lengthy periods of unemployment. His debts never seemed to go away, and he borrowed regularly from family and friends. The realization, too, that his younger son was perceptibly retarded and required special schooling added to the Marcus' household burdens. In the fall of 1984, Lily commenced divorce proceedings and turned to her father for counsel and aid. From Bern, he helped both as a devoted parent and a sagacious lawyer.[1]

All in all, as John understated his situation to his sister, "Life is very complicated for me these days."[2] And as winter approached, Cabot began an inexorable decline physically and mentally. The two brothers had last been together at John's swearing in, and he had held out the hope that Cabot and Emily might visit him in Switzerland. On November 7, Cabot wrote John a brief note, saying how saddened he was to think of the trouble that you are having. "In order to cheer you up, I am sending you a copy of 'Memories.' "[3] The short manuscript had the opposite effect. Cabot's account of his role in getting Italy into NATO after the war completely overlooked his brother's part, which John duly noted had already been spelled out in Italian diplomat Egidio Ortona's book on this subject, *Years of America*. John then proceeded to write his own recollection of the important event in order to set his brother straight.

The entire matter brought back John's hurt over being relegated to little more than a footnote in Cabot's autobiography, *The Storm Has Many Eyes*, and then totally ignored in his later memoirs on politics in the 1950s and 1960s, *As It Was*.[4] Even in his dotage, deliberately or unknowingly, Cabot never stopped piquing John, who really never saw through it and constantly fell into his brother's trap. "In that sense, the two of them never grew up," observed Cabot's son Henry Sears Lodge. "They reverted to ages six and seven. All the robes of high office—governor, ambassador—fell to the ground as Uncle John saw red and responded to his brother's needling. The continual teasing, the fierce competition, never stopped."[5]

Before the end of 1984, the White House and the State Department were well aware of John's health problems. On his last visit to Washington, they noted his stiff, slow gait. He looked his age. Now they wondered about his effectiveness in Bern. Was he physically frail, and maybe noticeably senile like his brother? Rather than returning to the States for full medical diagnosis and treatment, John decided to stay overseas for his recuperation. With Reagan's solid re-election victory, he felt that he would be kept in Switzerland for another two or three years. Moreover, after the 1984 election, Reagan requested that his diplomatic appointments not send in their resignations, as traditionally had been done after past elections. Lodge looked forward to more productive years on the Reagan team.

One morning just after the year-end holidays, Lodge received a call from his office. "Have you listened to the radio news today?" an aide asked. When Lodge said he had not, the embassy member relayed the unexpected and unconfirmed report that Lodge would be leaving his post in Bern. "That's not possible," John stated. "I haven't heard from the Secretary of State or anybody." That day several European newspapers ran the story. Former Ambassador to Switzerland Faith Whittlesey, they reported, was leaving the White House and taking John's job in early 1985.

John immediately contacted Secretary of State George Shultz, who was in Geneva to attend a meeting on arms control with Soviet Foreign Minister Andrei Gromyko. Shultz knew nothing about the recall. "John read about it out of the blue," he explained several years later. "He was upset and I was very upset because that's not the way to do things at all with anybody, let alone John Lodge. This was a very sad way to end his public career."[6]

Lodge gathered all the news he could on the matter and asked Shultz to look into it. Perhaps it was only a rumor. Former Ambassador to Bern, Shelby Cullom Davis, a house guest of the Lodges at the time, remembered Lodge spending most of his time that week on the phone trying to get an explanation. "Everyone in Switzerland will think I've done a poor job," John exclaimed to Davis, who had served there under Nixon and

Ford for six years. "We all knew John was an ideal fit for Bern," Davis later said. "And the Swiss felt that they had an envoy from the States who was close to the White House."[7]

But the White House was going through a stormy period, marked by personnel conflicts that were leading to a weeding out of those who were butting heads with chief of staff James Baker. Competent and able, Faith Whittlesey nonetheless tended to be power-hungry and outspoken in her dealings with other key members in the "ring of power." One day she apparently expressed a wish to return to the accommodating atmosphere of Bern. The combative Faith soon got her wish but at Lodge's expense. And she wasted no time in telling her friends of the move, leaking it to the press and ignoring official channels of communication. Naturally, such news spread rapidly and hit the wire services overseas. Neither Reagan nor the State Department had a chance to contact Lodge in advance and make a bona fide public announcement.[8]

John lost little time in writing Faith, whom the Lodges considered a friend. They had entertained her in Bern, and at her request, retained her DCM and other staffers. John even wrote a glowing letter of recommendation to Harvard on behalf of her college-bound son. John noted that *Der Bund* carried an article on his replacement by Faith, while a day earlier the Paris-based *Herald Tribune* ran a story on her taking the place of Jeane Kirkpatrick as Ambassador to the UN. "We here in Switzerland are very interested in your plans," he wrote Whittlesey. "It would also enable us to answer questions. You can imagine that anybody who has been in politics and diplomacy as I have does not believe everything that he reads in the paper. Indeed, you would find it difficult to be Ambassador to Switzerland while also Ambassador to the UN."[9]

Whittlesey replied in a handwritten note, stating she accepted the post only after learning that a change in Bern "had already been decided upon at higher levels." If she had not accepted the offer immediately, she added, the post would have been offered to another very interested candidate: "I do not know why there was a delay in notification which no doubt caused considerable embarrassment to you after word leaked to the press."[10]

John answered almost immediately. "From the point of view of successful diplomacy," Lodge tartly reminded Whittlesey, "the whole episode is something of a disaster. My effort now is to attempt to repair the damage before my departure from Switzerland. It is in such traumatic moments that one finds out who one's real friends are."[11]

Richard Nixon was among John's angered friends. He contacted the White House for some answers and termed the whole matter "a lousy deal" for Lodge. In a letter to John, he wrote: "I am sure the President feels exactly the same way in view of the fact that his loyalty to his supporters is one of his most admirable traits. You were the first Eastern Establishment heavyweight to come out for him, and your support at that early date was a decisive factor in his successful race for the nomination."[12]

On January 25, Reagan dashed off a personal note. The decision, he explained, was not based on dissatisfaction with John's performance. The President, in a face-saving move, wrote that he was honoring an earlier commitment to Whittlesey to complete her assignment in Switzerland, which had been cut short in early 1983 when he needed her back in Washington: "She has now completed her duties here, and I feel bound to give her the opportunity to resume her tour in Bern."[13]

Lodge conveyed his disappointment to the President, and noted that he had expected to stay for two years into his second term: "We shall always remember our time in Switzerland as a happy and rewarding experience which we owe to you." As he often had in the past, John emphasized that he looked forward to being of further service to the President and to the country during the next four years: "I do not plan to retire."[14]

"The affair was a fait accompli," said White House aide Tad Tharp, who had worked with the Lodges on the Reagan campaign in New England in 1979-80. "It had moved too far along to reverse and keep John there." Tharp too was relieved of his job at the White House. He believed his firing came about as a result of his inquiries on the Bern matter.[15]

On February 15, the State Department requested an official letter of resignation. Four days later, John acquiesced. He felt unnecessarily humiliated. The break from protocol and breach of etiquette were beyond his comprehension. He insisted on a minimum of six weeks to pay his final duty calls and pack for home.

A week after submitting his resignation, John received word that Cabot had died. The last of America's great patrician history makers, in the words of the *Manchester Guardian*, he was widely praised for a life well-spent in public service. The gifted, elegant, and experienced Henry Cabot Lodge had occupied the last of his eighty-two years in teaching, lecturing, and writing.

At once, John and Francesca flew to Boston for the private service. Devastated by the loss, John uncharacteristically remained subdued and silent during the sad journey and family gathering at Beverly. When his grandniece Emily Pidgeon remarked that she wished the old songs so often sung around the piano by her grandfather and Uncle John had been preserved on tape, he could barely reply. The thought that the Lodge brothers would never again enliven a get-together numbed John to the point of tears. The long and stressful trip back compounded his physical aches and public harassment. In March the pain in his shoulder became so acute that a second operation was performed, but it did not do much good.[16]

As the Lodges' departure date of April 30 neared, John remarked to Francesca that the old line "No good deed goes unpunished" certainly held true in the circumstances of his recall and his relationship with Faith Whittlesey. "What a tangled web we weave when first we practice to deceive," he wrote in one final letter:

> You, Faith, have done me a great wrong. You must be aware of it. Yet, in spite of the rough and unfriendly treatment which you have accorded me, I am willing, in the best interest of our nation and in order to continue to serve our great President Reagan to the end, to turn the other cheek and try to help you to fulfill the responsibilities of Ambassador to Switzerland. Just let me know.[17]

Lodge expected to go to Washington for a debriefing, but the State Department took a dim view of this customary gesture. It was, instead, strongly suggested that he take care of the administrative formalities of his resignation in Bern and proceed directly to his home in Connecticut. After a round of farewell parties and accolades, John and Francesca sadly left the residence for Westport. A small group of aides and friends accompanied them to the airport. But their DCM was nowhere to be seen. No explanation for his absence had been given. John felt his chief aide's failure to bid him adieu at the end of a posting was an outright dereliction of duty. To John, it showed a lack of good judgment and such judgment to him was the greatest asset for a diplomat.[18]

Amidst all the anguish and upheaval, John experienced a recurrence of pain in his shoulder. Soon after he settled back in Westport, he entered Columbia-Presbyterian Medical Center in New York for tests. A few days of examinations revealed the necessity for another operation to remove more infected bone. After surgery, he remained in the hospital for huge I.V. doses of antibiotics. He quickly picked up a reputation as an impossible patient. As one of his doctors described him: "High strung and bombastic, he was always a bit of a bull in a china shop."[19]

That June he was unable to attend his sixtieth reunion at Harvard. But by mid-summer he was well enough to travel to Marbella for the customary holiday with Beatrice and his Spanish grandchildren. "John truly suffered long periods of agony from his shoulder," Francesca recalled. "Nobody knew what really caused the infection. Apparently it was a very rare and intense strain of streptococcus—a type so unusual that it apparently had been found chiefly in Egyptian mummies several thousand years old. After the operations in Switzerland failed to help completely, I tried to get him to the States for a complete checkup. He refused because there were so many important meetings in Switzerland. During the third operation, his upper arm bone was removed, and afterwards he had limited use of his right shoulder. He was so concerned that the extent of movement with his right arm would limit his customary 'abrazos.' "

In a telephone interview from Spain with reporter Thom Duffy of the *New Haven Register*, John reviewed his political career for the paper's series on state governors. He described the construction of the controversial Connecticut Turnpike as one of the most traumatic experiences of his entire life. He told Duffy that a bill was kicking around Hartford that would rename the route the John Davis Lodge Thruway. "I don't mind being remembered for that," he said. But Lodge was looking not to the past but ahead to his next assignment.[20]

Vice President Bush had expressed regret, even anger, at the way Lodge's dismissal had been handled. Reagan too realized the enormity of the blunder and the shameless treatment of his early and loyal backer. To soothe the wounds, the President asked him to serve again as a delegate to the 40th Session of the UN General Assembly session that fall. "America cannot afford for your skills to lapse into desuetude," Reagan had cabled John as the Lodges prepared to leave Bern.[21] George Shultz also had a hand in the appointment: "I thought it was a good thing to do by way of having a little grace note, as well as something that would be of interest to him."[22]

For its fortieth anniversary, the UN General Assembly also planned a week of large-scale events in October to mark its founding in 1945. Some 100 heads of state and government prepared to visit New York that month. Lodge looked forward to serving as a participant in the special occasion. Reagan nominated him to serve under Lt. Gen. Vernon Walters, chief U.S. representative. In all there were four public representatives: Congressmen Gerald Solomon and Daniel Mica, Lodge, and retired Air Force Brig. Gen. Robinson Risner. (Clare Boothe Luce, the fifth delegate, declined because of poor health.)[23]

General Walters had first met John in Madrid when, as an interpreter, he accompanied President Eisenhower on his world tour in 1959. During Reagan's first term, the sixty-eight-year-old retired Army officer had visited over 100 countries as Ambassador at Large. It was pointed out that Walters had mastered seven languages, and John was glad that the delegation leader intended whenever possible to speak to colleagues in their own tongue. So would John. The General also intended to increase support for American positions at the UN by refusing to tolerate unfair criticism of the United States. Lodge turned out to be an ideal ally when other countries sought to achieve, in the word of Walters, the "lynching of the United States by resolution."[24]

John realized that the idea of inviting private citizens to serve as delegates was a way to interject public opinion into the country's UN policy in the tradition of the democratic process. John's predecessors as citizen representatives had included such diverse and prominent figures as Eleanor Roosevelt, William F. Buckley, Shirley Temple Black, and a host of lesser-known political appointees.

Lodge conscientiously followed the many debates on such topics as apartheid in South Africa, Latin America's $370 billion debt, the widespread African famine, and the anticipated summit meeting between the United States and the Soviet Union. Day after day, he listened to long-winded speakers in the Assembly Hall. Many of their remarks disparaged John's homeland; their words often disgusted him. His frequent grunts of displeasure, General Risner remembered, were readily audible to those fellow delegates beside him.

"The slurs against our country, especially by the Third World bloc, discouraged John a lot," remembered Francesca. "It really was too much of a strain on him to hear those debates every day. He had recovered enough to carry out his duties, but still I cautioned him to slow down. There were days I was terrified by his drive and anxiety. Sometimes he would say, 'I want to get this job done well, then go to Marbella and collapse. At that point, all my ambitions will be fulfilled.' But I doubted he'd really ever quit."

On Thursday, October 24, President Reagan met the delegation and UN leaders, then addressed the packed chamber, proposing that the Russians and Americans accept joint responsibility for fostering peace in five countries—Ethiopia, Angola, Afghanistan, Cambodia, and Nicaragua—where the presence of Soviet or Soviet-backed troops were causing "war with the people." Reagan surprised his audience with his call on Moscow to help resolve conflicts in these trouble spots and by not responding directly to Gorbachev's current proposal for a 50 percent reduction in ballistic missiles. "It marked the turnaround in U.S.-Russian relations," observes Herbert S. Okun, who served as deputy American representative at the UN from 1985 to 1989.[25]

The visit of the President and numerous heads of state, while invigorating John, also taxed his energy. Francesca had welcomed the chance to take him away from his duties with an evening at the theater to celebrate his eighty-second birthday.

On Monday, it was back to the usual round of delegation and General Assembly meetings. The morning newspapers that day and the next, October 29, carried a number of stories that piqued John's interest: U.S. concern about the security of American bases in the Philippines, the Walker Navy spy case, and the state of siege imposed by Argentine

President Alfonsín because of a series of bombings and bomb threats. He also noted with pleasure that New Jersey's Governor Thomas Kean seemed well on his way to re-election. The New York Stock Exchange ended its trading that Tuesday with the Dow Jones industrial index at 1,368, less than a point below its record close. As he often did, John checked out IBM's closing price. At $130½ a share, it neared its high for the year and reassured him that he, indeed, had made a wise investment in the computer firm forty years before.

A welcome home party at the Women's National Republican Club on October 29, although a gathering the Lodges thoroughly encouraged and happily anticipated, demanded much preparation. Both Lodges exerted extra effort to invite friends whom they had not been able to see since their return from Bern because of John's hospitalization, recuperation, and then his assignment at the UN. John was exhilarated by the thought of the forthcoming tribute and his after-dinner speech.

His first speech outside the UN since his return to America would underscore his life-long tenet of individual responsibility. "I believe," he had written in 1978 for a biographical entry in *Who's Who*, "that freedom and responsibility are inseparable; that the exercise of freedom requires a sense of responsibility. . . . I believe that, in general, the questions are more important than the answers. . . . Since, fortunately we cannot foresee the future, a backward glance may at least provide a basis for future action." Recalling his extraordinary life, full of challenges, adventures, and honors, he had added, "I remember much of the past and I wouldn't mind a bit repeating quite a lot of it. I have had an exhilarating life!"[26]

Lodge spent many free moments preparing his address, "The View from Bern." He had always tailored every word of his to the possible appraisal of posterity, and labored hour after hour over the text, writing in longhand on legal pads. As with most of his prepared talks, Francesca became his "sounding board." She pointed out their merits and shortcomings, and suggested cuts and revisions.

"Your talk at the Women's Club, John, desperately needs trimming," Francesca advised after hearing John's run-through. "You'll lose your audience's attention with so much detail on the complex world situation. After all, it's a celebration, not a political debate. You had better cut it by 25 percent or more." Lodge eliminated several sections, but not without protesting vociferously: "How can I stand before this group and not provide a full picture of the perils our country faces today? I simply cannot do it half way." "I think it's more important to give time to mention the ambassadors from Spain, Ecuador, Argentina and Switzerland who are coming to New York to honor you," she said. His address, nevertheless, filled over fifty file cards. Francesca expected John to allow her one more opportunity to comment on the final version. But his agenda at the UN, made more complex and entangled by the visit of President Reagan, ruled it out.

Shortly after four o'clock, John slowly walked back to his apartment building at UN Plaza and entered the elevator that carried him to his suite. Little time remained before the cocktail hour, just enough to go over his address alone once more. He completed a hurried review of his speech cards, then there was time for a short nap. At six P.M. they dressed: John, in the prescribed tuxedo, with a Legion of Honor rosette in his lapel representing just one of the seven decorations presented to him by foreign governments; Francesca, in a bright orange gown, with glittering earrings and necklace.

Clusters of formally attired guests greeted the Lodges at the club. Soon they were welcoming scores of acquaintances, colleagues, and supporters, virtually comprising a cross section of those people who had shared their good fortune and keen disappointments. Indeed, it represented the far-reaching network of those accomplished, influential partisans the Lodges had always attracted and nurtured. When he spotted his daughters, John toasted the family reunion with a glass of Scotch and soda.

Francesca moved about the room, greeting Elsie and Douglas Leigh, Joan and Stevan Dohanos, Veronica and Alfred Simson, Carla and Michael Rea, and Margaret and Thomas Melady. From time to time, she cast an admiring glance at her husband, whose hearty laugh frequently broke through the din of innumerable conversations. She wondered whether he had exceeded the two-drink quota his doctors urged he follow. As she returned to his side, he whispered, "Oh, Cesca, I'm so tired, I wish I could get off my feet and sit down. I'm exhausted."

"Why don't you, John? Please!"

"I can't greet all these people, especially women, sitting down in a chair."

By 8:15 P.M., the reception broke up, and the 200 guests moved into the banquet room, aglow with light from clusters of candles on every table. John accompanied dinner chairman Katharine Davis to the dais. The wife of Ambassador Shelby Cullom Davis, she welcomed the Lodges back to America, adding warm praise for her dinner committee co-workers and noting that the Swiss wine came from Francesca's ancestral vineyards in Neuchatel. Before introducing John, Davis read congratulatory messages from Richard Nixon, President Reagan, and Clare Boothe Luce.

Lodge acknowledged the applause as he stood at the podium. "This is a wondrous occasion," he exclaimed, "It is good to be home." His message emphasized the old Lodge values, all underscored by an uncomplicated patriotism. But his words also recognized new global changes and pressures. "Today, cornered by events, the nations of the world must perforce deal with new realities," he pointed out. Two years in a solidly neutral enclave of order and peace in the middle of Europe had tempered Lodge's views and outlook. But first John turned to a basic premise built into nearly all his speeches since the 1940s: "Ladies and gentlemen, if we don't actively love America, we will lose America, and with that loss, Western Civilization's patient accumulation of forty centuries of culture and achievement will go down the drain."

The words that followed acknowledged the overriding role that women played in the preservation of this culture and American values: "They protect our homes and loved ones. They are the preservers of life; they are the principal protectors of our children. I would never have been elected without the active support of the women of Connecticut." John then summed up his predominant philosophy: "A life of service is still a life well spent!"

Ever the loyal Republican Party stalwart, Lodge also praised the Reagan Administration for its imaginative leadership in economic policies as well as worldwide defense measures: "We are convinced, as I have said many times, that peace is a product of strength, that war is a derivative of weakness, and that appeasement merely multiplies the hazards of war."

His audience heartily applauded these deeply-felt words. Francesca smiled at the outpouring of support. But she hoped John would cut short his talk. The room had become unbearably warm and stuffy. A number of guests were obviously restless, tired, and drowsy. Few were really interested in an expansive review of U.S. foreign policy and defense mechanisms. She hoped someone would get up and open one of the windows in back of the podium. Fresh air from the street at least might perk up both the audience and John, whose voice seemed a bit strained. He even looked a little pale.

Lodge turned to his vision of the Communist menace, which he had warned of in speeches on the floor of the House in Washington and in talks on village greens in New England: "Accommodation with Russia means domination by the Soviet Union," he chided, "with all the regimentation, the obscene torture chambers, the absence of freedom, all the dreadful paraphernalia of tyranny which this comports." His fervid exhortation of life under a Soviet hegemony left him short of breath, but he quickly recovered and continued with a brief description of the different languages and cantons of Switzerland. Suddenly, he paused, asking for a glass of water, before elaborating on the variety of customs in that diverse yet united country.

A dozen speech cards remained in Lodge's hand as he sounded a call to create a society harmoniously mixing the best of the old with the best of the new. "Let us build a society in which justice is tempered with mercy," he inveighed, "a state so strong that neither enemies from abroad nor from within can destroy it. Look at a map of the world in 1974 and then look at it now in 1985. It will give you . . ."

The words suddenly grew breathy; his voice broke.

Herbert Brownell, for one, recognized that something was wrong. He wanted to jump up and ask John whether he could read aloud the rest of his speech. Lodge struggled to finish the paragraph on the hand-held card. "Let us be alert," he uttered in a frightening timbre, "to the danger . . ."

He stopped, staring down with a confused, almost painful, look. He removed his eyeglasses and pushed them into his jacket pocket. A slow-building round of applause greeted this gesture, a signal to him that he could or should end his talk and stop struggling to find the words. Lodge's hands gripped the podium. His expressionless face turned ashen. Lily Lodge sprang from her chair to help. Her father resisted efforts to pull him down into a chair. He shook his head, but finally gave in, assisted by one of the head-table guests. Once seated, he swayed to the right, falling to the floor in a state of unconsciousness.

Francesca rushed to him, loosening his bow tie, opening his dress shirt, and struggling to remove his dinner jacket. Perspiration covered his neck and chest. A doctor in the room tried to revive him; others phoned for paramedics and his physician. Attempts to resuscitate Lodge failed. To many observers, it seemed that outside medical help was slow in arriving, and when it did, ill-equipped for the emergency.

Guests had been asked to clear the dining room, but many remained in the lobby until the 198-pound Lodge was carried to the street and a waiting ambulance. Both Lily and Beatrice tried to get their mother into the car of Westport friends who would follow the hospital vehicle. But Francesca made it clear: "My place is with him." She pushed everyone aside and jumped in beside the paramedics. During that short, hurried ride to St. Clare's Hospital, John drew his last breath.

What on Tuesday had begun as a celebration in his honor became at week's end a gathering in his memory. Word of his death from cardiac arrest spread quickly. By morning a 500-word obituary by reporter Glenn Fowler ran in the *New York Times* along with a photograph taken at the time of his appointment to Argentina. On the following day, an expanded account of his life by Pulitzer Prize writer Eric Pace appeared in the *Times* with a more recent portrait. "What a memorable, dramatic, baroque ending to a stately giant of a man," exclaimed Jo Fox, a reporter from Lodge's hometown who had attended the homecoming. "The great scriptwriter in the sky knew his actor and gave him a finale of high style," she wrote for the *Westport News*.[27]

Over the next two days, several hundred friends and acquaintances paid their respects: diplomats, military officers, actors, artists, college classmates, lawyers, politicians, neighbors—a veritable cross section of the worlds Lodge had entered and enhanced. Surrounding his bier at the Frank Campbell Funeral Chapel were floral tributes from dozens of individuals and organizations, including Helen Hayes, Richard Nixon, the Order of the Sons of Italy, Herbert Brownell, University of Bridgeport President Leland Miles, Boys Town of Italy, and UN General Assembly President Jaime de Pinies. On hearing of John's sudden death, Nixon also dashed off a letter to Francesca. As John was speaking in New York, the ex-President noted, he too was mounting a podium in Chicago. "He was a major actor in enlisting support for my nomination as Vice President in 1952 in Chicago," he wrote, "and one of my most trusted, wise & loyal supporters in all the years since—in the bad times as well as the good."[28]

John's wallet and pockets that final night held the usual cluster of ID passes and membership and credit cards. But stuck around them were several slips of paper with notes and sayings. One treasured quotation, a statement by Churchill, reflected John's feelings about his country in a world of many "isms": "The vice of capitalism is inequitable distribution of blessings. The virtue of socialism is the equitable distribution of misery." The words on another piece of paper referred to the much-debated subject of nuclear freeze: "It doesn't do the sheep much good to pass a resolution on vegetarianism when the wolves are of a different opinion."

An Episcopal service at Christ and Holy Trinity Church in Westport brought together political workers from his days in office and current Governor William O'Neill. Neighbor Stevan Dohanos read the last part of the speech that John had been unable to complete. Lodge's closing remarks had looked to the future: "We Americans have a solemn obligation to persevere and to enhance our heritage and pass it on with its increment to succeeding generations." On his final page, he concluded: "Let us then, in whatever time is left to us, so conduct ourselves that 200 years from now, when our descendants look back on our gruesome scene, our grim Gethsemane, they may say of us: 'They too understood the challenges of their time and generation, they stood resolutely in the breach, and they prevailed.' "

Two days later, on Monday, November 4, a service of thanksgiving for the life of John Lodge took place at Christ Church in Washington. His staunch friends and allies there filled the front pews of the old parish and joined to sing the familiar and traditional hymns "Eternal father, strong to save," "Abide with Me" and "Onward, Christian Soldiers." Adm. George Anderson spoke, as did John's nephew George Cabot Lodge, who read several selections from Bay's book, *Poems and Dramas*.

John's wish to be buried among his country's honored war dead at Arlington was fulfilled late that afternoon. Placed on a caisson at the cemetery entrance, his flag-draped coffin slowly moved behind a mounted military honor guard and three riderless black horses, the highest Naval and Presidential honors any patriot could receive. After the burial, the small group of mourners met at the F Street Club, the once-private dwelling where John had first seen the light of day eighty-two years earlier. National Republican Committee Chairman Frank Fahrenkoff spoke of John in a brief tribute as "ever the statesman . . . ever the party man."[29] Later, Clare Boothe Luce rose to speak. Still a charismatic and outspoken individual, she quickly gained the attention of her select audience with her observation that she had pushed Lodge into public service: "I made John Lodge. I created him. He came to me after the War and asked, 'What should I do?' I urged him to run for my seat in Congress."

In New York later that week, John's colleagues and co-workers at the United Nations conducted a memorial service at the UN chapel. Organized by Ambassador Joseph Verner Reed, it was led by the Rev. John Andrew, rector of nearby St. Thomas Church. Ambassador Vernon Walters gave a stirring eulogy, expressing his unbounded admiration for John: "There was no break in his life of service. In his long life, every moment was dedicated to his country, to his fellow man and increasing the number of his country's friends and his own friends."[30]

Then a month later, in December 1985, John's life was again celebrated at a Catholic Mass at the Church of the Assumption in Westport, where Francesca had worshipped for nearly forty years. Sympathetic friend and conservative colleague William Buckley praised the multi-faceted, multi-careered Lodge and reminded the congregation of his antipathy for inactivity and retirement. The Rev. Kevin Fitzpatrick in his sermon described John as an "unabashed, unashamed public patriot." Father Fitzpatrick added an aside: "According to Francesca," he said, "John always thought it would be wonderful to come back as a seagull—to swim along the shore in the clear water and sunshine, to eat the best food cast from ocean liners and never pay taxes!"[31]

Buckley later published his eulogy of Lodge in his *National Review*:

> On that final day . . . an elderly man, while still on the platform, requested the refreshment of a glass of water, and received instead eternal refreshment, his boots still on.
>
> John Davis Lodge was an exemplary citizen, husband, father and friend. The best he'd have wished to hear about himself was that he merited his country's affections. And the best that can be said of his country was that it merited the loyalty of John Davis Lodge.[32]

And in a tribute in Congress, Connecticut Senator Chris Dodd, the son of Senator Tom Dodd who had defeated Lodge in the 1960s, concluded: "Whatever one's political orientation, it was hard not to admire John Lodge."[33]

The day after hearing of John's passing, President Reagan wrote a long letter to Francesca, recording his grief over the loss to John's family, his country, and the world. "For it is not only John's innumerable friends and admirers who mourn him, it is the grateful Nation he served so long with such ardor and such fidelity."[34] Reagan, through Ambassador Walters, suggested that Francesca take her husband's place as a member of the U.S. delegation for the remaining five weeks of the UN session. She was deeply moved and overwhelmed by the gesture. But the sudden loss of her beloved Jeannot was a numbing blow. "The shock has been greater than I can describe," she replied to the President, "and I do not feel that I can at this time fill such an important role with all of my best faculties."[35]

To her closest friends, she expressed an aversion to going back to their apartment at UN Plaza. "And I couldn't bear sitting for hours at the UN and hearing anti-American insults. I could hardly stand it when John had to do it. Walters really wanted me on the team, and, since he was a bachelor, available, too, as a companion for the official social events. Clare Luce urged me to take the post. Apparently she had suggested to Reagan that I'd be the ideal one to replace John. She called my refusal 'idiotic.' Quite mad about the whole matter, she insisted that one couldn't say no to the President. But I did."

The fact of her close partnership with John in every phase of his full life seemed to call forth from the White House such a comforting and honorific gesture. Francesca, however, couldn't truly face or fathom stepping into the shoes of her husband. Yes, they worked together, played together, like one for over fifty-six years. But John, she concluded, would always be The One.

CHAPTER 27

A Life of Service

In death, John Lodge returned to the city of his birth and youth. In Washington he had learned the rudiments of government and statesmanship, often at the side of his illustrious grandfather. There he became captivated by the idea of public service in the worthy style of Theodore Roosevelt and William Howard Taft, patricians and born leaders who were possessed of sensitive refinements of character and intellectual honesty. Years later, after careers in law, the movies, and the military, Lodge moved on to Capitol Hill, where he proved to be a man of admirable instincts, of considerable theoretical intelligence, and of high courage. In some instances, he was one of the most advanced post-war foreign policy thinkers in Congress—even somewhat visionary, somewhat outside the rigid line of approved party policy.

John Lodge seemed headed for a long and distinguished career in Congress, first in the House, then surely in the Senate. Yet he never achieved his goal to become a Senator from Connecticut, nor his other coveted objective, Secretary of State. Brother Cabot and his mother vetoed the idea of a seat in the Senate when John had the opportunity at his fingertips. Instead, a governorship brought Lodge into a milieu that tested his executive and political skills in every respect. He did not kowtow to regional ward heelers, and it cost him dearly. "My years as Governor were full of interest and challenge," he noted with understatement twenty years after leaving Hartford. "A person's ability, character and education, in a word, mettle, are challenged more in one day as Governor of an industrial state like Connecticut than in many years of ordinary life."[1] Defeated for a second term by a painfully slim margin, he had given the state an honest, efficient, and economical administration. Indeed, in a few short years, he had turned a $11 million deficit into a $17 million surplus.

With a lively interest in international relations and a broad cosmopolitan outlook on the world and its dangers, Lodge fitted well into the mold of ambassador. The ideal mid-twentieth century envoy, explained ambassador and lawyer Myron Cowen, should be an administrator, a business expert, a linguist, a gentleman, a diplomat, and a foreign affairs scholar as well as a master of public relations techniques and a confident and articulate though discreet spokesman for the foreign policy of his country—and his spouse, he added, must love and live his job twenty-four hours a day: "Together, they must have a zest for human contact and a keen awareness of the strivings of their host population."[2] Ever alert, tactful, and wise, Lodge acquitted himself with the best of this special breed, as did Francesca in her role.

Basically an old-school New Englander, this prudent Yankee became noticeably more understanding and mellow from his long sojourn under Iberian skies. Certainly his days in Spain brought a newness into his life, into his family. He often remarked that if he had received 1,600 more votes in 1954 and not gone to Madrid, he would have had a different son-in-law and a different set of grandchildren.

The son of a poet, he readily admitted he was never cut out for the bar or bench. His artistic bent surfaced early; a theatrical flair emerged in every public role he assumed. Not necessarily conscious of it, he projected himself, even cast himself, as a governor, senator, or admiral. A decade of professional acting honed and solidified his real zeal and enthusiasm for the public service arena. A gifted public speaker and orator whom few politicians surpassed on a podium, he readily injected a certain affability in his message. If he could express his views and opinions through anecdotes and humorous tales, he did so with relish.

In later years, he evolved into a bit of a boy scout in terms of conservatism—enthusiastic and naive to the realities of political and social change. To some observers his patriotism was touching but saddening, especially when he proclaimed multitudinous alien forces everywhere at work in America and beyond. Nonetheless, all but a few truly believed in his honesty, loyalty, and dedication.

A man who enjoyed life and appreciated talent, he was closer to the average person than many people were able to see or willing to admit. Effervescent and amiable with remarkable staying power, he seemed tireless but rarely tiresome. Yet he struck some acquaintances as frequently too hearty in his greetings, no matter how sincere they really were. A rather complicated, paradoxical fellow to others, he appeared to wear a mask of buoyant extroversion that hid some basic insecurity or shyness. To a close few, he seemed at times to be worrying about where he fit in, how to begin anew, or whether he was "making it" in the real world. The loss of his father at a very young age and a sibling rivalry influenced him profoundly, leading to a degree of egocentricity and insecurity. His long-time friend Dick Aldrich once remarked that he needed to have people admire and love him more than most, perhaps because in his youth, "he had always been sort of pushed around—except by his mother."[3]

When Francesca Braggiotti entered his life during his student days in Boston, a more gentle and less self-centered individual gradually unfolded. Much of his maturity, his success, his sureness, his serenity of spirit stemmed from this partner, who at first glance in 1929 seemed an unlikely choice as a wife for a Brahmin-bred barrister. But together they forged an unbreakable alliance and created an exciting and complementary togetherness as well as extraordinary accomplishments. Six months before his death, John was asked to describe his greatest personal achievement. Without hesitation, he replied, "my marriage, which has been wonderfully successful. Without my wife, I could not have accomplished what I have." It was his good fortune to have Francesca give his life continuity, warmth, and meaning.[4]

Together, John and Francesca combined intelligence, intuition, vitality, and faith: "I've always believed the entire sum of existence is the magic of being wanted," she believed. "And John always wanted me to be with him at every event, important or insignificant. To love one another is the greatest experience in one's lives. It sounds banal, but how many couples remember, feel and live the marriage vows. We thanked the Lord day and night for the faith he gave us for our complete love. We cared and were interested and ambitious for one another. I say, 'for a web begun, God sends thread'—and he did and kept us together with a golden thread."

After John's death, a staunch Francesca continued to weave the thread. There was one important loose end. A long-discussed proposal to name the Connecticut thruway for John came up for consideration. Since the time of his governorship, proponents had urged the state legislature to name the route in his honor, but without success. When the modern superhighway opened in 1958, Lodge journeyed from Spain to help dedicate the project, so controversial in its concept and construction that it had contributed to his defeat. However, it remained nameless, merely I-95 on road maps.

A generation later, Lodge's friends again urged the Democratic-controlled state to acknowledge his foresight and courage in getting it built, and thus rename it in time for his eightieth birthday. Then an outcry over the lack of much-needed road maintenance and repairs, a concern over several devastating toll plaza crashes and other serious accidents, and most alarming, a worry about more bridge collapses similar to the Mianus River Bridge disaster, discouraged name-change advocates. They decided to wait until the route's negative image of "blood alley" was faced and overcome. John replied that he had been responsible for the road, whether in the eyes of travelers it now struck them as good, bad, or somewhere in-between. The vital route lost him an election; he had nothing to lose by being identified with it a generation later. Still the proposal floundered in committee meetings.

In the wake of Lodge's death, key proponent of the measure Rep. Julie Belaga of Westport again urged the Transportation Committee of the General Assembly and the Governor to support the idea. With their bipartisan backing, the bill readily passed. In October 1986, at a turnpike service area in Darien, Gov. William O'Neill unveiled a granite marker with a bronze plaque naming the route for Lodge. In his remarks before a group of Lodge admirers and state dignitaries, including former governors Dempsey and Meskill, O'Neill spoke of John as "a brave and courageous man" for his foresight in advancing the superhighway to reality: "It was not necessarily a popular thing to do and it may have cost him politically. But it was the proper thing to do."[5] The Lodges' 30-year dream of having the road bear the designation "Governor John Davis Lodge Turnpike" had come true. A tearful Francesca thanked the Legislature for passing the bill to honor John. "I feel that this is marvelous beyond words, and words can't express a dream."

After nearly six decades as John's spouse, partner, and helpmate, Francesca, now alone, entered a trying period of solitude and frustration as well as readjustment. The widow of a public figure, particularly one in government, often faces pressing decisions, new obligations, and additional responsibilities. Francesca recognized this and accepted it.

Plans for the dedication of Interstate 95 as the John Davis Lodge Turnpike and a large reception she organized for invited guests occupied much of the first year of her widowhood. Once that event passed, the ever-dutiful Francesca focused on the design of a very special tombstone in Arlington. This undertaking moved slowly. She insisted on hiring a stone mason to carve the intricately detailed crests of each of John's seven decorations from foreign governments—France, Italy, Poland, Spain, and Argentina—as well as listing with dates his various careers, plus choosing a quotation summing up his philosophy of service to mankind: "To be useful to our fellow man is a noble aspiration. A life of service is still a life well spent." These engravings would fill all four sides of the large granite marker and require nearly two years to complete before its unveiling in 1989.

Correspondence files, career scrapbooks, and photo collections had long piled up in much disarray throughout Villa Lodge. Francesca slowly engaged in the task of bringing order to this mountain of material. She would never complete the Herculean chore to her satisfaction. Her family, health, and church always remained priorities in the years that remained.

John's accomplishments were never far from every move Francesca made, especially his vintage films, more and more shown on cable TV and reissued as video cassettes. From her own resources, she supported the restoration and preservation of his rarely seen foreign motion pictures housed at the British Film Institute. In 1993, this author, with Francesca's encouragement, initiated and produced film tributes to Lodge at the Amateur Comedy Club in New York, where both John and Francesca had acted in the early 1930s, and at the Library of Congress in Washington. Similar showings of his pictures by Francesca soon became a feature of the annual October gatherings in Washington on the anniversary of John's birth. These reunions of his closest friends and aides consisted of a Saturday evening banquet, usually at the Army and Navy Club, and a Sunday morning pilgrimage to Arlington, where a memorial service took place. Francesca carefully planned eight such gatherings, beginning in 1989.

Francesca herself continued to be recognized as an innovative civic leader, far-reaching humanitarian, and loyal Republican, receiving tributes from the Women's National Republican Club, Boys' Town of Italy, 4th Congressional District Republican Women's Association, and the Italian American Caucus of the Connecticut General Assembly. And the Hollywood Bowl acknowledged her innovative contribution to modern dance by prominently featuring in the Bowl's new museum rare film footage of the performance of her corps de ballet there in 1933.

Then, on the occasion of her ninety-fifth birthday in October 1997, the Westport Historical Society mounted an extensive exhibit of her life and achievements. At the gala opening, Francesca—for the first time too frail to travel from Spain to America—received in absentia citations from Connecticut Governor John Rowland, the State Legislature, and Westport Town officials. A highlight of the tribute came from The Seeing Eye, with the presentation of its prestigious Buddy Award, given to individuals who demonstrate exceptional commitment to the program of dog guides. The organization also named a young dog in training "Francesca."

By then Francesca had sold Villa Lodge and its remaining seven or so acres for subdivision. Saddened by the prospect of giving up her much-loved home after fifty-two years, Francesca, in the midst of the move, had developed pneumonia. It was the third serious health crisis since John's death. Earlier, she had undergone major knee surgery, and in 1991 suffered a heart seizure while visiting daughter Beatrice in Tokyo, obstacles she never dwelled upon. Talk of aches and pains, she had long concluded, was only a bore. She was more attuned to reminding others of good diet and the importance of daily early morning exercises, a regimen she had carried out all her life. A generous hostess, she liked to have people around every day. Often dressed in a bright red suit, a striking designer scarf, and chic white boots, she greeted visitors with a luminous smile and a light kiss on each cheek in the European manner.

But she missed America desperately and longed to go back to Connecticut for a visit. She pleaded with Harriet Manning, her secretary in Westport, to think up some way, some excuse to travel there from Marbella: "Comfort and certain luxury does not make up for *loneliness*. The more this place is beautiful & full of comfort & luxury—the *sadder* I feel to enjoy it *without* John."[6] Her friends in Connecticut missed her too—her warmth, her wit, her determination. "She knew how to approach people, circumvent conflict—that's a gift," observed close friend Carla Rea.[7]

The vagaries of extreme old age clouded Francesca's last months. Yet, with the dawn of 1998, she still looked across the sea to America, ever hopeful of enjoying the familiar Connecticut countryside, experiencing the New York theaters and shops, and seeing her Washington friends and family. But her last and ultimate journey began on February 25. Twelve years earlier, John Lodge had "gone his way"—and Francesca as she had in life, with her heart filled with love, joy, and anticipation, again followed.

Notes

The following abbreviations have been used: TAD (Thomas A. DeLong), EDL (Elizabeth Davis Lodge), FBL/P (Francesca Braggiotti Lodge/Papers), GCL (George C. "Bay" Lodge), HCL (Henry Cabot Lodge, Sr.), HCLJr (Henry Cabot Lodge, Jr.), JDL (John Davis Lodge), RN (Richard Nixon), RR (Ronald Reagan).

1. An Illustrious Lineage

1. No official record of his birth exists. Apparently, the attending physician, Dr. Tabor Johnson, neglected to make an official report. A notarized document, signed by his mother on December 2, 1925, testified to the 1903 birth.

2. Emma DeLong Mills, Journals, vol. 4 (unpublished), Oct. 8, 1919.

3. "Lodge Works Hard At His Movie Job," *Philadelphia Bulletin*, Mar. 6, 1934.

4. John W. Crowley, *George Cabot Lodge* (Boston: Twayne Publishers, 1976), 26-27.

5. Crowley, 33.

6. Crowley, 45.

7. Crowley, 23.

8. Crowley, 26.

9. Alden Hatch, *The Lodges of Massachusetts* (New York: Hawthorn, 1973), 84.

10. Crowley, 46.

11. Stephen Hess, *America's Political Dynasties* (Garden City, NY: Doubleday, 1966), 457.

12. Hatch, 86.

2. A Young Francophile

1. Quoted in Crowley, 48.

2. JDL to John W. Crowley, May 11, 1970.

3. Crowley, 95.

4. Hatch, 91.

5. Hatch, 91.

6. In conclusion, Crowley views Bay as a minor author: "He belonged to a transitional generation of poets, and his work fused the forms and themes of the nineteenth-century New England tradition with the tone of disillusionment so characteristic of twentieth-century poetry" (122, 128).

7. Hatch, 159.

8. Remarks by JDL, Annual Banquet of Federation of Franco-American Clubs, New Britain, CT. (ms), Apr. 18, 1953.

9. JDL to Anna Mills Lodge, Oct. 19, 1913.

10. JDL to Anna Mills Lodge, Oct. 19, 1913.

11. Henry Cabot Lodge, *The Storm Has Many Eyes: A Personal Narrative* (New York: Norton, 1973), 23.

12. John Lodge, "Les Enfants Terribles de Madame Lodge," unpublished recollections, 1975, FBLP.

13. Hatch, 163.

14. Hatch, 164.

15. Henry Cabot Lodge, 26-27.

3. In Class and On Stage

1. Helen Howe, *We Happy Few* (New York: Simon and Schuster, 1946), 7.

2. Halsey DeW. Howe to TAD, Mar. 6, 1989.

3. William J. Miller, *Henry Cabot Lodge* (New York: James Heineman, 1967), 38.

4. Miller, 38.

5. Miller, 38.

6. Miller, 38-39.

7. Henry Cabot Lodge, Sr., *Anna Cabot Mills Lodge* (Boston: Merrymount Press, 1918), 20.

8. Head Master Report of J. D. Lodge, Class VI, Feb. 12, 1916.

9. Luis A. Baralt to JDL, Mar. 13, 1964.

10. Finley Peter Dunne, Jr., to TAD, July 7, 1989.

11. HCL to EDL, May 14, 1916.

12. Hatch, 113.

13. "Maj. Gardner Dies at Camp Wheeler," *New York Times*, Jan. 15, 1918.

14. Miller, 48.

15. R. H. Howe to EDL, June 16, 1918.

16. Henry Woodbridge int. TAD, June 7, 1988.

17. R. H. Howe to EDL, Dec. 22, 1918.

18. Catalog, Evans School for Boys, 1918.

19. JDL to Sybil Ellinwood, Apr. 6, 1971.

20. Frederic Coudert to JDL, Jan. 1919.

21. EDL to JDL, Feb. 9, 1919.

22. Evans School Report, Nov. 10, 1919.

23. EDL to JDL, Oct. 1919. According to Francesca, John recited poetry aloud to himself to help overcome his twitch.

24. Frederick Winsor to EDL, Apr. 18, 1921. An unidentified Middlesex master in a handwritten analysis wrote of John in his senior year: "Suffers a little from being the grandson of his grandfather, and therefore having been too much in the reflection of the lime-light and from being a younger brother, and therefore having had too little chance to make his own decisions. In other words his character is pretty undeveloped as yet, though his sense of his own importance is not."

25. Miller, 56.

26. Rudolph Kass and Andrew E. Norman, "The Class in '21-'24 . . . A Look Back," 1925 Souvenir Issue, Harvard College, June 20, 1950.

27. Finley Peter Dunne, Jr., to TAD, July 7, 1987.

28. William Nichols int. TAD, Apr. 9, 1988.

29. George Blake Johnson to TAD, Mar. 20, 1989.

30. Hamilton Eames int. Alden Hatch, c. 1969.

31. Paul W. Williams int. TAD, Feb. 1, 1988.

32. JDL, "On the Other Hand," Letter to Editor, *Harvard Crimson*, Feb. 1, 1923.

33. P. W. Hollister, "Reviewer Finds 'Who's Who' Another of Hasty Pudding's Best Ever Shows—Declares Comedy is of Very High Order," *Harvard Crimson*, Apr. 1924.

34. Theatre Guild of Boston to JDL, June 4, 1924.

35. Charles F. Stanwood to TAD, Sept. 16, 1988.

36. John W. Spaeth to JDL, Nov. 9, 1950.

37. Miller, 62.

4. Francesca

1. Gloria Braggiotti, *Born in a Crowd* (New York: Thomas Y. Crowell, 1957), 87. Gloria, the youngest sister of Francesca Braggiotti Lodge, relied extensively on Francesca's recollections for this family portrait.

2. Braggiotti, 242. One of the students recalled that "We met every Saturday morning during nine months, a group of teenagers, mostly from my suburb in Chestnut Hill. . . . We loved every minute and it gave us a chance to know much classical music." Esther Bemis Goodwin to TAD, Apr. 22, 1991. "We wore short little white cheesecloth dresses, and learned the ballet foot positions and bar exercises, and also how to fall down gracefully." Louise Russell Jackson to TAD, May 15, 1991.

3. Louis Untermeyer, ed., *The Complete Poetical Works of Amy Lowell* (Boston: Houghton Mifflin, 1955), 581-82.

4. Braggiotti, 253.

5. Stage-Door Johnny

1. William C. Widener, *Henry Cabot Lodge and the Search for an American Foreign Policy* (Berkeley: University of California Press, 1980), 308.

2. JDL to FBL, c. July 1928.

3. JDL int., Oral History Research Office, Columbia University, Oct. 5, 1967, 2.

4. JDL, "Harvard's Role in a World Capable of Self-Destruction," Remarks at Mid-Century of Harvard Class of 1925 Reunion, June 21, 1950.

5. Paul W. Williams int., TAD, Feb. 1, 1988.

6. Joseph P. Kennedy, ed., *The Story of the Films* (Chicago: A. W. Shaw Co., 1927), v.

7. In some quarters, it was believed that Berta's death stemmed from an aborted pregnancy. Braggiotti dance students remembered hearing that she had contracted an infection from going to a backstreet abortionist and then sought help at Parkway Hospital. Her death certificate lists pelvic infection as the contributory cause of death on February 16, 1928. Certificate of Death, Commonwealth of Massachusetts, W. P. Graves, M.D.

8. JDL to FBL, June 28, 1928.

9. JDL to FBL, June 28, 1928.

10. JDL to FBL, July 17, 1928.

11. JDL to FBL, July 17, 1928.

12. JDL to FBL, July 26, 1928.

13. JDL to FBL, July 26, 1928.

14. HCL, *Anna Cabot Mills Lodge*, 15-16.

15. JDL to FBL, July 30, 1928.

16. Shari Benstock. *No Gifts From Chance: A Biography of Edith Wharton* (New York: Scribner, 1994), 316.

17. John L. Ellinger to FBL, Oct. 5, 1987, FBLP.

6. Marriage, the Law, and Greasepaint

1. Harvard Law School to Director of Naval Intelligence, Oct. 19, 1939.

2. Paul Williams int. TAD, Feb. 1, 1988. John's gift to each usher, a penknife, featured individual monograms designed by Francesca's father. Iva S. V. Patcevitch int. TAD, Aug. 15, 1989. A suitor of Berta, Patcevitch in 1929 was assistant to the president of Condé Nast Publications; he became president in 1942.

3. Richard Stoddard Aldrich began producing plays on Broadway in the 1930s and operated the Cape Playhouse and Falmouth Playhouse on Cape Cod. His theatrical endeavors included *Goodbye, My Fancy, The Devil's Disciple*, and *Caesar and Cleopatra*. In 1940 he married actress Gertrude Lawrence. *Biographical Record of The Harvard College Class of 1925, 25th Reunion*, June 1950.

4. JDL to Isidore Braggiotti, c. 1931.

5. Paul Cravath to JDL, Sept. 23, 1931. That year Cravath was elected president of the board of the Metropolitan Opera. He also served as a director of The Juilliard School, a vice president of the Philharmonic Symphony, and board chairman of Fisk University.

6. Thomas E. Dewey to JDL, Oct. 19, 1931.

7. JDL to FBL, May 6, 1932.

8. Memorandum, JDL to Nancy Smith, Dec. 11, 1934.

9. "Law Training Led to Film Bow of Actor John Lodge," *Boston Sunday Advertiser*, June 23, 1940.

7. Personality in Pictures

1. "A Fresh Look at Lodge," *Life*, Sep. 14, 1953. A distant Cabot cousin and contemporary of John, Eliot Cabot (1899-1938) Harvard '22, chose the stage for a career. He had leads with the Hasty Pudding Club, appeared in major productions on Broadway, and was leading man to Helen Hayes in *Coquette* (1927).

2. Mayme Ober Peak, "Hollywood Picks Senator Lodge's Grandson Because It Needs 'The Gentleman Type,'" *Boston Daily Globe*, Nov. 13, 1932.

3. Richard Watts, Jr., "On The Screen: 'The Woman Accused'—Paramount," *New York Herald Tribune*, Mar. 11, 1933.

4. The critic for the *Herald Tribune*, Richard Watts, Jr., wrote: "One of the murderer's victims is Mr. John Lodge, whose dying screams burst in upon Mr. Ruggles's comedy so insistently that for a moment I took him for a critic." Apr. 3, 1933.

5. Elliot Norton, "No Thrill Making Love to Marlene," *Boston Post*, Mar. 11, 1934.

6. Verna Hillie int. TAD, Feb. 19, 1991.

7. JDL, "John Davis Lodge Tells Hard Work Side of Screen Life in Hollywood," *Boston Sunday Advertiser*, Apr. 16, 1933.

8. JDL to EDL, Apr. 13, 1933.

9. Hillie int. TAD.

10. Kent A. Hunter, "Blueblood Son of Lodges to Act in Films," *Minneapolis Evening Journal*, Oct. 13, 1932.

11. JDL, Apr. 16, 1933.

12. Victoria H. Oakie int. TAD, Nov. 8, 1989.

13. Louise R. Jackson to TAD, May 15, 1991.

14. Katharine Hepburn to TAD, Aug. 2, 1990.

15. Josef von Sternberg, *Fun in a Chinese Laundry* (New York: Macmillan, 1965), 161.

16. Marlene Dietrich, *Marlene D.* (Paris: Bernard Grasset, 1984), 93.

17. von Sternberg, 265.

18. Richard Watts, Jr., "On The Screen: 'The Scarlet Empress'—Capitol," *New York Herald Tribune*, Sep. 15, 1934.

19. "Cinema: The New Pictures," *Time*, Sep. 3, 1934.

20. John Kobal, *Marlene Dietrich* (London: Studio Vista, 1968), 82.

21. Andre Sennwald, "The Screen: 'Menace,'" *New York Times*, Nov. 22, 1934.

22. JDL, radio int. Gertrude Ross, Los Angeles (not dated precisely, but c. Sep. 1934).

23. Nancy Smith, "The Man Without a Social Country," *Shadowplay Magazine*, Apr. 1935.

24. Evelyn Venable int. TAD, Nov. 12, 1989.

25. "Scandal Mongers Take Notice," *Los Angeles Times*, Jan. 11, 1935.

26. Smith, "The Man Without a Social Country."

27. Mayme Ober Peak, "Reel Life in Hollywood," *Boston Globe*, July 29, 1935.

8. Britain's Clark Gable

1. "Landi, Lodge Excellent in French Film 'Koernigsmark,' " *Hollywood Reporter*, Dec. 26, 1935.

2. "Moving Pictures Influencing Stage, Lodge Tells American Club Here," *Paris-New York Herald*, Dec. 13, 1935.

3. "Elstree Makes a Star of Man Hollywood Neglected," *London Evening Standard*, July 18, 1936. Graham Greene may have acknowledged Lodge's star status, yet in his *Spectator* review of *Ourselves Alone*, he noted that John "continues to suffer from a kind of lockjaw, an inability to move the tight muscles of his mouth, to do anything but glare with the dumbness and glossiness of an injured seal." *The Spectator*, Dec. 11, 1936. This film also carried the title *River of Unrest*.

4. Cavin O'Connor int. TAD, Mar. 13, 1988.

5. *London Daily Sketch*, Dec. 9, 1936. In a close-up piece, that journal noted that "a rather Hibernian nose promptly betrays his sense of humour—that is, in conjunction with a pair of very dark and twinkling eyes!" Edna Barnes, "Six-Feet-Three of Personality," *London Daily Sketch*, Apr. 6, 1936.

6. FBL to Gloria Braggiotti, Aug. 1936.

7. Richard Haestier, "A Slick Film," *London Star*, Jan. 29, 1937.

8. Throughout her life, and long after history's condemnation of Mussolini, Francesca viewed Il Duce as "a hero, a saviour, a great man." As late as the 1990s she remembered his magnetic personality: "I heard him speak . . . his sincerity was loud and convincing. . . . Mussolini was adored around the world." Among her prized photographs was an autographed portrait of the dictator. Recollections of 1936-1939, FBL to TAD, c. 1990.

9. Bosley Crowther, "At the Squire: 'Scipio Africanus,' " *New York Times*, Sep. 23, 1939.

10. A. T. Borthwick, "Bulldog Drummond Knocks His Man Out," *London News Chronicle*, Jan. 11, 1937.

11. William K. Everson, *The Detective in Film* (Secaucus, NJ: Citadel Press, 1972), 67.

12. EDL to JDL, May 31, 1937.

13. "English Day Out: A Film of Bank Holiday," *Liverpool Post*, Mar. 9, 1938. "The role is a graceless one. He is called upon to suffer, usually to music, and it is not his fault if you suffer too." *New York Herald Tribune*, June 2, 1938.

14. Jeff Walden, BBC Archives Centre to TAD, May 24, 1988.

15. Jack Dunfee to JDL, Dec. 22, 1937.

16. FBL to JDL, c. 1938.

17. EDL to JDL, July 4, 1938.

18. EDL to JDL, Aug. 14, 1938.

19. EDL to JDL, Aug. 14, 1938.

20. EDL to JDL, Sep. 13, 1938.

21. Lucius Beebe, "Stage Asides: In Spite of Boston's Dismay," *New York Herald Tribune*, Feb. 1, 1942.

22. EDL to JDL, Aug. 10, 1938.

23. "At the World: 'The Pasha's Wives,' " *New York Times*, Apr. 6, 1942.

24. Assia Noris to TAD, Oct. 6, 1997. French and American screen treatments followed: *Battement De Coeur* (1939), with Danielle Darrieux and Claude Dauphin, and *Heartbeat* (1946), with Ginger Rogers and Jean Pierre Aumont.

25. FBL to Gloria B. Etting, Sep. 1938.

26. Colin Ives to JDL, June 23, 1939.

27. FBL to Gloria B. Etting, Aug. 1, 1939; June 10, 1939.

28. Edwige Feuillère int. TAD, Apr. 12, 1988.

29. Feuillère int. TAD.

30. FBL to Gloria B. Etting, Aug. 27, 1939.

31. Charles Higham, *Rose: The Life and Times of Rose Fitzgerald Kennedy* (New York: Pocket Books, 1995), 210.

9. Watch on the Rhine

1. Radio talk, WQXR-New York, Oct. 27, 1939.

2. JDL to Eugene Tuscherer, Nov. 2, 1939.

3. "Lisa Sergio's Column of the Air," WQXR-New York, Mar. 14, 1940.

4. "Lisa Sergio's Column of the Air."

5. Tuscherer to JDL, c. July 1940.

6. Bosley Crowther, "The Screen," *New York Times*, Oct. 30, 1940.

7. "Ogunquit Playhouse: 'Amphitryon 38,' " *Boston Globe*, Aug. 6, 1940.

8. The non-musical version starred Melvyn Douglas opposite his future wife Helen Gahagan. A stage and film actress, she entered politics in the early 1940s and was elected to Congress from California in 1944.

9. JDL to HCLJr, Dec. 19, 1940.

10. John's performance was not written off by all critics. For example, John Mason Brown noted that "Mr. Lodge, who is given some awful things to say and do manages to get away with them surprisingly well. He is handsome, has a flair for comedy, has an excellent speaking voice, has lost all of his early stiffness as a movie actor, and appears behind the footlights not only as a man but as a gentleman, which is rarer still." " 'Night of Love' Comes to the Hudson Theatre," *New York Post*, Jan. 8, 1941.

11. Brooks Atkinson, "Watch on the Rhine," *New York Times*, Apr. 2, 1941.

12. William Wright, *Lillian Hellman: The Image, The Woman* (New York: Simon and Schuster, 1986), 176-77.

13. JDL to Maxwell Rabb, Jan. 29, 1941; Max Ophuls to JDL, Sep. 4, 1941.

14. JDL to EDL, Feb. 27, 1942.

15. " 'Watch on Rhine' Seen By President," *New York Times*, Jan. 26, 1942.

16. Script of Lucille Watson's Proposed Talk over CBS Radio, Feb. 1952.

17. "Unite Now To Win War, Walsh Says," *Boston Post*, Mar. 18, 1942.

18. Warner contractee Donald Woods played David. The film, released in 1943, brought the studio much prestige but very little profit. Paul Lukas won an Academy Award and Lucille Watson was nominated in the category of supporting actress.

10. A Military Bearing

1. Thomas W. Dewart int. TAD, Dec. 7, 1987.

2. E. O. Kollmorgen to Cmdr. R. A. Brown, Oct. 23, 1942.

3. JDL, Speech at War Labor Recruiting Drive, c. 1945.

4. Robert Morris int. TAD, Sep. 6, 1988. Morris afterwards served as president of the University of Dallas and was a perennial candidate for the U.S. Senate.

5. The key narrative source for Lodge's wartime experiences in the Mediterranean is Oral History Research Office, Columbia University, interview by John T. Mason, Jr., Oct. 5, 1967, 5-21.

6. JDL to Matilda Frelinghuysen, July 13, 1943.

7. JDL to Matilda Frelinghuysen, July 13, 1943.

8. Memorandum (classified SECRET) on U.S. Relations with French Navy, JDL to Rear Admiral Lyal A. Davidson, USN, Feb. 12, 1945.

9. Memorandum (classified SECRET) on U.S. Relations with French Navy.

10. "U.S. Senators Tell Cairo Newsman Allied Unity Will Assure The Peace," U.S. Office of War Information Press Release, Aug. 18, 1943.

11. Henry A. Dudley int. TAD, Oct. 6, 1988.

12. Like Lodge, Fairbanks learned to speak French well when he was nine and living in Paris with his mother. After the war, he became a commander in the U.S.N. Reserve and Knight Commander of the British Empire. As much a diplomat as an actor, he was once described "as a one-man signpost in Anglo-American friendship." Geoff Jeffreys, "Doug Invited The Queen to Dinner," *Singapore Times*, Jan. 4, 1953.

13. Excerpts, Quartermaster's Log, Aboard USS *Ancon*, Sep. 6-10, 1943.

14. Samuel Eliot Morison, *History of United States Naval Operations in World War II: Sicily-Salerno-Anzio, January 1943-June 1944*, vol. 9 (Boston: Little Brown, 1954), 252-53.

15. "There was no surprise. They were waiting for us. . . . They blanketed that whole beach of Salerno. . . . We were subjected to constant bombardment." JDL, Oral History, 15.

16. Quartermaster's Log.

17. JDL, Oral History, 16.

18. JDL, Notes on Salerno invasion, Sep. 11, 1943.

19. JDL, Notes on Salerno invasion, Sep. 15, 1943.

20. Philip Francoeur int. TAD, July 14, 1988.

21. JDL to Sherman Prindiville, Jan. 2, 1944.

22. Robert Prindiville to JDL, Mar. 14, 1944.

23. JDL to HCLJr, Jan. 26, 1944.

24. JDL to HCLJr, Jan. 26, 1944.

25. JDL to Major General Willis D. Crittenberger, May 4, 1944.

26. "I guess it was a relatively small minority (of naval officers) that actually saw battle. So I think I was rather lucky, because I'm not an indoctrinated naval officer. . . . I'm not qualified to take command of a ship." Oral History, 20.

27. Anson C. Piper to TAD, Aug. 25, 1988.

28. JDL to PRO COMTHREE, July 29, 1944.

29. JDL to Lt. Frank A. Sinon, Aug. 13, 1944.

30. *The Navy Reports*, WHN-New York, May 3, 1945.

31. Memorial Day Address, WEAF-New York, May 30, 1945.

32. JDL to Captain G. Francis Mentz, Nov. 20, 1945.

33. Address, "The Challenge of Peace," Bronx, NY, Rotary Club, Nov. 20, 1945.

11. Politics: The Family Business

1. "There is a Tide," (unpublished ms), 1945.

2. Lily Lodge int. TAD, Apr. 6, 1988.

3. Lily Lodge int. TAD, Apr. 6, 1988.

4. William I. Nichols int. TAD, Apr. 20, 1995. Nichols graduated from Harvard in 1926.

5. Olive Montgomery int. TAD, June 6, 1989.

6. Denis W. Brogan, *The Free State* (New York: Alfred A. Knopf, 1945), 49.

7. Henry Dudley int. TAD, Oct. 6, 1988.

8. Francesca, baptized in the Anglican Church, converted to Catholicism about the same time. Some viewed it as a political move as much as a spiritual step in order to attract the Italian-American vote.

9. "New Canaan Marks Memorial Day with Hundreds Taking Part," *New Canaan Advertiser*, June 6, 1946.

10. "New Canaan Marks Memorial Day with Hundreds Taking Part."

11. Florence Wessels, "Scion of Noted Family Battles for Tax Slash," *New York Journal-American*, c. Oct. 1946.

12. "I think she was ultimately sad over giving up her House seat, and gambled on the hope she would be in line for something bigger, such as a Cabinet post." Letitia Baldridge int. TAD, Aug. 5, 1988. Baldridge served as an aide to Luce during her ambassadorship to Rome in the 1950s.

13. Stephen Shadegg, *Clare Boothe Luce* (New York: Simon & Schuster, 1970), 214-15.

14. JDL, Acceptance Speech, Congressional Convention for Congress, 4th District, Sep. 14, 1946.

15. Robert McG. Thomas, Jr., "Henry A. Mucci Dies at 88; Rescued Survivors of Bataan," *New York Times*, Apr. 24, 1997.

16. JDL, "Mr. Lodge Recalls Brennan's Antagonism," *Hartford Courant*, July 2, 1971.

17. "C.I.O. Union Leaders Endorse Lodge and Mucci in Broadcasts," *Bridgeport Post*, Oct. 29, 1946.

18. JDL, Remarks, South Norwalk, CT (ms), Nov. 3, 1946.

19. JDL, Oral History, Oct. 5, 1967, 24-25.

20. Leland Miles int. TAD, June 15, 1988.

21. Campaign flyer (undated and unsigned).

22. "Lodge Gets Tidings from Predecessor, Expresses Gratitude," *Norwalk Hour*, Nov. 6, 1946.

23. "G.O.P. Facing Challenge To Keep Peace, Lodge Says," *Bridgeport Telegram*, Nov. 15, 1946.

24. Robert E. Rogers, "This is Life," *Boston American*, Sep. 13, 1934.

25. Baldridge int. TAD.

26. Sig Sakowicz int. JDL, Chicago radio, Feb. 1967.

27. Shirley Temple proved the on-screen centerpiece with Reagan in *That Hagan Girl* (1947). George Murphy and Reagan teamed up for *This is the Army* (1943).

28. At the end of his Administration, Reagan said acting had prepared him for the criticism that comes to any President, no matter how popular. Julie Johnson, "The Soviets Still Leave Reagan Uneasy," *New York Times*, Jan. 19, 1989.

29. JDL to Edward G. Robinson, Oct. 19, 1953.

12. Challenge of the Hour

1. Robert Jackson to JDL, Nov. 15, 1946.

2. "Rendezvous with Countess Fairfield," *Bridgeport Herald*, Feb. 9, 1947.

3. JDL, Speech, House of Representatives, June 6, 1947, as reported in Report From Your Congressman, No. 6, June 1947.

4. Report From Your Congressman, No. 4, Apr. 1947.

5. JDL Diary, European Trip, Sep.-Nov. 1947.

6. Peter Stephaich to TAD, Mar. 5, 1989; Peter Stephaich int. TAD, Apr. 25, 26, 1989.

7. Walter Judd int. TAD, Jan. 8, 1988.

8. "U.S. Congressmen at Petkov's Grave," *New York Times*, Oct. 2, 1947.

9. Judd. Judd described Lodge as a progressive conservative—"one to build on what has been successful . . . to move ahead to improve on it."

10. "Communist Surge Pictured," *New York Times*, Nov. 14, 1947.

11. JDL, Address, "The Challenge of the Hour" (Washington: U.S. Printing Office, 1947), 3.

12. Lodge, "Challenge," 15.

13. Paul H. Nitze int. TAD, Oct. 5, 1988.

14. Lee Edwards, *Missionary for Freedom* (New York: Paragon House, 1990), 155.

15. "Remarks of his Excellency, John Lodge, Governor of Connecticut at Annual Dinner of Faetana Society of Bridgeport," *La Lucerna*, Apr. 1953

16. "Communism is Seen At Halt in Europe," *New York Times*, Dec. 12, 1947.

17. Report From Your Congressman, No. 1, Jan. 1949.

18. JDL to HCLJr., Dec. 5, 1984.

19. HCLJr, "Some Random Memories" (ms), 1984.

20. Egidio Ortona, *Anni D'America: La Ricostruzione—1944/1951* (Bologna: Il Mulino, 1984), 225-29, 287-89.

21. John Patrick Carroll-Abbing, *A Chance To Live: The Story of the Lost Children of the War* (New York: Longmans, Green, 1952), 6.

22. Elizabeth B. Lamont, "Origins and History of the Darien Book Aid Plan" (ms), c. 1960.

13. Congressional Camaraderie

1. Tere Pascone, "Gaston's Campaign to Unseat Lodge as District's Congressman Has All the Hoopla of Vaudeville, Plays Every Town in County," *Bridgeport Post*, Oct. 17, 1948.

2. William A. Gaston to TAD, Oct. 15, 1988. Lodge also prospered from his Boston-managed trust left by his grandfather. Of his 1947 reported income of some $31,000, over $11,400 came from this trust and $5,000 from his own portfolio. His Congressional salary and travel allowance totaled $13,750, and he wrote off all but $2,000 as expenses for travel, lodging and meals, and business entertainment. Francesca earned $980 from dancing and writing. Their tax bill for 1947: $3,745.84.

3. "Gaston Still Chasing John 'Dodging' Lodge," *Bridgeport Sunday Herald*, Oct. 17, 1948.

4. "Rep Lodge Rounds Out Campaign With a Punch," *New York Journal-American*, Oct. 31, 1948.

5. Rama Braggiotti int. TAD, Dec. 21, 1988.

6. Gerald R. Ford to TAD, July 6, 1989.

7. "$200,000,000 Help Asked for China," *New York Times*, Aug. 9, 1949.

8. JDL to Walter Judd, Feb. 21, 1951.

9. JDL int. Former Members of Congress Oral History Collection, 1976, 2.

10. Glenn Davis int. TAD, Jan. 7, 1988. Lodge voted with his party 82 percent of the time in his first term and 64 percent in his second term. *Congressional Quarterly Almanac*, vol. 6, 1950, 60.

11. Donald Deschner, *The Complete Films of Cary Grant* (Secaucus, NJ: Citadel Press, 1973), 58.

12. Davis int. TAD.

13. *Bulletin of America's Town Meeting of the Air*, Nov. 15, 1949, 3-8.

14. "J. D. Lodge Scores Policy on Formosa," *New York Times*, Jan. 29, 1950.

15. JDL, Remarks on the Floor of the House of Representatives, May 18, 1950.

16. JDL, Remarks on the Floor of the House of Representatives.

17. HCLJr, "Grandson Backs His Elder," *LIFE*, Sep. 14, 1953. A more recent pro-Lodge analysis is the letter to the editor by John Karol, "Wilson Brought the League of Nations Debacle on Himself," *New York Times*, Jan. 19, 1988.

18. Frances Bolton to JDL, Dec. 1950.

19. Judd int. TAD.

14. Affairs of State

1. Raymond E. Baldwin int. Oral History Research Office, Columbia University, May 6, 1971.

2. Until his interim appointment, Benton had never registered as a Democrat and had even contributed to Mrs. Luce's congressional campaign.

3. Katharine A. H. Smith int. TAD, Sep. 9, 1988.

4. Stanley Marcus to TAD, Aug. 31, 1988.

5. Jack Zaiman int. TAD, Feb. 4, 1989.

6. Chester Bowles, *Promises To Keep: My Years in Public Life, 1941-1969* (New York: Harper & Row, 1971), 176.

7. Joseph I. Lieberman, *The Legacy: Connecticut Politics 1930-1980* (Hartford: Spoonwood Press, 1981), 40. Connecticut Attorney General from 1983 to 1988, Lieberman was elected U.S. Senator in 1988.

8. "Lodge Receptive in Racing Bowles," *New York Times*, Apr. 16, 1950.

9. Frank A. Wooding, "Lowdown on Lodge," *Bridgeport Herald*, July 15, 1951.

10. "The Tragedy of Harold Mitchell," *Bridgeport Herald*, June 25, 1950.

11. JDL, Oral History, Oct. 9, 1967, 47-48.

12. JDL, Acceptance Speech as nominee for CT governor (ms), June 15, 1950.

13. Charles S. House int. TAD, Nov. 17, 1987.

14. H. I. Phillips, "Hollywood, Congress, Points East," *Waterbury Republican*, June 24, 1950.

15. "Bailey says Lodge 'Leans on Tinsel' in Bowles Attack," *Milford Citizen*, Aug. 25, 1950.

16. JDL, television talk, WNHC-New Haven, Nov. 3, 1950; "Bowles and Lodge Battle Over ADA," *Bridgeport Telegram*, Nov. 4, 1950.

17. JDL, Oral History, 34-36.

18. "Candidate's Wife Rides Truck To Attend Dinner in This City," *New Britain Herald*, Oct. 13, 1950.

19. Henry Woodbridge int. TAD, June 7, 1988.

20. In Connecticut, ethnic minorities tended to be Democratic and largely Catholic. For any hope of election, both Lodges needed to court such groups.

21. HCLJr, Remarks, New Haven, CT (ms), Nov. 4, 1950, 1.

22. Bowles, 238. Adds Bowles: "Lodge was an example of an amateur politician who thinks that professional politics involves foul play as a matter of course. He was also a good example of a conservative without a program" (234).

23. Prescott S. Bush, Jr. int. TAD, Dec. 12, 1988.

24. Hatch, 239.

25. "Governor-Elect Lodge," *New Haven Register*, Nov. 8, 1950.

26. "Victory as Governor," *Hartford Times*, Nov. 8, 1950.

27. Edward N. Allen to JDL, Dec. 7, 1950.

28. "McMahon Voted Man of the Year," *Bridgeport Herald*, Dec. 31, 1950.

29. Joseph I. Lieberman, *The Power Broker: A Biography of John M. Bailey, Modern Political Boss* (Boston: Houghton-Mifflin, 1966), 153.

30. Tere Pascone, "The Lodges Take Over As Connecticut's First Family," *Bridgeport Post*, Jan. 7, 1951.

31. "Father's Play Gives Lodge Theme of Talk," *Bridgeport Herald*, Jan. 7, 1951; JDL, Governor's Inaugural Message, Jan. 3, 1951.

32. "Connecticut Follies," *New York Times*, Jan. 6, 1951.

15. Strife and Fair Play in the Political Arena

1. Bowles once calculated that in order to live in equal comfort, an individual would have required a private income of at least $150,000 a year. Bowles, 191.

2. Florence Berkman int. TAD, May 19, 1988.

3. A. B. McGinley, "Saints, Sinners Singsong Lodge Winter 'Fall Guy,' " *Hartford Times*, Feb. 26, 1951.

4. Raymond Watt to Francis McCarthy, Jan. 19, 1951.

5. Lieberman, *The Legacy*, 49-51.

6. Allan Jackson News Program, CBS Radio, Dec. 10, 1952.

7. Lodge's special assistant in Madrid from 1959 to 1961, Fred Sacksteder notes that John even "thanked people for their thank-you letters. His semi-personal correspondence always opened and closed in long hand. It was very British." Fred Sacksteder int. TAD, Oct. 21, 1995.

8. "Lily Lodge Plays The Lead," *Connecticut Circle*, Apr. 1952, 18.

9. JDL to George Santayana, Sep. 5, 1951.

10. Edward Allen to JDL, Aug. 23, 1951.

11. Jack Zaiman, "State Trend Seen Away From GOP," *Hartford Courant*, June 12, 1951; Zaiman, "Lodge's Acts Cause Rift In State GOP," *Hartford Courant*, June 13, 1951.

12. Henry S. Lodge int. TAD, May 24, 1988.

13. Dwight D. Eisenhower, *Mandate for Change: The White House Years, 1953-56* (Garden City, NY: Doubleday, 1963), 16.

14. "Gov. Lodge Starts Drive to Swing Connecticut Behind Eisenhower," *New York Herald Tribune*, Feb. 6, 1952.

15. "Gov. Lodge Starts Drive to Swing Connecticut Behind Eisenhower."

16. Stewart and Joseph Alsop, "The Lesson of New Hampshire," *Hartford Courant*, Mar. 14, 1952.

17. Morty Freedman, "Lodge Comes Out for Ike; Scores Administration," *St. Petersburg Times*, Feb. 23, 1952.

18. JDL, Oral History, Oct. 9, 1967, 68-69.

19. John W. Wood to JDL, Apr. 7, 1952.

20. Mrs. Lodge generally followed Cabot's "line" of thinking in such matters. In family conferences, he declared that "there is room for only one Lodge in the Senate." John O'Donnell, "Capital Stuff," New York *Daily News*, July 29, 1952. "The Lodge brothers both wanted Cabinet posts and obviously both couldn't. I was in the middle of that problem at times." Meade Alcorn int., Oral History Collection, Columbia University, June 5, 1967.

21. Prescott Bush, Jr. int. TAD, Dec. 12, 1988.

22. John paid $10 a day for his room at the Inn. When other delegates raved about their quarters at the posh Edgewater Beach Hotel, he injected, "There are no luxury hotels in the United States." John Alsop int. TAD, Nov. 18, 1987.

23. Quoted in Roslyn Kaiser, "W'porters Remember Ike," *Westport News*, Apr. 3, 1969.

24. Max Rabb int. TAD, Aug. 15, 1996.

25. Herbert Brownell int. TAD, Aug. 15, 1988. For an in-depth account, see Herbert Brownell, *Advising Ike* (Lawrence, KS: University Press of Kansas, 1993).

26. "Lodge's Connections Gave State Key Convention Role," *New Haven Register*, July 11, 1952; Meade Alcorn int. TAD, May 18, 1988.

27. JDL, Remarks, Republican National Convention, Chicago, July 7, 1952.

28. JDL, Remarks, Republican National Convention.

29. John Alsop int. TAD.

30. "Governor Lodge for Vice President?" *New Britain Herald*, July 8, 1952.

31. JDL, Oral History, 73; Peter Edson, "Here's How Nixon Picked as Ike's Running Mate," *Fremont (NE) Guide & Tribune*, Jan. 26, 1953.

32. The list reportedly consisted of Nixon, Thornton, Arthur Langlie, Driscoll, Knowland, Harold Stassen, and Cabot Lodge. Apparently, two months before the convention Dewey had sounded out Nixon and a "deal was made." Brownell, too, let it be known that vice presidential "lightning could strike Nixon" in return for the latter's support within the seventy-member delegation from California, which nominally was committed to favorite son Earl Warren. William Costello, *The Facts About Nixon: An Unauthorized Biography* (New York: Viking Press, 1960), 84, 89-92.

33. Brownell int. TAD.

34. JDL, Oral History, 78.

35. Alan Olmstead, "Twixt Connecticut and Rome," *Waterbury Republican*, Dec. 9, 1952.

36. Frank Wooding, "Lowdown on Lodge," *Bridgeport Herald*, July 29, 1951; A.H. Olmstead, "Connecticut Yankee," *Bridgeport Telegram*, Aug. 28, 1952.

37. "Mrs. Luce Says Lodge Refuses to Back Her," *Bridgeport Telegram*, Aug. 29, 1952.

38. "Mrs. Luce Plans to Carry Fight to Convention Floor," *Bridgeport Telegram*, Aug. 30, 1952.

39. Bush, Jr. int. TAD.

40. Henry R. Luce to JDL, Sep. 5, 1952.

41. JDL to Henry R. Luce, Sep. 1952.

42. Zaiman int. TAD.

43. "The Other Republicans," *Life*, Sep. 29, 1952. Earlier *Life* noted that Kennedy is "a fine young man . . . is smart and has smart advisers—as witness the fact that he fired the first big gun of his campaign last week with a demand that President Truman call a special session of Congress to pass a new price control law" (Aug. 25, 1952).

44. HCLJr to Henry R. Luce, Oct. 1952.

45. House int. TAD.

46. Donald L. Jackson to JDL, Oct. 22, 1952.

47. Dwight D. Eisenhower to JDL, Nov. 10., 1952.

48. Brooks Harlow to JDL, Sep. 11, 1952. Harlow was a Harvard classmate and loyal supporter of John.

49. Robert Cutler to JDL, Nov. 14, 1952.

50. JDL int., Oral History, 91.

51. "Lodge Steals Show Visiting Puerto Rico," *Hartford Courant*, Jan. 23, 1953.

16. A Lincoln Republican

1. Roger Dove, "Connecticut," *Town & Country*, Mar. 1953.

2. Florence Berkman int. TAD, May 19, 1988; Rockwell Hollands, "People

and Politics: Lodge and Brennan," *Stamford Advocate*, Apr. 11, 1953. See JDL, "Mr. Lodge Recalls Brennan's Antagonism," *Hartford Courant*, July 2, 1971.

3. John W. Boyd int. TAD, Aug. 6, 1998.

4. Lawrence Gilman int. TAD, June 14, 1988.

5. "House Stifles Gilman Attack By Democrats," *New Haven Register*, Feb. 26, 1953.

6. JDL, Oral History, 42.

7. Gilman; "Mr. Steinkraus' Dinner," *Bridgeport Post*, Feb. 4, 1953.

8. Richard Ficks int. TAD, July 5, 1990; Richard Ficks to JDL, Mar. 12, 1974. Prior to serving JDL, Ficks was a reporter on the Hartford bureau of the United Press International.

9. Gilman int. TAD.

10. JDL, Oral History, 41.

11. John H. Pinkerman, "GOP Seen Bypassing Ray Baldwin as Chief Justice," *Westport Town Crier*, Jan. 29, 1953. The anti-Baldwin feeling was so strong that he once was greeted politely but not cordially by a group of Republicans. One of them caustically said to another, "I thought I heard the sound of 30 pieces of silver." When Inglis retired in 1958, Democratic Governor Ribicoff named the 65-year-old Baldwin Chief Justice.

12. Richard Joyce Smith int. TAD, Jan. 19, 1989. Smith observed that Lodge had the "fatal mistake" of being too good-looking for a politician.

13. JDL, Oral History, Oct. 5, 1967, 37. Commission members included Lt. Gen. Leslie R. Groves, former head of the Manhattan Project; Dr. Karl T. Compton of MIT; Dr. Shields Warren of New England Deaconess Hospital, and William Webster of New England Electric System. Press Release, Gov. Lodge's Office, Mar. 18, 1954.

14. "John Bailey plays the game as he understands the game," observed JDL in 1967. "You know, he aims for the jugular all the time, and sometimes it's quite effective. What you call a gut player." JDL, Oral History, 94.

15. Keith Schronrock, "Extra Curricular Demands Complicate Governor's Job," *Hartford Courant*, Dec. 13, 1953.

16. "Governor's Diary," *Connecticut State Journal*, July 1954.

17. Meade Alcorn, "Let Us Keep Pace with His Greatness," Mar. 1953.

18. JDL, Oral History, 89; John Foster Dulles to JDL, Oct. 1953.

19. Jack Neal int. TAD, Oct. 24, 1988.

20. JDL, Oral History, 90-91.

21. JDL, Remarks, CBS Radio-WDRC-Hartford, Nov. 22, 1953, FBLP.

22. "Mrs. Luce Hailed at Dinner Marking Farewell Tribute," *Bridgeport Post*, Apr. 11, 1953.

23. Clare Boothe Luce to JDL-FBL, July 29, 1953. By 1959 Luce wanted to be the first woman nominated for Vice President and maneuvered to gain Eisenhower's support. Meade Alcorn int., Oral History, Columbia University, Feb. 8, 1967.

24. Deane Keller to Regina Tomlin, Dec. 10, 1954.

25. "Official Lodge Portrait Unveiled," *Hartford Times*, Oct. 16, 1954.

26. John was a master of "off the cuff" remarks, but Coote pushed scripted talks which often were too long and esoteric. "Coote kept Lodge on a leash. Lodge was an aristocrat but not standoffish. He had a lot of friends in labor-type jobs." Ficks int.

27. Zaiman int. TAD.

28. JDL, Oral History, 66.

29. Sen. Prescott Bush long urged him to run. "You have a splendid record. . . . No one else we could nominate would have such a record. Furthermore, I think it is widely appreciated at the voting level, and that is what counts." Prescott Bush to JDL, Apr. 22, 1954.

30. Edmund O'Brien int. TAD, Oct. 19, 1987.

31. George E. Sokolsky, "Today's Connecticut Story," *Long Island Press*, July 6, 1954.

32. Alcorn int., Oral History.

33. JDL, 43.

34. JDL, "Politics Is Everybody's Business," *New York Times Magazine*, Sep. 19, 1954.

35. "Lodge Absentee Governor Bailey Charge," *Meriden Record*, Aug. 31, 1954.

36. Abraham Ribicoff int., Oral History, Columbia University, Jan. 24, 1989.

37. Ribicoff int., Oral History.

38. "John Bailey Must Be Worried," *New Britain Herald*, Oct. 26, 1954.

39. "McGuire Backs Lodge in Split with Party," *New Haven Journal-Courier*, Oct. 29, 1954.

40. "Where John Lodge Lost," *Connecticut State Journal*, Nov. 1954.

41. John L. Ericson, "Lodge Remembered," *New Britain Herald*, Nov. 4, 1985.

42. Ribicoff int., Oral History.

43. Ribicoff int., Oral History.

44. "Lodge Victory Celebration Crushed by Prediction Error," *New Haven Register*, Nov. 3, 1954.

45. "Lodge Victory Celebration Crushed by Prediction Error,"

46. Roger Dove, "Republicans' Joy Turns to Gloom at Mansion," *Hartford Courant*, Nov. 4, 1954.

47. Alsop int. TAD.

48. Ribicoff int., Oral History, May 15, 1989.

49. Keith Schronrock, "Lodge Received $11,455 in Campaign Donations," *Hartford Courant*, Nov. 23, 1954.

50. Tere Pascone, "Francesca Held Not to Blame for Husband's Election Defeat," *Bridgeport Post*, Nov. 8, 1952.

51. Zaiman int. TAD.

52. Moses Berkman, "World of Politics," *Hartford Times*, Dec. 11, 1954.

17. New Constituents

1. JDL to Frederic R. Coudert, Jr., Mar. 27, 1958. Coudert served six terms (1947-59) as a Republican Congressman from Manhattan.

2. Rama Braggiotti int. TAD, Dec. 21, 1988.

3. HCLJr to JDL, Nov. 4, 1954.

4. Thomas Dewart int. TAD, Dec. 7, 1987.

5. In 1988, Francesca stated that Cabot did encourage Eisenhower to appoint John to Spain, adding it was the "only good thing Cabot ever did." But soon thereafter Cabot thought his brother too unwell to handle a diplomatic post. Vice President Nixon wrote: "I want you to know that if you could be prevailed upon to take a position in Washington you will find me in your corner." RN to JDL, Nov. 19, 1954.

6. Chadwick Braggiotti int. TAD, Feb. 1, 1988.

7. Chadwick Braggiotti int. TAD.

8. Former Senator William Benton suggested that he consider a career in the Foreign Service: "I do not say this out of any desire to induce you to turn your back on Connecticut. . . . I think you might find it a very rewarding career. . . . I remember too your constructive interest in my problems in the State Department when you were a member of the Foreign Affairs Committee." William Benton to JDL, Dec. 3, 1954.

9. By 1957 the U.S. Information Service was answering 2,000 letters a week from Spaniards asking about American life. This agency also furnished news of America to radio stations and newspapers. William J. Clew, "Lodge Hailed In Spain As Great Ambassador," *Hartford Courant*, Sep. 27, 1957.

10. American and Spanish architects criticized the Embassy because it did not harmonize with the surrounding buildings. One suggested it followed the "Hitlerian style." Some referred to it as a pocket edition of the UN headquarters in New York. "8 Story Embassy in Madrid for U.S.," *London Times*, Apr. 26, 1955.

11. Chadwick Braggiotti int. TAD.

12. "When he lost the race for re-election as Governor of Connecticut, I never saw him as dejected as he was (It was really bad) but some two years later when he invited me to a party at the Embassy in Madrid he was his old bouncey self." Edward W. Marshall to TAD, Nov. 14, 1988.

13. "Lodge Presents Credentials, His Family Impresses Press," *Spanish-American Courier*, Mar. 24, 1955.

14. Benjamin Welles, *Spain: The Gentle Anarchy* (New York: Praeger, 1965), 291.

15. Welles, 242.

16. Cabot Sedgwick to TAD, June 8, 1998.

17. JDL to Albert W. Coote, Aug. 5, 1955.

18. EDL to JDL, June 7, 1955.

19. Beatrice Lodge Oyarzabal int. TAD, Feb. 26, 1988.

20. Don Ross, "The Brothers Lodge Confer Here on Strategy to Get Spain Into U.N.," *New York Herald Tribune*, Dec. 7, 1955.

21. Joaquín Calvo Sotelo int. TAD, Feb. 29, 1988.

22. Arthur Krock, "In the Nation," *New York Times*, May 23, 1957.

23. Albert Gelardin int. TAD, Feb. 29, 1988.

24. "Spaniards always wore military dress at diplomatic dinners," Lily Lodge int. TAD, May 6, 1988.

25. Drew Pearson, "Envoy Is Spared Porter's Tirade," (The Washington Merry-Go-Round), Bell Syndicate, 1959.

26. JDL, Oral History, Feb. 20, 1969, 152.

27. Antonio Carrigues int. TAD, Feb. 25, 1988.

28. HCLJr to JDL, Jan. 24, 1956; Feb. 24, 1956.

29. Brownell int., Feb. 11, 1988.

30. Jack Noel int. TAD, Feb. 3, 1988.

31. Welles, 261.

32. Katherine Pinto-Cuello int. TAD, Feb. 27, 1988.

33. Archibald Roosevelt int. TAD, Oct. 6, 1988. Upon Roosevelt's selection as a Rhodes Scholar in 1938, the 20-year-old Harvard senior was reported to have mastered 13 languages. "Archibald B. Roosevelt, Jr. Wins Rhodes Award on 4 Hours Sleep," *New York Herald Tribune*, Dec. 18, 1938.

34. Roosevelt; Frederick Sackstader int. TAD, Oct. 21, 1995. Roosevelt described Spain as a moderate dictatorship with occasional censorship and some discrimination against non-Catholics.

35. William B. Sowash to TAD, May 20, 1990.

36. "Sen. Mansfield Apologizes to Envoy Lodge," *Stars and Stripes*, Jan. 17, 1958.

37. "Time Clocks for Ambassadors?" *Hartford Courant*, Oct. 23, 1958.

38. JDL, "Spain Today," Address at University of Bridgeport (ms), Jan. 9, 1957, 4.

39. JDL, "An Ambassador Looks At His Embassy," Address at University of Bridgeport (ms), Jan. 9, 1957, 2.

40. JDL, "An Ambassador Looks At His Embassy," 8.

18. Life in Spain

1. Aline, Countess of Romanones int. TAD, Mar. 6, 1989.

2. Aline, Countess of Romanones, *The Spy Wore Red* (New York: Random House, 1987).

3. Bob Hope, *I Owe Russia $1200* (Garden City, NY: Doubleday, 1963), 172.

4. Hope, 172.

5. Marcella Cisney to TAD, Oct. 30, 1988.

6. Maria Rodriguez int. TAD, Mar. 29, 1988.

7. Christina Hawkins int. TAD, Oct. 6, 1988; Christina Hawkins, "A Tale of Three Horses" (ms), Oct. 5, 1989, FBLP.

8. George S. Moore, *The Banker's Life* (New York: Norton, 1987), 274.

9. George S. Moore to FBL, Aug. 14, 1987, FBLP.

19. A Spanish *Abrazo*

1. JDL to HCLJr, Apr. 25, 1958.

2. HCLJr to JDL, May 1, 1958.

3. JDL to HCLJr, May 26, 1958.

4. HCLJr to JDL, June 9, 1958.

5. JDL to HCLJr, June 16, 1958.

6. JDL to HCLJr, June 16, 1958.

7. JDL to HCLJr, Sep. 12, 1958.

8. Chadwick Braggiotti int. TAD, Feb. 1, 1988.

9. Robert L. Bliss to FBL, Dec. 5, 1958; Benjamin Welles int. TAD, Oct. 21, 1990.

10. Milton Barall int. TAD, Jan. 6, 1988. "John preached economic modernization of Spain and its entrance into Europe, both politically and economically. That was laudable and probably the position of Eisenhower as well—certainly that of some of his Cabinet." Barall to TAD, Apr. 10, 1998.

11. In 1959 Spain was admitted as a full member into the organization for European Economic Cooperation and the IMF.

12. JDL to Mathias Plum, July 16, 1958.

13. Gene Tunney to JDL, Nov. 8, 1957.

14. HCLJr to JDL, Nov. 22, 1957.

15. Frank Oram int. TAD, Jan. 7, 1988.

16. Barbara T. Eisenhower Foltz to TAD, Jan. 21, 1990.

17. Benjamin Welles, *Spain: The Gentle Anarchy*, 248.

18. Vernon Walters int. TAD, June 24, 1988.

19. Foltz int. TAD.

20. Welles, 249-50.

21. Dwight D. Eisenhower, *Waging Peace: The White House Years, 1956-1961* (Garden City, NY: Doubleday, 1965), 509-10.

22. Eisenhower, 509-10.

23. Welles, 252.

24. Welles, 252.

25. JDL to HCLJr, Sep. 9, 1959.

26. JDL to HCLJr, Sep. 25, 1959.

27. "Morton Says Nixon Has Wide-Open Field," AP Release, Feb. 11, 1960.

28. Keith Schonrock, "John Lodge Ready to Campaign," *Hartford Courant*, July 26, 1960.

29. HCLJr to JDL, Aug. 30, 1960.

30. JDL to HCLJr, Sep. 8, 1960.

31. HCLJr to JDL, Sep. 10, 1960.

32. JDL to HCLJr, Sep. 13, 1960. John also contacted Nixon with an offer to return home and campaign. Nixon replied that it was not in the nation's best interest for ambassadors to engage in partisan activities "in these critical times." "Lodge Offer Declined By Nixon," *Waterbury American*, Sep. 12, 1960.

33. Edward C. Burke, "Lodge Foresees Negro in Cabinet," *New York Times*, Oct. 19, 1960.

34. JDL to RN, Nov. 9, 1960.

35. JDL to RN, Jan. 11, 1961.

36. RN to JDL, Jan. 19, 1961.

37. Christian A. Herter to JDL, Jan. 4, 1961; JDL to John F. Kennedy, Feb. 9, 1961.

38. JDL, Oral History, Oct. 9, 1967, 101.

39. Beatrice Lodge Oyarzabal int. TAD.

40. Temple Fielding to JDL, Jan. 24, 1961.

41. Quoted in Benjamin Welles, "Ambassador Remains Popular Although Spaniards Assail U.S.," *New York Times*, Apr. 17, 1961.

42. "Farewell to a Cordial Bostonian" (editorial), Madrid *El Pueblo*, Feb. 16, 1961.

43. "This Beautiful Friendship of Ours" (editorial), Barcelona *La Vanguardia*, Feb. 5, 1961.

44. FBL to JDL, Apr. 13, 1961.

20. Casting About

1. JDL, "John Davis Lodge Breaks Long Silence In Article," *Meriden Journal*, Aug. 5, 1961.

2. JDL, "John Davis Lodge Breaks Long Silence In Article."

3. JDL, Address, Middlebury College Commencement, Middlebury, VT (ms), June 12, 1961, 2.

4. A certain amount of aversion to Lodge still remained because of the Turnpike. To confront the matter once and for all, Republican Town Committeeman Allen Raymond suggested a billboard along this highway with the words: "Enjoying the Turnpike? John Lodge built it." Allen Raymond int. TAD, Mar. 10, 1997.

5. Bush, Jr. int.; "Politics: How Now, Nutmeg State?" *Time*, May 25, 1962.

6. John L. DeForest, Diary (unpublished), Yale University Library, May 17, 1962.

7. JDL, "I Don't Like What I See," Remarks at meeting of Young Republican League of New Haven County" (ms), May 22, 1962.

8. Statement, Lodge for Senator Committee, Westport, CT (ms), 1962.

9. Stamford attorney Donald Zezima was briefly considered as a nominee for Congressman-at-large and Lieutenant Governor. John Lupton and Joseph Adorno, however, won these nominations, respectively.

10. DeForest, June 4, 1962.

11. DeForest, June 6, 1962. The GOP, for the first time in Connecticut history, nominated a black, Atty. William D. Graham of Hartford, for a statewide elective office, that of State Treasurer.

12. Jack Zaiman, "Lodge's Defeat," *Hartford Courant*, June 11, 1962.

13. Lily Lodge to JDL, June 7, 1958.

14. Martin Arnold, "The Three Lives of Marcus: Charmer, Dreamer, Imposter," *New York Times*, June 24, 1968.

15. "205 Degrees Conferred At Colorful Ceremony," *The Alumni News: Hobart and William Smith Colleges*, June 1962.

16. Charles A. Mosher to JDL, Nov. 17, 1962.

17. E. H. Mosler, Jr. to JDL, July 27, 1962.

18. Press Release, Junior Achievement, Inc., Nov. 30, 1962.

19. Gerry Pratt, "Veteran Campaigner Thunders Eloquence," Portland *Oregonian*, Feb. 17, 1963.

20. Joseph J. Francomano int. TAD, Dec. 29, 1987.

21. Francomano int. TAD.

21. Political Tightropes

1. Anne Blair, *Lodge in Vietnam: A Patriot Abroad* (New Haven: Yale University Press, 1995), 4.

2. Miller, 352.

3. Blair, 72.

4. JDL to HCLJr, Dec. 9, 1963.

5. HCLJr to JDL, Dec. 16, 1963.

6. Alice Harlow int. TAD, Feb. 1, 1988.

7. Marge Chain Ellinger int. TAD, Sep. 17, 1988.

8. DeForest, Feb. 21, 1964.

9. DeForest. Lily Lodge gave birth to a son, James L. Marcus, Jr., the following day, February 22, 1964.

10. Helena de Streel to JDL, cMar. 1964.

11. Eugene Scalise int. TAD, Jan. 8, 1990. Scalise received 139 convention votes to Lodge's 330.

12. JDL, Acceptance Speech, Republican State Convention, Hartford (ms), June 13, 1964.

13. "John Lodge Addresses Convention," *Hartford Courant*, July 17, 1964.

14. Barry Goldwater, Acceptance Speech, Republican National Convention, San Francisco (ms), July 16, 1964.

15. JDL to Thruston Morton, July 19, 1964. At one point, the 16-vote Connecticut delegation pushed John for Vice President on the Goldwater ticket.

16. DeForest, Oct. 10, 1964.

17. Helen Hayes, Campaign luncheon, Cheshire, CT (audiotape), Sep. 28, 1964.

18. Hayes, Campaign luncheon.

19. "Cabot Lodge Pushes Care In Foreign Policy," *Waterbury Republican*, Oct. 25, 1964.

20. "Cabot Lodge Pushes Care In Foreign Policy."

21. "Connecticut and the Elections," *New York Times*, Oct. 22, 1964. In an earlier editorial on September 29, the *Times* described both Dodd and Lodge as "reasonably progressive on domestic issues, though their respective records in public office share a common thinness and superficiality. Mr. Lodge was a competent but uncreative Governor. His six years as Ambassador to Spain passed without incident, although he exhibited an uncritical enthusiasm for the Franco regime." "Questions for Connecticut," *New York Times*, Sep. 29, 1964.

22. JDL to RN, Nov. 7, 1964.

23. Barry Goldwater to JDL, Dec. 11, 1964; JDL to Barry Goldwater, Jan. 14, 1965.

24. JDL to William J. Miller, Dec. 12, 1964.

22. Relations, Foreign and Domestic

1. JDL, "Can NATO Be Restored?," *Orbis*, 10, No. 3 (Fall 1966), 724-36.

2. John A. Howard to JDL, Oct. 29, 1963.

3. John A. Howard to TAD, Nov. 30, 1988.

4. "Rare Lincoln Photo Presented By Lodge," *Bridgeport Sunday Post*, Feb. 12, 1967.

5. John Hallisey, " 'No Alternative' In Viet Nam," *Monterey Peninsula Herald*, June 23, 1965.

6. Cabot Lodge declined an honorary degree at Fairfield that May because he was going to take a vacation. JDL to FBL, Apr. 22, 1967. His refusal, once again, avoided "the brother act"—and an unusual dual degree presentation to the Lodges.

7. John's post-defeat pursuits in 1965, in the eyes of Francesca, put a "great wall" between them. "People, activities and fatigue have separated us and we have been miles apart. I have been very sad," she wrote en route to Spain. July 17, 1965.

8. Robert H. Michel to TAD, Nov. 17, 1988.

9. Diane Monk, "Mrs. Lodge 'outsocks' reporter," *Chicago Daily News*, Dec. 9, 1967.

10. JDL, "A Member Looks at the Constitutional Convention" (ms), Nov. 1965; "Why is There A Convention?" *Connecticut State Journal*, July-Aug. 1965, 18.

11. JDL to The Editor, "Policy Toward Spain," *New York Times*, Jan. 4, 1962.

12. Robert Mosher int. TAD, Mar. 3, 1988.

13. Jo and Luis Villalon, "Connecticut's Prophet Without Honor Seems To Be Riding A 'Winner' Again," *Westport Town Crier*, Feb. 15, 1968.

14. "Mrs. Lodge Takes Spotlight in Hub," *Boston Post*, Sep. 8, 1952.

15. JDL, " 'Losers' Who Came Back," editorial, *Westport Town Crier*, July 9, 1967.

16. JDL, "Guest Editorial," *New York Daily News*, Oct. 19, 1967; "Capital Bulletin," *National Review Bulletin*, May 23, 1967, 4-5.

17. RN to JDL, May 22, 1967. In 1968 Lodge visited a number of high-level Nixon backers in Palm Springs, including Walter Annenberg, Amory Houghton, and Thomas Gates. JDL to RN, Mar. 26, 1968.

18. RN to JDL, Nov. 14, 1967.

19. JDL to Chadwick Braggiotti, Jan. 13, 1968.

20. Richard Reeves, "Marcus, Ex-Lindsay Aide, Held with Corallo, a Mafia Leader, in Kickbacks on City Contract," *New York Times*, Dec. 19, 1967; Edward O'Neill and Paul Meskil, "Friends Say Marcus' Debts Exceed 200G," *New York Daily News*, Dec. 22, 1967.

21. "The Corrupters," editorial, *New York Times*, Dec. 20, 1967.

22. Bernard L. Collier, "Marcus Draws 15 Months on Federal Bribery Count," *New York Times*, Sep. 10, 1968.

23. John V. Lindsay to JDL, Dec. 28, 1967.

24. JDL to Elaine Ainley, Sep. 16, 1968.

25. John H. Fenton, "John Lodge Opens Campaign for Nixon in New Hampshire," *New York Times*, Jan. 17, 1968.

26. RN to JDL, Mar. 25, 1968.

27. Dwight D. Eisenhower to FBL, Mar. 30, 1968.

28. "Win On Second Ballot Predicted For Nixon," *Oregon Journal*, Apr. 30, 1968, 8J.

29. JDL to RN, July 29, 1968.

30. JDL to RN, July 29, 1968.

31. JDL to RN, Aug. 10, 1968.

32. Martha Kearney, "Man Supreme, Says Wife of John Lodge," *Boston Evening American*, Aug. 13, 1947.

33. "Sign Spells 'Nixon' on Great White Way," *New York Times*, Sep. 26, 1968; Douglas Leigh int. TAD, Mar. 13, 1991.

23. The Road to Argentina

1. JDL to RN, Dec. 19, 1969.

2. JDL to RN, Dec. 19, 1969.

3. FBL to JDL, Mar. 29, 1969.

4. Antonio de Oyarzabal int. TAD, Apr. 1, 1988.

5. Flora Lewis, "Why John Lodge Didn't Get Spain," *Hartford Courant*, June 29, 1969.

6. Benjamin Welles, "John Davis Lodge May Get O.A.S. Post," *New York Times*, Apr. 5, 1969.

7. JDL to RN, Apr. 1, 1969.

8. FBL to JDL, Apr. 1, 1969. Cabot urged John to take the O.A.S. post, if offered.

9. Benjamin Welles, "The Mystery of John Davis Lodge," *New York Times*, Apr. 13, 1969.

10. JDL to William P. Rogers, Apr. 19, 1969.

11. JDL to RN, Apr. 20, 1969.

12. Francesca strongly believed Cabot had convinced Eisenhower not to appoint John as Ambassador to Italy in the 1950s because she was Italian-born. For the rest of her life, she expressed dismay over Cabot's lack of support for John's endeavors.

13. President Ongania (1914-1995) moved to buttress his power with repressive measures extraordinary even in the country's dictatorship-studded history. Eric Pace, "Gen. J.C. Ongania, Ex-Argentine Dictator, 81," *New York Times*, June 10, 1995; Carey Cronan, "Interrogation of John Lodge," *Bridgeport Sunday Post*, May 25, 1969.

14. Betty Beale, "VIPs Have Fun With Lodge Movie," *Washington Evening Star*, June 25, 1969.

15. The ubiquitous Lodge canines were aboard: a collie and a dachshund. Their passage cost $35 and $25, respectively.

16. Frank Oram int. TAD, Jan. 7, 1988.

17. "A Savvy Ambassador," *La Mañana* (Corrientes), Oct. 18, 1969.

18. Donald Stewart int. TAD, Oct. 3, 1988.

19. Peter B. Smith int. TAD, July 13, 1989.

20. Stewart int. TAD.

21. Milton Barall int. TAD, Jan. 6, 1988.

22. Richard Nixon, "U.S. Foreign Policy for the 1970s: Shaping A Durable Peace," A Report To The Congress, May 3, 1973, 115-30.

23. David Rock, *Argentina 1516-1987* (London: T. B. Tauris & Co., 1987), 320.

24. Smith int. TAD.

25. "No Rules in B.A., Says Meyer," *Buenos Aires Herald*, May 19, 1970.

26. "Generals in Argentina Make Grab for Power," *Hartford Courant*, June 9, 1970.

27. Jonathan Dugan int. TAD, May 24, 1988.

28. Stewart int. TAD.

29. David F. Belnap, "Wife of U.S. Envoy Charms the Argentines," *Los Angeles Times*, Sep. 16, 1972.

30. DeForest, July 31, 1969.

31. DeForest, Aug. 2, 1969.

24. Showing the Flag

1. JDL to Helena de Streel, Sep. 12, 1970.

2. Most American Cabots disclaim descent from Sebastian Cabot and his father John Cabot, Italians who adopted an English surname when they lived in that country in the early sixteenth century. See William M. Bulkeley, "Founding Families: Lacking an Aristocracy, Americans Confer Role on Clans Like Cabots," *Wall Street Journal*, May 7, 1979.

3. JDL, Remarks (English translation), Lincoln Library Presentation, Buenos Aires, Dec. 1, 1970.

4. John Kriendler int. TAD, Feb. 22, 1990.

5. JDL, Antarctica travel notes, Feb. 17, 1971.

6. Kriendler int. TAD.

7. JDL to Charles A. Meyer, Sep. 19, 1972.

8. JDL, "The Watergate Affair," statement (ms), Aug. 22, 1973.

9. Betty Beale, "U.S. Diplomacy is at Its Best in Argentina," *Washington Star-News*, Oct. 1, 1972.

10. Betty Beale int. TAD, Oct. 3, 1988.

11. Lewis H. Diuguid, "Ambassador Lodge: 'Urgente,' " *Washington Post*, Feb. 18, 1973.

12. Diuguid, "Ambassador Lodge: 'Urgente.'

13. Diuguid. Lodge's Connecticut friend Jonathan Dugan points out a certain characteristic: "John compartmentalized things. In the office, you discussed certain matters; at social gatherings, less serious things." Dugan int. TAD.

14. JDL to Department of State (telegram-unclassified), Feb. 22, 1973.

15. JDL to Department of State (telegram-unclassified), Feb. 22, 1973.

16. "BA wits whet tongues on life style of Lodges," *Buenos Aires Herald*, Mar. 3, 1973. Lodge has described the *Herald* as "by and large anti-American, inaccurate, and rather to the left." JDL to William F. Buckley, June 1, 1973.

17. Max V. Krebs, Statement by DGM of U.S. Embassy, Feb. 24, 1973.

18. Shirley Temple Black int. TAD, Jan. 14, 1988.

19. Kriendler int. TAD.

20. JDL to William F. Buckley, Apr. 18, 1973; "Envoy to Argentina to Get Sack," New York *Daily News*, Apr. 14, 1973.

21. Lodge had learned from the sour experience of a predecessor there, Ambassador Spruille Braden. In the closing days of World War II, Braden made a series of speeches which were considered open American pressure on the neutral Argentina government. As a result, Perón was swept to electoral victory with the slogan "Perón or Braden." Lodge deliberately kept a low profile and America's name out of Argentine presidential campaigns in 1973. JDL to Richard M. Nixon, Mar. 2, 1973.

22. JDL to Gerald R. Ford, June 26, 1973.

23. RN to JDL, June 28, 1973.

24. By mid-1973, Nixon was tearing great divisions within the ranks of his party, even within the loyal Chowder & Marching circle. "If Nixon couldn't even hold C&M it was only a matter of time before he lost everything." Glenn R. Davis as quoted in Kevin B. Smith, *The Iron Man: The Life and Times of Congressman Glenn R. Davis.* (Lanham, MD: University Press of America, 1994), 323.

25. William Sowash to TAD, Apr. 2, 1990.

26. "The Story behind the Krebs Memorandum," *Buenos Aires Herald,* Aug. 4, 1973; JDL to Gerald R. Ford, Aug. 21, 1973; JDL to Kenneth Rush, Under Secretary of State, Sep. 18, 1973.

27. Carl T. Curtis to JDL, Oct. 17, 1973.

28. Alberto J. Vignes, Remarks, Buenos Aires, Sept. 24, 1973.

29. Woody Klein, "The Role He Treasures Most Is Governor of Connecticut," *Connecticut Magazine,* Mar. 1974.

30. Joseph Verner Reed int. TAD, June 16, 1988.

31. Reed int. TAD.

32. Reed int. TAD.

33. HCLJr to JDL, Sep. 7, 1973.

34. JDL to HCLJr, Sep. 30, 1973.

35. Liz Barzda, "John Lodges Share Argentine News with Vice President," *Hartford Times,* Jan. 27, 1974.

36. In 1974 terrorism in Argentina had accelerated. Some 180 people were kidnapped or assassinated that year. U.S. Ambassador Bob Hill stood as a prime target, more so than Lodge, because he had been outspoken about Cuba while serving in Mexico. His public appearances were curtailed and irregularly scheduled. The Embassy became an armed fortress. Cecilia Hill int. TAD, Oct. 5, 1988.

37. JDL, "On revisiting Argentina and Uruguay: Jan. 30-Feb. 16, 1977" (unpublished notes), FBLP.

38. JDL to Robert H. Michel, July 5, 1975.

39. JDL to Robert H. Michel, July 5, 1975.

40. JDL to Gerald R. Ford, Oct. 18, 1975.

41. JDL, Address, Convention of Foreign Language Teachers, Hartford (ms), Oct. 25, 1974.

42. JDL, Address, Meeting of American Coalition of Patriotic Societies, Washington (ms), May 1, 1976, 7.

43. JDL, Remarks, Luncheon of Woman's Auxiliary to New Haven County Medical Association (ms), Nov. 5, 1975, 6.

44. JDL, "Why Chile?" (unpublished article), Feb. 1979, FBLP.

45. JDL, "Looking at Spain," *New York Times*, Nov. 20, 1975; Jim Ameling to Editor, "Franco's Spain: What the Envoy Didn't See," *New York Times*, Dec. 6, 1975. In the 1970s Lodge published 13 by-line articles.

46. "University honors Francesca Lodge," *Westport News*, June 9, 1978.

47. Elizabeth G. Curren, "Fun 'whirl' For GOPs Young At Heart," *New Haven Register*, Aug. 22, 1976.

48. JDL to Jimmy Carter, Dec. 1, 1976.

25. Man of the Right

1. Ronald Reagan, Presidential Remarks for Campaign Rally (press release), Fairfield, CT, Oct. 26, 1984.

2. Jack Zaiman, "Six From State To Help Reagan," *Hartford Courant*, Mar. 8, 1979; Statement by JDL, cMar. 1979.

3. JDL, Speech, Woman's National Republican Club, New York, Oct. 15, 1980, 8.

4. Lodge suggested two names in response to a letter from Reagan on his running mate: Bush and Alexander Haig. Jack Kemp also was mentioned. JDL to RR, July 8, 1980.

5. FBL, "Detroit: The GOP puts on a good show," *Westport News*, July 23, 1980.

6. FBL, "Detroit: The GOP puts on a good show."

7. Charles Gamzey, "At GOP headquarters, elation, butterflies, former Governor Lodge," *Greenwich Time*, Nov. 5, 1980.

8. A. Krebs and R. McG. Thomas, Jr., "Notes on People: An Ex-Governor Waiting in the Wings," *New York Times*, Mar. 19, 1981.

9. JDL to RR, Aug. 21, 1981.

10. George Bush to JDL, Aug. 12, 1981.

11. George Bush to JDL, Sep. 8, 1981.

12. Leland Miles int. TAD, June 15, 1988.

13. Paul Dietrich int. TAD, Oct. 4, 1988.

14. Serving with Lodge were Kenneth Adelman (Deputy Representative), Charles H. Percy, Hernan Padilla, Milton Gray, William C. Sherman, José S. Sorzano, and Charles M. Lichenstein.

15. JDL to Jeane J. Kirkpatrick, Dec. 22, 1982.

16. JDL, Statement, Right of Reply to Afghanistan before UN General Assembly (press release), Oct. 14, 1982.

17. Jeane J. Kirkpatrick to JDL, Jan. 11, 1983.

18. JDL to RR, Dec. 20, 1982.

19. JDL to William F. Buckley, Jr., May 28, 1982.

20. William R. Leute int. TAD, Mar. 18, 1989.

21. Helene Von Damm, *At Reagan's Side* (New York: Doubleday, 1989), 247.

22. Von Damm, 248.

23. "Look out Bern, here comes Lodge," *Washington Times*, Mar. 2, 1983.

24. JDL to Tad Tharp, Mar. 8, 1983.

25. "Ambassador John Davis Lodge?" Stamford *Advocate*, Jan. 22, 1983.

26. Carol Giacomo, "At 79, State's John D. Lodge Takes on New Challenge," *Hartford Courant*, Apr. 16, 1983.

27. JDL, Remarks at Swearing-in Ceremony, Washington, Apr. 15, 1983, 2-3.

28. Quoted in Ignaz Staub, "Gnaden-Brot in Bern," *Schweizer Illustrierte*, Mar. 1983.

29. Sally Ardrey int. TAD, July 8, 1988.

30. Hans W. Selhofer to TAD, Mar. 23, 1988.

31. Virginia Steiger int. TAD, Mar. 22, 1988.

32. DeForest, May 8, 1984.

33. DeForest, "John Davis Lodge, Active Ambassador," Stamford *Advocate*, July 9, 1984.

34. JDL to Hans H. von Thyssen-Bornemisza, Apr. 20, 1984.

35. Richard Dugstad int. TAD, Oct. 4, 1988.

36. RR to JDL, Nov. 17, 1983.

37. JDL to RR, Mar. 5, 1984.

38. RR to JDL, July 17, 1984.

26. The Last Homecoming

1. Jim and Lily Marcus were divorced in 1985; he died of leukemia in Phoenix, Arizona in January 1988 at age 57.

2. JDL to Helena de Streel, Nov. 24, 1984.

3. HCLJr to JDL, Nov. 7, 1984.

4. HCLRJr, *The Storm Has Many Eyes* (New York: Norton, 1973); *As It Was* (New York: Norton, 1976).

5. Henry S. Lodge int. TAD, May 24, 1988.

6. George Shultz int. TAD, Oct. 26, 1989.

7. Shelby Cullom Davis int. TAD, Dec. 10, 1987.

8. Joyce Gemperlein and Robin Clark, "Whittlesey reportedly to return to embassy," *Philadelphia Inquirer*, Jan. 8, 1985.

9. JDL to Faith Whittlesey, Jan. 8, 1985.

10. Faith Whittlesey to JDL, Jan. 16, 1985.

11. JDL to Faith Whittlesey, Jan. 8, 1985.

12. RN to JDL, Jan. 16, 1985. In a handwritten postscript, Nixon added: "Since dictating this letter I hear the decision may be reversed. Good!"

13. RR to JDL, Jan. 25, 1985.

14. JDL to RR, Feb. 8, 1985.

15. Tad Tharp int. TAD, Jan. 7, 1988.

16. Hamilton Southworth, M.D., int. TAD, June 16, 1988.

17. JDL to Faith Whittlesey, Apr. 2, 1985. Whittlesey's second stint in Bern was troubled. She was investigated for alleged abuses of an embassy entertainment fund put together by U.S. businessmen and for her hiring practices. She also reportedly spent most of the $82,300 fund entertaining and lodging American officials and leading conservatives, even though the money was meant to be used for entertaining Swiss nationals. No action was taken against her, but in 1987, as a result of an investigation,

the State Department barred all embassies from accepting private gifts. Reagan recalled her before the end of his second term. Howard Kurtz, "Whittlesey faces probe on funds," *Philadelphia Inquirer*, Sep. 26, 1986.

18. JDL to Richard Burt, May 2, 1985.

19. Southworth int. TAD.

20. Thom Duffy, "Gov. Lodge, 81, ready for new role—at United Nations," *New Haven Register*, Sep. 15, 1985.

21. RR to JDL, Apr. 1, 1985.

22. Shultz int. TAD.

23. Esther B. Fein, "At U.N., Black Tie and Political Ties," *New York Times*, Oct. 7, 1985.

24. Vernon Walters int. TAD, June 24, 1988.

25. Herbert S. Okun int. TAD, Jan. 30, 1991.

26. *Who's Who in America*, 40th Edition 1978-1979, vol. 2 (Chicago: Marquis Who's Who, 1978), 1988.

27. Jo Fox, "The ambassador from a better time," *Westport News*, Nov. 6, 1985.

28. RN to FBL, Oct. 30, 1985.

29. Eulogy by Frank J. Fahrenkopf, Jr., Washington, Nov. 4, 1985.

30. Eulogy by Vernon Walters, Memorial Service (ms), Nov. 6, 1985, 3.

31. Kevin P. Fitzpatrick, Memorial Mass, Westport, CT, Dec. 14, 1985.

32. William F. Buckley, Jr., "John Davis Lodge, RIP," *National Review*, Nov. 29, 1985.

33. Christopher Dodd, *Congressional Record*, Proceedings and Debates of the 99th Congress, First Session, vol. 131, No. 157-Part II, Nov. 14, 1985.

34. RR to FBL, Oct. 31, 1985.

35. FBL to RR, Nov. 6, 1985.

27. A Life of Service

1. JDL profile, *Fiftieth Anniversary Report: Harvard Class of 1925*, Cambridge, MA, June 1975, 393.

2. Myron M. Cowen, "Model of a Modern American Ambassador," *New York Times Magazine*, Dec. 1, 1957. Cowen served as U.S. Ambassador to Australia, the Philippines, and Belgium during the Truman Administration.

3. Richard Aldrich to Alden Hatch, undated, Alden Hatch Papers, Special Collections, University of Florida, Gainesville.

4. JDL to Dwayne R. McMurren, Mar. 21, 1985.

5. "I-95 Now Gov. John Davis Lodge Turnpike," *Bridgeport Telegram*, Oct. 2, 1986.

6. FBL to Harriet Manning, Jan. 1997.

7. Marian Gail Brown, "Connecticut Lodge Legend Lives," *Connecticut Post*, Mar. 12, 1995.

Bibliography

BOOKS

Adams, Henry. *The Life of George Cabot Lodge*. Boston: Houghton Mifflin, 1911.

Amory, Cleveland. *Who Killed Society?* New York: Harper & Bros., 1960.

Baldwin, Raymond. *Let's Go Into Politics*. New York: Macmillan, 1952.

Blair, Anne. *Lodge in Vietnam*. New Haven: Yale University Press, 1995.

Braggiotti, Gloria. *Born in a Crowd*. New York: Thomas Y. Crowell, 1957.

Brogan, D. W. *The Free State; Some Considerations on its Practical Value*. New York: Alfred A. Knopf, 1945.

Brownell, Herbert, with John P. Burke. *Advising Ike: The Memoirs of Attorney General Herbert Brownell*. Lawrence: University of Kansas, 1993.

Bruccoli, M. J. and Richard Layman. *American Decades: 1950–1959*. Detroit: Gale Research Institute, 1995.

Cercle Française de l'Université Harvard: 1874–1923. Boston: McGrath-Sherrill Press, November 1923.

Cohen-Stratyner, Barbara. *Biographical Dictionary of Dance*. New York: Schirmer Books, 1982.

Coote, Albert W. *Four Vintage Decades: The Performing Arts in Hartford 1930–1970*. Hartford: Huntington Publishing Co., 1970.

Costello, William. *The Facts About Nixon*. New York: Viking Press, 1960.

Crassweller, Robert D. *Perón and The Enigmas of Argentina*. New York: 1987.

Cutler, Robert. *No Time for Rest*. Boston: Atlantic Monthly Press, 1966.

Davis, Charles H. *The Life of Charles Henry Davis, Rear Admiral, 1807–1877*. Boston: Houghton Mifflin, 1899.

de Comes, Philippe and Michel Marmin. *Le Cinéma Français: 1930–1960*. Paris: Editions Atlas, 1984.

Dietrich, Marlene. *Marlene D.* Paris: Bernard Grasset, 1984.

Edwards, Lee. *Missionary for Freedom: The Life and Times of Walter Judd*. New York: Paragon House, 1990.

Eells, George, and Stanley Musgrove. *Mae West*. New York: William Morrow, 1982.

Eisenhower, Dwight D. *Crusade in Europe*. Garden City: Doubleday, 1949.

_____. *Waging Peace: The White House Years, A Personal Account 1956–1961*, Vol. 2. Garden City: Doubleday, 1965.

Everson, William K. *The Detective in Film*. Secaucus, NJ: Citadel Press, 1972.

Fairbanks, Douglas, Jr. *A Hell of a War*. New York: St. Martin's Press, 1993.

Feuillere, Edwige. *Les Feux de la Mémoire*. Paris: Albin Michel, 1977.

Francomano, Joseph J., and Wayne and Darryl Lavitt. *Junior Achievement: A History*. Colorado Springs: Junior Achievement, Inc., 1988.

Garraty, John A. *Henry Cabot Lodge: A Biography*. New York: Alfred A. Knopf, 1953.

Griffis, Stanton. *Lying in State*. Garden City: Doubleday, 1952.

Haldane, Sean. *The Fright of Time: Joseph Trumbull Stickney, 1874–1904*. Ladysmith, Quebec: Ladysmith Press, 1970.

Hatch, Alden. *The Lodges of Massachusetts*. New York: Hawthorn Books, 1973.

Hechinger, Fred M. *An Adventure in Education: Connecticut Points the Way*. New York: Macmillan, 1956.

Hempstone, Smith, ed. *An Illustrated History of St. Albans School*. Glastonbury, CT: Glastonbury Press, 1981.

Hess, Stephen. *America's Political Dynasties From Adams to Kennedy*. Garden City: Doubleday, 1966.

Hoffman, Paul. *Lions in the Street: The Inside Story of the Great Wall Street Law Firms*. New York: Saturday Review Press, 1973.

Hope, Bob. *I Owe Russia $1200*. Garden City: Doubleday, 1963.

Hyman, Sidney. *The Lives of William Benton*. Chicago: University of Chicago Press, 1969.

Jarratt, Vernon. *The Italian Cinema*. London: Falcon Press, 1951.

Karnow, Stanley. *Vietnam: A History*. New York: Viking Press, 1983.

Lears, T. J. Jackson. *No Place of Grace: Antimodernism and The Transformation of American Culture, 1880–1920*. New York: Pantheon, 1981.

Lewis, R.W.B. *Edith Wharton*. New York: Harper & Row, 1975.

Lieberman, Joseph I. *The Legacy: Connecticut Politics 1930–1980*. Hartford: Spoonwood Press, 1981.

_____. *The Power Broker: A Biography of John M. Bailey, Modern Political Boss*. Boston: Houghton Mifflin, 1966.

Lockard, Duane. *New England State Politics*. Princeton: Princeton University Press, 1959.

Lodge, Henry Cabot, Sr. *Anna Cabot Mills Lodge*. Boston: Merrymount Press, 1918.

_____. *Early Memories*. New York: Charles Scribner's Sons, 1913.

Lodge, Henry Cabot. *The Storm Has Many Eyes*. New York: Norton, 1973.

Martin, Ralph G. *Henry and Clare: An Intimate Portrait of the Luces*. New York: G. P. Putnam's Sons, 1991.

Miller, William J. *Henry Cabot Lodge*. New York: James H. Heineman, 1967.

Moore, George S. *The Banker's Life*. New York: W. W. Norton, 1987.

Mordden, Ethan. *The Hollywood Studios: House Style in the Golden Age of the Movies*. New York: Alfred A. Knopf, 1988.

Morison, Samuel Eliot. *History of U.S. Navy Operations in World War II*, Vol. 9. Boston: Little, Brown, 1954.

Morris, Roger. *Richard Milhouse Nixon: The Rise of an American Politician*. New York: Henry Holt, 1989.

Moss, Robert F. *The Films of Carol Reed*. London: Macmillan, 1987.

Murphy, Robert. *Diplomat Among Warriors*. Garden City: Doubleday, 1964.

O'Neill, William L. *American High: The Years of Confidence 1945–1960*. New York: Free Press, 1986.

Ortona, Egidio. *Anni d'America: La Ricostruzione, 1944–1951*. Bologna, Italy: Mulino, 1984.

Patterson, Dradley H., Jr. *The Ring of Power: The White House Staff and Its Expanding Role*. New York: Basic Books, 1988.

Patterson, Jerry E. *The Best Families: The Town & Country Social Directory 1846–1996*. New York: Harry N. Abrams, 1996.

Phillips, Cabell. *The 1940s: Decade of Triumph and Trouble*. New York: Macmillan, 1975.

Riva, Maria. *Marlene Dietrich*. New York: Alfred A. Knopf, 1993.

Roosevelt, Archie. *For Lust of Knowing: Memoirs of An Intelligence Officer*. Boston: Little, Brown, 1988.

Samuels, Ernest. *Henry Adams: The Major Phase*. Cambridge: Harvard University Press, 1964.

Schaffer, Howard B. *Chester Bowles: New Dealer in the Cold War*. Cambridge: Harvard University Press, 1993.

Shneidman, J. Lee, ed. *Spain and Franco: Quest for International Acceptance 1949–59*. New York: Facts on File, 1973.

Smith, Kevin B. *The Iron Man: The Life and Times of Congressman Glenn R. Davis*. Lanham, MD: University Press of America, 1994.

Stanwood, Charles F. *Portrait of Pasquaney*. Bristol, NH: Pasquaney Trust, 1985.

Steinberg, Jonathan. *Why Switzerland?* Cambridge, England: Cambridge University Press, 1976.

Studlar, Gaylyn. *In The Realm of Pleasure: Von Sternberg, Dietrich and the Masochistic Aesthetic*. Urbana: University of Illinois Press, 1988.

Swaine, Robert T. *The Cravath Firm and Its Predecessors 1819–1948*, Vol. 3. New York: Ad Press, 1948.

Van Dusen, Albert E. *Connecticut: A Fully Illustrated History of the State from the Seventeenth Century to the Present*. New York: Random House, 1961.

von Sternberg, Josef. *Fun in a Chinese Laundry*. New York: Macmillan, 1965.

von Damm, Helene. *At Reagan's Side*. New York: Doubleday, 1989.

Walters, Vernon. *Silent Missions*. Garden City: Doubleday, 1978.

Watson, Steven. *Strange Bedfellows: The First American Avant-Garde*. New York: Abbeville Press, 1991.

Welles, Benjamin. *Spain: The Gentle Anarchy*. New York: Praeger, 1965.

Wharton, Edith. *A Backward Glance*. New York: Appleton-Century, 1934.

Wright, William. *Lillian Hellman: The Image, The Woman*. New York: Simon and Schuster, 1986.

Yeomans, Henry A. *Abbott Lawrence Lowell: 1856–1943.* Cambridge: Harvard University Press, 1948.

Zeiger, Henry A. *The Remarkable Henry Cabot Lodge.* New York: Popular Library, 1964.

Zúñiga, Angel. *Una Historia del Cine.* Barcelona, Spain: Ediciones Destino, S.L., 1948.

ARTICLES

Alden, Betty. "Braggiotti Sisters Lead Six Best Dancers in Smart Set, Says Betty Alden." *Boston American*, Aug. 22, 1922.

"Ambassador Lodge—Running Strong," *Newsweek*, Mar. 23, 1964.

"An Engineering Report on Estimated Cost for Greenwich-Killingly Expressway." State of Connecticut State Highway Dept., Nov. 1953.

"A Plan for the Solution of the Post Road Congestion Problem." Prepared for the Connecticut State Highway Dept. by H. W. Lochner & Co., Chicago, Feb. 1952.

Bell, Nelson B. "Washington Entertains Young Leading Man." *Washington Post*, Mar. 15, 1934.

Berkman, Florence, "My Neighbor, The Governor." *Northeast-Hartford Courant Sunday Magazine*, Aug. 8, 1993.

Borland, John K. "Lodge Played Cautious Role in First Year of Long Term." *Hartford Times*, Dec. 29, 1951.

Carroll, Harrison. "Boston Blue-Blood Teamed with Mae West for Starter." *Los Angeles Herald-Express*, Oct. 29, 1932.

Clew, William J. "Lodges in Spain." *Hartford Courant*, Oct. 27, 1957.

Coffin, Patricia. "Mrs. John Davis Lodge: Washington's Most Discussed Woman." *Look*, Sept. 30, 1947.

Cohn, Herbert. "Tennis Game, 2 Telegrams Convert Lawyer into Actor." *Brooklyn Eagle*, Oct. 8, 1940.

Cole, Gloria. "The Lodges come home." *Fairpress*, Dec. 12, 1973.

"Connecticut: The Windstorm." *Time*, Jun. 26, 1950.

Craig, Paul. "Our Embassy in Spain is a Family Affair." New York *Sunday Mirror Magazine*, Feb. 19, 1956.

Crowley, John W. " 'Dear Bay:' Theodore Roosevelt's Letters to George Cabot Lodge." *New York History*, 53, No. 2 (Apr. 1972).

Davenport, Walter. " '52 Buttons for Bowles?" *Collier's*, Aug. 27, 1949.

DeLong, Thomas A. "Westporter John Lodge Played in Early Version of 'Little Women.' " Westport *Minuteman*, Jan. 26, 1995.

_____. "Westport's First Lady of the World." Westport *Minuteman*, Aug. 3, 1995.

DePascal, Vincent. "American Dancing Beauty Chosen by Il Duce for Star Role in Biggest Production." *Columbus Record Monthly*, Jan. 1937.

Deval, Paul. "On a tourné à Boug-de Peage 'De Mayerling à Sarajevo.' " Grenoble *Petit Dauphinois*, Aug. 23, 1939.

Dixon, Kenneth. "Lodge, Honored by UB, Warns on Soviet." *Bridgeport Telegram*, Feb. 23, 1984.

Dove, Roger. "Connecticut." *Town and Country*, Mar. 1953.

Ellinwood, Sybil. "East Meets West in the Field of Education." *Journal of Arizona History*, 15, No. 3 (1973).

Fenton, John H. "Cabots and Lowells of Boston Society are Less Isolated—To a Degree." *New York Times*, Jan. 28, 1957.

_____. "John Lodge Opens Campaign for Nixon in New Hampshire." *New York Times*, Jan. 17, 1968.

"Former Governor's Screen Career Remembered." *Westport News*, Oct. 15, 1993.

Garrett, William A. "Lodge, Decorated by Italy, Sees Ike, Flies to Panama." *Hartford Times*, Oct. 30, 1953.

"Governor Lodge, Gaining Experience in Office In First Half of Term, Takes Stronger Hold." *Hartford Times*, Dec. 29, 1952.

Hope, Barbara. "Which Is John?" *Film Pictorial*, May 20, 1939.

"Ike's Victory Increases Lodge's Political Stature." *Bridgeport Post*, Jul. 12, 1952.

"John Lodge Wins Screen Success by Own Efforts." *Minneapolis Evening Tribune*, Mar. 5, 1934.

Kaferie, Dan. "Ribicoff: Retired now—but staying involved." *New Haven Register*, Sept. 22, 1985.

Keavy, Hubbard. "Movie Future is Uncertain." *Sacramento Union*, Dec. 25, 1933.

Knowlton, John E. "Middlesex Remembered." *Middlesex School Bulletin*, Summer 1997.

Lee, Sonia. "John Lodge Sheds his Ancestors," *Motion Picture*, Aug. 1934.

"The Life Story of John Lodge." *Picture Show*, Apr. 8, 1939.

Lodge, John Davis. "The Canal: A Rampart." *New York Times*, Nov. 29, 1977.

_____. "Can NATO Be Restored?" *Orbis*, 10, No. 3 (Fall 1966).

_____. "Criticism of Ronald Reagan's Age is Historically Unjustified." *New Haven Register*, Jan. 9, 1980.

_____. "Hollywood Stars I've Met." *Boston Sunday Advertiser*, Apr. 9, 1933.

_____. "John Davis Lodge Tells Hard Work Side of Screen Life in Hollywood." *Boston Sunday Advertiser*, Apr. 16, 1933.

_____. "Know Thy Enemy." *New York Times*, Apr. 1, 1977.

_____. "Looking at Spain." *New York Times*, Nov. 20, 1975.

_____. "Mr. Lodge Recalls Brennan's Antagonism." Letter to Editor, *Hartford Courant*, Jul. 2, 1971.

_____. "On Summitry: A Plea for the Old." *National Review*, May 26, 1978.

_____. "Our Real 'Problem' Generation." *This Week Magazine*, Oct. 17, 1954.

_____. "Politics is Everybody's Business." *New York Times Magazine*, Sep. 19, 1954.

_____. "Problems of Nomenclature." *New Haven Register*, Jul. 17, 1978.

"Lodge of 'Mayerling,' The." *New York Times*, Oct. 27, 1940.

"Lodge Raps Truman View of Eisenhower." *Los Angeles Times*, Oct. 1, 1952.

Norton, Elliot. "Spurns Stardom for Her Husband," *Boston Post*, Aug. 7, 1940.

Papazian, Rita. "Here's To Francesca!" *Connecticut Post*, Nov. 20, 1997.

Pascone, Tere. "The Lodges Take Over as Connecticut's First Family." *Bridgeport Post*, Jan. 7, 1951.

Peak, Mayme Ober. "Hollywood Picks Senator Lodge's Grandson Because It Needs 'The Gentleman Type.' " *Boston Daily Globe*, Nov. 13, 1932.

_____. "John Lodge Wanted to Change his Name for Movies." *Boston Morning Globe*, Feb. 25, 1934.

"Pour Tourner Trois Jours, John Lodge a Voyagé Six Semaines." *Cinémonde*, Feb. 14, 1940.

Radcliffe, Donnie. "Preparing a Lodge for Switzerland." *Washington Post*, Apr. 16, 1983.

Robinson, Grace. "No Glamor in Politics?" *New York Sunday News Magazine*, Oct. 31, 1954.

Ross, Don. "Connecticut's Three-Ring Election." *New York Herald Tribune-This Week*, Oct. 29, 1950.

Ross, Rita. "Westport's Francesca Lodge still enjoying life at 93." *Westport News*, Nov. 3, 1995.

"Slow, But Sure: U.S. Bases in Spain Take Shape." *U.S. News & World Report*, May 17, 1957.

Sokolsky, George E. "Today's Connecticut Story." *Long Island Press*, Jul. 6, 1954.

"Spain Builds New Era of Economic Expansion." *New York Herald Tribune*, Sect. 12, Apr. 12, 1956.

Tazelaar, Marguerite. "Henry Cabot Lodge's Grandson Reflects on the Law and Films." *New York Herald Tribune*, Mar. 10, 1935.

Thayer, Charles W. "Our Ambassadors: an intimate appraisal of the men and the system." *Harper's Magazine*, Sep. 1959.

Todd, Nancy. "This is the Time . . ." *Carousel Magazine*, Fall 1993.

"U.S.-Spain Trade Seen Expanding." *New York Herald Tribune*, Jan. 6, 1956.

Veale, William H. "John Lodge—'A Good Governor, A Better Dad.' " *Hartford Courant Magazine*, Jun. 21, 1953.

Walsh, William J. "Ribicoff Enters Race in '54 With Attack on Lodge." *Bridgeport Post*, Apr. 12, 1953.

Welles, Benjamin. "John Lodge Finally Lands Post: He Is New Envoy to Argentina." *New York Times*, May 1, 1969.

Welch, Deshler. "The European Playground." *Boston Courier*, Jan. 28, 1911.

Wooding, Frank A. "Lowdown on Lodge." *Bridgeport Herald*, Jul. 8, 15, 22, 29, 1951.

Index